Introduction
to
Nursing:
An Adaptation Model

Contributing Authors

Sue Ann Brown, R.N., M.N.
Assistant Professor, School of Nursing, University of Portland, Portland, Oregon

Edda Coughran, R.N., M.N.
Nursing Instructor, School of Nursing, Los Angeles County/USC Medical Center

Marie Driever, R.N., M.N.
Extended Nursing Program Coordinator, Assistant Professor, University of Portland,
Portland, Oregon

Jeannine R. Dunn, R.N., M.N.
Formerly, Instructor of Nursing, Department of Nursing, Mount St. Mary's College,
Los Angeles, California

Janet Dunning, R.N., M.N.
Assistant Professor, School of Nursing, University of Portland, Portland, Oregon

Edythe Ellison, R.N., M.S.N.
Formerly, Assistant Professor, Department of Nursing, Mount St. Mary's College,
Los Angeles, California

Barbara Gruendemann, R.N., M.N.
Assistant Professor, Department of Nursing, Mount St. Mary's College, Los Angeles, California

C. Margaret Henderson, R.N., M.N.
Instructor in Nursing, Department of Nursing, Mount St. Mary's College, Los Angeles,
California

Sonja Liggett, R.N., M.N.
Program Director, American Association of Critical Care Nurses, Irvine, California

Sister Theresa Marie McIntier, R.N., M.N.
Inservice Instructor, St. Joseph's Hospital, Tuscon, Arizona

Nancy Malaznik, R.N., M.N.
Instructor in Nursing, Department of Nursing, Mount St. Mary's College, Los Angeles,
California

Cecilia Martinez, R.N., M.N.
Psychiatric Clinical Specialists, Gifford Mental Health Clinic, San Diego, California

Nancy Zewen Perley, R.N., M.N.
Instructor in Nursing, California State University, Long Beach, California

Mary Poush, R.N., M.N.
Assistant Professor, Department of Nursing, Mount St. Mary's College, Los Angeles, California

Brooke Randell, R.N., M.N.
Assistant Clinical Professor, School of Nursing, University of California, Los Angeles,
California

Sister Callista Roy, R.N., M.S.
Assistant Professor, Department of Nursing, Mount St. Mary's College, Los Angeles,
California

Ann Macaluso Schofield, R.N., M.S.
Associate Professor, Assistant Chairman, Department of Nursing, Mount St. Mary's College,
Los Angeles, California

Sharon Vairo, R.N., M.N.
Assistant Professor, Department of Nursing, Mount St. Mary's College, Los Angeles,
California

Sister Joyce Van Landingham, R.N., M.S.
Assistant Professor, Department of Nursing, Mount St. Mary's College, Los Angeles, California

Introduction to Nursing: An Adaptation Model

SISTER CALLISTA ROY

Prentice-Hall Inc., Englewood Cliffs, New Jersey

Library of Congress Cataloging in Publication Data

Main entry under title:

Introduction to nursing.

    Includes bibliographies and index.
      1.–Nursing. 2.–Nursing–Psychological aspects.
I.–Roy, Callista. [DNLM: 1.–Nursing. 2.–Models,
Theoretical. 3.–Adaptation, Psychological. WY100
R888i]
RT41.I57   610.73   75-43612
ISBN 0-13-491290-X

Printed in the United States of America

10 9 8 7 6

PRENTICE-HALL International, Inc., *London*
PRENTICE-HALL of Australia, Pty. Limited, *Sydney*
PRENTICE-HALL of Canada, Ltd., *Toronto*
PRENTICE-HALL of India Private Limited, *New Delhi*
PRENTICE-HALL of Japan, Inc., *Tokyo*
PRENTICE-HALL of Southeast Asia Pte. Ltd., *Singapore*

Contents

v

Preface

Nursing is rapidly making its way into the domain of a scientific discipline. The development of conceptual frameworks for nursing is one advance that is potentiating this progress. When nursing knows what phenomenon it is studying, and what it aims to accomplish, then it is in a position to classify, relate, predict, and proscribe regarding that phenomenon. As the various nursing theorists have approached their task of defining nursing, they have all taken the person as the phenomenon for study. Nursing's goal has been variously stated, but generally involves helping the person to cope with situations of health and illness. This book is an attempt to take the Roy adaptation model of nursing and to specify in one unified text the classification, relationships, predictions, and proscriptions that the authors have identified as currently known about the person coping with health and illness.

Most current textbooks in nursing use a medically based approach. They focus on a clinical specialty such as medical-surgical or maternity nursing. The person in health and illness is their general topic, but there is no integrated delineation of the components of a science of nursing. At the same time, texts are being developed which focus on certain aspects of that total science, for example, on pain. What seems to be needed is a text that will outline the dimensions of a science of nursing based on a conceptual framework and will fill in that outline with the nursing knowledge that is rapidly developing.

The development of a scientific text on the adaptation model of nursing may take either of two approaches. Since this concept is relatively new, it would be appropriate to develop in great depth the concept itself on a theoretical level. This approach would have the advantage of contributing to the theoretical and scientific foundations of nursing. A second approach is to take the present knowledge of the Roy adaptation model of nursing and the knowledge related to it and to develop a popular textbook for students of nursing. This text might be on a less secure scientific footing since it is putting into print the rudiments of a science before it can be fully developed. On the other hand, it can place in the hands of practicing nurses of this and the next generation, the authors' present thinking of what nursing is. The latter approach was chosen for this book for two main reasons. Adaptation is being used as the theoretical framework for increasing numbers of schools of nursing. In working with the concept in our own program at Mount St. Mary's College in Los Angeles, and in consultant visits to other nursing programs throughout the country, the great need for a student textbook is apparent. Faculty who have chosen to integrate their nursing curriculums often cannot find adequate textbooks. They are desperate for these materials. In addition, we have developed the Roy adaptation model of nursing as the basis of a curriculum to a much greater degree than any other aspect of the model. If we could get into print what we have done, this in itself would be a contribution to theoretical development. Thus the book takes the form of an introduction to nursing based on the Roy adaptation model.

This text, then, is intended to present what the authors believe to be knowledge essential for basic nursing preparation. It may be used appropriately in associate in arts and diploma nursing programs, as well as beginning courses in baccalaureate programs. In addition, it may be helpful to the graduate student or student of another field who is studying concepts of the specific nature of nursing. Hopefully, it can give one framework for practice to the nurse already in the field.

The content for this text was selected by outlining the adaptive modes of man. According to the adaptation framework, behaviors and influencing factors within each mode are discussed. Finally, the known nursing interventions for given adaptation problems are delineated. It should be pointed out that medical pathology is discussed as only one of the factors influencing adaptive behaviors. It will be necessary to use medically based texts in conjunction with this book. The aim of this book will be to maintain a focus on nursing science.

The text incorporates some learning aids which will be helpful to the student and to the nurse studying the Roy adaptation concept of nursing for the first time. Each chapter begins with definitions of key concepts. These can serve as an overview of the contents of the chapter and as a handy reference for clarifying the major concepts. Each chapter also has at the beginning the objectives for the chapter so that readers can focus on what they are expected to be able to do as a result of studying the chapter. A summary overview of the nursing model can be seen in Appendixes I and II, which outline the factors the nurse assesses and the interventions she uses in each of the adaptive modes. For ease in reading, clients are referred to as male and nurses are referred to as female even though both writers and readers recognize that there are both male and female clients and nurses. We do not wish to reinforce sex stereotyping but found alternate wording too cumbersome.

The authors present this text with the hope that the use of the Roy adaptation model of nursing may be a step in improving the health care of clients. It is also our hope that this text will make a contribution to the development of the science of nursing.

There are many persons to whom the author is endebted for both encouragement and assistance. Many will go unmentioned, but nonetheless appreciated. I am especially grateful to the contributors to this text and other faculty members from Mount St. Mary's College who have made significant contributions to the development of the Roy adaptation model. The students we teach have also had a role in that development. Cecilia and Radames Martinez deserve special thanks for providing me a hide-away for working as well as constructive criticism and encouragement. I appreciate the help of the capable typists: Ruth Garrick, Theresa De la Pena, and June McClure, who produced the manuscript. My religious community and family have contributed to the project by their supportive acceptance of me throughout this demanding time. Lastly, I would like to thank in a special way Dorothy E. Johnson, my teacher, who has been a continual focal stimulus for the development of the adaptation model.

Department of Nursing
Mount St. Mary's College   Sister Callista Roy
Los Angeles

I

Introduction to the Nursing Model

This text introduces the student and the practicing nurse to nursing as based on an adaptation nursing model. Part I begins this process by discussing specifically the Roy model of nursing practice and by outlining the nursing process based on this model.

1

Adaptation as a Model of Nursing Practice

Sister Callista Roy

KEY CONCEPTS DEFINED

Nursing in General: A theoretical system of knowledge which prescribes a process of analysis and action related to the care of the ill or potentially ill person.

Adaptation Nursing: An approach to nursing which views man as a biopsycho-social being with modes of adapting to changing environment, and which acts through a nursing process to promote man's adaptation in each of these modes in situations of health and illness.

Biological Nature of Man: The living nature of man, that is, human anatomical parts and how they function physiologically.

Psychological Nature of Man: The perceiving, learning, acting part of the human being; that is, the psychic organization which produces meaningful behavior.

Social Nature of Man: The part of man which relates behavior to other persons on group levels, such as family, community, and work groups.

Adaptive Mechanisms: Innate or acquired ways of coping with the changing
environment.

Adaptation Level: The condition of the person relative to adaptation, which
helps to determine whether the response to a changing environment will
be adaptive or maladaptive.

Adaptive Response: Behavior that maintains the integrity of the individual.

Maladaptive Response: Behavior that disrupts the integrity of the individual.

Adaptive Mode: A way or method of adapting or coping with the changing
environment.

Need: A requirement within the individual which stimulates a response to
maintain integrity.

Adaptation Problems: The occurrence of situations of inadequate responses to
need deficits or excesses.

Health Illness Continuum: A continuous line representing states of degree of
health or illness that a person might experience at any given time.

After studying this chapter the reader will be able to:

1. Define the key concepts of this chapter.
2. Compare and contrast the elements of nursing models proposed by
   Nightingale, Henderson, Johnson, Rogers, and Roy.
3. Describe the following elements of the Roy adaptation model of nursing:
   a. Man the recipient of nursing care
   b. The goal of adaptation nursing
   c. Nursing activities according to the adaptation model

Nursing is a scientific discipline which is practice oriented. That is, nursing
has a body of knowledge, and the purpose of that knowledge is to provide a
service to people. In a general sense, nursing is a theoretical system of knowledge which prescribes a process of analysis and action related to the care of the
ill or potentially ill person. There are a number of theoretical approaches to
nursing, each of which outlines specifically what the practice of nursing is.
This text explores one of these approaches, the adaptation concept of nursing.
It describes how the beginning level nurse uses this approach to nursing in her
nursing practice.[1] There are other theoretical approaches to nursing. These
approaches are called nursing models. Just as any model is made up of the essential parts of what it represents, so the nursing model is made up of essential
parts, or elements. How each model describes these elements determines the
type of nursing practice based on the model.

---

[1] Although it is recognized that an increasing number of young men are entering the
nursing field, for the purpose of simplicity we will continue to refer to the nurse as female.
Clients are referred to as male for ease of reading and not to reinforce stereotyping.

ELEMENTS OF NURSING MODELS

In recent years nursing has made greater efforts to define its theoretical basis of practice. Each of these efforts has been aimed at defining more clearly the *person* who receives nursing care, the *goal* or purpose of nursing, and nursing *intervention,* that is, what the nurse does. The elements of a nursing model are, thus, the nurse's view of the human being, nursing's goal, and nursing activities.[2]

It has long been recognized that human beings, at one time or another, require nursing care. From the earliest Christian times certain members of the community have been designated to care for the ill and infirm. Persons who were suffering were the focus of attention. Florence Nightingale (1820–1910) initiated the modern era of nursing and described more clearly man as the recipient of nursing care. As we will discuss later, she looked at man as responding to the laws of nature whether the person was healthy or sick. She began schools of nursing that taught how to put people in the best condition for nature to act upon them. Textbooks in those schools were initially largely procedure manuals, which described what the nurse was to do for her patient. Later the nursing program began to look more closely at the nature of the human being, the patient. At first this study focused on the biological being, and biological sciences such as anatomy, physiology, and microbiology became basic to nursing. Finally nursing educators recognized the significance of the psychosocial person, and the behavioral and social sciences became an important part of the nursing curriculum. Various nursing theorists will provide different frameworks for viewing the biopsychosocial person, the recipient of nursing care.

The goal of nursing has always been to contribute to the overall goal of health care; that is, to promote the health of individuals and of society. The particular way that nursing makes its contribution—the unique goal of nursing— has developed throughout nursing's history. Initially nursing was aimed at care and comfort of the ill and injured. This care and comfort involved the meeting of basic needs such as cleanliness, nutrition, and elimination. Again, it was Nightingale who expressed the purpose of these activities when she described nursing's goal as putting the person in the best condition for nature to act upon him. At that time her focus was largely on the healing process for the sick and injured. With the later emphasis on preventive medicine, nursing's goal took on the broader context of promotion of health as well as curing disease and injury. Each nursing theorist has a somewhat different way of expressing the goal of supporting people in health and illness.

[2]For a more detailed discussion of the elements of nursing models see: Joan P. Riehl and Sister Callista Roy, *Conceptual Models for Nursing Practice* (New York: Appleton-Century-Crofts, 1974).

The concept of the activities of nursing intervention has undergone an evolution similar to the evolution of nursing's concept of man and of its goal. As we have noted, care and comfort activities aimed at meeting basic needs have always been a part of nursing. To carry out these activities appropriately, nurses gradually placed more emphasis on the skill of observation. As nursing education became organized in hospital schools of nursing, nursing's dependency on the field of medicine was emphasized. The nurse reported her observations to the physician, who in turn made judgments about the course of treatment. The physician then delegated certain tasks to the nurse. Such tasks might include giving medications, at first only orally, then later intramuscularly, and finally intravenously. The scope of medically delegated tasks widened. Yet at the same time nursing theorists became concerned about the independent role of the nurse and the activities this might include. A detailed nursing process was developed. The earlier emphasis on observation was now expanded into a total process of patient assessment. Assessment is a process of gathering data about the patient. Based on this data, the nurse makes a judgment about patient situations that require nursing intervention. This judgment is called nursing diagnosis. At this point the nurse intervenes; that is, she selects an approach to solve the patient problem or to meet the patient need. Following her intervention the nurse evaluates her care in relation to the effect it has had on the patient. The nursing theorists outlined here will describe this basic nursing process with some variations. The most thoroughly developed models will provide a scheme of nursing approaches that can predictably bring about the goal of patient care. Some basic models of nursing are compared in Table 1.1 and discussed in the following pages.

OTHER MAJOR NURSING MODELS

Nightingale Florence Nightingale's concept of nursing has already been mentioned; historically she made a major contribution to nursing theory. We will outline here the elements of a nursing model revealed in Nightingale's writings (1859).

Nightingale viewed *man* as a passive instrument of nature. As has been noted, she identified the fact that man responds to the same laws whether healthy or sick. The subject of man's total response in health and illness is still the core of nursing knowledge. For Nightingale, the *goal* of nursing was to put the human being in the best condition for nature to act upon him. This goal was to contribute to the overall reparative process. Secondarily, she dictated that nurses should also aim at preventing unnecessary suffering. In regard to the nursing process *activities,* Nightingale emphasized the observation aspect of assessment by stating that "a careful nurse will keep constant watch over her sick" (Nightingale reference at end of chapter, p. 59). She detailed the

TABLE 1.1
Comparison of Models of Nursing

	Nightingale	Henderson	Johnson	Rogers	Roy
View of man	A passive instrument of nature responding to the same laws whether healthy or sick.	A whole, complete, and independent being who has 14 basic activities: breathe, eat and drink, eliminate, move and maintain posture, sleep and rest, dress and undress, maintain body temperature, keep clean, avoid danger, communicate, worship, work, play, and learn.	A behavioral system composed of 8 subsystems: affiliative, achievement, dependency, aggressive, eliminative, ingestive, restorative, sexual.	A unified whole possessing integrity and manifesting: wholeness, openness, unidirectionality, pattern and organization, sentence and thought.	A biopsychosocial being in constant interaction with a changing environment and having four modes of adaptation: physiologic needs, self-concept, role function, and interdependence
Goal of nursing	To put man in the best condition for nature to act upon him.	To substitute for what the patient lacks in physical strength, will, or knowledge to make him complete, whole, or independent.	To bring about the patient's behavioral stability.	To promote harmony between man and his environment with the ultimate goal of reaching the highest state of health possible.	To promote adaptation in the four adaptive modes.
Nursing activities	"A careful nurse will keep constant watch over her sick." To provide the proper use of fresh air, light, warmth, cleanliness, quiet, and diet.	To know the patient (assessment), identify what patient lacks (diagnosis), help supply this lack (intervention), and evaluate success (evaluation).	To assess behavioral stability, decide on the dynamics of behavioral instability, intervene by restricting, defending, inhibiting, or facilitating, and evaluate resulting patient behavior.	To gather data about man in his environmental field, and to use technical activities, manual skills or human relations to repattern man and the environment.	To assess patient behaviors and factors which influence adaptation level and to intervene by manipulating the influencing factors (focal, contextual, and residual stimuli).

approaches of nursing intervention by specifying that the nurse was to provide the proper use of fresh air, light, warmth, cleanliness, quiet, and the proper selection and administration of diet. The nurse whould accomplish all of these activities at the least expense of vital power to the patient. The influence of Nightingale's model of nursing is seen in the writings of later nursing theorists, who refer frequently to her writings.

Henderson Virginia Henderson wrote extensively in the 1950s and early 1960s on the nature of nursing. Her writings provided a theoretical basis which influenced the thinking of that day by being included in a popular nursing text (Bertha Harmer's *Textbook of the Principles and Practice of Nursing*, reference Harmer, 1955) and by publication of a monograph containing Henderson's concepts by the International Council of Nurses (Henderson, 1960).

Henderson added to Nightingale's concept of man, the recipient of nursing care, by emphasizing that *man* is a whole, complete, and independent being. Her view is further specified by her enumeration of the activities the human being must perform. These activities include the following:

1. Breathe normally.
2. Eat and drink adequately.
3. Eliminate body wastes.
4. Move and maintain desirable posture.
5. Sleep and rest.
6. Select suitable clothes—dress and undress.
7. Maintain body temperature within normal range by adjusting clothing and modifying the environment.
8. Keep the body clean and well groomed and protect the integument.
9. Avoid dangers in the environment and avoid injuring others.
10. Communicate with others in expressing emotions, needs, fears, and the like.
11. Worship according to one's faith.
12. Work in such a way that there is a sense of accomplishment.
13. Play or participate in various forms of recreation.
14. Learn, discover, or satisfy the curiousity that leads to "normal" development and health, and use the available health facilities.

These activities clearly delineate the aspects of the biopsychosocial person that are the focus of nursing.

The specific *goal* of nursing, for Henderson, is to substitute for what the patient lacks to make him complete, whole, or independent. The lack may be of physical strength, will, or knowledge. She sees nursing, then, as primarily complementing the patient by supplying what the patient needs to perform daily activities and also to carry out the treatment prescribed by the physician.

Henderson spelled out more clearly the nursing process as the procedure of nursing *activity*. She emphasized that the nurse must make efforts to know her patients, to understand them, "to get inside their skin" (assessment). The nurse then identifies what the patient lacks (diagnosis) and helps to supply this lack (intervention). Finally, Henderson stresses that the nurse evaluates her success according to the degree to which the patient establishes independence in all activities (evaluation). Although Henderson did not provide a scheme of nursing approaches to be used in nursing intervention, the approaches she would consider as nursing are implied in the activities of man, which the nurse is to facilitate.

Henderson's writings pointed out the need for nursing practice to be based on sound theoretical framework. The following two decades showed an increase in nursing model development. Two prominent authors of this period are Dorothy E. Johnson and Martha Rogers.

Johnson   Dorothy E. Johnson developed her nursing model at the University of California at Los Angeles, where the model became the basis of the undergraduate nursing curriculum. The development of curriculum on the basis of nursing models soon became a trend in nursing education.

Through the years, Johnson has developed a very comprehensive view of man as the recipient of nursing care. *Man* is a behavioral system which has a tendency to achieve and maintain stability in patterns of functioning. Like Nightingale, Johnson sees that similar patterns occur in both health and illness. Johnson postulates that the whole behavioral system of the human is composed of eight subsystems: affiliative, achievement, aggressive, dependency, eliminative, ingestive, restorative, sexual. The goals of the total behavioral system are the survival, reproduction, and growth of the human organism. To maintain the stability of the system, and thus to meet its goal, each subsystem must receive adequate functional requirements or sustenal imperatives. Johnson defines these as input in the form of protection, nurturance, and stimulation. As Grubbs, writing on the Johnson model (Riehl and Roy, 1974), points out, a patient becomes a patient when his behavioral system is threatened by the loss of order and predictability through illness.

Based on this concept of man, the *goal* of nursing is to bring about the patient's behavioral stability. Nursing aims at establishing regularities in behavior so that the goal of each subsystem will be fulfilled. Behavioral stability exists when: a minimum expenditure of energy is required, continued biological and social survival are insured, and some degree of personal satisfaction is accrued. Behavioral instability might be observed either as physiological changes or as behavioral changes such as disorder, purposelessness, or unpredictability.

Johnson outlines more specifically than the earlier theorists the four stages of the nursing process: assessment, diagnosis, intervention, and evaluation. The assessment process involves a thorough examination of the patient behavior and the significant variables that affect it. Johnson categorizes these variables as: biological, sociological, and a general category called level of wellness. If the nurse finds an actual or potential problem, she closely analyzes the unstable subsystem.

The nurse then makes a diagnosis by deciding what are the dynamics of the behavioral instability. Johnson outlines four diagnostic categories. The first two, originating within any one subsystem, are manifested by insufficiency or discrepancy. The second two, manifested within more than one subsystem, are either incompatability or dominance. Grubbs (Riehl and Roy, p. 185) explains that under each of these categories for each subsystem, specific nursing problems or subcategories can be listed.

In regard to nursing *intervention*, according to the Johnson model, the nurse has four choices: to restrict, defend, inhibit, or facilitate. Finally, the outcome of nursing intervention is evaluated by comparing the resulting patient behavior with the expected outcome expressed as a behavioral objective.

Johnson's behavioral systems model is one of the most completely developed models of nursing. Her main source of influence has been through her contact with undergraduates and graduates at the University of California, Los Angeles, her occasional writings, and her consultation with other schools of nursing.

Rogers   The last major model in nursing we will consider was developed by Martha Rogers at New York University. Roger's main contribution to the development of nursing models was her emphasis upon unitary man. She pointed out that *man* is a unified whole, possessing his own integrity and manifesting characteristics that "are more than and different from the sum of his parts" (Rogers, 1970, p. 46). Rogers focuses on the life processes of the human and points out that these processes have the following characteristics: wholeness, openness, unidirectionality, pattern and organization, sentence, and thought. These life processes are like an energy field embedded in an environmental matrix. The human energy field evolves rhythmically along life's nonlinear spiralling axis in a way that can be represented by the child's coiled toy, known as "Slinky."

Rogers has stated the *goal* of nursing as "to promote symphonic interaction between man and environment, to strengthen the coherence and integrity of the human field, and to direct and redirect patterning of the human and environmental fields for realization of maximum health potential" (Rogers, p. 122). Thus, the nurse aims to promote harmony between man and his environment with the ultimate goal of reaching the highest state of health possible. Roger's emphasis on the evolutionary nature of the human being expands the nursing goal beyond the more common concepts of maintenance and promotion of health and rehabilitation to what at this time is the unknown destiny of the human being.

Rogers' concept of the nursing process is similar to the process outlined by other nursing theorists. When the nurse gathers data (assessment) she considers the person in his environmental field at a given point in space-time. She identifies individual differences in the sequential patterning of the life process. Based on this data the nurse makes a nursing diagnosis and determines immediate and long-range goals for the individual, family, and society. Nursing *interventions* are designed to help the patient reach the goal. Technological activities, manual skills, or human relationships are geared toward repatterning man and the environment for the development of the total human potential. Rogers emphasizes that the science of nursing is a prerequisite to the process of nursing. She and her colleagues continue to study the implications of her model for a science of nursing.

THE ADAPTATION MODEL OF NURSING

The focus of this book is on the adaptation model of nursing. A number of nursing authors have included patient adaptation as basic to the framework of nursing (for example, references Levine, 1973; and Byrne, 1972). However, this book will present the theoretical framework developed by one author, Sister Callista Roy. Roy began her work on the nursing model while she was a graduate student at the University of California, Los Angeles, and continued it as a faculty member at Mount St. Mary's College in Los Angeles. The model became the basis of both the baccalaureate and associate in arts degree nursing programs of the college and later was utilized by other schools of nursing in their curriculum development.

The model clearly defines its elements: the recipient of nursing care, the goal of nursing, and nursing activities.

Man, the Recipient of Nursing Care

According to Roy, man is a biopsychosocial being in constant interaction with a changing environment. This means that the nature of man includes the biological level with components such as anatomical parts which function physiologically. For example, man has a circulatory system made up of the heart, arteries, and veins. These anatomical parts function as a whole to contribute to the biological constancy of man. At the same time, man has a psychological nature. His various biological systems, headed by the complex nervous system, together produce meaningful behavior. This behavior is organized in such a way that man has constancy in his life of perceiving, learning, and acting. Lastly, man is a social being, and his behavior is related to the behavior of others on group levels such as family, community, and work groups. This total being that man is interacts with a constantly changing environment. The weather changes, sources of motivation change, group membership changes. Alvin Toffler (1970) has written well of the accelerated pace of change that modern man faces.

To cope with this changing environment, man has certain innate and acquired mechanisms (See Figure 1.1). These mechanisms are biologic, psychologic, and social in origin. Some mechanisms are genetically determined, such as the amount of antihemophilic factor in the blood, a substance necessary for blood clotting. Other innate mechanisms are common to the species and include such factors as the self-sealing mechanism of the blood vessels. When it is disrupted, the cut end of a blood vessel constricts, thus helping to prevent excessive bleeding. Mechanisms may also be acquired through such processes as learning. For example, every student nurse learns to apply pressure to the site to control local bleeding. Psychological defense mechanisms act in a similar way. If a fact is too anxiety provoking, one can block it out by use of the mechanism of denial.[3] Whatever the change in the environment, be it a direct assault that causes injury or a subtle variation in psychological climate, man has mechanisms to cope with the changing world.

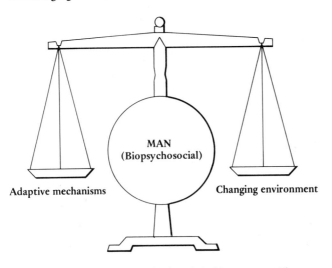

Figure 1.1   Man's adaptive mechanisms help him to cope with a changing environment.

Man's positive response to a changing environment is commonly known as the process of adaptation. Roy draws from the work of Harry Helson (Helson, 1964) to describe this process further. Man's ability to respond positively, or to adapt, depends upon the degree of the change taking place and the state of the person coping with the change. Thus, if the weather changes by the temperature dropping 20 degrees in 24 hours, and the person is normally healthy and has frequently experienced such changes in temperature, he responds positively, or adapts to the change. On the other hand if the temperature change is extreme, say 150 degrees in 24 hours (not unheard of when it is possible to fly from the equator to the North Pole in a matter of hours), the person may

---

[3] A complete list and explanation of psychological defense mechanisms can be found in any introductory psychology text.

not adapt without special efforts or assistance. Similarly, if the change is not so extreme, but a person's ability to adapt is limited, for example, through an illness such as pneumonia or through limited experience such as living only in a very mild climate, there will be difficulty in adapting.

Helson calls the degree of change the *focal stimulus*.[4] The condition of the person relative to adaptation he calls *adaptation level*. The adaptation level is determined by the pooled effect of three classes of stimuli: (1) focal stimulus, or stimulus immediately confronting the person, which has already been discussed as the degree of change, such as temperature variation; (2) *contextual stimuli,* all other stimuli present, such as the degree of humidity during the temperature change; (3) *residual stimuli,* stimuli such as beliefs, attitudes, experience, or traits which have an immeasurable effect on the present situation, for example, a history of limited exposure to temperature fluctuations.

Helson conceptualizes the adaptation level as setting up a zone within which stimulation will lead to a positive or adaptive response. This is illustrated in Figure 1.2.

Figure 1.2

On the other hand, stimuli that fall outside of the zone lead to negative or maladaptive responses as shown in Figure 1.3.

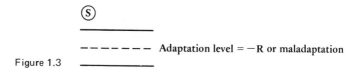

Figure 1.3

An adaptive response in general is behavior that maintains the integrity of the individual. A maladaptive response is one that does not maintain integrity and is disruptive of the person.

We have seen that man has mechanisms which help to cope with a changing environment. These mechanisms are part of the stimuli that make up the adaptation level. If we can clearly validate the effect they have on the present situation, for example, a laboratory report tells the level of antihemophilic factor in the blook, then they are focal or contextual. That is, they are an immediate or environmental contributing cause of the present response. If their

[4]In general, a stimulus is anything that provokes a response. If you prick your finger while sewing, the needle is the stimulus that provokes the response of bleeding and pain.

influence is less determined, such as the effect of previous experience, then they are considered residual stimuli.

Roy (1970) has identified two major types of adaptive mechanisms—the regulator and cognator. She discusses these as follows:

The regulator mechanism works mainly through the autonomic nervous system[5] to set up a reflex action, which readies the person for coping with the stimulus by approach, attack, or flight. The cognator identifies, stores, and relates stimuli so that symbolic responses can be made. It acts consciously by means of thought and decision, and unconsciously through the defense mechanisms. Pronounced autonomic activity with cognator ineffectiveness signals an adaptation failure. Pronounced regulator activity can be observed by an increase in heart rate or blood pressure, tension, excitement, or loss of appetite.

Cognator ineffectiveness is seen behaviorally in the following: (1) lack of awareness of the need state; (2) inability to identify the goal object; (3) inability to select means to an identified end; and (4) failure to reach a goal object (1970, p. 44).

The cognator and regulator, as primary adaptive mechanisms, are significant in analyzing clients' adaptive responses and in planning appropriate nursing care. Analysis of their effects on client behavior is just beginning by nurses developing the adaptation model of nursing. However, where appropriate this relationship will be pointed out as the nursing process and specific nursing diagnoses are discussed.

The Adaptive Modes

We have seen that Roy views man as a biopsychosocial being. When she analyzes man as an adaptive organism she further describes man as being composed of four adaptive modes. A mode is a way or method of doing or acting, and an adaptive mode is a way of adapting. Based on a survey of 500 samples of patient behavior (Roy, 1971), Roy has tentatively identified the following ways in which man adapts: *physiological needs, self-concept, role function,* and *interdependence.* Each of these adaptive modes, their component parts, how they develop, and the resulting patient problems are explored in detail later in this book. Here we can look briefly at how the adaptive modes are related to man's needs.

Categorizing man according to his various needs is a common practice in the study of human behavior. Various authors have their own classification systems.

---

[5]The autonomic nervous system consists of the sympathetic division, which increases heart action, inhibits salivation and gastrointestinal activity, raises blood pressure, dilates the bronchioles, and stimulates perspiration; and the parasympathetic division, which facilitates smooth muscle contraction, increases salivation, and decreases the heart rate.

A. H. Maslow (1954) places his classification of needs in a hierarchy according to their importance for survival. He lists these needs as: (1) physiologic needs, (2) safety needs, (3) belonging and love needs, (4) need for social esteem, and (5) need for self-actualization. This classification system has been used frequently by nursing authors in their discussion of patient needs (for example, Du Gas, 1972).

Roy's particular classification of needs stems from observations of man's attempts to cope with internal and external changes. She views a *need* as a requirement within the individual which stimulates a response to maintain integrity. These responses stimulate activity on the part of the organism. This activity is manifested in behavior. Behaviors in man are geared toward *physiologic integrity, psychic integrity,* and *social integrity,* according to the nature of man described earlier. As internal and external environments change, the degree of satiety or satisfaction of any needs changes. When satiety changes, a deficit or excess is created. This deficit or excess triggers off the appropriate adaptive mode. Activity results, and behaviors to cope with the situation are emitted. The adaptive mode is the intervening variable[6] and organizing concept between need changes and behavior. The coping mechanisms are the functional or working part of the adaptive modes. Basic needs, then, underlie each adaptive mode. For example, as satiety of the need for fluids reaches a low level, a fluid deficit is created. The physiologic adaptive mode is activated and appropriate coping behaviors, such as taking a drink of water, are initiated.

The physiologic adaptive mode, then, has as its basis man's need for physiological integrity. Roy subdivides this mode according to the following types of physiological needs: exercise and rest, nutrition, elimination, fluid and electrolytes, oxygen, circulation, and regulation, including temperature, the senses, and the endocrine system.

Man can be analyzed according to how well he is adapting to the deficits or excesses within each of his physiological needs. This analysis is discussed in detail in Chapters 3 through 10. Nurses learn methods for gathering the pertinent data regarding the activities stimulated by each type of physiological need, for example, how to measure the level of body temperature or of the person's blood pressure. Repeated observations of patients' adaptation in each of these areas lead to identification of common situations in which usual mechanisms to meet the need deficit or excess are inadequate. The occurrence of situations of inadequate responses to need deficits or excesses are referred to as adaptation problems. Roy has tentatively identified some of the most frequently occurring adaptation problems relative to each physiological need. Thus, for

[6]An intervening variable is something that stands between two other things and helps to explain their relationship. For example, a person can understand your behavior better if you tell him your motivation. Your motivation is the intervening variable between you and what you do.

example, immobility, fatigue, and insomnia are identified as frequently occurring conditions of inability to cope with need deficits and excesses in the realm of exercise and rest.

In addition to the need for physiologic integrity, students of human behavior recognize man's need for psychic integrity as well. Man needs to know who he is so that he can *be*, or exist. Just as the physiologic need for integrity has a subdivision of types of needs, so the psychic need for integrity can be subdivided into the aspects of self that require integrity. Roy has followed the work of Marie Driever (1970) to outline these subdivisions. The self-concept is composed of the physical self and the personal self. The personal self is further subdivided into the moral-ethical self, self-consistency, self-ideal, and self-esteem. Satiety of the need for integrity of each of these aspects of self-concept will vary according to internal and external changes. For example, if a series of social obligations places a student nurse in the position of eating a number of rich meals, she may gain three or four pounds. As a result there is a deficit in the integrity of her physical self. The student may begin to think of herself as overweight. Her self-concept adaptive mode is activated. This may initiate the behavior of cutting down on calorie intake to return to her normal weight and thus restore physical self-integrity. Once again, adaptation problems, or situations in which usual mechanisms are inadequate to meet need deficits or excesses, can be identified in each subdivision of the self-concept. These problems are further explored in Chapters 13 through 17.

The last two adaptive modes—role function and interdependence—are related to the need for social integrity. Man needs to know who he is in relation to others and what are the expectations of society regarding the positions he holds so that he can *act* appropriately. This need relates to his roles. In addition, he needs to know that he is loved and supported so that his being and acting have *meaning* through gaining the affection and achievement he seeks. This need is referred to as interdependence.[7] Both of these modes are subdivided according to types of behaviors manifested in each mode.

To perform a role is to be in a position in society and to carry out a pattern of interaction with another person who also occupies a position in society. Role function involves both instrumental and expressive behaviors. Instrumental behaviors are oriented toward specific goals. Thus, a mother feeds her child so that he will grow and develop. Expressive behaviors are oriented toward immediate gratification. A mother may cuddle her child for the immediate satisfaction it gives her. Each person acts in a variety of roles throughout any given day. To maintain his social integrity the person needs cues as to the appropriate instrumental and expressive behaviors for each role. In addition he needs the other to interact with and needs access to the facilities for role performance. If any of these requirements is lacking, a deficit is created which

---

[7]This way of looking at these needs was first developed by Sister Joyce Van Landingham, instructor at Mount St. Mary's College.

activates the role function adaptive mode. The three major adaptive problems in this mode are: role distance, role conflict, and role failure. These problems are discussed in Chapter 20.

By interdependence, we mean a comfortable balance between dependence and independence. This form of the need for social integrity involves a person's need to be related to others and to achieve. It includes the need for nurturance and affection, as well as the need for self-sufficiency. The types of dependency behaviors are based on the work of Robert R. Sears and others (1957) in observations of children. These include: help-seeking, attention-seeking, and affection-seeking. Independent behaviors include initiative-taking and obstacle mastery. Each person varies in his need for dependency and independency according to many conditions of time and place. When the necessary means for meeting the current need are changed, deficits or excesses develop. If usual mechanisms to handle the deficit or excess are not adequate, adaptation problems result. These problems can be generally called dysfunctional dependence and dysfunctional independence. These problems and the specific forms they take are the subject of Chapters 23, 24, and 25.

Relationship Among the Adaptive Modes

Man functions as one unified being. It is possible to look at man from a variety of viewpoints and to divide him up for purposes of analysis. However, each part of his nature is intimately interrelated in complex ways. As the nurse views man she must keep in mind the complexity and interrelatedness of the total person.

An internal or external change may affect more than one adaptive mode at a time. For example, when a man loses his job, his role as family breadwinner may be primarily affected. At the same time his self-concept also suffers. Even his physiological needs may reach the point of deficit if the unemployment is prolonged. Any given focal stimulus may simultaneously cause adaptation problems in any or all of the adaptive modes.

Man's integrated nature also makes it possible for one behavior to be a manifestation of disruption in more than one mode. The behavior must be looked at in relation to all influencing factors before a diagnosis can be made as to which mode is disrupted primarily. For example, if a student comes to class late, one cannot judge whether rest deficits or role deficits are primarily involved until one knows the focal, contextual, and residual stimuli that led to the behavior. Looking at behavior from Helson's framework of causality helps to avoid simplistic conclusions of one behavior having one meaning.

Finally, the integrated nature of man is seen particularly through the affect that one mode has upon another. As a young mother develops in her mothering role, one of the primary residual factors influencing the situation is how she feels about herself—her self-concept. Similarly integrity of one's physiological self may be the focal stimulus for a change in self-concept. An example of this would be getting a severe sunburn, which leads to the thought, "I was stupid to let it happen." Each adaptive mode may act as a focal, contextual, or residual stimulus for each other mode.

The Goal of Adaptation Nursing

The goal of nursing according to the adaptation model is clearly implied in the earlier discussion of man, the recipient of nursing care. This nursing model views man as having four adaptive modes which help him to cope with the changing environment. Furthermore, nursing historically has dealt with persons who have problems of a health-illness nature. Thus, nursing's goal is to promote man's adaptation in each of the adaptive modes in situations of health and illness. The states of varying degrees of health or illness can be represented by a continuous line called the health–illness continuum (see Figure 1.4). Adaptation problems have been defined as situations resulting from inadequate responses to meet need deficits or excesses. As man moves along the continuum between maximum wellness and maximum illness, he will encounter adaptation problems. These problems are the concern of the nurse. Her goal will be to solve the problem and bring about adaptation.

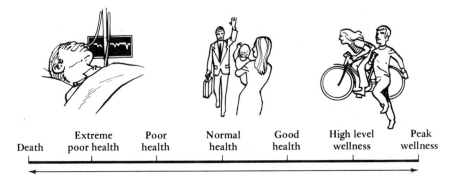

| Death | Extreme poor health | Poor health | Normal health | Good health | High level wellness | Peak wellness |

Figure 1.4   Health-illness continuum.

Nursing Activities According to the Adaptation Model

The adaptation model of nursing implies a process similar to that which has been developed over the years of nursing history. The nurse first assesses client behavior in each of the adaptive modes. This is called first level assessment. Then she selects areas of concern, either maladaptive behaviors or adaptive behaviors needing reinforcing. For each of these she moves to second level assessment and determines the focal, contextual, and residual stimuli contributing to each behavior. Based on this assessment, the nurse diagnoses the related adaptation problem. Since she has clearly identified the client behavior to be changed or reinforced, she can easily establish her nursing goal. This goal is stated in terms of the behavioral outcome for the patient. Nursing approaches are then selected to accomplish the nursing goal. In general these approaches are aimed at removing the focal stimulus or changing the contextual or residual stimulus. In this way the cause of the behavior is removed or the client's ability to cope—adaptation level—is broadened. The nurse manipulates stimuli by removing them, increasing them, decreasing them, or altering them. Behavioral outcomes are then evaluated, and nursing approaches modified as necessary. This total nursing process is explored in Chapter 2.

SUMMARY

Nursing is a scientific way of providing care for the ill or potentially ill person. The Roy adaptation nursing model is an approach to nursing which views man as a biopsychosocial being with modes of adapting to changing environment and which acts through a nursing process to promote man's adaptation in each of these modes in situations of health and illness.

REFERENCES

Byrne, Marjorie and Leda F. Thompson, *Key Concepts for the Study and Practice of Nursing.* St. Louis: C. V. Mosby Co., 1972.

Driever, Marie, Unpublished lecture notes. Los Angeles: Mount St. Mary's College, 1970.

DuGas, Beverly, *Kozier-DuGas Introduction to Patient Care.* 2nd ed. Philadelphia: W. B. Saunders Company, 1972, p. 70.

Harmer, Bertha, *Textbook of the Principles and Practice of Nursing.* Rev. by Virginia Henderson. 5th ed. New York: The Macmillan Company, 1955.

Helson, Harry, *Adaptation Level Theory.* New York: Harper and Row, Publishers, 1964.

Henderson, Virginia, *Basic Principles of Nursing Care.* London: International Council of Nurses, 1960.

Levine, Myrna, *Introduction to Clinical Nursing.* Philadelphia: F. A. Davis, 1973.

Maslow, A. H., *Motivation and Personality.* New York: Harper and Row, Publishers, 1954.

Nightingale, Florence, *Notes on Nursing: What It Is, and What It Is Not.* A facsimile of the first edition printed in London, 1859, with a foreword by Annie W. Goodrich. Philadelphia: J. P. Lippincott Company, 1966.

Riehl, Joan P. and Sister Callista Roy, *Conceptual Models for Nursing Practice.* New York: Appleton-Century-Crofts, 1974.

Rogers, Martha E., *An Introduction to the Theoretical Basis of Nursing Practice.* Philadelphia: F. A. Davis, 1970.

Roy, Sister Callista, "Adaptation: A Conceptual Framework for Nursing," *Nursing Outlook,* March 1970, pp. 42–45.

____ , "Adaptation: A Basis for Nursing Practice," *Nursing Outlook,* April 1971, pp. 254–57.

Sears, Robert R., E. E. Maccaby and H. Levin, *Patterns of Child Rearing.* New York: Harper and Row, Publishers, 1957.

Toffler, Alvin, *Future Shock.* New York: Random House, Inc., 1970.

2

The Nursing Process

Sister Callista Roy

KEY CONCEPTS DEFINED

Nursing Process: A problem-solving procedure for gathering data, identifying problems, selecting and implementing approaches, and evaluating results in relation to care of the ill or potentially ill person.

Client: The person receiving nursing care. The client may be healthy or ill.

Human Behavior: Actions or reactions under specified circumstances.

Behavior the Nurse Assesses: The person's responses to changes in need states which require an adaptive response. These responses can be observed or measured or are subjectively reported.

First Level Assessment: Gathering data about client behavior in each adaptive mode by skillful observation, accurate measurement of response, and communicative interviewing.

Nursing Interview: Structured interaction with the client to obtain subjective data about his responses to changes in health and illness.

Norm: A standard of behavior to guide judgment about what promotes integrity.

Second Level Assessment: Identification of the focal, contextual, and residual factors that influence client behavior.

Focal Stimulus: The degree of change or stimulus most immediately confronting the person and the one to which the client must make an adaptive response; that is, the cause of the behavior.

Contextual Stimuli: All other stimuli present that contribute to the behavior caused by the focal stimulus.

Residual Stimuli: Factors which may be affecting behavior but whose effects are not validated.

Problem Identification: The step of the nursing process in which the nurse makes a statement of the client's adaptive and maladaptive behavior with the most relevant influencing factors.

Nursing Diagnosis: The summary statement or conclusion based on the data gathered in the nursing assessment process. The same as problem identification except that in its higher form it is a short label that communicates the total nature of a unique client problem.

Setting Priorities: A procedure inherent throughout the nursing process by which the nurse determines the hierarchy of importance of client problems.

Goal Setting: Establishing clear statements of the behavioral outcomes of nursing care for the client.

Intervention: Selection and carrying out of an approach to change or stabilize adaptation by manipulation of stimuli.

Evaluation: Judging the effectiveness of the nursing intervention by looking at the effect it had on client's adaptive behavior.

After studying this chapter the reader will be able to:

1. Define the key concepts of this chapter.
2. Illustrate reasons for using a problem-solving based nursing process.
3. Distinguish between all human behavior and behavior the nurse assesses.
4. Specify methods of assessing client behavior.
5. Differentiate focal, contextual, and residual stimuli.
6. Contrast problem identification and nursing diagnosis.
7. Identify a nursing goal that is stated as a behavioral outcome for the client.
8. Apply the nursing judgment model to an ordinary decision in life.

The nursing process has been identified as the specific activity that distinguishes nursing from other health care disciplines. Each nursing theorist has her own way of specifying this process. The specification identifies her view of the uniqueness of nursing. However, the general outline of any nursing process follows the procedure used by other professionals giving health service. This procedure is the problem-solving process. In using this process, the person first gathers data, then identifies the problem. An approach to the problem is selected from among possible alternatives, and finally the results of the approach are evaluated. As we explore the Roy adaptation nursing process in this chapter, this general outline will be apparent, but the specifics of nursing, based on this model, will also be clarified. The adaptation model determines what data to collect, how to identify the problem, what approach to use, and how to evaluate the approach.

RATIONALE FOR THE NURSING PROCESS

There are two major reasons why nursing uses a problem-solving based nursing process. The first reason is the client-centered goal of nursing. The second is the accountability of the professional as a scientific discipline which is service-oriented.

We have described nursing's goal as to promote man's adaptation in situations of health and illness. Man as an individual, as a member of a family, or as a member of the community is the recipient of nursing care. In this text we refer to the person receiving nursing care as the client. Each person copes differently with changes in his status of health and illness. Since nursing is to help man adapt to these changes, the nurse must be able to clearly identify the person's level of adaptation and to define his difficulties so that she may intervene to promote adaptation. Thus she must gather data, define a problem, and select an approach. Any nurse who has cared for clients can verify that no two clients are alike. Even given a common medical diagnosis, clients will present unique ways of coping with their situations. One client will be able to cope well with the pain following an appendectomy. Another will find the pain intolerable. Since the goal of nursing is to promote adaptation, the nurse must go through the process of assessing adaptation and planning accordingly.

As a scientific discipline, nursing must be accountable for the service it provides to society. To maintain itself as a needed service nursing must be able to verify that its activities make a difference in terms of what is valued by society. The experience of fluctuations in health and illness is a universal phenomenon. Even the most robust of persons will at some time in his life experience such fluctuations. It seems accurate to say that most people will also at some time experience difficulty in coping with these changes. According to the adaptation concept of nursing, nursing aims to promote this adaptation in health and illness. It is a basic assumption of the model that this service is valued by society. Nursing must then validate that it can in fact effect client adaptation. It can do this only if it can demonstrate by using a scientific approach that nursing activities can change a situation of maladaptation into a situation of adaptation. To do this the nurse must assess adaptation, plan care, and evaluate the effectiveness of her approach.

Thus the problem-solving nursing process is required by the client-centered goal of nursing and by the need to verify the service that the nurse provides. The rest of this chapter shows how this process is developed according to the Roy adaptation model.

STEP ONE—ASSESSMENT OF CLIENT BEHAVIORS

The first step of the problem-solving based nursing process is data collection. The adaptation concept outlines the data the nurse collects. Since the nurse's goal is to promote adaptation, she must first evaluate the current level of client adaptation. The nurse turns to the nursing model's concept of man to select areas for data collection. Man is viewed as having four adaptive modes or ways to cope with changes in the environment. These modes are conceptualized as real areas of man's adaptive being, just as the human circulatory system is part of man's anatomical being. These modes are physiologic, self-concept, role function, and interdependence. Behind each mode is a basic need. In general these are the needs for physiologic integrity, psychic integrity, and social integrity. When a change in the environment causes a deficit or excess in the need, then the appropriate adaptive mode is activated. This action is like that of an

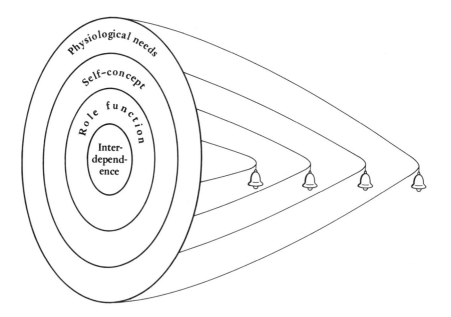

Figure 2.1   Model of the adaptative modes and their relationship to behavior.

arrow hitting one ring within a total target. Once the ring is hit, the functional unit of that ring is activated. This would be like the ring having a built-in mechanism to ring a bell or flash on a light. This is known as the response to the stimuli (Figure 2.1). The functional or working unit of the adaptive mode is the coping mechanisms within the mode. These mechanisms emit responses in the form of human behavior. This behavior is the nurse's first unit of observation in the assessment process.

Behavior the Nurse Assesses

Human behavior is defined generally as actions or reactions under specified circumstances. Thus if a psychologist is testing a person's learning of nonsense syllables, the measured behavior is the response of repeating the syllables under the conditions specified, for example, in a dark room with no sensory input. At the same time, the person will have internal responses, which the psychologist can also monitor. The psychologist may also have leads attached to the subject to measure any increase in heart rate. Since this increase is also a response to the situation, it is also called a behavior. Behaviors, then, may be internal or external. Some internal behaviors can be easily measured, such as heart rate. Other internal behaviors, at the present stage of sophistication of behavioral science, can only be subjectively reported. If the subject who is repeating the nonsense syllables knows that he has performed poorly, he may feel disappointed. For the psychologist to be aware of this internal response, the subject must give some report of his feelings either verbally or in some clearly manifested, nonverbal communication.

We can now describe generally the object of the nurse's first level of assessment. The nurse looks at the person's responses, internal or external, that can be observed or measured or which are subjectively reported.

Our definition of human behavior stated that it was reactions under specified circumstances. The nursing model must point out what those circumstances are. The adaptation concept of nursing states that changes in satiety of given needs trigger adaptive responses. The specific circumstance under which the nurse observes human behavior, then, is changes in need satisfaction requiring an adaptive response.

Our general description of behavior that the nurse assesses can be summarized as follows: *The person's responses to changes in need states which require an adaptive response. These responses can be observed or measured or are subjectively reported.*

If the nurse is to look at behavior in relation to changes in each of the need states of man, she must know what behavior manifests responses to change in each need. The outline of what responses to observe is part of the body of nursing science. Nursing texts and nursing instructors must clarify for the developing practitioner what observations will give her data about human responses to changes in need states. At the present time we may define the client's heart rate, or pulse, and respiration as measurements indicating responses to change in need for oxygen. The nurse will thus observe these measurements. Subjective reports regarding self-worth may be indicators of responses to changes in the need for self-esteem. Thus the nurse will be aware that these are some of the behaviors she assesses. Specifying behaviors to observe in each of the adaptive modes is one objective of the remaining chapters of this book. Each chapter should be read with the purpose of outlining clearly what behavior to assess. A summary list of what the nurse looks at in her assessment is included in Appendix I.

Methods of Assessing Client Behavior

How the nurse assesses client behavior is basically the same process for all nurses, but how the process unfolds is largely a function of the circumstances in which she meets the client. When the student nurse is learning to assess client behavior she may look at only one need and adaptive mode at a time. Thus she may describe only one set of client behaviors relative to that mode. When the independent nurse practitioner[1] is describing the total adaptation problems of her client she may systematically gather data regarding each adaptive mode. Similarly the clinical specialist[2] in the hospital situation may make a total assessment of the client on admission to initiate the plan for nursing care. The team leader may update that plan by quickly assessing behavior in each mode for a group of clients. The nurse in an acute situation, such as an emergency room or coronary care unit, may be summoned by one presenting client behavior such as gasping for breath. Assessment of needs related to this behavior takes precedence over a total client assessment. Although such variations in use of the client assessment process are recognized, the basic process of assessment will be discussed.

In assessing client behaviors—that is, making first level client assessment—the nurse systematically looks at client behavior in each adaptive mode. She does this by means of her observation skills, her ability to measure internal and external responses, and her interviewing skills to obtain subjective data.

---

[1] The independent nurse practitioner is a nurse who has established a private practice to help clients with needs within the realm of nursing, for example, solving adaptation problems.

[2] The clinical specialist is a nurse who by reason of additional education and experience has expertise in meeting particular client needs, for example, physiological needs or needs for psychic integrity.

In using her observation skills the nurse uses all her senses to obtain data about a client's responses to changes in need states. She may see cyanotic skin color, hear rales, feel weakened pulse, or smell foul excreta. When she is making an initial assessment of the client, she goes through a systematic process of gathering data through her senses regarding each of the client's adaptive modes. The specific data to be gathered are discussed in the chapters on the adaptive modes and are outlined in Appendix I. When she makes contact with the client later she quickly turns her attention to each known area of importance. The data enters the nurse's perception and is quickly processed as a behavior indicative of responses in regard to given adaptive modes. There are times when a behavior may be indicative of responses in more than one mode. For example, if the nurse observes hard, dry stools, this may be a response to the body's need to adapt to changes in food and fluid intake, for example, after surgery. On the other hand, this behavior may be indicative of slowing peristalsis due to self-concept changes taking place following a loss. Behaviors that the nurse observes through her senses are classified as clearly as possible according to the adaptive mode about which they speak. Sometimes alternative modes are identified awaiting the more definitive second level assessment.

At the present time, the nurse's ability to measure internal and external responses is somewhat limited. Certain measurements, for example, determining arterial and venous pressures of the blood, are well established and defined. Every nurse learns these in basic nursing education, and techniques can be found in any basic textbook of nursing skills. Other measures are only in the early stages of testing. For example, some nurses have experimented with paper and pencil tests to measure relative degrees of feelings of powerlessness (Grubbs, 1968).

For other responses to need changes in health and illness, there are as yet no known nursing tests. For example, we do not know how to measure the body's response to the increased need for rest during convalescent stages. Nor do we know how to measure the adequacy of expressive role responses when there is a role change in health and illness.[3] At this point we can say that the nurse systematically utilizes the known tools for measuring internal and external responses to changes in need satisfaction in health and illness. At the same time the nurse is alert to the development and testing of new methods of measuring client adaptive behavior.

The client interview is one generalized tool the nurse uses to assess behavior. It is potentially her most important tool. Adaptive responses to situations of health and illness have a largely subjective element. When the body is adjusting to an increased need for oxygen, only the person can feel the subjective state of anxiety and panic. The feeling of loneliness when there is an increased need for

---

[3]One tool for measuring adequacy of instrumental role behaviors of the mother of the hospitalized child has been developed. See Sister Mary Callista Roy, "Role Cues and Mothers of Hospitalized Children," *Nursing Research* (Spring 1967), pp. 178-82.

affection in the absence of the loved partner is perceived only by the person.
Thus the nurse must be able to structure her interaction with the client in such
a way as to obtain this subjective data. The term "interview" is used to describe
this process, whether it involves a structured set of questions asked at one time,
or the purposeful listening without comment spaced throughout the nurse-client
relationship. The client and his subjective experience of responses to changes
in health and illness are the subject of the nursing interview. To obtain this data,
the nurse must maintain open lines of communication with her client. The process of communication involves a sender, a message, and a receiver. Communication has been successfully accomplished when a message is understood by the
receiver in the appropriate manner in which the sender intended (Ruesch, 1961).
Since the nurse is trying at this point in the nursing process to receive a message
from the client, she should encourage his or her participation.[4] She does this
by open-ended questions, paraphrasing, reflection of perceived meaning, and
gesturing such as nodding and leaning forward. The nurse must also be skillful
in nonstructured interviewing and in the purposeful use of silence within the
trusting nurse–client relationship to get the maximum benefit of the client's subjective perception of his own adaptive status.

Thus as any nurse begins the process of client assessment, whether her client
be a person in the intensive care unit or a pregnant woman in the prenatal clinic,
or whether her client be a family or the community at large, the nurse notes
client behavior in each adaptive mode by means of skillful observation, accurate
measurement of responses, and communicative interviewing. This is the process
of first level nursing assessment.

Judgment of Behavior as Adaptive or Maladaptive

The first step in the nursing process, assessment of client behavior, cul-
minates in a nursing judgment about whether the behavior is adaptive or maladaptive. In general a behavior is adaptive when it promotes the goal of the
adaptive mode, that is, integrity. Thus when the client with a fluid deficit
drinks water, this behavior is adaptive since it will promote physiologic integrity. On the other hand, if the client refuses to drink, the behavior may be
considered maladaptive since it is detrimental to his physiologic integrity not
to do so. Similarly, when a client suffering a loss cries and moans in such a
way and to such an extent as to move successfully through the grieving process,
then this behavior is adaptive. If, however, the behavior continues to the point
that psychic integrity is jeopardized, then the behavior may be considered maladaptive. For certain human responses, we have norms to guide our judgments

[4]The use of communication as a therapeutic tool is discussed in Chapter 23.

of what promotes integrity. For example, there is a range of pulse rates, blood pressures, and temperature readings for various age groups which are considered indicators of physiologic integrity for that group. For other behaviors such norms do not exist. For example, we do not know what level of expression of guilt about an illness is actually helpful to promote psychic integrity. In all areas, norms are merely general guidelines. They are not applied rigidly and to the same extent in all instances. For example, pulse varies by age groups, and expression of pain varies by culture.

To judge adaptability in areas where norms are not available, the nurse applies the general criteria hypothesized by the adaptation concept of nursing to the specific circumstances. The general signs of adaptation failures were identified as pronounced autonomic activity with cognator ineffectiveness. Observations indicative of pronounced regulator activity are: increase in heart rate or blood pressure, tension, excitement or loss of appetite. Behaviors that demonstrate cognator ineffectiveness include: (1) lack of awareness of the need state, (2) inability to identify the goal object, (3) inability to select means to an identified end, and (4) failure to reach a goal object. In general, the nurse asks herself whether the behavior she observes is a useless waste of energy that does not leave the client free to respond to other stimuli and particularly to use energy for getting well.

Thus if the nurse observes excessive bleeding, she knows that pronounced regulator activity will be present and that bodily energies are drained from the getting-well process to the process of coping with the emergency of hemorrhage. In this case, the behavior can be labeled quite clearly maladaptive. In the psychosocial realm, if a mother whose newborn infant died several days previously continues to ask the nurse whether she in any way contributed to the death of the infant, the nurse should recognize cognator ineffectiveness in that the mother cannot reach the goal of psychic integrity unaided. Her energies are being bound up with the same self-accusatory questions and are not free for other activities, such as relating to those closest to her. At the present time, the nurse may consider this behavior maladaptive.

As the nurse makes judgments about the adaptability of human behavior, she must be continually aware that the client should be involved in this judgment process. The client can often be the best judge of whether or not his behavior is effective in coping with a given stimuli. For example, a client may tell the nurse that the hospital bedtime routines do not result in a good night's sleep for him. Or the son of an elderly client may share with the nurse the fact that he is having a very difficult time making a decision about how to provide convalescent care for his father. The nurse should always take the client's observations of his own behavior into account in making her judgment about the adaptability of the behavior. The range of adaptive responses is wide. Norms are broad and not to be applied rigidly.

Summary of First Level Assessment

In the first step of the nursing process, the nurse gathers data about the client's behavior in each of the adaptive modes. The behavior she assesses are the person's responses to changes in need states. These changes in need states require an adaptive response. The resulting response can be observed or measured or it can be subjectly reported. The behaviors to be observed in each mode are further identified throughout this book. The nurse uses skillful observation, known tools of measurement, and the client interview to gather data about client behavior. First level assessment is completed with a tentative judgment about whether the behavior is adaptive or maladaptive. Criteria used in making this judgment include: whether or not the behavior promotes integrity of the adaptive mode, whether or not there is regulator and cognator effectiveness, whether or not the client perceives his behavior as adaptive.

STEP TWO—ASSESSMENT OF INFLUENCING FACTORS

Once the nurse has tentatively labeled behaviors as adaptive or maladaptive, she can proceed to the next step of the assessment process called second level assessment, which is the identification of the factors that influence these behaviors. She is interested in maladaptive behaviors because she wants to change them to adaptive behaviors. And she is interested in adaptive behaviors because she wants to maintain or reinforce these behaviors, particularly if they are threatened by negative influencing factors. With the realities of time constraints and other limitations of the nursing situation, the nurse cannot consider all behaviors equally important to analyze. At this point she will have to begin setting priorities about what behaviors are most important for her consideration. Principles for setting priorities are discussed below. When she has set priorities and identified the most significant client behaviors, then she identifies the focal, contextual, and residual stimuli influencing or contributing to these behaviors.

Identifying Focal Stimuli

The focal stimulus has been identified as the degree of change which precipitated the behavior being observed. This stimulus is the one most immediately confronting the person and the one to which the client must make an adaptive response. It is, as described earlier, the arrow that hits the target. It may be an environmental change, such as the occupancy of a single bed in a double hospital room instead of occupancy of a double bed in a private bedroom. Or it may be a change in a relationship, such as increased presence and solicitude of in-laws after the birth of a baby. Possible focal stimuli for given behaviors are identified throughout the chapters on the specific adaptive modes. The nurse uses the same method in assessing the focal stimuli that she used in assessing patient behaviors. That is, she makes skillful observations, collects measurements for which she has appropriate tools, and interviews the client. When she has made a hypothesis about with what stimulus the client is having difficulty coping, she shares this hunch with the client, if possible, to obtain validation of her assessment. Ida Jean Orlando (1961) emphasized the importance of sharing such observations with the client. With the current emphasis on client rights and with the adaptation concept of value of the individual person, it is extremely important that the client be involved in every phase of the plan for his care. This involvement has already begun in the step of first level assessment and is continued in the second level assessment—assessment of influencing factors.

We should point out that what is behavior observed in one adaptive mode may become the focal stimulus for another mode. Thus grieving behavior, when loss is the focal stimulus affecting self-concept, may itself be focal to causing behavior indicative of role function. For example, the fact that the client is crying and moaning regarding a loss is the very change that leads to disruption in his role as consoler of the family. At the same time one focal stimulus can affect more than one adaptive mode. This would be like the arrow bouncing off one ring of the target and hitting another, thus ringing more than one bell. Hemorrhage is an immediate threat to circulatory integrity, but at the same time the client may feel his self-consistency threatened by the fear of death. In any case, in assessing the focal stimulus, the nurse is looking for the most immediate cause of the observed behavior.

Identifying Contextual Stimuli

Contextual stimuli are those contributing to the behavior caused by the focal stimulus. They are all other stimuli present that affect the behavior being observed. It is like observing the atmosphere through which the arrow travels for determining anything that will influence its effect upon the target, and observing the target apparatus for anything that will influence the ringing of the bell. Again the stimuli may be external, such as environmental factors, or internal, such as factors within the person. For example, as we will see in a situation used in Chapter 20, a school-age boy has the maladaptive role behavior of not studying. The focal stimulus has been identified as the fact that his usual schedule is missing. However, contributing to the effect of this stimulus are the internal factor that until yesterday he felt "sick" and the external factors of being in isolation and of the usual rewards of school and home being missing. These are considered contextual stimuli. Contextual stimuli are identified by the same process of observation, measurement, interview, and validation.

Nurses sometimes ask whether contextual stimuli can be both positive and negative. That is, does the nurse identify factors that make the behavior less maladaptive at the same time that she searches for those that contribute to making it maladaptive? The answer is that at times it may be important to know stimuli which are tugging in a direction opposite to the focal stimulus because these can be capitalized on to change the effect of the focal stimulus. According to the image used earlier, this positive contextual stimulus may become the focal arrow which hits the target and causes an adaptive response. For example, if a supportive mother is contributing to making a young woman less maladaptive to her new mothering role, she should be identified as a positive contextual stimulus. In the intervention phase, to be discussed later, the nurse may be able to make this stimulus more focal.

In developing the adaptation concept of nursing certain classes of relevant contextual stimuli are being identified for certain circumstances. For example, the chapter on role theory explains that the following are contextual to role function: consumer, reward, set of circumstances, and objects for cooperation. Nursing instructors who have worked with the adaptation model as applied to nursing of children have identified these as relevant contextual stimuli: separation from family, developmental age, stress of illness, response to authority figures, and restricted activities (Schofield and Poush, 1973). Significant contextual stimuli are discussed throughout this text, and are summarized in Appendix I. Some contextual factors that seem to influence all adaptive modes are: genetic makeup, sex, developmental stage, drugs, alcohol, tobacco, self-concept, role functions, interdependence, social interaction patterns, coping mechanisms and styles, physical and emotional stress, cultural orientation, religion, and environment. A careful assessment of all relevant contextual stimuli will be important for both problem identification and for nursing intervention.

Identifying Residual Stimuli

When the nurse is assessing the factors that influence client adaptive and maladaptive behavior, she often identifies stimuli that she presumes from previous knowledge are affecting the behavior. These may be such things as beliefs, attitudes, experience, or traits. However, she is unable to validate the effect they have on client behavior. As a group these stimuli are called residual stimuli. Figuratively, it may be factors present to influence the impact of the arrow, but which are impossible to substantiate at present, for example, the motives of the invisible archer who shot the arrow, or some elusive malfunction in the apparatus which initiates the sound of the bell. These stimuli come from the same external and internal forces as the focal and contextual stimuli, but they are differentiated by the fact that they cannot be substantiated. Thus, for example, toilet training or cultural beliefs may be affecting current bowel elimination.

However, it is difficult for a nurse to validate exactly what affect they have. She then categorizes these factors as residual stimuli. Appropriate residual factors influencing behavior are discussed in the chapters on adaptation problems.

STEP THREE—PROBLEM IDENTIFICATION

When the process of nursing assessment has been accurately carried out, whether completely and painstakingly as by a clinical specialist, or in isolated areas in haste by a critical care nurse, then the step of identifying client problems becomes relatively simple. The problem is simply a statement of the client's adaptive or maladaptive behavior with the most relevant influencing factors. In keeping with our earlier example, we can say that we identify the particular sound of the bell and say it is due to a particular arrow also influenced by other specified circumstances. Thus a problem in bowel elimination may be described as "hard, dry stools due to decreased fluid intake and limited mobility." A problem of interdependence relative to aggression may be described as "abusive language due to lack of control of aggressive drive in the face of excessive alterations in the environment." Behaviors which are currently adaptive but which may become maladaptive unless reinforced may be stated as potential problems. For example, "Currently performing taking-in and taking-hold maternal behaviors, but potential role failure due to mother-in-law's comparisons of her with other relatives."[5]

We have called this phase of the nursing process the step of problem identification. This step is related to what is currently called nursing diagnosis. A nursing diagnosis is defined as the summary statement or conclusion based on the data gathered in the nursing assessment process. When we have summarized our assessment by stating the behavior observed and the factors influencing it, we have, in a sense, made a nursing diagnosis. This, however, is diagnosis in its most elementary form. A higher level of the diagnostic process is reached when the summary statement is a short label that communicates the total nature of a unique client problem. Nursing is now in the process of developing a typology of such labels or diagnoses. The First National Conference on Nursing Diagnosis, sponsored by St. Louis University, met in the fall of 1973 (Gebbie and Lavin, 1975). Since that time a national task force has been working to develop a standard typology of diagnoses for nursing, which would have a standard, codifiable nomenclature. Many models of nursing have their own typologies of client problems. The problems currently identified as commonly recurring according to the Roy adaptation concept of nursing are referred to throughout this book. However, since nursing does not yet have a commonly accepted typology of diagnoses and since the adaptation labels have neither been tested nor are they commonly understood, the author feels it is best for nurses present-

---

[5]The problems used here as examples are discussed in detail in later chapters.

ly using this model to employ the problem-identification method described here rather than to use diagnostic labels. Stating behaviors and influencing factors has the advantage of being an accepted form of clear communication for nurses (see, for example, Mayers, 1972).

CRITERIA FOR SETTING PRIORITIES

Setting priorities is viewed not as a separate step of the nursing process, but rather as a procedure inherent throughout the process. As the nurse identifies client behavior, she selects those behaviors on which she will focus in doing her second level of assessment, identifying influencing factors. Once she does her assessment, she will identify the problems. She then places these in a hierarchy of importance. Her setting of goals is influenced by the relative importance of the problem. The nature and timing of interventions will also depend on the priorities set. Even the time and effort given to the evaluation process is relative to the priority of the problem. Thus it is important for the nurse to have principles or criteria on which to base her setting of priorities.

Priority is defined as precedence, especially established by order of importance or urgency. Fay Louise Bower (1972) identifies criteria for determining a hierarchy of importance of client problems as follows:

" 1.   those problems that threaten the life and integrity of the individual, family, or community;
  2.   those problems that threaten to change destructively the individual, family, or community; and
  3.   those problems that affect the normal development and growth of the individual, family, or community."[6]

Thus the nurse will always give top priority to problems in the first category, then move on down the list. At times she can plan to meet needs in more than one category with one nursing intervention. While she is teaching a new mother to nurse her baby, she has the child's need for life-giving nourishment as one priority, but the potential effect of the mother-child relationship on the infant's development is also being considered. In planning with an individual client, the client's view of the priority of the problem is also used as data in establishing a hierarchy of importance.

This same author adds the following criteria for use when the nurse is setting priorities for groups of patients.

[6]Fay Louise Bower, *The Process of Planning Nursing Care* (St. Louis: C. V. Mosby Co., 1972). p. 14.

"1. Safety—severity of health problems, potential for recovery, attainment of high-level wellness.
2. Efficiency—time needed by the client, nurse, or health team.
3. Cost—expense in money and energy to client, nurse, agency, society.
4. Receptivity to care."

These two sets of criteria interact in any given situation. For example, in a disaster area, the nurse may find that many lives are threatened. The further criteria of potential for recovery helps her to decide where to concentrate her energies. When a problem reaches the point of greater threat to integrity, greater costs may be tolerated. For example, with the continuing drug problem in society with its potential for destroying the integrity of the community, the government is willing to undertake the high cost of preventive drug abuse programs.

The nurse can use these criteria for setting priorities throughout each phase of the nursing process.

STEP FOUR—GOAL SETTING

When the nurse has made a clear behavioral description of the client problem, she can establish her nursing goal. Her goal, in general, is to change maladaptive behavior to adaptive behavior, and to reinforce adaptive behavior. Thus the goal is stated in terms of the resulting behavior expected of the client.

For the sample problems discussed earlier, the following statement of goals is appropriate.

Problem	Goal
1. Hard, dry stools due to decreased fluid intake and limited mobility.	Client will have stools of normal consistency and frequency.
2. Abusive language due to lack of control of aggressive drive in face of excessive alteration in the environment.	Client will not use abusive language but will express aggressive drive within limits of environment, for example, in decision-making about time of care.
3. Currently performing taking-in and taking-hold maternal behaviors, but potential role failure due to mother-in-law's comparisons of client with other relatives.	Client will continue to manifest role mastery by taking-in and taking-hold maternal behaviors.

Goals, then, are clear statements of the behavioral outcomes of nursing care for the client.

STEP FIVE—INTERVENTION: SELECTION OF APPROACHES

The next step of the nursing process, intervention or selection of approaches, is based directly on the way the nursing model views the process of client adaptation. We have pointed out that man's ability to respond positively, or to adapt, depends upon the degree of change taking place and the state of the person coping with the change; that is, client adaptation depends upon the focal stimulus and the client's adaptation level. If the nurse wants to effect change or to stabilize adaptation, she can manipulate the focal stimulus or she can broaden the adaptation level by manipulating the other stimuli present. In selecting which stimuli to manipulate, Roy points out that the nurse uses the nursing judgment method outlined by F. J. McDonald and Mary Harms (1966). This method is a way of listing possible approaches, then selecting the approach with the highest probability of achieving the valued goal. Combining this method with the Roy adaptation model, we can say that the various stimuli affecting patient behaviors are listed. Then the consequences of manipulation of each stimuli are outlined. The probability of each consequence is determined. In addition, the value of the outcomes of the approach are judged. The approach with the highest probability of reaching the valued goal can then be selected. For example, in the problem of elimination identified earlier, this method of analysis would provide the outline in Table 2.1.

TABLE 2.1
Nursing Judgement Method Combined with Adaptation Nursing Model

Alternative Approach	Consequences	Probability	Value
Manipulate stimuli of decreased fluid intake	Improve bowel function	.70	desirable
	Do not improve bowel function	.30	undesirable
	Cause circulatory overload	.05	undesirable
Manipulate stimuli of limited mobility	Improve bowel function	.70	desirable
	Do not improve bowel function	.30	undesirable
	Cause disturbance of spinal fusion site	.90	undesirable

In this example, the first approach, manipulating the focal stimulus of decreased fluid intake, has a fairly high probability of achieving a desirable consequence, which is the goal of the intervention. At the same time the undesirable consequences of this approach, not improving bowel function and causing circulatory overload, have a low probability. On the other hand, one undesirable outcome of the second approach, causing disturbance of spinal fusion site, has a very high probability. Thus the first approach, manipulating the stimuli of decreased fluid intake, is selected for nursing action. It should be pointed out that whenever possible the focal stimulus should be manipulated since it is seen as the primary cause of the behavior being considered.

STEP SIX—EVALUATION

The final step of the nursing process is the evaluation of the effectiveness of nursing intervention. This effectiveness is judged by the result that the nursing approach had regarding the client's adaptive behavior. The nurse simply asks herself whether or not the desired client goal was attained. Did the client manifest the behavior listed in the stated goal? To gather data to answer this question, the nurse uses the same methods that she used in gathering data in the first and second steps of the nursing process—she makes skillful observations, uses tools of measurement, and interviews the client. In the three problem areas used as examples in this chapter, the nurse would simply measure current client behavior against the behavior stated in the goal; does the client have stools of normal consistency and frequency? Or, does the client not use abusive language, but expresses his or her aggressive drive in such ways as decision-making about time of care? Or, does the client continue to manifest role mastery by taking-in and taking-hold maternal behaviors? When the nurse determines the effects of her intervention, she returns to the first step of the nursing process. She looks more closely at behaviors that continue to be maladaptive and reassesses the factors influencing these. For behaviors that have become adaptive, with no threat of returning to maladaptive, she may delete this behavior as a priority of nursing concern. For behaviors that are still maladaptive she reassesses influencing stimuli to see if her nursing approach should be modified by manipulating another stimulus. Evaluation, then, is a crucial tool in updating the plan for nursing care.

SUMMARY

In this chapter we have considered the nursing process as specified by the Roy adaptation model of nursing. This process is built on the problem-solving process used by other professionals in giving health care service. However, the nursing model has been used to determine the specific data to collect, that is, assessment of client behavior in each adaptive mode and focal, contextual, and residual factors influencing these behaviors. To gather this data, the nurse uses skillful observation, the known tools of measurement, and the client interview. A method of identifying the problem by describing adaptive or maladaptive behavior and the primary influencing factors was described. This method was seen as a beginning step in what can soon become a sophisticated process of nursing diagnosis. The nursing model also was used to describe the steps of stating goals in terms of expected client behaviors. The discussion of selecting approaches to meet that goal combined the Roy model emphasis on adaptation being a function of adaptation level with the nursing judgment model proposed by McDonald and Harms. The final step of evaluation came as a logical conclusion of the earlier discussion. Client behavior is reassessed to decide whether or not the nursing approach has achieved the stated goal. Modifications are made or new priorities are set based on this evaluation. This process is illustrated in Figure 2.2.

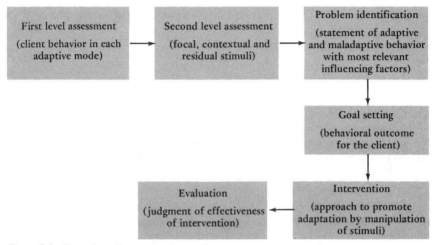

Figure 2.2   Flow chart illustrating the nursing process based on the Roy adaptation model of nursing.

REFERENCES

Bower, Fay Louise, *The Process of Planning Nursing Care.* St. Louis: C. V. Mosby Co., 1972, p. 14.

Gebbie, Kristine and Mary Ann Lavin, *Classification of Nursing Diagnoses.* St. Louis: C. V. Mosby Co., 1975.

Grubbs, Judy, "Powerlessness among Mothers of Chronically-Ill Children," unpublished Master's thesis. Los Angeles: University of California, 1968.

McDonald, F. J. and Mary Harms, "Theoretical Model for an Experimental Curriculum," *Nursing Outlook,* vol. 14, no. 8, August 1966, pp. 48-51.

Mayers, Marlene G., *A Systematic Approach to the Nursing Care Plan.* New York: Appleton-Century-Crofts, 1972.

Orlando, Ida Jean, *Dynamic Nurse-Patient Relationship.* New York: G. P. Putnam's Sons, 1961, pp. 31-40.

Roy, Sister Callista, "Adaptation: A Basis for Nursing Practice," *Nursing Outlook,* vol. 19, no. 4, April 1971, p. 256.

Ruesch, Jurgen, *Therapeutic Communication*. New York: W. W. Norton and Company, Inc., 1961, pp. 452-55.

Schofield, Ann and Mary Poush, *Unpublished lecture notes*. Los Angeles, Mount St. Mary's College, 1973.

II

Basic Physiological Needs

Sister Joyce Van Landingham, *Coordinator*

The preceding chapters dealt with the concept that a person requires help in adapting to his changing environment in health and illness, and that through the use of the nursing process the nurse can more effectively promote the client's physiological and psychosocial adaptation on the health illness continuum. The ways in which man adapts have been called adaptive modes. Behind each mode are needs that fluctuate in degree of satiety according to the changes in the internal and external environments. Deficits or excesses bring the mode and its functional part, the copying mechanisms, into action. Activity results which is observed as behavior.

Part II of this text focuses on the physiological needs. Each need is looked at in relation to the behaviors the nurse observes which show activity to adapt to changes in satisfaction of the need. Factors that influence adaptation in the physiological mode are reviewed in relation to each need. Finally, in each chapter on the needs there is a discussion of the common adaptation problems of deprivation and overload, and the nursing intervention to promote adaptation.

41

3

Exercise and Rest

Sister Teresa Marie McIntier

KEY CONCEPTS DEFINED

Posture: An anatomical arrangement of body parts either while moving about or while still.

Supine: Lying on the back.

Lateral: Lying on the side.

Prone: Lying with face downward.

Foot Drop: Deformity in which person is no longer able to hold his or her foot in a normal position.

Muscle Atrophy: A decrease in muscle size and contractility.

Muscle Contracture: A condition of fixed, high resistance to the passive stretch of a muscle.

Hypertrophy: Enlargement resulting from increased use.

Rest: A relative cessation of activity in which energy requirements are minimal.

Sleep: A state of rest in which the person has a decreased ability to interact with the external environment.

Immobility: Relative inactivity beyond the period of rest.

Fatigue: A subjective feeling of aversion to activity connoting mental or physical weariness and exhaustion.

Insomnia: A sleep disturbance that consists of difficulty in falling asleep, difficulty staying asleep, early final awakening, or a combination of these.

Passive Exercise: Movement of the joint for the person.

Active-Assistive Exercise: Exercise in which the client carries out motions to fullest potential and then is assisted to complete them.

Active Exercise: Exercise of using muscles without personal or mechanical assistance.

Resistive Exercise: Exercise the person accomplishes against resistance such as by adding weight.

After studying this chapter the reader will be able to:

1. Define the key concepts of this chapter.
2. Describe correct standing and lying postures.
3. Demonstrate the principles of body mechanics.
4. List factors affecting exercise and rest (see Appendix I).
5. Identify problems of immobility, fatigue, and insomnia if given case studies illustrating these problems.
6. Specify nursing interventions to be used in problems of exercise and rest (see Appendix II).

Exercise and rest are essential to the human body in a way similar to the more obvious need for food and fluids. Presumably, the organism will demand the proper ratio of both rest and exercise. The ideal ratio in a physiologically and psychologically adjusted individual is for rest and exercise to be nearly equally divided. However, even in the most well-adjusted person, stresses do occur that change the ratio. It can become unbalanced at times due to the demands of situations, such as a weekend tennis tournament or an acute illness that necessitates staying in bed for a person accustomed to much physical activity.

BEHAVIORAL ASSESSMENT OF EXERCISE

In assessing exercise, the nurse must gather data concerning the client's posture and mobility. These are man's basic activities in relation to the need for exercise.[1] Posture is defined as an anatomical arrangement of body parts

[1] Looking at activities in relation to physiological needs is an approach being developed by Sister Joyce Van Landinghan and Dorothy Clough at Mount St. Mary's College, Los Angeles.

either in a dynamic or static condition. The posture of an ambulatory[2] client is described as being dynamic, whereas any attempt to hold the body stationary is considered a static position. The more common static positions are lying, sitting, and standing. The correct posture of the standing body is aligned vertically with the center of gravity of the head, arms, and trunk in a plane slightly behind the hip joints and in front of the knee joints (see Figure 3.1). Correct posture promotes proper functioning of the body systems, while incorrect posture places undue strain on muscles, ligaments, and joints.

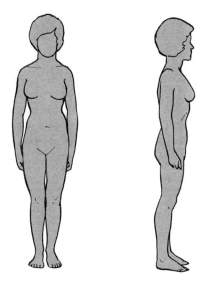

Figure 3.1   Correct standing posture.

The lying positions are the supine, lateral, and prone. In each position correct posture must be maintained.

Supine means lying on the back. In the supine position special attention is given to the neck and feet. The person's body should be in full extension resembling the upright position. Placing a small pillow under the head helps to maintain the neck in extension.[3] Careful positioning of the trunk minimizes undue flexion[4] on the hips. The arms should then be gently flexed at the elbows with the hands resting on the abdomen. Extend the legs; a small pillow under the knees prevents strain on the abdominal muscles. The feet are placed

---

[2]Ambulatory means being able and allowed to move about and walk from place to place.

[3]Extension means to straighten out.

[4]Flexion is the act of bending.

firmly against a footboard, keeping the heels free of the mattress as a preventive measure against decubiti, or bed sores. If the feet are left unsupported a deformity called *foot drop* results, and the person is no longer able to hold his foot in a normal position.

Lateral relates to the side. When placing the person in the lateral position, body alignment can best be maintained if a full-size pillow is arranged lengthwise from the shoulders to the buttocks. Keeping the head in line with the spine enhances body alignment. Flex the upper leg at the hip or knee, and support it in slight abduction.[5] Extending the lower leg in a straight line with the spine and placing a pillow between the knees prevent pressure and provide comfort. Body alignment can be further maintained by pulling the buttocks slightly back. Flex the lower arm at the elbow and shoulder, and support it with a small pillow. Place the upper arm at the person's side.

Prone refers to lying with face downward. The prone position is usually the one of choice in caring for the unconscious person. The person's head is extended in a lateral rotation and in alignment with the rest of the body. Abduct and externally rotate the arms at the shoulder joint and flex the elbows. Placing a small pillow from the umbilicus to midthigh will support the pelvis. The lower legs should also be supported to maintain the feet in a neutral position against a footboard. As the heels were kept free of the mattress in the supine position, so should the toes be suspended over the edge of the mattress in the prone position.

In the sitting position, the torso is held vertically with firm support under the buttocks. The arms are flexed at the elbows and supported in position. Both feet are flat on the floor.

Mobility, or dynamic posture, depends on the coordinated activity of bones, muscles, and nerves. Bones provide attachments for muscles and ligaments, and act as levers. The muscles contract to produce motion. Nerves conduct impulses from the central nervous system (sometimes simply referred to as C.N.S.) and carry impulses back from the sensory receptors.

Applying the scientific principles of mobility enables the nurse to determine the type and range of movement of which the person's body parts are capable. Bony structure is capable of many movements, which may range from the maximum mobility of the shoulder joint to the complete immobility of the joints of the skull.

Joints are usually formed of fibrous connective tissue and cartilege. They are classified structurally as freely movable, slightly movable, and immovable. In functional terms they are categorized as gliding, ball and socket, hinge, and saddle and pivot joints.

The location of body movement is found in articulation, but its source is in muscular contraction. Even when muscles are at rest a certain tautness remains

[5]Abduction is movement away from the center of the body.

called muscle tone. Although the mechanism that produces muscle tone is not fully understood, it is known physiologically to be due to nerve impulses. By means of tonic contraction in skeletal muscles, a person's posture can be maintained for relatively long periods with little or no fatigue. This absence of fatigue is due to different groups of muscle fibers contracting in relays, allowing alternating periods of rest and activity for a given muscle fiber group. Muscle tone is greater during periods of excitement and in positions of readiness and is lower in standing and sitting positions. During sleep the tone is progressively lessened.

As fatigue sets in, the muscle contracts over a shorter range and does not return completely to its normal length when relaxation is permitted. However, the recovery process is hastened by external application of heat, warm showers, and light massage.

When muscles are not in use (such as when a joint is immobilized), they lose much of their contractility, become flaccid, and decrease in size. This condition is known as *muscle atrophy*. If this disuse and lack of joint motion lasts over a period of time, a maladaptive response of *muscle contracture* develops. This is a condition of fixed, high resistance to the passive stretch of a muscle. On the other hand, increased use of a muscle results in enlargement, or *hypertrophy*.

In assessing the adaptability of body movement the nurse will assess whether or not the principles underlying body mechanics are being used. Commonly accepted principles are listed below:

1. Large muscles fatigue less quickly than small muscles—for example, does the person lift a heavy object by flexing the knees rather than bending from the waist.
2. The stability of an object is greater when there is a wide base of support and a low center of gravity, and when a vertical line from the center of gravity falls within the base of support—for example, does the person also stand with feet apart while flexing the knees.
3. The amount of effort required to move a body depends upon the resistance of the body as well as the gravitational pull—for example, does the client push up in bed while lying down rather than sitting.
4. The force required to maintain body balance is greatest when the line of gravity is farthest from the center of the base of support—for example, does the person hold a weight close to his body rather than out with extended arms.
5. Changes in activity and position help to maintain muscle tone and avoid fatigue—for example, does the client change positions in bed, or move from lying to sitting and standing as able.
6. The friction between an object and the surface upon which the object is moved increases the amount of work needed to move the object—for example, is the bed smooth before a client tries to push himself up.

7. Pulling or sliding an object requires less effort than lifting it, because lifting necessitates moving against the force of gravity (adapted from DuGas, 1972).

Recognizing the body's need for exercise, the nurse should observe her client and use other methods of collecting data to describe the client's posture and mobility. These are assessed as to amount of exercise and use of the principles just discussed.

ASSESSING FACTORS INFLUENCING EXERCISE

There are many factors that influence the amount and quality of exercise at any given time for a person. Perhaps the most significant factor, and thus a frequent focal stimulus, is the intactness of the skeletal-muscular system. Many pathological conditions interfere directly with posture and mobility, for example, fractured bones or paralysis.

Contextual and residual factors affecting exercise include the following:

1. Sedentary culture—we do not walk, but ride; do not play sports, but watch.
2. Age—there is a natural "slowing down" in physical activity associated with middle and later years.
3. Personality makeup—by temperament some people are more inclined to physical activity.
4. Habit patterns—physical fitness may have become part of an individual's way of life.
5. Physical factors such as altitude and climate—when the Olympic Games were held in Mexico City, the loss of performance in endurance events was 1 to 2 percent.
6. Use of drugs such as tobacco and alcohol—one researcher reports that nonsmokers were able to continue with a progressive treadmill test for 16.5 minutes, compared with 13.2 minutes in smokers of the same age (Shephard, 1972).
7. Air pollution—recent observations from California have suggested a concentration of air pollutants has affected performance in running events (Shephard, 1972).
8. Understanding of the need for activity—research has shown that the postoperative patient who knows the reasons for early ambulation is more likely to cooperate in this procedure.
9. Availability of and skill in using needed appliances—in stages of re-habilitation, crutches, walkers, braces, and artificial limbs may all affect mobility.

10. Activity cycles—allowing for individual differences, swings from rest to activity are approximately one and one-half hours apart.
11. Fear and pain—at times mobility may be limited by fear, such as fear of opening an incision following surgery, or by the pain caused by movement, such as getting out of bed with an abdominal incision.

BEHAVIORAL ASSESSMENT OF REST

Rest and sleep are the means that the body uses for restoration and repairs. During these two states, there is a relative cessation from activity. The skeletal and muscular systems are immobile, but physiological activity remains, although it may be sharply reduced. The heart, lungs, and colon continue to function. At *rest,* either sitting or lying, the person's cell metabolism is decreased, and energy requirements are minimal. During sleep the reduction in cell metabolism and energy requirements is even greater.

The resting positions of sitting and lying do not always guarantee this reduction of metabolism and energy. On first observation the nurse might assume the person to be at rest, when in fact he may be dissipating energy on pain, temperature, discomfort, or anxiety. Since the nurse cannot directly observe metabolism and energy expenditure, in assessing the client's state of rest she must validate with the client her observations of comfort and freedom from energy expenditure.

Rest becomes *sleep* when the person has a decreased ability to interact with his external environment. During sleep sympathetic activity markedly decreases and there is little or no muscle tone. Arterial pressure falls, pulse rate decreases, gastrointestinal function slightly increases, and the muscles assume a relaxed state.

Two sleep states have been defined by the use of electroencephalograph (EEG) readings, impulses from chin muscles, and eye movements. The first state, nonrem sleep, is characterized by slow waves, spindles, and K-complexes in the EEG record; no eye movements except transient and slow ones as the sleeper enters this stage; electrical activity of the chin EMG (electromyogram, which records changes in electric potential of muscles) decreases as one passes from wakefulness to nonrem sleep. These characteristics have been noted with machines called polygraphs. However, the behaviors the nurse may note during nonrem sleep include: a few gross body movements, regular, deep respirations, slow, regular heart rate; blood pressure below waking level; thoughtlike processes reported by the client; and, frequently, a galvanic skin response.[6] Nonrem sleep is divided into four stages.

---

[6] A galvanic skin response is an electrical reading related to perspiration. It is not presently a common assessment tool used by nurses, but it may be so in the future.

The second type of sleep is called the rem state and is distinguished by the following characteristics: low voltage EEG activity mixed with bursts of theta waves; frequent conjugate eye movements (from which it is named rem, standing for rapid eye movements); and greatly decreased electrical activity of the chin. Observations at this time show the following: twitching body movements; variable shallow respirations; variable rapid heart rate; variable blood pressure; penile erection; dreamlike, dramatic cogitation; and, rarely, the galvanic skin responds.

The usual pattern of nightly sleep begins with nonrem sleep. After about two hours the sleeper suddenly enters rem sleep. Periods of nonrem and rem sleep then alternate, with cycles averaging 90 minutes. Four to six rem periods occur during a night, making up a fifth to a quarter of the total sleep time. Although there are mental occurrences during nonrem sleep, most reported dreams occur during rem sleep.

The effects of sleep disruption are often the subject of scientific studies. Apparently, fulfilled sleep satisfies the need for slow wave sleep, which is fairly constant in each person. Rem sleep is responsible for psychological restoration. The cause of rem sleep is not fully known, but a need for rem sleep is postulated or proposed. Although research is not totally conclusive, it is commonly held that repeated disruptions of rem sleep can have deleterious effects on a person's physical and mental well-being.

In assessing the client's sleep the nurse not only observes this state directly, but seeks information from the client about the length of time it usually takes him to go to sleep, the number of times he awakens during the night, the preparation he goes through for sleep, and the methods he usually employs in returning to sleep.

Behaviors associated with insufficient rest and sleep include: irritability, dizziness, nervousness, uncoordinated muscular activity, darkened areas around the eyes, puffy eyelids, yawning, reddened conjunctiva, lassitude, inability to concentrate, and burning eyes.

ASSESSING FACTORS INFLUENCING REST

Just as with exercise, there are many factors that influence the rest and sleep a person gets in both health and illness. Any of the following factors may be focal, contextual, or residual stimuli, depending on the type of influence it is having at a given time.

1. Age—the following are general norms for hours of sleep per 24 hours:
   Infants   18-20
   Children   10-14
   Adults   7-9
   Elderly   5-7

2. Habit patterns—sleep and rest patterns are learned over time.
3. Amount of exercise—sleep is generally improved in those who get adequate physical exercise.
4. General physical condition—painful disease may interfere with sleep, while certain neurological conditions such as encephalitis may increase it.
5. Cortical activity—anxiety is a frequent cause of restlessness and sleeplessness.
6. Familiarity and lack of stimulation are important factors in inducing sleep.
7. Circadian rhythmns—periods of rest and activity generally conform to the rhythmns of night and day. Within sleep there are rhythmic alterations of type of sleep about every one and one-half hours.
8. Drugs—research generally shows that alcohol and barbiturates increase total sleep time and decrease the percentage of time in rem sleep.

PROBLEMS OF EXERCISE AND REST

The most significant problem of a deficit in exercise is the condition generally termed immobility. *Immobility* is relative inactivity beyond the period of rest. This condition is important because of its effect on other bodily functions.

First, there is the effect of immobility on the maintenance of skin integrity. For the person unable to move freely in bed, there is a problem of pressure on the skin itself. In addition, the underlying tissue over bony prominences are deprived of an adequate blood supply, which in turn diminishes the amount of oxygen and other nutrients vital to cell metabolism. Furthermore, the maintenance of normal joint motion is greatly influenced by immobility. Joints that are not moved tend to become stiff, and muscle contractures soon occur.

The effect of immobility on nutrition and elimination cannot be overlooked. Inactivity dulls the appetite. Lack of fluid in the fecal material and sluggish propulsion of the intestinal tract lead to constipation, which may result in impaction. On the other hand, the stress that inactivity often engenders may cause intestinal mobility leading to diarrhea. Waste products are also expelled from the body through the skin, lungs, and kidneys. The amount of waste products lost through the skin is dependent on such factors as physical exercise. The elimination of carbon dioxide from the lungs plays an important role in the person's acid base balance, and fluid and electrolyte balance.

The metabolic effect of immobility is important. In the absence of activity catabolism is accelerated causing a breakdown of cellular material. The end result is protein deficiency and retardation of tissue repair.

A person's need for oxygen is also affected when muscular activity and metabolism are decreased. Prolonged periods of bed rest diminish the muscular power needed to facilitate adequate oxygen exchange. Decreased respiratory movement inhibits the action of secretions, which in turn upsets the balance of oxygen and carbon dioxide. Oxygen absorbed from the lungs is transported to the cardiovascular system, but the physiological actions of respiration and circulation are dependent on the central nervous system. Respiration, circulation, and inervation are so interdependent that a disruption in the function of one leads to disturbance in another.

There are extensive effects of immobility on the cardiovascular system. Thrombus formation is often caused from venous stasis or stagnation of blood in the veins, associated with prolonged bed rest. A thrombus is a blood clot that remains fixed at the point where it begins forming. The lower extremities are common sites for the formation of thrombi. Orthostatic hypotension, another cardiovascular problem in which blood pressure is lowered in the standing position, results from lack of activity. This condition is generally caused by loss of muscle tone in the veins of the legs. Finally, immobility places greater demands on the heart itself while the person is in a supine position. Studies have demonstrated increased cardiac output when the person is lying down.

Common problem deficits in rest and sleep are fatigue and insomnia. *Fatigue* is a subjective feeling of aversion to activity. It connotes mental or physical weariness and exhaustion. The elements leading up to this subjective feeling include impairment, disorganization, discomfort (largely in the muscles), and work decreases. Simple causes of fatigue include boredom, and intellectual or physical exertion. Fatigue may also be the result of more complex situations, such as debilitating disease, lack of motivation, nervous tension and anxiety, depression, hysteria, and chronic inhibition of ego function.

The common fatigue situations include: (1) those that require considerable expenditure of energy (for example, labor and delivery), (2) those demands that pace or otherwise restrict the individual's performance (for example, reading or writing tasks frequently given the bedridden client), (3) tasks that become prolonged (for example, sitting for a difficult dressing change), (4) tasks in which the goals are quite remote (for example, learning to use eating utensils by a paralyzed person), and (5) situations resulting in frustration (for example, first ambulation experiences after a stroke).

Insomnia is a sleep disturbance that consists of difficulty in falling asleep, difficulty staying asleep, early final awakening, or a combination of these. It may be a symptom associated with illness, including cardiovascular, endocrine, gastrointestinal, or genitourinary diseases, or any condition where pain is a significant symptom, such as arthritis. Psychological disturbances, especially depression, may also lead to insomnia.

However, it has been reported that in the United States about 20 percent of young, healthy people have difficulty falling asleep. When poor sleepers are compared with good sleepers by electroencephalography, they have greater sleep latency, more awakenings, a higher percentage of nonrem stage two, and shorter rem periods giving an overall decreased percentage. Other physiological factors, such as heart rate, peripheral vasoconstriction, and rectal temperature indicate a higher level of physiological arousal for poor sleepers during sleep. Insomnia is usually presumed present when general well-being and performance are clearly disrupted following pronounced loss of sleep.

With this knowledge of behavioral manifestations, influencing factors, and problem areas, the nurse whould be able to identify basic types of problems in exercise and rest.

NURSING INTERVENTIONS IN PROBLEMS OF EXERCISE AND REST

The major problem of exercise discussed is the problem of immobility, or a deficit of exercise. This condition is usually the result of some pathological condition which makes exercise impossible, such as paralysis, or contraindicated, such as heart disease. The nurse may be carrying out functions under the direction of a physician (called dependent nursing functions) to alleviate the disease condition responsible for the immobility. At the same time, she has a major responsibility for preventing the harmful effects of this condition noted earlier. This is her independent function.

The goals of intervention in the problem of immobility are to prevent complications in other body functions and to maintain the intactness of the neuromuscular system in preparation for eventual ambulation. Her means of intervention are to manipulate the influencing factors of proper positioning, exercise, and physical and psychological preparations for ambulation.

Proper positioning in the supine, lateral, and prone positions have been described. The important point to remember is that no position should be maintained for more than two hours. Thus each time the immobile client is positioned, the nurse whould immediately plan the next time for repositioning. It is the nurse's responsibility that every member of the health team is aware of and strictly adheres to the schedule for repositioning. The skin is also inspected at pressure points when repositioning the client. When an area is red or mottled (blotchy in appearance), the nurse should carry out measures, such as bathing and massaging, to promote circulation to the affected area.

For every immobile client, the nurse plans a daily program of exercise. The type and extent of exercise depend on the needs and ability or disability of the client. There are four basic types of exercise. The first is *passive exercise.* This type is movement of the joint for the person either because he is unable to do so or it is undesirable for him to move unassisted. The nurse carries out passive exercise for the following reasons: (1) to maintain the person's potential range of motion, (2) to restore function, and (3) to prevent deformities and complications. The second type of exercise is *active-assistive exercise,* in which the person carries out motions to his fullest potential and then is assisted to complete them either through personal or mechanical help. The purpose in this case, in addition to the same purposes as for passive exercise, is to encourage normal function and strength, and maintain normal joint function. *Active exercise* is the third type of exercise. In this type the client uses muscles without personal or mechanical assistance. This type of exercise is used whenever possible to achieve the same goals as passive and active-assistive exercise. The fourth is *resistive exercise,* which the person accomplishes against resistance. The resistance may be manual as in exerting pressure against the motion or it may be mechanical by adding weight. This type of exercise would be initiated to increase muscle strength.

For the client who has a part of the body in a cast or otherwise immobilized, the nurse directs the client in muscle setting exercises. This means alternately contracting and relaxing the muscle while keeping the joint in a fixed position.

Minimal exercise for the immobile client is full range of motion for all joints several times a day. Each joint is extended, flexed, abducted, adducted, and rotated. These movements are illustrated in Figure 3.2. This can be done during the bath and while repositioning the client.

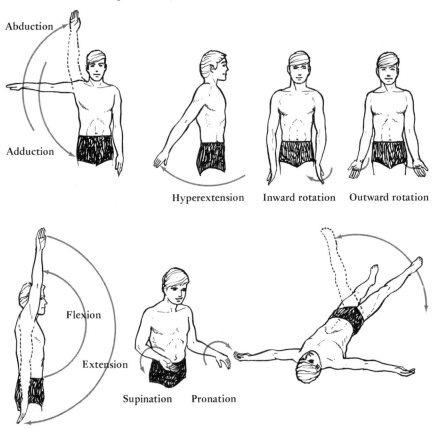

Figure 3.2   Range of motion movements.

This exercise is the first step in preparing the client physically for ambulation since it maintains muscle strength. In addition, the nurse helps the client develop sitting balance, then standing balance. Finally, physical preparation for ambulation includes training in shifting body weight. At the same time, the nurse prepares the client psychologically for ambulation. This includes: (1) familiarizing the client with equipment to be used by explanation and demonstration, (2) assuring him that sufficient help will be available, (3) giving the client the opportunity to express his fears, and (4) praising and encouraging all efforts while merely listening to negative or resistive comments.

The nurse then plans for meeting the exercise needs of all her clients, particularly those who are immobile. Selecting and implementing proper positions, exercises, and ambulation are dependent on the nursing assessment described earlier and on the limitations imposed by the prescribed medical therapy.

Fatigue and insomnia are the major problems noted with deficits in the need for rest. Nursing interventions indicated when these problems are identified include the manipulation of the stimuli that are causing or contributing to the maladaptive behavior noted.

To induce adequate rest and sleep, the nurse will first of all meet the exercise needs of the client as noted earlier. Physiotherapy, and occupational and recreational therapy can be helpful here.[7] In providing exercise, she is careful that undue fatigue is not induced. She does this by limiting fatigue situations, such as great expenditures of energy, tasks requiring constricted performance, prolonged tasks, tasks with remote goals, and frustrating tasks.

The nurse capitalizes on the client's habit patterns by making the conditions for rest and sleep consistent with them. She provides the means for the client to carry out bedtime rituals, for example, brushing teeth. Often hospital routines can be altered to take account of the client's pattern, for example, serving a midmorning breakfast to the latesleeper.

Since the client's general physical condition influences his rest and sleep, the nurse will utilize comfort measures to induce rest. Thus she sees that the client is warm enough and that the bed is comfortable. She relieves pain by medication and positioning as indicated. A back rub and warm drink may also be provided.

Decreasing the environmental stimulation is an important factor in inducing sleep. Both lighting and noise should be kept to a minimum. At the same time, the internal stimulation of cortical activity must be decreased. Relief of anxiety, to be discussed in Chapter 15, is particularly applicable since it is commonly the stimulus interfering with sleep.

The final measure that the nurse could utilize in promoting sleep and rest is the administration of sedative and hypnotic drugs as ordered by the physician.

[7]Physiotherapy refers to healing and rehabilitation measures dealing with the muscular-skeletal system. Occupational therapy deals with helping clients to develop new skills or to regain skills which have been lost during illness. Recreational therapy involves activities for refreshment and relaxation particularly aimed at improving general well-being.

TABLE 3.1
Nursing Process Guide Focusing on Adaptation to Need for Exercise and Rest for
48-Year-Old Male Truck Driver Confined to Bed with a Back Injury.

Behavior	Adaptation Status	Influencing Factors		
		Focal	Contextual	Residual
Lying very still except for fidgety hand movements	M*	Order for bed rest	Used to more physical activity Used to being alert and occupied on the road Pain on movement Fear of disturbing traction apparatus Little knowledge about meaning of bed rest Expressed former interest in music	At active developmental stage Role of breadwinner
Reports difficulty falling asleep and frequent awakening during night Eyes reddened with darkened circles under them	M	Lack of physical and mental activities	Used to sleeping at unusual hours and in different places, but not in double room Used to drinking beer before going to bed Likes room very dark	As above.

*M=maladaptive.

A sample nursing process guide[8] for a forty-eight-year-old male truck driver
who is confined to bed with a back injury, is given in Table 3.1. This guide
focuses only on the client's adaptation to his need for exercise and rest.

SUMMARY

This chapter has looked at the client's need for exercise and rest from a
Roy adaptation nursing approach. The nurse assesses the client's response to
exercise needs by looking at the amount and quality of mobility and posture,

[8]The nursing process guide is one formal way the nurse records and communicates
her nursing activities from assessment through evaluation. In some hospitals and other
health agencies only the problems and approaches are recorded. This abbreviated format
if often referred to as a Nursing Care Plan.

Problem Identification	Goal	Intervention
Lying very still due to order for bed rest, but is fidgety.	Having mobility within limits of bed rest and showing signs of restfulness.	Explain nature of bed rest and importance of mobility within limits. Explain traction apparatus and how to move without pain. Initiate active exercise program for uninvolved joints. Have family bring in radio.
Difficulty sleeping due to lack of physical activity and change of routine.	Having a good night's sleep and waking refreshed.	Provide physical and recreational activities as above. Arrange for having beer at bedtime. Turn out night light in room, and screen his bed off.

and at the variety of factors that affect this need. She assesses response to the need for sleep and rest by looking at sleep and relaxation patterns and at manifestations of insufficient rest and sleep. Based on her assessment, the nurse can identify the common adaptation problems of immobility, fatigue, and insomnia. Nursing interventions for these problems involve manipulating the stimuli that influence them.

REFERENCES

DuGas, Beverly, *Kozier-DuGas Introduction to Patient Care.* 2nd ed. Philadelphia: W. B. Saunders Company, 1972.

Shephard, Roy, *Alive Man! The Physiology of Physical Activity.* Springfield, Ill.: Charles C. Thomas, Publisher, 1972.

ADDITIONAL READINGS

Bartley, S. Howard, *Fatigue, Mechanism and Management.* Springfield, Ill.: Charles C. Thomas, Publisher, 1965.

Freemon, Frank, *Sleep Research.* Springfield, Ill.: Charles C. Thomas, Publisher, 1972.

Ganang, William F., *Review of Medical Physiology.* Las Altas, Calif.: Lange Medical Publication, 1969.

Gragg, Shirley Hawke and Olive M. Rees, *Scientific Principles in Nursing.* 6th ed. St. Louis: C. V. Mosby Co., 1970.

Kales, Anthony, *The Evaluation and Treatment of Sleep Disorders by the General Physician.* Pennsylvania State University.

Kales, Anthony, *Sleep Physiology and Pathology.* Philadelphia: J. B. Lipincott Company, 1969.

Larson, Elizabeth R., "Turning the Bed Patient." *American Journal of Nursing,* 63:100, February 1963.

Nordmark, Madelyn T. and Anne W. Rahwedor, *Scientific Foundations of Nursing.* 2nd ed. Philadelphia: J. B. Lipincott Company, 1967.

Olson, Edith V., "The Hazards of Immobility." *American Journal of Nursing,* 67:779-96, April 1967.

Snyder, Morish and Rebecca Baum, "Assessing Station and Gait," *American Journal of Nursing,* 74:1256-57, July 1974.

Web, Wilse B., *Sleep: An Active Process.* Glenview, Ill.: Scott, Foresman and Company, 1973.

4

Nutrition

Nancy Malaznik

KEY CONCEPTS DEFINED

Daily Recommended Dietary Allowances: A description of the quantities of
necessary nutrients in relation to the individual's sex, age, height, and
recommended weight issued by the Food and Nutrition Board of the
National Research Council.

Four Basic Food Groups: Division of foods into milk group, meat group, fruit
and vegetable group, and bread and cereal group for estimating adequate
daily nutritional intake.

Nutritional Status: The condition of health of the individual as influenced by
the utilization of nutrients.

Nausea: A subjective feeling of sickness in the throat or the stomach with a
desire to vomit.

Vomiting: The forceful expulsion of gastric contents through the mouth.

Emesis: The act of vomiting.

Anorexia: Loss of appetite or lack of desire for food.

After studying this chapter the reader will be able to:

1. Define the key concepts of this chapter.
2. Analyze her own daily food intake according to the Four Basic Food Groups.
3. List factors influencing nutritional behavior (see Appendix I).
4. Identify problems of nutritional adaptation status if given case studies illustrating these problems.
5. Specify nursing interventions to be used in problems of nutrition (see Appendix II).

The purpose of this chapter is to illustrate the application of the adaptation nursing process to the physiological mode component, nutrition. To accomplish this purpose, we will (1) look briefly at the theoretical framework of the science of nutrition; (2) describe the assessment process with regard to client behaviors and factors or stimuli-influencing behaviors; (3) identify some problems of nutrition; and (4) apply the problem-solving approach within the framework of the nursing process guide to promote adaptive nutritional behaviors.

OVERVIEW OF NORMAL NUTRITION

A basic understanding of the science of nutrition is necessary prior to application of the adaptation nursing process to the physiological status of the client. To attain and/or maintain a physiological status that is on the health side of the health-illness continuum, the body needs certain quantities and types of nutrients.

Research studies in nutrition have led to the development of a daily nutritional guide known as the Recommended Dietary Allowances (1973). This schedule describes quantities of necessary nutrients in relation to the individual's sex, age, height, and recommended weight. The nutrients are divided into five categories: (1) calories, (2) protein, (3) fat soluble vitamins, (4) water soluble vitamins, and (5) minerals. More specific classifications of these categories are as follows:

1. Calories
2. Protein
3. Fat soluble vitamins
   a. Vitamin A
   b. Vitamin D
   c. Vitamin E
4. Water soluble vitamins
   a. Vitamin C
   b. Folacin

     c. Niacin
     d. Riboflavin
     e. Thiamine
     f. Vitamin B_6
     g. Vitamin B_{12}
5. Minerals
     a. Calcium
     b. Iodine
     c. Iron
     d. Magnesium

In addition to the Recommended Dietary Allowances for daily intake of nutrients, another guide was developed to recommend foods from which the necessary nutrients can be obtained. This schedule, known as the Four Basic Food Groups, divides all foods into four categories: (1) milk group, (2) meat group, (3) fruit and vegetable group, and (4) bread and cereal group, and recommends quantities of each group necessary for daily adequate nutrient intake.[1]

Finally, tables listing the nutrient composition of foods are available to guide individuals more specifically in choosing foods from the four food groups that meet recommended daily nutrient requirements as listed in the Recommended Dietary Allowances. The reader is referred to a basic nutrition textbook for in-depth details of the guides and the specifics of nutrient values.

With the aid of these guides as a framework of the science of nutrition, balanced dietary planning, evaluation, and thereby promotion of a healthful nutritional status are possible.

FIRST LEVEL ASSESSMENT

"Nutritional status is the condition of health of the individual as influenced by the utilization of nutrients" (Robinson, 1972, p. 6). First level assessment of nutritional behaviors may be through direct observation, that is, objective observation of the client's eating or food habits, or through subjective reports from the client, client's family, or others with regard to the client's nutritional behaviors. Further, observation of the client's weight with regard to height, age, sex, and body structure may be indicative of the client's nutritional status. Finally, physiological behaviors indicating a disease process due to dietary disruptions provide first level assessment data for the nutrition component.

[1]One guide recommends for daily eating: two or more glasses of milk, two or more servings of meat, cheese, fish, or poultry; four or more servings of vegetables and fruit; and four or more servings of cereal and bread (see Figure 4.1, Courtesy of National Dairy Council.)

A Guide to Good Eating

Use Daily:

Milk Group

3 or more glasses milk — Children
smaller glasses for some children under 8

4 or more glasses — Teenagers

2 or more glasses — Adults

Cheese, ice cream and other milk-made foods can supply part of the milk

Meat Group

2 or more servings

Meats, fish, poultry, eggs, or cheese—with dry beans, peas, nuts as alternates

Vegetables and Fruits

4 or more servings

Include dark green or yellow vegetables; citrus fruit or tomatoes

Breads and Cereals

4 or more servings

Enriched or whole grain
Added milk improves nutritional values

This is the foundation for a good diet. Use more of these and other foods as needed for growth, for activity, and for desirable weight.

The nutritional statements made in this leaflet have been reviewed by the Council on Foods and Nutrition of the American Medical Association and found consistent with current authoritative medical opinion.

Figure 4.1   An example of the use of the four basic food groups.

Build Meals Around These FOUR IMPORTANT FOOD GROUPS

MILK GROUP . . . Use daily

> 3 or more glasses milk—children; 4 or more—teenagers (smaller glasses for some children under 8)
> 2 or more glasses—adults
> 3 or more glasses—pregnant women
> 4 or more glasses—nursing women
> (a glass—8 ounces or ¼ quart of milk)

Needs of some younger children may be met by smaller servings. That is, a 6-ounce glass may replace an 8-ounce glass.

These quantities of milk provide about ¾ of the day's calcium recommended for good nutrition.

Milk is our main source of calcium in foods. For calcium . . .
1 slice American cheese (1 oz.) = ¾ glass milk
½ cup creamed cottage cheese = ⅓ glass milk
½ cup (¼ pint) ice cream = ¼ glass milk

Milk also contributes fine quality protein, vitamins—especially riboflavin and vitamin A—and many other nutrients.

For children, 3 glasses of milk supply ⅔ to all the protein recommended daily and all the riboflavin.

For adults, 2 glasses of milk supply about ¼ the protein and about ½ the riboflavin.

Skim milk lacks whole milk's fat and vitamin A (unless fortified); other food values are the same, calories less.

One glass of skim milk plus 1 scant tablespoon of butter equals the food values of whole milk.

Butter supplies milk's flavorful and easily digested fat along with its vitamin A.

Use milk as a beverage and in cooking—in hot cereals, milk soups, white sauces, puddings, and custards. Pour on fruit, cereal, and puddings.

The combination of milk with cereal or bread is excellent, especially in meals where little or no meat or eggs are served. The proteins in milk make those in cereals and bread more useful in the body.

MEAT GROUP . . . Use 2 or more servings daily

> Meat, fish, poultry, eggs, or cheese—with dry beans, peas, nuts or peanut butter as alternates

Use amounts of these foods to supply at least as much protein as that in 4 ounces of cooked lean meat (about ⅓ pound raw).

Good practices to follow are

An egg a day or at least 3 to 5 a week

Liver, heart, kidney, or sweetbread about once a week

Other kinds of meat, fish, poultry, or cheese: 4 to 5 or more times a week

With dried beans, peas, nuts or peanut butter, serve milk or cheese. The animal protein makes the vegetable protein more useful in the body.

Foods in the meat group are counted on to supply about ½ the protein recommended daily for good nutrition.

Two servings for an adult might be, for example . . .
1 medium serving meat (3 ounces, cooked) + 1 egg

Choose combinations from the following which are about equal in amount of protein . . .
1 ounce cooked lean meat, poultry, or fish
1 egg
1 slice cheese, American or Swiss (1 ounce)
2 rounded tablespoons creamed cottage cheese (2 ounces)
2 tablespoons peanut butter (1 ounce)
½ cup cooked dried beans or peas

Eggs and meat, especially liver, are important for iron; also for B-vitamins. Pork supplies large amounts of the B-vitamin, thiamin. The legumes—dried beans, peas, nuts—are good sources of iron and thiamin, but their protein should be supplemented with an animal protein.

VEGETABLES & FRUITS . . . Use 4 or more servings daily

> Include a dark green leafy or deep yellow vegetable or yellow fruit at least 3 to 4 times a week for vitamin A; a citrus fruit, or tomatoes, or other good source of vitamin C every day.

Use other vegetables and fruits for variety as well as their minerals, vitamins, and roughage.

Use potatoes frequently for all these food values plus food energy.

Use fresh, canned or frozen vegetables and fruits.

Save food values and flavors of vegetables by cooking quickly in small amount of water.

Dried fruits are valuable for iron.

A serving is ½ cup or more.

Foods in this group should supply over half the vitamin A and all of the vitamin C recommended daily for good nutrition.

Vegetables & fruits high in vitamin A	These are about equal in vitamin C
broccoli, chard	1 medium orange, ¾ cup juice
all "greens"	½ grapefruit, ¾ cup juice
kale, spinach	2 medium tomatoes, 2 cups juice
carrots	½ large cantaloupe
sweet potatoes	1 cup strawberries
tomatoes	¾ cup broccoli
cantaloupe, apricots	1½ cups cabbage, raw, shredded

BREADS & CEREALS . . . Use 4 or more servings daily

> Use enriched or whole grain products. Check labels!

Choose from breads, cooked and ready-to-eat cereals, cornmeal, crackers, grits, spaghetti and macaroni, noodles, rice, quick breads and other baked goods if made with whole grain or enriched flour.

A serving is 1 slice bread; ½ to ¾ cup cereal.

Foods in this group supply valuable amounts of protein, iron, several B-vitamins, and food energy.

Cereals cooked and/or served with milk and breads made with milk are improved in quality of protein as well as quantity of protein, minerals, and vitamins.

ADDITIONAL FOODS . . . The foods recommended form the foundation for a good diet. In general, use smaller servings for young children; more or larger servings may be needed by teenagers, pregnant and lactating women.

Most nutrient needs are met by the amounts of foods suggested by the Guide. Special attention must be given to food sources of iron for young children, teenagers, and women. Liver, eggs, meat, legumes, dried fruit, dark green leafy vegetables, enriched or whole grain breads and cereals are good iron sources.

More food for energy, calories, is usually required. The amount varies with age, size, and activity. Food from the four groups helps to achieve an adequate diet.

Calorie restricted diets can be pleasing and satisfying when energy comes mostly from foods in these four groups.

Some source of vitamin D should be included for infants and children, pregnant and lactating women, and adults getting little sunshine. Good sources are vitamin D milk, fish liver oils, and direct sunshine.

B76, 21 1973, 3rd Edition, Copyright © 1958, 1964, National Dairy Council, Chicago 60606. All rights reserved. Printed in U.S.A.

Determination as to whether the assessed behaviors are adaptive or maladaptive should be made with regard to the principles of the science of nutrition, which promote behaviors on the health side of the health-illness continuum. Tools such as the Recommended Dietary Allowance Guide, the Four Basic Food Groups, and the nutrient composition of foods may be helpful in making evaluations of the behaviors as adaptive or maladaptive. In Table 4.1 we have four examples of client behaviors, which can be judged as adaptive or maladaptive in relation to nutritional status.

TABLE 4.1
First Level Assessment of Nutritional Status

Behavior	Adaptation Status	Principle of Judgement
Client #1: Client ate all of food served at breakfast (4oz. orange juice, 2 poached eggs, 1 slice toast with butter, 8 oz. milk)	A	Foods included (iron, each of the basic four food groups) promote healthy nutritional status.
Client #2: Client states, "I never eat fruits and vegetables."	M	Diets deficient in foods from one or more of the basic four food groups do not promote healthy nutritional status (unless nutrients are obtained in alternate manner than food intake).
Client #3: Height 5'2" Weight 210 lbs.	M	Gross weight discrepancies between height and recommended weight allowances promote an unhealthy nutritional status.
Client #4: Hemoglobin (Hgb) 8.8 13-year-old female	M	Low iron capacity, due to diet deficiency or blood loss, promotes unhealthy nutritional status.

SECOND LEVEL ASSESSMENT

Second level assessment of factors directly causing or at least contributing to the assessed client behaviors may again be either subjective or objective observations or both. With regard to nutritional behaviors, some known factors or stimuli should be considered, and an attempt is made to validate whether they may be focal or contextual stimuli for the client's presenting behavior(s). Such stimuli include:

1. Hunger.
2. Palatability of the food.
3. Cultural preferences.
4. Values of food and eating patterns as stressed or not stressed in the home environment.
5. Amount of exposure to different types of foods.
6. Economic status of the client and/or the client's family.
7. Moral values associated with food (for example, foods used for bribery, punishment, reward).
8. Client's age, sex developmental stage.
9. Peer group influences.
10. Client's emotional makeup and possible attachment to food as security or to fill a need.
11. Client's desire to gain or lose weight.
12. Pregnancy.
13. Lactation.
14. Amount of activity.
15. Growth process.
16. Knowledge about "good nutrition."
17. Availability of someone to prepare meals.
18. Amount of time set aside for eating.
19. Food fads.
20. Recommended daily nutrient intake.
21. Illness or disease process (for example, loss of appetite due to drug or radiation therapy, nausea and/or vomiting, decreased sugar intake for diabetics, doctor's orders for nothing by mouth or special diet).
22. Anxiety, loneliness, pathology affecting absorption, such as gastric ulcers or ulcerative colitis (see medical texts for discussion of such diseases).

Table 4.2 shows factors which may be influencing the behavior of the four clients discussed in Table 4.1.

PROBLEM IDENTIFICATION: NUTRITIONAL ADAPTATION STATUS

From the assessment process comes the identification of maladaptive client behaviors that the nurse hopes to change to adaptive behaviors, or adap-

TABLE 4.2
Application of Second Level Assessment Influencing Factors

Client	Focal	Contextual	Residual
#1	Client states, "I'm hungry."	On regular diet. Food served hot and attractively. Made out own menu. 13-year-old male (growth spurt). Ambulatory. Goes to physio-therapy 3 times per day.	Probably eats a good breakfast every day at home.
#2	Client says, "Too much of a bother to buy and fix for myself."	"Some fruits give me diarrhea." "I've gotten along fine without them to this point." "They never taste good when I fix them."	Maybe he is lonely and therefore eats very little.
#3	Client says, "I don't know why I weigh so much; I really don't eat a thing." Quote in discrepancy with observed eating habits.	2-lb. box of candy at bedtime, half gone in one day. Ordered two doughnuts for breakfast, chocolate eclair for dessert at lunch, and ice cream for dessert at dinner. Had hamburger, french fries, and milk for lunch. "Sometimes at work I don't even get a lunch break." Both parents are overweight. States mother is an excellent cook—lasagne and spaghetti are her specialties. "I don't eat many fruits and vegetables."	Probably "munches" all day instead of eating regularly scheduled meals, so doesn't realize that she is eating a lot of calories, which contribute to her overweight problem.
#4	Client intake deficient in iron.	13-year-old female. Menses for 2 years. On reducing "crash diet"—eating grapefruit, eggs, and cottage cheese.	

tive client behaviors the nurse wants the client to continue. When these behaviors are stated with their influencing factors, we have the identification of the problem. When summary labels are used for the nutritional component of the physiological mode, we have: (1) good or healthy nutritional status, (2) malnutrition, (3) nausea and vomiting, (4) nutrient deficiency, (5) overweight, (6) underweight. These problems, except for nausea and vomiting, have been illustrated in the examples on the previous pages.

Nausea and vomiting accompany illnesses of many kinds. *Nausea* is a subjective feeling of sickness in the throat or the stomach with a desire to vomit. The client who is nauseated may also feel faint and weak, and the nurse may observe salivation, pallor, perspiration, and a rapid pulse. *Vomiting* is the forceful expulsion of gastric contents through the mouth. The act of vomiting is called *emesis*. In addition to the illnesses that cause nausea and vomiting, psychic stimuli such as odors, sights, tastes, thoughts, and feelings may also trigger these problems. The nurse should also be aware of the drugs (such as anesthetics) and treatments (such as radiation) that are likely to produce nausea and vomiting. Nursing interventions which manipulate the stimuli causing the various forms of maladaptive nutrition are discussed below.

NURSING INTERVENTION IN MALADAPTIVE NUTRITION

Once the adaptive or maladaptive nutritional behaviors have been identified and the problem cited or a nursing diagnosis made, client goals (adaptive behaviors) and nursing interventions that manipulate the validated stimuli can be formulated. It should be recognized that intervention for the disease process itself is primarily directed by the physician. However, nursing interventions may manipulate any of the stimuli presented under the heading of "second level assessment," or any other stimuli the nurse may validate to cause a specific client's behaviors which does not interfere with the prescribed medical regime and is within the realm of nursing functions of the institution by which the nurse is employed.

Following are suggested interventions for posed stimuli.

Stimuli	Intervention
1. Lack of knowledge about nutritional requirements.	a. Teach nutritional requirements through use of guides such as Recommended Dietary Allowances, Basic Four Food Groups, and content of dietary evaluation of foods client is eating.
	b. Teach how stresses and strains of illness and other stimuli, such as increased activity, may indicate increased daily nutrient intake.

c. Compare calorie requirement and intake with height, suggested weight, age, sex, body frame, and activity.

d. Teach that dieting with proper nutrient intake can not only promote weight loss but good nutritional status.

2. Cultural, moral, religious convictions.

a. Teach the nutrients in the foods that are permitted, showing how the individual can incorporate different foods daily that meet nutritional requirements.

b. Explore possibility of dietary supplements such as vitamin tablets.

3. Hunger, food palatability, likes and dislikes, or *anorexia,* that is, loss of appetite or lack of desire for food.

a. Provide snacks to fit in with diet regime if client is hungry between meals.

b. Let client choose own foods on selected menu.

c. Make effort to serve food at correct temperatures, on time, and attractively.

d. Arrange surroundings so they do not detract from food.

4. Economic status.

a. Assist client in choosing foods that meet nutritional needs and also fit into budget.

b. Explore sources such as social services to get financial aid if eligible.

c. Refer to public health department for follow-up after hospitalization.

5. Peer group influence.

a. Teach how to choose foods that peers eat to fit nutritional and/or dietary needs and still fit within the social context.

6. Emotional need for food.

a. Explore these feelings with the client.
b. Listen.
c. Offer suggestions if asked for them.
d. If doctor has restricted the diet, explore client's feelings about the imposed restrictions and whether the client is willing to go along with them.

7. Loneliness, depression, availability of someone to cook meals.

a. Explore community or private groups such as meals on wheels, senior citizen meetings, to get food to the client.

b. Refer to public health department for follow-up in the home.

    c. Evaluate nutritional value of simple-to-prepare, such as T.V. dinners, canned meals such as ravioli.

    d. Explore the client's interests and groups that might also share the same interests.

    e. Explore reasons why lonely or depressed, and intervene with those stimuli.

8. Eating patterns regarding time, value of food, and other factors.

    a. Explore client's understanding of how eating patterns affect nutritional status.

    b. Teach the affect if not understood.

    c. Encourage client to suggest alternate eating patterns that would fit into his schedule and still meet nutritional needs.

9. Illness.

    a. Follow medical regime to promote a healthy status.

    b. Decrease intake if nausea and vomiting present.

    c. Record intake and output.

    d. Offer 7-Up, ginger ale, tea, dry toast, soda crackers if they fit into medical treatment regime and client can tolerate intake.

    e. Keep food or anything producing nausea out of client's sight and smell.

    f. If client has emesis, clean client and environment immediately.

    g. Decrease client's activity, even movement in bed.

    h. Report maladaptive nutritional behaviors to the physician.

The preceding list offers only a few examples of interventions the nurse can formulate to promote adaptive nutritional client behaviors. Completion of the nursing process guide of the adaptation nursing model to the client behaviors used as examples in first and second level assessments would incorporate (1) problem identification, (2) client goals for adaptive nutritional behaviors, (3) nursing interventions that promote adaptation, (4) evaluation, and (5) modification, if necessary. Table 4.3 presents a summary of the problems, goals, and interventions used with these clients.

Evaluation of client behaviors as to whether or not goals were met after interventions were performed is a necessary component of the nursing process. If adaptive behavior is not observed in the evaluation, modification of either the goals or interventions is necessary until adaptation is attained. Adaptive nutritional behaviors should be congruent with a healthy nutritional status.

TABLE 4.3

Completion of Nursing Process Guide for Adaptive Nutritional Behaviors

Problem	Client Goal	Nursing Interventions
Client #1: Client ate well because of increased appetite with activity regime. Nursing intervention should be directed toward continuing the client's adaptive nutritional status.	1. Client will continue to eat at least 3/4 of all meals served while in the hospital setting.	1. Nurse will encourage client to continue activities of physiotherapy and ambulation to keep client's appetite good. 2. Nurse will praise these activities so client will continue them.
Client #2: Client diet is deficient in fruits and vegetables because client does not think they are necessary enough in the diet to bother to fix for self. Nursing intervention should be directed toward including fruits and vegetables in client's diet.	1. Client will eat at least 2 fruits and 3 vegetables (approximately ½ cup each) each day while in hospital and make plans to include in diet when discharged.	1. Nurse will teach client importance of the nutrients in fruits and vegetables through use of charts on Daily Allowance Guide. 2. Nurse will encourage client to choose fruits and vegetables each day that meet at least 3/4 of nutrients requirement listed in DNR with chart for basic four group and lists describing number of nutrients in food. 3. Nurse will encourage client to choose fruits and vegetables that may be eaten raw or require little preparation. 4. Nurse will contact discharge planning nurse for possible referral to PHN for follow-up on dietary knowledge patterns and plans after client returns to home setting.
Client #3: Client overweight for height but does not indicate knowledge of reasons why, or understand-	1. Client will lose one pound per day while in hospital setting.	1. Nurse will provide health teaching regarding calorie requirements for

ing of excessive calorie intake. Nursing intervention will be directed toward getting client to lose some weight.

	height and suggested weight.
	2. Nurse will explore further to try to validate whether client does indicate reasons why she may be overweight.
	3. Nurse will encourage client to count number of calories in foods ordered on menu and compare with suggested caloric intake.
	4. Nurse will encourage client to order balanced diet with suggested number of calories.

Client #4:

Hgb 8.8 due to anemia resulting from intake deficient in iron. Nursing intervention should be directed toward increasing hgb.	1. Client will have hgb of 9.4 within 4 days when next hgb study is ordered.	1. Nurse will give ferous sulfate daily per doctor's orders.
		2. Nurse will teach importance of including foods containing iron in the diet of an individual with high demands for iron (such as female having started menses).
		3. Nurse will teach which foods are high in iron content.
		4. Nurse will help client choose foods that are high in iron content and are palatable to the client.

SUMMARY

In summary, this chapter has demonstrated application of the Roy adaptation nursing model to the physiological mode component, nutrition. The process draws on the nurse's knowledge of the science of nutrition to (1) assess client behaviors as adaptive or maladaptive, (2) assess stimuli that cause or contribute to the nutritional behaviors, and (3) problem-solve to complete a nursing process guide that includes client's goals, nursing interventions, evaluation, and possible modification. The adaptation nursing process within the framework of the science of nutrition makes it possible to promote adaptive nutrition client behaviors on an individual client basis.

REFERENCES

Robinson, Corrine, *Normal and Therapeutic Nutrition.* New York: The Macmillan Company, 1972.

Recommended Dietary Allowances, 8th ed., 1973. National Academy of Sciences, Printing and Publication Office, 2101 Constitution Avenue, Washington, D. C. 20418.

ADDITIONAL READINGS

Chappelle, M. L., "The Language of Food," *American Journal of Nursing,* vol. 72, July 1972, pp. 1294-95.

Harper, Alfred E., Ph.D., "Recommended Dietary Allowances: Are they what we think they are?" *Journal of the American Dietetic Association,* vol. 64, February 1974, pp. 151-56.

Hegsted, D. Mark, Ph.D., "Food and Nutrition Policy—Now and in the Future, "*Journal of the American Dietetic Association,* vol. 64, April 1974, pp. 367-71.

Leverton, Ruth M., Ph.D., R.D., "What is Nutrition Education? "*Journal of the American Dietetic Association,* vol. 64, January 1974, pp. 17-18.

Rubin, R., "Food and Feeding: A Matrix of Relationships," *Nursing Forum,* vol. 6, no. 2, 1967, pp. 195-205.

Treadwell, Dawn D., R.D., "Planning the Nutrition Component of Long-Term Care," *Journal of the American Dietetic Association,* vol. 64, January 1974, pp. 56-60.

5

Elimination

Janet Dunning

KEY CONCEPTS DEFINED

Defecation: Evacuation of the intestinal tract.

Flatulence: Excessive gas in the gastrointestinal tract.

Tenesmus: Ineffectual and painful straining.

Constipation: Difficult defecation with occasional passage of dry, hard stools.

Diarrhea: Passage of liquid or excessively unformed feces.

Parenteral therapy: Feeding by routes other than oral.

Anal incontinence: Inability of the anal sphincter to control discharge of fecal matter and gases voluntarily.

Oliquria: Infrequent voidings with less than 150 cc (cubic centimeters) each time.

Anuria: Lack of production of urine.

Polyuria: Excretion of large amounts of urine.

Urinary retention: Failure to expel urine from the bladder.

Urinary catheterization: Introduction of a catheter through the urethra into the bladder for purposes of withdrawing urine.

Perspiration: The functional excretion of sweat.

After studying this chapter the reader will be able to:

1. Define the key concepts of this chapter.
2. Describe normal intestinal elimination and the factors that affect it (see Appendix I).
3. Identify problems of intestinal elimination if given case studies illustrating these problems.
4. Specify nursing interventions to be used in problems of intestinal elimination (see Appendix II).
5. Describe normal urinary elimination and the factors that affect it (see Appendix I).
6. Identify problems of urinary elimination if given case studies illustrating these problems.
7. Specify nursing interventions to be used in problems of urinary elimination (see Appendix II).

A third major area in the assessment and planning of client care aimed at physiological integrity is related to the need for elimination. Physiological man needs to expel waste products from the body by way of the skin, rectum, urinary bladder, and lungs. This chapter will deal with elimination from the rectum, urinary bladder, and skin. Elimination of wastes from the lungs will be covered in the chapter on oxygen and circulation. Changes in the level of need create activity seen in behaviors. Assessment of behaviors in elimination will be described and factors influencing these will be outlined. Major problems in elimination will be cited and nursing intervention to solve these problems will be indicated.

BEHAVIORAL ASSESSMENT OF INTESTINAL ELIMINATION

When assessing intestinal elimination, the nurse should evaluate the following factors: the color of the stool or fecal material from the bowel, the odor of the feces, the presence or absence of gas pains, the consistency of the feces, the quantity of the stool, and the frequency of *defecation,* that is, evacuation of the intestinal tract.

The color of the feces is a result of its contents, which include digested and undigested material and bacteria, intestinal secretions, by-products of decomposed bacteria, purine basis, pigments, and inorganic salts. A pigment called stercobilin or urobilin, which is derived from bilirubin or bile, gives the stool its normal color—medium brown. Other colors, such as dark brown, dark red, black or melanotic, green, yellowish, clay-colored, tarry, grayish or putty-colored, and bright red, may indicate a problem. These abnormal colors may occur from disease, drugs, or ingested foods. The odor of the feces is mainly due to skatole and indole, which is produced by the action of bacteria on the amino acids in the intestines. Usually the odor is characteristic smelling.

Many times intestinal elimination is accompanied by *flatulence,* excessive gas and/or gas pains preceding and during defecation. The flatulence and gas pains are the result of several factors. Swallowed air, containing 70 percent nitrogen, passes through the intestines and produces gas. Some of the other factors that contribute to the production of gas are the presence of inorganic salts, the formation of lactic and acetic acids from certain bacteria working on carbohydrates, and the breakdown of protein. A hardened abdomen, a rolling feeling in the abdomen, abdominal distention, and the expelling of a foul-smelling odor are often factors that the nurse observes, and may be indicative of flatus.

The variation in the consistency of the feces is explained by the fact that as waste products of digestion pass through the large intestine, water is absorbed from the feces. The consistency varies to a certain extent on the length of time the food is in the gastrointestinal tract. The normal consistency of the stool is formed to soft. If the stool is liquid, semiliquid, watery, hard, frothy, or if it contains undigested food, excessive mucus, pus, stones, and parasites, a problem or some form of pathology may exist.

The quantity of the stool will vary with the amount of food consumed and absorbed. A normal quantity will vary from small, moderate, large to copious. Peristaltic mass movements, which propel the fecal material through the intestines, occur up to three or four times in one day; and are often stimulated by the entrance of food into the stomach. These movements push the food into the sigmoid and pelvic colon, where it is stored. Defecation is stimulated by the movement of fecal material from the large intestine to the rectum. There is a wide variation in normal frequency of defecation; one to four times a day are possible. Other factors to assess or evaluate are pain on defecation and the nature of the pain, any problem or pathology such as hemorrhoids that might change one or all of the above factors, any incontinence of feces, any *tenesmus,* (ineffectual and painful straining), any abdominal distention, and any change in the shape of the stool.

ASSESSING FACTORS THAT AFFECT NORMAL INTESTINAL ELIMINATION

The focal stimuli affecting intestinal elimination would vary depending upon the behaviors with which you are dealing. Some general factors found to affect directly the eliminative status of an individual are as follows: emotional status, faulty personal habits; diet—either too high or too low in roughage or not nutritionally adequate; immobility; the intake of too much or too little fluids; disease; pregnancy; lack of privacy; weak musculature; and the chronic

use of such medications as laxatives, diuretics, narcotics, enemas, and suppositories. The contextual factors might be the eating habits of friends and family,
one's own likes and dislikes in foods, the availability of adequate toilet facilities,
and age. Residual factors can be many, but such things as being toilet trained
too early or having punitive measures imposed to accomplish toilet training, and
developmental level can also affect habits of elimination. Cultural beliefs about
regularity and privacy also influence bowel elimination. Assessment of intestinal
elimination is summarized in Table 5.1.

TABLE 5.1
Assessment of Intestinal Elimination

Behavioral Assessment	Influencing Factors
Color of fecal material	Emotional status
Odor of feces	Faulty personal habits
Presence of gas pains	Diet, especially roughage intake
Consistency of feces	Fluid intake
Quantity of stool	Immobility
Frequency of defecation	Disease
	Pregnancy
	Lack of privacy
	Weak musculature
	Chronic use of medications
	Toilet facilities
	Age or developmental level
	Toilet training
	Cultural beliefs about
	regularity and privacy

GENERAL NURSING INTERVENTIONS FOR
ENCOURAGING NORMAL INTESTINAL ELIMINATION

The ways in which the nurse can help the client to maintain normal elimination patterns are to manipulate the stimuli affecting elimination. These include: reducing uncomfortable emotional factors to a minimum, providing for
the client's privacy, encouraging the client to respond to the urge to defecate
in an unrushed manner, encouraging the client to set aside a time each day for
this purpose, and eliminating uncomfortable or foul odors in the environment.
The client should be encouraged to sit in a natural way during bowel movements. A toilet or a commode most frequently provides the best position. If
a bedpan is required, it should be warmed and placed in a comfortable position
with the head of the bed elevated. Children should use a potty chair rather than
using an elevated toilet seat. Short-legged adults whould use a block of wood or
a stool for their feet so that it is possible to flex the thighs against the abdomen.

The nurse should discourage the chronic use of laxitives, the excessive use of constipating medications, such as antacids and mixtures containing codeine, and excessive consumption of such constipating foods as milk, cheese, and white bread. A diet high in residue, such as vegetables with long fibers (celery, cabbage, and greens), whole fruits with skins (prunes, apricots, figs, dates, and dried fruits), and whole grain cereals and breads, helps to maintain normal peristaltic functioning. The nurse should educate the client to drink six to eight glasses of water each day. Omission of breakfast, which stimulates the strongest gastrocolic reflex of the day, can often result in problems in intestinal elimination. The nurse would include this fact as part of her teaching to promote normal elimination.

COMMON PROBLEMS OF INTESTINAL ELIMINATION

Constipation, which is difficult defecation with occasional passage of dry, hard stools, is perhaps the most common abnormality of intestinal elimination. When the nurse assesses the patient with constipation, she might observe the stool to be dark brown in color, to have a foul odor, to have a consistency which is unduly dry and hard and may even form ball-shaped masses, and to vary in quantity from a small to a moderate amount of hard round masses. The client may defecate as often as once a day to as little as once a week. Other factors the nurse might assess when a client is constipated are tenesmus, leakage of watery brown drainage from the anal area, malaise, foul breath, a furred tongue, abdominal distention, belching, and dizziness.

The focal factors that might cause constipation are numerous. The client may consistently refuse to heed the urge to defecate, causing the awareness of rectal fullness to become dulled and the urge to disappear. Such factors as the demands of one's occupation, stress and rush of modern life, modern travel, reluctance of children to interrupt play, and the neurotic habit of delay can be focal causes of constipation. After the use of laxatives repeatedly and over long periods of time, one completely loses the regular bowel habit, since fecal matter is never allowed to accumulate in sufficient quantity to stimulate the urge to defecate. Many types of pathology can directly influence intestinal elimination and cause constipation. Hypertonic colon, associated with emotions, produces spastic constipation. Painful lesions make defecation uncomfortable and an activity which one tries to avoid. Systemic diseases, such as acute illness, cancer of the bowel, subnormal hydration, congenital anomalies, narcotic addiction, lead poisoning, and mechanical obstructive lesions, can be contributing factors toward constipation. Other factors are the use of such drugs as narcotics, analgesics, tranquilizers, and bismuth compounds; a diet poor in bulk and fluids, prolonged bed rest or immobility, and pregnancy. When a person has had no intake of food, for example, after surgery, he will not have frequent or regular bowel movements. The contextual and residual factors are the same as those discussed under factors that affect elimination.

The nursing interventions will relate to the focal, contextual, and residual stimuli. The client may have to be taught to alter his life-style and set aside a time to accommodate elimination needs; usually this is best after breakfast. If the client has utilized laxatives, enemas, or suppositories to relieve a chronic constipation problem, he should be encouraged to see a member of the health team for evaluation of a possible physical or emotional problem. The client needs to have his dietary needs assessed and should be encouraged to consume a diet high in foods containing fiber or residue.

If these interventions are not sufficient to relieve the problem of constipation, a more thorough physical and psychological assessment may be done by the physician or nurse specialist. In some instances it may be necessary to order an *enema,* which is the introduction of solution into the lower intestine; or a *suppository,* a semisolid fusible substance that is introduced into the anal orifice where it dissolves; or a *cathartic,* a drug to induce defecation. Types of enemas, suppositories, and cathartics, and the techniques for their safe administration, are discussed in texts on nursing skills.

Diarrhea, which is the passage of liquid or excessively unformed feces, is usually light brown to medium brown in color, has a foul odor, may contain solid particles, and can vary in quantity from one stool with a small amount of liquid to many stools with an excessive amount. The client may defecate at frequent intervals.

Other factors the nurse might observe with a client who is having diarrhea are complaints of pain which has a piercing or a gripping nature, complaints of an urgency for defecation, poor tissue turgor, weight loss, the presence or absence of a temperature elevation, weakness, emaciation, fatigue, and general malaise.

The focal stimuli may be allergy to ingested foods; allergy to drugs such as antibiotics, sulfonamides, cathartics, reserpine, and diuretics; dietary indiscretions; infections from viruses, bacteria, fungi, protozoa, or metazoa; psychological problems such as neurosis; tumors of the gastrointestinal tract; and inflammatory conditions such as ulcerative colitis. The contextual and residual factors will be much the same as those mentioned under general factors that affect elimination.

The client may be discouraged from taking any foods by mouth as long as this active peristalsis persists. Depending on the extent of the fluid loss, the client may be considered for *parenteral therapy,* that is, feeding by routes other than oral. When the active peristalsis ceases, the client is usually given a bland diet that is low in sugar and warm in temperature. Cleansing of the anal orifice after each defecation is imperative, since breakdown of the skin occurs readily due to the constant source of irritation.

The nurse may also participate in the drug therapy for the treatment of diarrhea, a dependent nursing function.

Another problem in intestinal elimination is *anal incontinence,* which is the inability of the anal sphincter to control discharge of fecal matter and gases voluntarily. The color, odor, consistency, and quantity of the stool will be characteristic for that person. The frequency of defecation will vary, because of the individual's inability to control the anal sphincter. Psychological problems, developmental stage, pathology relating to the spinal cord, and damage to the anal sphincter may be focal factors. The contextual and residual factors will vary.

The nurse may be responsible for initiating the bowel training program. She should enlist the client's cooperation and understanding by explaining the program and its expectations. The training should start with a clean bowel, and a regular evacuation time daily or on alternate days should be established. The client should be encouraged to maintain maximum mobility, should have a well-balanced diet at regular times, and a fluid intake of 2,500 to 3,000 cc per day. Any results of the plan should be recorded for reference by all those caring for the client. The program should not be interrupted, and its progress should be reported to all members of the health team. These programs generally continue for 14 to 21 days.

Some of the general nursing actions that can be carried out to promote client comfort when an abnormality in intestinal elimination is present are to make sure that the anal area is clean, to allow the client an opportunity to wash his hands after wiping, to remove soiled bedclothes or linens, to use sprays and good ventilation when odors are present, to keep the bedpan readily available for the client, to apply emollient creams or powder to irritated skin, to encourage adequate fluid intake unless they are contraindicated, and to encourage the client to avoid cold fluids and rich foods.

ASSESSMENT OF URINARY ELIMINATIVE BEHAVIORS

When assessing urinary elimination, the nurse should observe the following factors: color of the urine, odor of the urine, consistency of the urine, frequency of urination, the amount voided each time, and any other data that might indicate a problem. The characteristic color of urine is mainly derived from the pigment urochrome, which is a constant product of metabolism and may vary in amount under abnormal conditions. Urine is generally light yellow or amber in color, but under abnormal circumstances it may be dark amber, brown, bright red, dark red, blue, green, black, or brick-colored. Drugs, blood, and food may alter the color of normal urine. A substance in the urine called urinod gives the urine its characteristic odor, which is faintly aromatic. As urine stands and bacteria are allowed to ferment it, an odor of ammonia develops. Other abnormal odors of urine are musty, the odor of new-mown hay, stercoraceous or fecal smelling, or sweet smelling. The consistency of the urine varies according to the amount of solids in it. Urine generally gives a dilute appearance because it is composed of 95 percent water, 3.7 percent organic salts, and 1.3 percent inorganic salts. The normal specific gravity of urine is 1.010 to 1.030. Urine is usually clear, but under normal circumstances it may be cloudy or contain sediment, stones, or calculi.

The frequency of urination and the amount voided each time can be related to three physiological phenomena: first, the musculature of the bladder is capable of great distention to hold urine that is constantly accumulating, and the urge to urinate does not occur until approximately 300 cc have accumulated; second, the desire to urinate is due to the stimulation of the stretch receptors in the bladder; and third, the internal sphincter, which is located at the opening of the bladder into the urethra, relaxes and allows urine to escape. The usual daily amount of urine excreted by an adult is from 1,200 to 1,500 cc. *Oliquria* is defined as infrequent voidings with less than 150 cc each time. If an individual has a lack of urine production, a condition called *anuria* exists, and if a client is excreting large amounts of urine in one voiding, it is called *polyuria*.

Other factors to assess that may indicate a problem are the presence of pain or burning sensations when voiding, a feeling of fullness with an inability to void, redness or swelling around the urinary meatus, edema, or swelling, around the eyes, feet, ankles, hands, and sacral area, changes in skin pigmentation, a temperature elevation, and signs of neuromuscular dysfunction, such as incontinence. Lassitude, headache, and other cerebral symptoms can result from the accumulation of waste products such as urea nitrogen and creatinine in the blood plasma. If a urinary problem is suspected and the nurse observes any of these signs of cerebral dysfunction, she should check any available laboratory reports to see if the blood urea nitrogen [normal range—15 to 25 milligrams (mg)/100 milliliters (ml) of blood] and the blood creatinine (normal—1.2 to 13 mg/100 ml of blood) are within normal ranges (DuGas, 1972, p. 384).

ASSESSING FACTORS THAT AFFECT
NORMAL URINARY ELIMINATION

The focal factors affecting urinary elimination would vary depending upon the behavior with which you are dealing. Such factors as the use of a bedpan; the fear of wetting the bed; the intake of fluids; the use of such medications as hormones or diuretics; such diseases as pyelitis, pyelonephritis, cystitis, glomerulonephritis, diabetes, and congestive heart failure; pregnancy; the availability of toilet facilities; dehydration due to excessive climatic conditions or disease; and the presence of a catheter can all directly influence urinary elimination. The contextual factors might be restrictions in diet, poor eating habits, climate, and age. Punitive measures in child rearing, school phobias, cultural values, and developmental level are residual factors that may affect urinary elimination. Assessment of urinary elimination is summarized in Table 5.2.

TABLE 5.2
Assessment of Urinary Elimination

Behavioral Assessment	Influencing Factors
Color of urine	Use of bedpan
Odor of urine	Fear of wetting bed
Consistency of urine	Intake of fluids
Frequency of urination	Medications
Amount voided each time	Diseases
Presence of pain or	Pregnancy
burning when voiding	Toilet facilities
	Dehydration
	Catheter
	Restrictions in diet
	Poor eating habits
	Climate
	Age or developmental level
	Child rearing
	Cultural values

GENERAL NURSING INTERVENTIONS FOR ENCOURAGING NORMAL URINARY ELIMINATION

The client should have a relaxed environment and should be allowed to assume as normal a position as possible; usually the toilet or commode facilitate the best position. For clients in bed, the nurse should be extra careful to warm the bedpan and the urinal and put them into proper position. This is important since, if the client is not able to control his position, he may fear wetting the bed. Other methods to help the client maintain normal elimination from the bladder are running water in audible distance, dangling of fingers in water, providing for privacy, pouring water over the perineum, relieving anxiety or pain, encouraging an intake of a minimum of 1,000 to 1,500 cc in a 24-hour period, rubbing an ice cube over the lower abdomen for two to three second intervals for 30 seconds (DuGas, 1972, p. 389), and soft brushing in a rapid manner for two to three seconds for a period of 30 seconds.

COMMON PROBLEMS OF URINARY ELIMINATION

Whenever there is any problem with urinary elimination, the nurse should initiate an intake and output record. Intake should include all oral and intravenous fluids, and output should include all fluid lost in perspiration, feces, urine, vomitus, bleeding, gastric suctioning, or wound drainage. The perineal area should be kept clean and free of discharge.

Urinary retention, which is failure to expel urine from the bladder, is common after lower abdominal or pelvic surgery, with mechanical obstructions such as swelling of the urethra after childbirth, after gynecological or urinary surgery, with psychological conditions such as being too embarrassed to void, with delayed ambulation, and with such pathology as infections and neurogenic bladder. The contextual and residual factors would vary with the individual client. When a client has urinary retention, the color, odor, and consistency of the urine are characteristic. Other symptoms which the client may manifest are failure to expel sufficient quantities of urine with any one voiding in spite of sufficient intake, discomfort in the lower abdomen, and a bladder that is distended above the symphysis pubis.

If all the methods for encouraging normal urinary elimination fail, a catheterization may have to be initiated. A *catheterization* is an introduction of a catheter, which is a hollow tube, through the urethra into the bladder for purposes of withdrawing urine. This procedure is done under aseptic conditions.

Urinary incontinence is another problem of urinary elimination, defined as an involuntary release of urine from the urinary bladder. The color, odor, and consistency of the urine can all be characteristic, but the nurse will observe very little consistency in frequency, in that the client can dribble almost constantly. In paradoxical incontinence, the dribbling of urine ends when the pressure in the bladder is reduced. Focal factors that might cause urinary incontinence include cerebral clouding. This is a lack of awareness of the need to empty the bladder and occurs in aging, in the acutely ill, and in the comatose client. Other focal factors are such pathology as urinary tract infections; disturbance of central nervous system pathways causing loss of voluntary control; spinal cord injuries; tumors; tissue damage to sphincters; relaxation of perineal structures from childbirth, developmental stage; psychological problems such as persistent enuresis in children; and an overfull bladder when sneezing or coughing. The contextual and residual factors will vary with the individual client. Frequent cleansing of the perineal area is essential when there is incontinence to prevent skin breakdown. Application of ointment such as zinc oxide may be necessary to reduce irritation to the skin. The client may have to be encouraged to do active and passive abdominal, perineal, and gluteal exercises to strengthen supporting musculature.

Many times the entire health team evaluates the individual client's situation to see if the bladder training program is feasible. A drinking schedule, which will permit convenient occasions for emptying the bladder, is generally instituted. The client is usually encouraged to sit in a comfortable, relaxed position with legs flexed. He should have times set aside each day for voiding, which will be determined by the client's intake of fluids. The client should be made aware of any stimulus or call to void, such as sensations in the abdomen, chilliness, sweating, and muscular twitching. He should be encouraged to assist in the process by bending forward in a slow rhythmic fashion to create pressure on the bladder, by pressing his hands over the bladder area, by drinking fluids, and by listening to running water (Fuerst et al., 1974, p. 370). Not until the client is able to use a specific method to stimulate and empty the bladder is the bladder training considered successful.

BEHAVIORAL ASSESSMENT OF ELIMINATION THROUGH THE SKIN

The nurse should observe the quantity and odor of perspiration. *Perspiration* is the functional excretion of sweat. Water and certain mineral salts, such as sodium chloride, are excreted by the sudorific glands of the skin. The main function of this perspiration is the cooling of the body by the evaporation of water to maintain normal body temperature. The amount of heat lost through evaporation and convection is affected by the amount of skin exposed, the quantity of moisture on the skin, and the surrounding environmental temperature and circulating air.

Perspiration can be absent, commonly called anhidrosis, to excessive, called diaphoresis, and still be normal or average for that individual. The odor of perspiration is due to the breakdown products produced by the bacteria, as well as the growth of those bacteria normally found on the skin. Perspiration normally smells salty, sour, musty, or ammoniacal. If it is unusually offensive it is called malodorous.

Other factors to assess or evaluate are whether the perspiration is located over the entire body, over the upper extremities, over the lower extremities, over the forehead or hands, and whether it is associated with temperature elevation. The nurse should also note whether the skin is pale or flushed and if there are any reddened or broken areas on the bony prominences of the skin.

ASSESSMENT OF FACTORS THAT AFFECT ELIMINATION THROUGH THE SKIN

Factors that directly increase the quantity of perspiration from the skin are activity, excitement, stress or fear, environmental factors such as temperature of the room or climate, disease pathology which cause temperature elevation, cleanliness, and basic metabolic rate. Contextual factors that affect the quantity and odor of the perspiration are the use of deodorants, the frequency of baths and perineal care, and age. Child-rearing practices in relation to cleanliness, culture, and hospitalization can also affect elimination from the skin.

TABLE 5.3
Nursing Process Guide Focusing on Adaptation to Need for Intestinal Elimination for
28-Year-Old Pregnant Woman

Behavior	Adaptation Status	Influencing Factors		
		Focal	Contextual	Residual
Dark brown, foul smelling, hard, dry stools Abdominal distention Belching Malaise	M	Displacement of of intestinal tract and other physiological changes of pregnancy	Poor fluid and bulk intake On iron tablets Decreased exercise Hemorrhoids Rushed schedule after breakfast	Former bowel habits

GENERAL NURSING INTERVENTIONS FOR ENCOURAGING NORMAL ELIMINATION THROUGH THE SKIN

Since odor is caused by the breakdown or growth of bacteria, it is important to help the client to keep clean by removing or helping him to remove the dirt, excretory products, and secretions in which these bacteria flourish. The bath not only accomplishes this goal, but also helps the client to relax and feel well-groomed, as well as to stimulate good circulation. Since the underarms are a warm, dark, and moist place, and thus furnish an excellent media for bacteria to grow, a deodorant should be used under the arms to eliminate odor. The perineal area is also warm, dark and moist, and as a result should be kept clean and dry. The client should also be encouraged to implement good oral hygiene, as this helps to reduce the plaque, which can cause tooth decay, periodontal disease, and halitosis or bad breath. Since rubber prevents the evaporation of moisture, rubber sheets should not be used on the client's bed unless some material is also used to absorb the perspiration. A sheepskin placed under the client who must be in bed can help to reduce perspiration, since air spaces in the wool allow for evaporation of moisture.

COMMON PROBLEMS OF ELIMINATION THROUGH THE SKIN

Malodorous perspiration, or that which has a very musty or strong smell, is caused by excessive secretions from the sudorific and sebaceous glands, coupled with excessive perspiration and bacteria on the skin. This can be caused by any one of the factors mentioned. Since bacteria flourish in a more alkaline

Problem Identification	Goal	Intervention
Hard dry stools due to physiological effect of pregnancy	Having a normal intestinal elimination pattern	Instruct to increase fluid intake, particularly prune juice. Help plan for more bulk in diet. Instruct on exercise within safe limits. Suggest second cup of coffee after house quiets down in morning.

environment, regular soap, which changes the skin's pH (symbol used to express the measure of alkalinity and acidity) from acid to alkaline (Gragg and Rees, 1970, p. 395), should not be utilized. Soaps with hexachlorophene do not change the skin's pH and may be advantageous for this reason. The client should be encouraged to bathe frequently and to use deodorants.

SUMMARY

This chapter has discussed the assessment and planning of care for the client in regard to the physiological need for elimination. Adaptive and non-adaptive behaviors in intestinal, urinary, and skin elimination were identified. Focal, contextual, and residual factors affecting each type of elimination were outlined. The major problems of excesses or deficits in each area were discussed. The commonly known nursing interventions to deal with these problems have been included throughout the chapter. The adaptation nursing process implied here is illustrated in the sample nursing process guide in Table 5.3 for a 28-year-old pregnant woman.

REFERENCES

DuGas, Beverly, *Kozier-DuGas Introduction to Patient Care*. 2nd ed. Philadelphia: W. B. Saunders Company, 1972.

Fuerst, Elinor, LuVerne Wolff, and Marlene Weitzel, *Fundamentals of Nursing*. Philadelphia: J. B. Lippincott Company, 1974.

Gragg, Shirley Hawke and Olive M. Rees, *Scientific Principles in Nursing.* St. Louis: C. V. Mosby Company, 1970.

ADDITIONAL READINGS

Delehanty, L. and V. Stravino, "Achieving Bladder Control," *American Journal of Nursing,* vol. 70, February 1970, pp. 312-16.

Elizabeth, Sister Regina, "Sensory Stimulation Techniques," *American Journal of Nursing,* vol. 66, February 1966, pp. 281-86.

Thompson, I. M., "Managing the Problems of Elimination," *Nursing Outlook,* vol. 14, November 1966, pp. 58-61.

Tudor, L. L., "Bladder and Bowel Retraining," *American Journal of Nursing,* vol. 70, November 1970, pp. 2391-93.

6

Fluids and Electrolytes

Nancy Zewen Perley

KEY CONCEPTS DEFINED

Tissue Turgor: Fullness and resiliency of tissue demonstrated by springing back of skin when it is pinched.

Edema: Excessive fluid stored in body tissue spaces.

Levels of Consciousness: The state of awareness of the client.

    Alert and oriented: Knows time and place.

    Stuporous: Partial unconsciousness; can be aroused with difficulty.

    Comatose: Profound unconsciousness; cannot be aroused.

Tetany: Excitability of the nervous system resulting in carpopedal spasm, laryngospasm, and convulsions.

Osmotic Equilibrium: Balance established by movement of water across cellular membranes from an area of lower concentration to an area of higher concentration.

Dehydration: Fluid volume deficit—decreased extracellular water volume.

Overhydration: Fluid volume overload—increased extracellular water volume.

Hyponatremia: Sodium deficit of extracellular fluid.

Hypokalemia: Potassium deficit of extracellular fluid.

Hyperkalemia: Potassium excess of extracellular fluid.

Hypocalcemia: Calcium deficit of extracellular fluid.

Hypercalcemia: Calcium excess of extracellular fluid.

pH: A measurement of the hydrogen ion concentration, and thus of acidity.

Metabolic Acidosis: Base bicarbonate deficit of extracellular fluid.

Metabolic Alkalosis: Base bicarbonate excess of extracellular fluid.

Respiratory Acidosis: Carbonic acid excess of extracellular fluid.

Respiratory Alkalosis: Carbonic acid deficit of extracellular fluid.

Homeostasis: That narrow range within which the body maintains its adaptation.

After studying this chapter the reader will be able to:

1. Define the key concepts of this chapter.
2. Identify behaviors indicating fluid and electrolyte imbalance and list the factors influencing these behaviors (see Appendix I).
3. Specify nursing interventions to be used in problems of dehydration, Edema, and electrolyte imbalance (see Appendix II).

Another component to consider in the assessment of the physiological mode is that of fluids and electrolytes. Disturbances in this area can contribute to or be a resultant effect of a disease process. They can occur in individuals with mild, moderate, or severe illnesses and can even precipitate death. Therefore, the maintenance of these bodily fluids and its dissolved substances (electrolytes) in an adaptive state is extremely important for the preservation of physiological integrity.

The nurse's role in preventing or alleviating fluid and electrolyte imbalances cannot be understated. Since the nurse is the individual who probably has the most consistent and frequent contact with the client, she is in an excellent position to assess both the subtle and obvious effects of these imbalances. Along with other members of the health team, the nurse plays an integral part in manipulating the stimuli so that the imbalance is either corrected or brought under control before serious and/or irreparable damage is done.

This chapter explores the topic of fluids and electrolytes as it relates to the adaptation nursing process. The assessment procedure in both health and illness will be discussed along with specific nursing interventions.

BEHAVIORAL ASSESSMENT OF FLUIDS AND ELECTROLYTES

Maintaining bodily fluids and electrolytes in their prescribed delicate proportions is absolutely vital for the sustenance of life. Cellular, extracellular, and systemic functioning will be disrupted and eventually fail without their activity. Since disruptions can occur on all three levels, fluid and electrolyte imbalances exhibit a wide range of clinical observations (behaviors). Some of these behaviors (for example, poor tissue turgor, muscle spasms) may be quickly associated with these imbalances. On the other hand, there are a number of manifestations (for example, anuria, weakness, rapid heart rate) that are not so obviously related, and may be misdiagnosed. Therefore, in the assessment process, it is essential that the nurse explore all of the components of the physiological mode when evaluating fluid and electrolyte status.

The status of fluid and electrolytes may be assessed by considering both subjective and objective data. In subjective assessment, the client or family will make certain key statements that will alert the nurse to the possibility of a fluid or electrolyte imbalance. Examples of these statements may be the following: "I just don't know what's the matter with me; I don't seem to have the pep that I did last week" or "We can't understand it, Aunt Mary used to be as sharp as a tack, but now she's suddenly so confused!" Although this subjective data does provide an important key, it must also be supported by objective data, which may be acquired through a combination of direct observation and clinical measurement (laboratory tests, electrocardiograms).

As discussed previously, many of the behaviors associated with fluids and electrolyte status are either so subtle or inconclusive that without careful assessment and validation, misdiagnoses can occur. In these cases validation is usually achieved through measurement. The laboratory test, for example, may be the only concrete evidence to show that an imbalance is present. The diversity of fluid and electrolyte manifestations are illustrated in Table 6.1, in which both adaptive and maladaptive behaviors are listed in relation to type of data and physiological component. Using the chart you will see what physiological factors to look at in doing a behavioral assessment of fluids and electrolytes.

TABLE 6.1
First Level Assessment—Fluids and Electrolytes

Behavior	Type of Data	Adaptive Status
1. *Rest and Exercise*		
a. Appropriate balance of rest and exercise for age and position on health-illness continuum.	S or DO	A
b. Fatigue (I'm so tired all of the time").	S	M
c. Restlessness or agitation.	DO	M
d. Muscular weakness.	S or DO	M
2. *Nutrition*		
a. Healthy appetite.	DO	A
b. Anorexia.	S	M
c. Nausea.	S	M
d. Vomiting.	DO	M
e. Fluctuations in weight (may be either acute or chronic).	DO	M

TABLE 6.1 (Continued)

Behavior	Type of Data	Adaptive Status
3. *Elimination*		
a. Normal urinary output (considering intake, age, and position on health-illness continuum).	DO	A
b. Urinary output increase or decrease.	DO	M
4. *Oxygen and Circulation*		
a. Respirations within normal limits.	DO	A
b. Dyspnea—difficulty breathing.	DO	M
c. Increase or decrease in rate of respiration.	DO	M
d. Apical or radial pulse rate within normal limits.	CM	A
e. Aberrations, in rate, regularity, and strength of pulse.	CM	M
f. Aberrations in electrocardiogram.	CM	M
g. Cardiac arrest.	DO or CM	M
5. *Fluids and Electrolytes*		
a. Normal intake of fluids (considering age, weight, output, and position on health-illness continuum).	DO	A
b. Good tissue turgor (when pinched, skin will spring back to normal position immediately).	DO	A
c. Moist mucous membranes.	DO	A
d. Serum electrolyte values within normal limits.	CM	A
e. Extreme thirst.	S	M
f. Poor tissue turgor (when pinched, skin remains raised for many seconds).	DO	M
g. Dry mucous membranes.	DO	M
h. Rough, dry, red tongue.	DO	M
i. Edema, excessive fluid stored in body tissue spaces (especially lower extremities, hands, and face).	DO	M
j. Aberrations in serum electrolyte values.	CM	M
k. Increased intraocular tension.	CM	M
l. Puffy eyelids.	DO	M
6. *Regulation*		
a. Neurological		
(1) Levels of consciousness.		
(a) Alert and oriented (knows time and place).	DO	A
(b) Stuporus (partial unconsciousness, can be aroused).	DO	M
(c) Comatose (profound unconsciousness, cannot be aroused).	DO	M

TABLE 6.1 (Continued)

Behavior	Type of Data	Adaptive Status
(2) Hallucinations and delusions.	DO	M
(3) Intestinal ileus (failure of intestines to propel contents forward).	DO	M
(4) Numbness and/or tingling in extremities.	S	M
(5) Muscle spasms.	DO	M
(6) Paralysis.	DO	M
(7) Tetany (excitability of the nervous system resulting in carpopedal spasm—feet turned down with toes flexed, laryngospasm—spasm of vocal cords, and convulsions).	DO	M
b. Senses		
(1) Pain or cramping.	S	M
(2) Voice changes (usually due to paralysis).	DO	M
(3) Tinnitus (ringing of ears).	S	M

Key: DO — Direct Observation
S — Subjective
CM — Clinical Measurement
A — Adaptive
M — Maladaptive

ASSESSING FACTORS THAT INFLUENCE FLUIDS AND ELECTROLYTES

Fluid and electrolyte disturbances may be caused by one factor alone (the focal stimulus) or a multiplicity of factors (focal, contextual, and residual stimuli), depending upon the individual situation. It is essential that the nurse be aware of situations that commonly cause these imbalances so that appropriate interventions can be initiated before serious consequences develop. Table 6.2 illustrates the major categories of conditions that influence and/or directly contribute to the development of these imbalances.

TABLE 6.2
Major Categories of Conditions Likely To Cause Fluid and Electrolyte Disturbances.

Category	Example
Imbalances occurring in clinical conditions[1]	
1. Acute illnesses	Adrenal insufficiency (deficient

TABLE 6.2 (Continued)

Category	Example
	aldosterone production results in loss of sodium and conservation of potassium).
2. Chronic illnesses	Renal disease (inefficient kidney has limited or absent ability to excrete hydrogen ions, potassium ions, and water).
3. Injuries	Massive crushing injuries (results in loss of extracellular fluid and release of cellular potassium).
Imbalances caused by medical therapy	Administration of potent diuretics (causes fluid, sodium, and potassium loss).
Imbalances resulting from loss of specific bodily fluids (gastric juice, intestinal juice, sensible and insensible fluid, bile, wound exudates, and pancreatic juice)	May occur due to the following: vomiting, diarrhea, gastrointestinal suctioning, fistulas, drainage.
Additional factors that may contribute to imbalances	1. Age (infant or elder). 2. Poor nutritional status. 3. Climate (intense heat may cause excessive perspiration resulting in fluid and sodium loss).

[1]Conditions likely to cause fluid and electrolyte disturbances are often related to pathological conditions. It is assumed that the nurse studying adaptation nursing is also receiving a background in pathophysiology, which will enable her to understand the examples given in this chapter and throughout this text.

ASSESSMENT OF SPECIFIC IMBALANCES

In the previous section, behaviors associated with fluid and electrolyte status and possible related stimuli were indicated. In order to make an accurate identification of the problem or nursing diagnosis and institute appropriate interventions, the nurse needs to have a specific knowledge of the more commonly occurring imbalances. Although there is a possibility of the occurrence of at least 16 fluid and electrolyte disturbances, the most common will be discussed in this chapter.

Fluid Imbalances

Bodily fluid constitutes approximately 60 percent of the total body weight and is divided between two compartments, intracellular (45 percent) and extracellular (15 percent). For the infant 70 to 80 percent of total body weight is in a fluid state (see Figure 6.1). For metabolic processes to take place in the body, a transport system is needed. Fluid serves that purpose by acting as an aqueous medium in which vital exchanges of electrolytes and other important substances occur. In addition, fluid also functions to maintain *osmotic equilibrium* by allowing free movement of water across the cellular membranes and capillaries. Movement is from an area of lower concentration to an area of higher concentration until equilibrium or balance is established.

Imbalances can occur when there are significant gains or losses of body fluid. Due to the two major functions of fluid as described above, these imbalances may also be accompanied by an abnormal concentration of various electrolytes, creating further disequilibrium for the client. The following list categorically illustrates the numerous behaviors and stimuli that are associated with fluid imbalances.

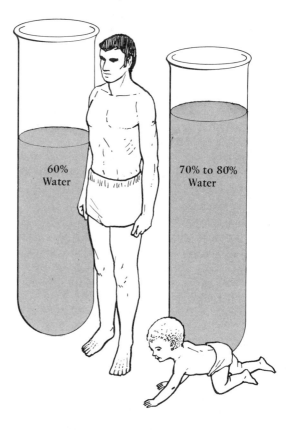

Figure 6.1 Body fluids in relation to total body weight.

Fluid Volume Deficit (Synonym: dehydration—decreased extracellular
water volume)

Behaviors

1. Clinical observations
   a. Poor tissue turgor—when pinched, skin remains raised for many
      seconds depending on degree of fluid loss.
   b. Dry, sticky mucous membranes.
   c. Decrease in weight—may occur on either an acute or chronic basis.
   d. Decreased intraocular tensions—loss of fluid in the eyeball decreases
      the intraocular tension. The result is a "sunken eyes" appearance.
   e. Sunken facial appearance.
   f. Oliguria or anuria—significant fluid loss results in decreased cardiac
      output. As a compensatory mechanism, the blood is shunted away
      from the kidney to provide oxygen to the more immediately vital
      tissues. As a consequence, there is decreased urine production.
   g. Tachycardia—the heart also attempts to compensate for the decreased
      cardiac output by accelerating its rate.
   h. Impaired sensorium—exhibited in the client by confusion, disorien-
      tation, stupor, and coma, and is due to cerebral cellular dehydration.
2. Laboratory data—fluid loss is reflected in laboratory data by the
   following reports: increased hemoglobin, increased hematocrit, and
   increase in number of red blood cells/ml.

Stimuli

1. Stimuli—may be due to any number of causes such as gastritis or pyloric
   obstruction.
2. Decreased water intake—major contributory factor in fluid volume loss
   that is especially observed in elderly or extremely ill clients.
3. Fever—causes significant water loss through the mechanism of
   perspiration.
4. Diarrhea—any pathological state that results in diarrhea may contribute
   to significant water loss. Examples are ulcerative colitis and parasitic
   disease.
4. Drainage from tubes or fistula.
6. Diuresis—examples are the administration of potent diuretics and
   diabetic acidosis.
7. Excessive perspiration due to increased environmental temperature.

Fluid Volume Overload (Synonyms: edema, overhydration—increased
extracellular water volume)

Behaviors

1. Clinical observations
   a. Puffy eyelids—due to edema around the eyes.
   b. Round, puffy facial appearance.

    c. Edema—may be observed in the extremities (especially ankles and fingers), face, or abdomen (ascites).

    d. Tachypnea and moist rales—these behaviors occur when the fluid volume overload results in pulmonary congestion.

    e. Increase in weight—as in fluid volume deficit, this maladaptive behavior may be acute or chronic in onset.

2. Laboratory data—although there is usually no change in the hematocrit, there may be a significant drop in the serum sodium concentration (below 125 milliequivalent [mEq] /ml).

Stimuli

1. Administration of excessive quantities of I.V. (intravenous injection) fluid.

2. Inappropriate A.D.H. (antidiuretic hormone). Syndrome—oversecretion of this pituitary hormone results in excessive water retention by the kidney tubules.

3. Congestive heart failure—since the heart is an inefficient pump, excessive fluid retention may result.

4. Renal disease—the kidney in the uremic state has limited capacity to produce urine; therefore, fluid intake may exceed fluid output.

Sodium Imbalances

Sodium, a cation that is chiefly found in extracellular fluid, functions primarily to control the distribution of water throughout the body. This is accomplished by maintaining osmotic equilibrium between the intracellular and extracellular compartments. The excretion of sodium is principally controlled by the kidney, which acts as a highly efficient organ (in the absence of pathology) to both conserve and excrete this electrolyte depending upon the serum concentration. This task is aided by two hormones, aldosterone (inhibits renal sodium excretion) and A.D.H. (promotes water reabsorption by the kidney tubules). Excretion of sodium from the skin is minimal under normal conditions. However, this loss may be accelerated considerably due to perspiration from muscular exercise, fever, or increased environmental temperature.

The major sodium imbalance that the nurse will encounter in clinical practice will be that of sodium deficit of extracellular fluid. Since this electrolyte has such a close relationship with water, the stimuli for a deficit imbalance should be grouped into three major categories: depletional hyponatremia (loss of sodium without a proportionate loss of water), dilutional hyponatremia (water replacement or retention without concomitant sodium replacement), and conditions with unclear etiology. Sodium excess of extracellular fluid is rarely observed clinically and will be discussed in the following list of behaviors and stimuli primarily for theoretical purposes:

Sodium Deficit of Extracellular Fluid (Synonyms: hyponatremia, low sodium syndrome)

Behaviors

1. Clinical observations
   a. Muscular weakness and fatigue.
   b. Apprehension and apathy possibly progressing to delusions and hallucinations—this maladaptive behavior is due to the automatic shift of fluid into the cerebral cells in an attempt to restore extracellular isotonicity.
   c. Convulsions, coma, and death in severe cases.
2. Laboratory data—a serum sodium concentration below 137 mEq indicates a sodium deficit of extracellular fluid. However, clinical symptoms usually are not apparent until the concentration drops to approximately 120 mEq/ml, with severe symptoms occurring at a 110 mEq/ml level.

Stimuli

1. Depletional hyponatremia
   a. Administration of potent diuretics.
   b. Loss of sodium-rich bodily fluids (wound exudates, bile and gastric, intestinal, and pancreatic juices)—usually occur in conjunction with diarrhea, drainage, fistulas, and G.I. (gastrointestinal) suctioning
   c. Adrenal insufficiency—decreased aldosterone production causes decreased renal conservation of sodium.
   d. Renal disease—damaged renal tubules cannot reabsorb sodium ion.
2. Dilutional hyponatremia
   a. Excessive perspiration plus drinking plain water—water is replaced, but not sodium.
   b. Inhalation of fresh water (drowning).
   c. Excessive plain water enemas.
   d. Administration of electrolyte free parenteral fluids.
   e. Psychogenic polydipsia—a neurotic condition in which the individual drinks large quantities of plain water.
3. Conditions with unclear etiology.
   a. Inappropriate A.D.H. syndrome—this syndrome is a pathological state in which the production of the antidiuretic hormone is increased. The result is an excessive conservation of water by the kidney tubules, thus diluting the serum sodium level.
   b. Congestive heart failure.
   c. Cirrhosis of the liver.

Sodium Excess of Extracellular Fluid (Synonyms: hypernatremia, salt excess)

Behaviors

1. Clinical observations—in this rarely encountered imbalance, the client may be asymptomatic. However, in symptomatic clients, there is usually

an associated dehydration with the clinical observations due to that particular condition.

2. Laboratory data—a serum sodium concentration above 147 mEq/ml is indicative of a sodium excess of extracellular fluid.

Stimuli

1. Diabetes insipidus—in this case, A.D.H. is deficient due to a tumor or surgical removal of the pituitary. The result is an excessive water loss without a proportionate sodium loss.
2. Inhalation of salt water (drowning).
3. Decreased water intake.

Potassium Imbalances

Potassium is the major intracellular cation with only 2 percent of total body potassium being found in the extracellular fluid. In addition to affecting intracellular integrity and osmolarity, this ion also participates in various metabolic processes and influences the conduction of nerve impulses and skeletal muscle function. In contrast to sodium, potassium is poorly conserved, thus depending heavily on adequate daily intake. In renal pathology, however, abnormal retention can occur.

Due to the factors mentioned above, potassium imbalances are frequently encountered in clinical practice, thus necessitating close nursing observation. The following categorically lists behaviors and stimuli related to these imbalances.

Potassium Deficit of Extracellular Fluid (Synonym: hypokalemia)

Behaviors

1. Clinical observations
   a. Weakness and fatigue—although these behaviors are very vague and easily misdiagnosed, they may be the only early signs of this imbalance.
   b. Muscular system involvement—as the imbalance becomes more severe, the muscular system is affected. Manifestations are: constipation progressing to paralytic ileus, shallow breathing (secondary to weakness or paralysis of the respiratory muscles) progressing to apnea and respiratory arrest, and cardiac arrhythmias.
2. Laboratory data—the following data would support the diagnosis of potassium deficit of extracellular fluid: serum potassium level below 3.5 mEq/ml and an electrocardiogram exhibiting a depression of the T wave, elevation of the U wave, and sagging of the S T segment.

Stimuli

1. Hyperaldosteronism—an oversecretion of this hormone results in excessive renal loss of potassium.

2. Chronic administration of adrenal cortical hormones—the mechanism involved is similar to the above.
3. Administration of potent diuretics—in this case, potassium is lost in conjunction with water and sodium.
4. Loss of gastric juices—since gastric juice is rich with potassium, its depletion may result in a hypokalemic condition. This may be due to gastric suctioning and any state that induces vomiting.
5. Loss of intestinal juices—since these juices also have a high concentration of potassium, the following conditions may induce a hypokalemic state: suctioning, fistulas, excessive water enemas, and diarrhea.
6. Decreased dietary intake.
7. Stress—may contribute to loss of potassium due to the increased cortisol

Potassium Excess of Extracellular Fluid (Synonym: hyperkalemia)

Behavior
1. Clinical observations
    a. No clinical observations in mild cases.
    b. Muscular system involvement—in severe cases, the client will exhibit behaviors similar to those associated with a hypokalemic state. These include: flaccid paralysis resulting in difficulty in speaking and shallow breathing, and depression of the myocardium with cardiac arrhythmias and death.
2. Laboratory data—in potassium excess of extracellular fluid, there is a serum potassium above 5.6 mEq/ml, and an abnormal electrocardiogram (high T wave with depressed S T segment and loss of P wave).

Stimuli
1. Adrenal insufficiency—a deficient or absent production of aldosterone will result in an excessive conservation of potassium.
2. Excessive parenteral administration of potassium.
3. Oral intake of potassium exceeding renal tolerance.
4. Acidosis—this pathological state causes intracellular potassium to be released into the extracellular fluid.
5. Renal pathology—the diseased kidney has a decreased or absent capacity to excrete potassium.

Calcium Imbalances

Calcium, the most abundant electrolyte in the body, has a 99 percent concentration in the bony skeleton with the remainder being found in the skin and extracellular fluid. The only chemically active form of calcium in the extracellular fluid is in the ionized form, with the rest being complexed or bound to protein. The functions of this electrolyte are numerous. In addition to its contribution to the bony skeleton, the calcium ion has several other important capacities: (1) it is necessary for normal blood coagulation; (2) it has a regulatory control over nerve impulses, perhaps by decreasing cell permeability; (3) it appears to influence contractility and excitation of the skeletal muscle.

Calcium imbalances can occur when the ionized form of this electrolyte is not maintained in the appropriate concentration in the extracellular fluid. The following list illustrates the behaviors and stimuli that are related to these imbalances:

Calcium Deficit of Extracellular Fluid (Synonym: hypocalcemia)

Behaviors
1. Clinical observations
    a. Muscle rigidity.
    b. Carpopedal spasm.
    c. Tingling sensation around lips.
    d. Numbness of extremities.
    e. Tetany.
    f. In severe cases—respiratory stridor and death.
2. Laboratory data—a hypocalcemic client may be diagnosed with a serum calcium level below 4.5 mEq/ml, or 8-9 mg%. However, this data reflects the total serum concentration and does not distinguish between the two major forms of serum calcium, ionized and protein-bound. Since ionized calcium is the only chemically active form, it is necessary also to consider the serum albumin (protein) level to arrive at an accurate diagnosis.

Stimuli
1. Hypoparathyroidism—since parathormone (a hormone secreted by the parathyroid glands) regulates the serum calcium level, an undersecretion will result in a hypocalcemic state. This condition is caused by primary failure or surgical removal.
2. Acute pancreatitis—lipase is liberated from the pancreas during an inflammatory process and acts on fat tissues in the abdominal cavity to cause a release of fatty acids. Since fatty acids can combine with the calcium ion and render it chemically inactive, the serum calcium level decreases as a result.
3. Renal failure—the serum phosphorus level increases in the presence of renal failure due to the inability of the kidney to excrete it. Phosphorus and calcium have an inverse relationship to each other in the extracellular fluid. Therefore, since the serum phosphorus level is increased, the serum calcium level will decrease as a consequence.
4. Excessive administration of citrated blood—citrate, a preservative used in transfused blood, can combine with the calcium ion, thus rendering it chemically inactive. Although this condition is rarely a focal stimulus for the development of a hypocalcemic state, it certainly can be an important contributory factor.

5. Alkalosis—this metabolic state results in decreased ionization of serum calcium. As above, this condition may not be focal, but rather contextual to the development of the extracellular calcium deficit.
6. Decreased dietary intake.

Calcium Excess of Extracellular Fluid (Synonym: hypercalcemia)

Behaviors

1. Clinical observations
    a. Flank pain due to kidney stones.
    b. Muscle flaccidity.
    c. Anorexia.
    d. Hypercalcemic crises—observed only in severe conditions and characterized by the following: nausea, vomiting, constipation, dehydration, thirst, stupor, coma due to C.N.S. (central nervous system) depression, and possibly cardiac arrest.
2. Laboratory data—a serum calcium level about 5.5 mEq/ml, or 11 mg%, may be diagnostic of calcium excess of extracellular fluid. As mentioned previously, this data must be interpreted in conjunction with the serum albumin level.

Stimuli

1. Hyperparathyroidism—may be due to an adenoma or malignant tumor; causes excessive amounts of calcium to be released from the bone. As a consequence, the serum calcium level increases.
2. Vitamin D intoxication—increased intake of vitamin D through food or tablets may cause a hypercalcemic state by increasing the absorption of calcium from the intestines.
3. Metastatic cancer of the bone—a breakdown of bone causing excessive amounts of calcium to be released into the bloodstream.
4. Prolonged immobilization—can also cause bony breakdown. Specific cases include osteoporosis and Paget's disease.
5. Acidosis—an acidotic state may contribute to the development of hypercalcemia due to the fact that acidosis causes increased ionization of serum calcium.

Hydrogen Ion Imbalances

The pH of extracellular fluid must be maintained between 7.35 and 7.45 to preserve adaptive matabolic processes. If the pH falls below 6.8 or rises above 7.8, death will eventually follow. Since acids and alkalis are constantly being introduced into the bloodstream (in normal conditions, cellular metabolism, exercise, and ingestion; in abnormal conditions, disease process), the body must enforce certain regulating mechanisms to uphold this intricate balance. These mechanisms, appropriately termed "the three lines of defense," include: the buffer system (primarily base bicarbonate and carbonic acid in a 20 to 1 ratio), the lungs (blow off or retain carbon dioxide), and the kidneys (excrete or conserve hydrogen and bicarbonate ions).

Hydrogen ion imbalances will evolve when the concentration of this ion in the extracellular fluid increases as in acidosis or decreases as in alkalosis, and may be respiratory or metabolic in nature. The following list outlines the behaviors and stimuli associated with these imbalances.

Metabolic Acidosis (Synonym: base bicarbonate deficit of extracellular fluid)

   Behaviors
   1. Clinical observations
       a. Lethargy.
       b. Deep, rapid breathing (Kussmaul respirations)—illustrates the compensatory effort of the lungs to excrete excessive acid in the form of carbon dioxide.
       c. Stupor.
       d. In severe cases, coma and death.
   2. Laboratory data—a serum pH below 7.35 and serum bicarbonate below 20 mEq/ml is diagnostic of metabolic acidosis. However, this condition is usually considered to be moderately severe when the base bicarbonate level drops to 15 mEq/ml, and very severe at an 8 mEq/ml level.
   Stimuli
   1. Diabetic acidosis—in uncontrolled diabetes, carbohydrates are not utilized for metabolism due to lack of insulin. Body fat is metabolized instead with keto-acids produced as a by-product. This increased amount of acid is in excess of the body's buffering capacity, with a fall in pH as a result.
   2. Decreased food intake (especially carbohydrates) or ketogenic diet (deficient in carbohydrate)—a depletion of the carbohydrate reserve will eventually result in body fat metabolism similar to the above stated.
   3. Diarrhea—loss of the bicarbonate ion in intestinal juice may be greater than loss of the hydrogen ion, resulting in a decreased pH.
   4. Renal disease—diseased kidney is unable to excrete the hydrogen ion.

Metabolic Alkalosis (Synonym: base bicarbonate excess of extracellular fluid)

   Behaviors
   1. Clinical observations
       a. Decreased rate and depth of respiration—due to a compensatory attempt of the lungs to conserve carbon dioxide (carbonic acid).
       b. Tingling of the fingers and toes — Alkalosis causes a decreased ionized calcium concentration.

    c. In severe cases, tetany, convulsions, coma, and death.

3. Laboratory data — a definite indication of metabolic alkalosis is a serum pH above 7.45 and a serum bicarbonate above 25 mEq/ml.

Stimuli

1. Excessive alkali intake.

2. Loss of gastric contents—since gastric contents contain a significant amount of hydrochloric acid, loss of these juices through suctioning or vomiting may result in a rise in pH.

3. Hypokalemia—a potassium deficiency due to administration of potent diuretics or loss of gastrointestinal juices, for instance, may cause a rise in pH.

Respiratory Acidosis (Synonym: carbonic acid excess of extracellular fluid)

Behaviors

1. Clinical observations
    a. Weakness.
    b. Dyspnea.
    c. Disorientation and confusion.
    d. In severe cases, coma and death.

2. Laboratory data—diagnostic of respiratory acidosis is: pH below 7.35, serum bicarbonate above 25 mEq/ml and a pCO_2 (carbon dioxide pressure) below 35 mHg.

Stimuli

1. Pneumonia, emphysema, asthma, and occlusion of breathing passages—these respiratory conditions may prevent the efficient elimination of carbon eioxide, thus resulting in a decreased pH.

2. Barbituate, morphine, and meperidine poisoning—these drugs depress the respiratory center with the result that carbon dioxide is inefficiently eliminated.

3. Breathing excessive amounts of carbon dioxide.

4. C.N.S. disturbances of the respiratory center.

5. Inaccurate regulation of the mechanical respirator.

Respiratory Alkalosis (carbonic acid deficit of extracellular fluid)

Behaviors

1. Clinical observations
    a. Tetany observations.
    b. Convulsions.
    c. In severe cases, coma and death.

2. Laboratory data—the following may be indicative of respiratory alkalosis: a serum pH above 7.45, a serum bicarbonate below 20 mEq/ml, and a pCO_2 below 35 mHg.

Stimuli

1. Intentional overbreathing.
2. Oxygen lack—in this condition, the respirations increase with an excessive amount of carbon dioxide being eliminated as a consequence.
3. Anxiety reaction—may induce hyperventilation, which will cause an excessive elimination of carbon dioxide.
4. C.N.S. disturbances of the respiratory center.
5. Inaccurate regulation of the mechanical respirator.

NURSING INTERVENTIONS IN MAINTAINING FLUID AND ELECTROLYTE BALANCE

Once the behaviors and stimuli have been carefully assessed, the nurse can identify the problem or make a nursing diagnosis. Common problems include: dehydration, edema, and electrolyte imbalance. The nurse is then prepared to formulate goals for the client to organize a plan of care. Ideally, the plan will be designed to manipulate the stimuli in such a manner that homeostasis is restored. However, in many conditions (for example, renal failure, diabetic acidosis), manipulation of the offending stimuli may not be feasible at that time or may not provide the most effective means for reestablishing the adaptive state. In these cases, various supportive measures must be instituted to modify the behavior until actual alteration of the stimuli is possible.

The nurse has an essential role in the re-establishment of fluid and electrolyte imbalances to an adaptive state. Although many of the interventions are medical, surgical, or pharmacological in nature, and are dependent upon the physician's order, the nurse has some unique, independent functions. These include: devising goals and implementing a plan of care for the client based upon the total assessment according to the adaptation theoretical framework; providing constant reassessment and modification of this care plan if necessary; establishing an environment that is conducive to adaptation; and instituting an educational program for the client (for example, diet counseling). Education is particularly essential in certain chronic disease processes in which fluid and electrolyte disequilibrium readily occurs. The client with renal failure, for instance, must be fully aware of diet restrictions such as fluid and potassium in order to prevent frequent electrolyte imbalance and promote as normal an existence as possible.

The following list illustrates by categories specific interventions associated with previously discussed fluid and electrolyte imbalances.

1. *Fluid Volume Deficit*
   a. Treat underlying cause (manipulate stimuli—for example, control fever).

    b. Continuous intake and output.

    c. Daily weights.

    d. Replacement of lost fluid to restore the normal composition of the extracellular fluid (may be accomplished either orally by pushing fluids or intravenously).

2. *Fluid Volume Overload*

    a. Treat underlying cause (manipulate stimuli—for example, monitor I.V. closely).

    b. Continuous intake and output.

    c. Daily weights.

    d. Restriction of fluids so that normal fluid concentration is restored without altering the electrolyte composition of the extracellular fluid.

3. *Sodium deficit of extracellular fluid*

    a. Treat underlying cause (manipulate stimuli—for example, control diarrhea).

    b. Replacement of sodium deficit so that sodium level of the extracellular fluid is restored without causing a fluid volume overload.

    c. Restrict fluids.

4. *Sodium Excess of Extracellular Fluid*

    a. Treat underlying cause (manipulate stimuli—for example, increase water intake).

    b. Administration of hypotonic fluid either orally or intravenously to dilute increased sodium concentration.

5. *Potassium Deficit of Extracellular Fluid*

    a. Treat underlying cause (manipulate stimuli—for example, increase dietary intake).

    b. Administration of potassium either orally or intravenously to restore this electrolyte to its normal concentration in the extracellular fluid.

6. *Potassium Excess of Extracellular Fluid*

    a. Treat underlying cause (manipulate stimuli—for example, monitor parenteral administration).

    b. Restriction of potassium in the diet.

    c. Administration of kayexalate (induces potassium excretion through feces).

    d. In renal disease:

        1. Administration of dextrose and insulin (glucose causes potassium to be deposited within the cells; insulin accelerates this action).

        2. Administration of alkali (causes shift of potassium to intracellular space).

        3. Peritoneal or hemodialysis (mechanically rids body of potassium).

        4. Kidney transplantation.

7. *Calcium Deficit of Extracellular Fluid*

    a. Treatment of underlying cause (manipulate stimuli—for example, increase intake).

b. Administration of calcium either orally or intravenously in such amounts necessary to restore normal calcium concentration.

c. Administration of vitamin D (increases intestinal absorption of calcium).

8. *Calcium Excess of Extracellular Fluid*

a. Treatment of underlying cause (manipulate stimuli—for example, provide exercises for those on bed rest).

b. Hydration (push fluids to dilute the excessive concentration of calcium in the extracellular fluid).

c. Administration of phosphate (results in calcium deposition in the bones).

d. Administration of lasix (causes calcium excretion in the urine).

e. Administration of calcitonin (suppresses calcium release from the bone, used experimentally).

f. Dietary restriction of calcium.

9. *Metabolic Acidosis*

a. Treatment of underlying cause (manipulate stimuli—for example, increase carbohydrate intake).

b. Administration of bicarbonate intravenously (buffers excessive hydrogen ions).

c. Administration of intravenous fluids (promotes renal excretion of the hydrogen ion).

10. *Metabolic Alkalosis*

a. Treatment of underlying cause (manipulate stimuli—for example, limit gastric suctioning).

b. Administration of saline (exchanges bicarbonate ions with chloride ions).

c. Correction of associated hypokalemia if present.

11. *Respiratory Acidosis*

a. Treatment of underlying cause (manipulate stimuli—for example, regulate respirators carefully).

b. Mechanical ventilators (promotes blowing off of carbon dioxide and may be used continuously or intermittently).

12. *Respiratory Alkalosis*

a. Treatment of underlying cause (manipulate stimuli—for example, decrease anxiety).

Nursing interventions, then, are based on the goal of promoting an adaptive response and involve a combination of manipulating stimuli causing the maladaptive behavior and other supportive or corrective measures. The total nursing process in relation to the need for fluids and electrolytes is summarized in Table 6.3, which gives an example of a six-week-old infant admitted to the hospital with diarrhea and vomiting.

TABLE 6.3
**Nursing Process Guide Related to Fluid and Electrolyte Needs of
Infant Admitted to Hospital with Diarrhea and Vomiting.**

Behavior		Influencing Factors		
		Focal	Contextual	Residual
Poor tissue turgor.	M	Fluid loss	Inexperienced	6 weeks old
Dry, sticky mucous		through	mother who	(greater body
membranes.	M	diarrhea	increased	weight in
6-oz. weight loss.	M	and	sugar intake	extracellular
Sunken eyes.	M	vomiting.	with initial	fluid).
Decreased urinary			symptoms.	
output.				
Weakness and		Potassium	No potassium	
fatigue	M	loss by	supplement.	
Lab report:		vomiting.	Crying due	
Potassium			to discomfort.	
below				
3.5 mEq/ml	M			
Currently has	Poten-	I.V. fluids.	In isolation	Fluid balance
signs of	tially		room.	labile because
dehydration but	M			of age.
receiving I.V.				
fluids.				

* When a client has an increased risk of developing a problem, it is stated as a potential
problem.

SUMMARY

The adaptation concept is related to bodily homeostasis. Adaptation involves changing levels of response to all types of stimuli and may include a wide
range of behavioral responses. Homeostasis refers to that more narrow range
within which the body maintains its adaptation. Generally the normal responses
in relation to fluid and electrolytes are due to homeostatic mechanisms. We have
noted many factors that interfere with these mechanisms and thus jeopardize
bodily homeostasis and, in a larger sense, total client adaptation. The nurse's
role in assessing maladaptive responses was highlighted. Finally, we outlined
some specific interventions to be used in restoring homeostasis of the fluid and
electrolyte system, thus promoting total client adaptation.

Problem Identification	Goal	Intervention
Dehydration due to fluid loss through diarrhea and vomiting.	Having good tissue turgor, moist mucous membranes, regained weight, eyes and urine output normal	Maintain intravenous fluids. Give fluids by mouth when tolerated. Record accurate intake and output. Record daily weight.
Hypokalemia due to potassium loss by vomiting.	Having increased energy and activity and increased potassium.	Instruct mother in infant diet adjustments and relationship between sugar and diarrhea.
Potential fluid* volume overload.	Not having behavioral signs of overload.	Maintain I.V. potassium intake. Control vomiting by limiting oral intake. Keep infant comfortable. Each hour regulate flow of I.V. Record accurate intake and output. Observe carefully for signs of overload.

REFERENCES

Brunner, Lillian Sholtis and others, *Textbook of Medical-Surgical Nursing*. Philadelphia: J. B. Lippincott Company, 1971.

Burgess, Audrey, *The Nurse's Guide to Fluid and Electrolyte Balance*. New York: McGraw-Hill, Inc., 1970.

Dutcher, Isabel E. and Sandra B. Fielo, *Water and Electrolytes—Implications for Nursing Practice*. New York: The Macmillan Company, 1967.

Fluids and Electrolytes. Chicago: Abbott Laboratories, 1968.

Frohlich, Edward D., *Pathophysiology—Altered Regulatory Mechanisms in Disease*. Philadelphia: J. B. Lippincott Company, 1972.

Harvey, A. McGehee, ed., *The Principles and Practice of Medicine*. New York: Appleton-Century-Crofts, 1972, pp. 55-113.

Heath, Joleen Klocke, "A Conceptual Basis for Assessing Body Water Status," *Nursing Clinics of North America,* vol. 6, no. 1, March 1971, pp. 189-98.

Metheny, Norma Milligan, *Nurses' Handbook of Fluid Balance.* Philadelphia: J. B. Lippincott Company, 1974.

Snively, W. D. and Donna R. Beshear, "Water and Electrolytes in Health and Diseases," *Advanced Concepts in Clinical Nursing.* Philadelphia: J. B. Lippincott Company, 1971.

Voda, Ann M., "Body Water Dynamics," *American Journal of Nursing,* December 1970, pp. 2594-2601.

7

Oxygen and Circulation

Sharon Vairo

KEY CONCEPTS DEFINED

Respiration: A combination of cardiovascular and pulmonary processes by which a sufficient amount of oxygenated blood to meet metabolic requirements is provided and the end products of metabolism are removed.

Systemic Circulation: The major circulation by which blood is pumped from the left ventricle of the heart through the arteries and arterioles to the capillaries.

Pulmonary Circulation: The lesser circulation by which blood is pumped through the pulmonary vessels and is equilibrated with the oxygen and carbon dioxide in the alveolar air.

Respiratory Center: The respiratory neurons located in the medulla oblongata and lower pons.

Hypoxia: Various degrees of oxygen deficiency.

Dyspnea: Difficult or painful breathing.

Orthopnea: Difficult or painful breathing while lying down.

Paroxysmal Noctural Dyspnea: Dyspnea at night.

Cough: A response to clear the airway.

Hemoptysis: Coughing up of blood.

Cyanosis: Bluish or purplish color of skin and/or mucous membranes.

Bradycardia: Slow heartbeat.

Respiratory Failure: The respiratory system is unable to maintain adequate oxygenation of the blood.

Cardiovascular Failure: The cardiovascular system is unable to provide a sufficient amount of oxygenated blood to meet the needs of the various body tissues.

Shock: Inadequate tissue perfusion.

Hypercarbia: Buildup of carbon dioxide.

After studying this chapter the reader will be able to:

1. Define the key concepts of this chapter.
2. Identify behaviors indicating oxygen deficiency (hypoxia and shock) and list factors influencing these behaviors (see Appendix I).
3. Specify nursing interventions to be used in problems of hypoxia and shock (see Appendix II).

Man's need for oxygen is another crucial factor in his total physiological adaptation. This chapter considers the oxygen need and the related process of circulation. The structure, function, and regulation of the cardiovascular and pulmonary systems are described. Nursing assessment of behaviors related to and factors influencing them are discussed. Problems of adaptation and maladaptation to excesses and deficits of oxygen are pointed out. Finally, appropriate nursing interventions are listed and then demonstrated in a nursing process guide.

STRUCTURES AND FUNCTIONS RELATED TO OXYGEN NEED

The cardiovascular and pulmonary systems are responsible for providing to all body tissues, under all conditions, a sufficient amount of oxygenated blood to meet the metabolic requirements of each tissue and to remove the end products of metabolism that have accumulated. This entire combination of processes is referred to as *respiration.*

In man, respiration is comprised of three parts. The first is external respiration, which involves taking in oxygen from the air and excreting carbon dioxide. This process is controlled by nervous and mechanical devices. Second, respiration includes the transport of oxygen and carbon dioxide. This is the chemical and physical process of gas exchange between blood and cells in the tissues. Third, internal respiration is the term used to cover the physiochemical and biochemical processes of cellular metabolism in which oxygen is utilized and carbon dioxide is produced.

The pulmonary system by itself is mainly concerned with the intake and exchange of respiratory gases. The system is basically composed of the lungs; the air passages to and from the lungs; the thoracic and abdominal muscles, which do the actual work involved in breathing; and the pleural spaces, which allow the movements of breathing. The actual exchange of the respiratory gases takes place in the numerous small alveoli of the lungs. This exchange is controlled by the laws governing the diffusion of gases, which are discussed in detail in any of the available medical-physics texts.

The cardiovascular or circulatory system is the transport system of the body. It is responsible for carrying the oxygen absorbed from the alveolar surfaces of the lung to the tissues of the body and returning carbon dioxide to the lungs to be removed. The vehicle for this movement is the blood. The blood is able to carry large amounts of oxygen because of the hemoglobin contained in the red blood cells. Oxygen combines reversibly with hemoglobin and is transported in this form to the individual tissues of the body. This oxyhemoglobin combination is influenced by the partial pressure of oxygen in the surrounding environment. Carbon dioxide is transported mainly in the form of bicarbonate ions in the blood plasma and in the red blood cells.

The blood, which is carrying these respiratory gases, is propelled through the system of blood vessels by the heart, which functions as a pump. In reality, in man the heart is two pumps joined together. From the left ventricle of the heart, blood is pumped through the arteries and arterioles to the capillaries, where the substances carried are transferred to the interstitial fluid and from there to the individual cells. The waste products of cell metabolism are picked up by the blood at this time and transported back to the right atrium of the heart through the venules and veins. This is called the major, or *systemic circulation*. From the right atrium, blood travels to the right ventricle, which pumps it through the pulmonary blood vessels to the left atrium and then on to the left ventricle. Circulation through the pulmonary vessels is known as the lesser, or *pulmonary circulation*. It is in the pulmonary capillaries that the blood equilibrates with the oxygen and carbon dioxide in the alveolar air. This entire circulation is controlled by a multiplicity of regulatory systems whose general function is to maintain adequate blood flow and thus adequate oxygenation to body tissues.

REGULATION RELATED TO OXYGEN NEED

Respiration is controlled and regulated by a neural and chemical balance within the body. The principle integration and regulation of breathing are achieved by respiratory neurons located in the medulla oblongata and lower pons.[1] This "respiratory center" is influenced by structures at higher levels of the nervous system as well as by changes in the chemical environment. For example, the cerebral cortical center provides for sufficient voluntary control of breathing to allow talking, laughing, holding of breath. The major chemical factor affecting breathing is considered to be the blood carbon dioxide concentration. An increase in arterial pCO_2 results in an increased pCO_2 in tissue fluids, and thus a decreased pH within the chemosensitive neurons of the respiratory center. These changes result in an increase in ventilation. This increased activity will then cause a decreased pCO_2 and ventilation will correspondingly decrease. This feedback control system maintains the arterial pCO_2 within narrow limits unless there is a disturbance of the respiratory center or the cardiovascular-pulmonary structure itself.

The circulatory system is capable of adjusting to varying demands of body tissues. Blood supply to active tissues is increased and heat loss can be increased or decreased. Flow of blood to vital organs such as the brain and the heart will be maintained at the expense of other less vital body tissues. These circulatory adjustments are brought about by neural and chemical mechanisms that change the caliber of the arterioles and other resistance vessels, increase or decrease blood storage in venous reservoirs, and vary the rate and stroke output of the heart.

NURSING ASSESSMENT OF BEHAVIORS RELATED TO OXYGEN NEED

Disruptions anywhere in the cardiovascular and pulmonary systems that cause an interference with oxygen supply to the tissues cause *hypoxia*. The term "anoxia" is also often used; however, hypoxia is more accurate in that it implies various degrees of oxygen deficiency whereas anoxia means an absence of *any* oxygen.

Nursing assessments are directed toward the early recognition of the signs and symptoms of hypoxia. It may be either acute or chronic. The signs and symptoms of acute hypoxia are similar to those of acute alcoholic intoxication. Indeed, acute alcoholic intoxication is an example of one type of hypoxia. The behaviors indicative of chronic hypoxia resemble those of fatigue.

Early objective changes in the vital signs resulting from cardiovascular response to hypoxia include an increased pulse rate indicative of tachycardia. Respirations may increase in depth (hyperpnea) and rate (tachypnea). Systolic blood

---

[1]These are structures of the brain stem, which may be located in a basic text on anatomy.

pressure rises slightly as cardiac output increases. The general norms for pulse, respirations, and blood pressure are given in Table 7.1.[2]

TABLE 7.1
General Norms for Pulse, Respirations, and Blood Pressure of Healthy Adult

Pulse	60-80 beats per minute
Respirations	16-20 per minute
Blood pressure	120/80 ml of mercury

When the hypoxic state becomes more advanced and the body's compensatory efforts fail, the pulse rate and blood pressure will fall.

Temperature changes are seen whenever the system disruptions change body metabolic requirements. For example, a moderately elevated central temperature is very common in clients in the early stages of an acute myocardial infarction (heart attack). If a client's temperature is elevated at the same time the skin temperature is normal or subnormal, it would indicate a cutaneous vasoconstriction resulting from a decreased cardiac output.

Dyspnea, cough, and hemoptysis are three common behaviors indicative of disruptions in the pulmonary and/or cardiovascular systems. *Dyspnea* is a subjective sensation and is defined as difficult or painful breathing. The degree to which this sensation is felt varies greatly with the individual. Dyspnea that develops when the person lies down is called *orthopnea.* When it occurs at night it is called *paroxysmal nocturnal dyspnea. Cough* occurs when there is a need to clear the airway. It is always considered abnormal since it has no role in the normal respiratory cycle. It may result from disturbances in the pulmonary system itself or in the cardiovascular system. *Hemoptysis,* or coughing up of blood, occurs when there is bleeding into the respiratory tract. It too may result from direct disturbances in the pulmonary system or as a result of cardiovascular disturbance.[3]

Skin color may or may not indicate the presence of hypoxia. It is inaccurate to assume that the patient who is not cyanotic (bluish-tinged) is not hypoxic. Very severe degrees of hypoxia can exist in the absence of cyanosis. For the bluish or purplish color of cyanosis to be seen in the skin and mucous membranes, the capillary blood must contain approximately 5 grams (g) per 100 ml or more of unoxygenated hemoglobin, and the surface capillaries must be dilated

---

[2]Methods for measuring these parameters and further discussion of variations in measurement can be found in texts on nursing skills.

[3]A comprehensive discussion of dyspnea, cough, and hemoptysis is found in the reference on signs and symptoms: Mitchell, R.I. and J.A. Pierce, "Cough," *Signs and Symptoms: Applied Pathologic Physiology and Clinical Interpretation,* 5th ed., eds. Cyril MacBryde and Robert Blacklow (Philadelphia: J.B. Lippincott Company, 1970). pp. 324-36, 341-57.

and must have blood circulating through them. Clients with carbon monoxide poisoning have a very characteristic cherry pink color to their skin resulting from the combination of carbon monoxide and hemoglobin (carboxyhemoglobin), which is a cherry-red colored compound. These clients are very hypoxic because the hemoglobin which is combined with carbon monoxide is not free to combine with oxygen, thereby depriving body tissues of an adequate oxygen supply.

Hypoxia is also accompanied by changes in the gastrointestinal and renal systems. These changes may occur as a direct result of the hypoxia on the involved tissues or indirectly through the effects of hypoxia on the nervous system. For example, anorexia, nausea, and vomiting frequently occur when oxygen tension falls.

Hypoxia of renal tissue results in oliguria and, unless corrected, eventually anuria. The kidney is very sensitive to hypoxia; for this reason frequent measurement of urine output is a very important part of the assessment of the client with acute hypoxia.

The first signs and symptoms of hypoxia result from the effects of oxygen deficit on the central nervous system. Since the most oxygen-sensitive tissue in the body is the retina, the earliest symptoms involve vision. However, this is usually unnoticed as the first change is a decrease in dark adaptation (night vision). As hypoxia increases a wide variety of central nervous system signs and symptoms may appear: headache, depression, apathy, dizziness, slowness of thought, euphoria, irritability, defective judgement and memory loss, diminished visual acuity, emotional disturbances, poor muscular coordination, fatigue, stupor, and finally unconsciousness. As can be seen from this partial list of behaviors, it is the cerebral cortex that suffers disturbances very early in the development of hypoxia. Three to five minutes is generally considered the approximate time period that the cerebral cortex can tolerate oxygen deprivation without irreversible damage.

Although fluid retention may not often be thought of in connection with hypoxia, it is a common occurrence in pulmonary and cardiovascular disturbances that result in circulatory congestion.

The emotional and psychological responses of the patient who is unable to get his breath are very evident. Any emotional stress has a marked effect on respiration, and these patients are very apprehensive and anxious. Frequently this will result in hyperventilation, thus compounding the problem. The client who is having difficult breathing will try to sit bolt upright if possible, and if an oxygen mask is being used may frequently try to push it away because of the sensation that it is stifling him. Respirations become increasingly gasping and rapid. Breath to be used in speaking is very limited. As the client's fear increases so does his energy requirement, which places an even greater load on the already overburdened respiratory system, and thus increases the hypoxia.

In addition to direct observation of the client the nurse has a wide range of laboratory test data to utilize in assessing the client's oxygen and circulatory status.[4] Certainly most clients admitted to a hospital have at least routine chest x-rays and hemoglobin or hemocrit determinations. These provide basic data which must be included in any nursing assessment of a client's pulmonary and cardiovascular status. The pH and arterial pCO_2 and pO_2 are very specific indicators of respiratory status, and the nurse must consider them. Very often the nurse is the first person to see these test results and is responsible for recognizing and interpreting deviations from normal and applying the interpretations to the condition of the client.

FACTORS INFLUENCING OXYGEN AND CIRCULATION

The cardiovascular and respiratory systems are responsive to changes in the environment. When the body is exposed to a hot environment, vasodilatation occurs, which results in a great increase in blood flow to the skin. This increases the amount of heat lost from the body surface. Because this vasodilating effect results in a large decrease in vascular resistance, there is also a compensating increase in cardiac output to maintain blood pressure. The respiratory system responds with hyperventilation. When exposed to cold there is a general vasoconstriction, with the blood pressure rising and the cardiac output decreasing. Sudden exposure to cold results in a quick inspiration followed by hyperventilation. In a state of hypothermia ventilation will decrease and the heart will slow. However, if the central body temperature falls below 30°C, ventricular fibrillation may occur.

Changes in altitude also result in cardiovascular and respiratory changes. The higher one goes, the lower the pO_2 of the air being breathed and therefore the pO_2 of the arterial blood. This results in an increase in respiratory rate and depth and in cardiac rate. Usually these changes are minimal until one reaches approximately the 10,000-foot level, unless added stress is encountered. Many people who normally live at sea level have had the experience of going to the mountains and rapidly discovering that their exercise tolerance is markedly decreased. Respiratory rate and depth quickly increase with exercise. Systolic blood pressure greatly increases and diastolic pressure usually rises a little. There is redistribution of blood flow with the exercising muscles receiving a large increase. This response to exercise is primarily under the control of neural mechanisms and occurs very rapidly.

[4]These are discussed in detail in Jacqueline F. Wade, *Respiratory Nursing Care: Physiology and Technique.* (St. Louis: C. V. Mosby Co., 1973), pp. 23-69.

Emotional and psychological changes will bring about a response in the cardiovascular and respiratory systems. These responses appear to be mediated through either the sympathetic nervous system or the parasympathetic nervous system. During feelings of anxiety and fear, sympathetic activity increases, which results in increased respiratory and cardiac rates and increased force of cardiac contractions. All of these actions result in increased cardiac output. Conversely, it appears that when sudden fright, extreme dejection, or hopelessness occur, the parasympathetic nervous system is stimulated. This brings about vagal stimulation and results in bradycardia (slow heartbeat), decreased blood flow to skin and viscera, and increased arterial pressure.

The individual with a healthy cardiovascular and respiratory system is able to compensate for, and physically tolerate very well, a wide variety of the environmental, physical, emotional, and psychological stresses he encounters, unless they are very severe or prolonged. However, the individual with a disease state causing function impairment of either or both systems has a tolerance that is reduced in direct proportion to the severity and extent of the disease state.

Failure of the respiratory system basically means that it is unable to maintain adequate oxygenation of the blood (hypoxemia). Many diseases and injuries can cause respiratory failure. Obstruction of the airway, emphysema, pulmonary tumors, and trauma to the chest are but a few examples.

Failure of the cardiovascular system may occur even if the arterial blood is adequately oxygenated. Here the cardiovascular system is unable to provide a

TABLE 7.2
Assessment of Need for Oxygen

Behaviors	Influencing factors
Hypoxia	Environmental heat
increased pulse rate	Altitude
increased respiratory rate	Emotional and psychological
and depth	changes
rise in systolic blood	Disease states
pressure	Respiratory failure
temperature elevation	Cardiovascular failure
Dyspnea	
Cough	
Hemoptysis	
Cyanosis or cherry pink color	
Anorexia, nausea, and vomiting	
Oliguria	
Central nervous system signs —	
headache, depression, dizziness	
Emotional responses including	
hyperventilation	
Laboratory test data	

sufficient amount of oxygenated blood to meet the needs of the various body tissues (hypoxia). This failure may result from a dysfunction of the heart pump itself or it may occur from damage in the vascular system resulting in an impairment of circulation. Examples include heart damage such as myocardial infarction or obstructions such as thrombosis. Hypoxia can also occur from other causes, which will be discussed in more detail later. Table 7.2 summarizes the assessment of the need for oxygen.

CARDIOVASCULAR AND PULMONARY ADAPTATION TO STRESS

A short term adaptation to stress is illustrated by the effects of a sudden acute blood loss of one to two liters. Peripheral vasoconstriction occurs; heart rate increases; sweating occurs with the skin becoming cold, pale, and moist; renal blood flow decreases with a resultant decrease in urine output; blood becomes diluted by interstitial fluid in an effort to restore volume; and an antidiuretic hormone is secreted. Respirations also increase in rate and depth. All of these compensatory changes are for the purpose of maintaining adequate tissue oxygenation by restoring blood volume and maintaining adequate arterial and venous pressure. Continued blood loss or other additional stresses will eventually exceed compensatory efforts.

A more long-term adaptation to stress by the cardiovascular and pulmonary systems is illustrated in those persons who live consistently at high altitudes. The highest known permanent habitation is located at an altitude of 17,500 feet. Any acclimatization to high altitude depends on the length of time exposed. Over a period of time pulmonary ventilation becomes increased, especially with exercise, and the arterial pCO_2 is reduced. The red blood cell count increases as does the hemoglobin concentration of the blood. The arterial blood thus is able to carry larger amounts of blood and meet the oxygen needs of body cells even though the pCO_2 is reduced.

CARDIOVASCULAR AND PULMONARY MALADAPTION TO STRESS

Although the cardiovascular and pulmonary systems are able to tolerate a wide range of stresses, eventually a point is reached where they can no longer compensate and fulfill their function. This can occur either with deprivation or with overload.

An example of deprivation is again hypoxia. Although moderate hypoxia can be compensated for over a prolonged period of time, this is not true of acute hypoxia. Man has essentially no oxygen reserve and when exposed to an acute interruption of oxygen quickly demonstrates the signs and symptoms of hypoxia.

These vary widely with individuals and their differing abilities to adjust physiologically. However, in general the higher levels of the brain will show the effects of oxygen deficit very early. Intellectual function is impaired quickly, and due to this factor the person is usually unaware of what is happening. The retina has the highest oxygen demand of any body organ, which is why one of the earliest functions lost is the ability to adapt to night vision. This can occur as low as 5,000 feet. Personality changes may occur, which are likened to those seen in alcoholic intoxication. Muscular coordination becomes progressively decreased. Indications of compensatory efforts are seen in increased rate and depth respirations, increased pulse rate and cardiac output, and increased blood pressure. Depending on the severity and duration of the oxygen lack, the compensatory efforts will eventually fail, and the person will proceed to unconsciousness and death.

There are various classifications of hypoxia; however, the following may be used as a very basic one:

1. Hypoxic hypoxia—caused by a decrease in oxygen pressure in the inspired air or in the lungs, or by conditions which prevent or interfere with the diffusion of oxygen across the alveolar membrane. Examples of causes are exposure to high altitudes, obstruction of the airway, asthma, pneumonia, congenital cardiovascular disease.
2. Hypemic (anemic) hypoxia—caused by a reduction in the ability of the blood to carry sufficient amounts of oxygen due to a decrease in hemoglobin. Examples of causes are anemia and carbon monoxide poisoning.
3. Histotoxic hypoxia—occurs when the ability of the cells to utilize oxygen is interfered with. Causative examples are alcohol, narcotics, and poisons such as cyanide.
4. Stagnant hypoxia—due to a malfunction of the circulatory system wherein there is inadequate circulation of the blood to the tissue cells even though the oxygen-carrying capacity of the blood may be normal. Examples of causes would be heart failure, arterial spasm, and shock.

Another example of oxygen deprivation is the phenomenon of *shock*. The shock syndrome can occur from a wide variety of causes. Detailed definitions of types of this condition can be found in medical texts. A common feature of all types of shock is that of inadequate tissue perfusion, that is, lack of oxygen permeation. The circulation becomes progressively inadequate and the behaviors exhibited by the client reflect this inadequacy. The person in shock appears very pale and the skin is cool and moist. Early in the chain of events he may be quite restless and agitated, but this progresses to apathy and confusion. Thirst is a common symptom but usually little water can be tolerated because of nausea. Urinary output is progressively decreased. Breathing is rapid and shallow, and as shock becomes more severe the pulmonary function progressively deteriorates. Pulse rate is rapid but thready. Arterial blood pressure, particularly systolic pressure, rises early in shock for a brief period and then falls. The pulse pressure also tends to be narrow. These behaviors are all indicative of very severe stress and unless the cause of the shock can be corrected, and supportive measures instituted, the prognosis is very poor.

An overload of either carbon dioxide or oxygen also constitutes stresses on the cardiovascular and respiratory systems. The effects of a buildup of carbon dioxide (hypercarbia) occur more slowly than do the effects of hypoxia. Effects are seen on the central nervous system, and the client may appear anywhere on a continuum from somnolence to coma. The usual early signs are drowsiness, inability to concentrate, confusion, and irritability. Clients will often complain of a headache and being unable to sleep. This carbon dioxide narcosis usually occurs either from excessive oxygen therapy or from sedation.

It is not really known why oxygen when present in excess will cause convulsions and other nervous aberrations. The first signs, which will occur within twenty-four hours, are substernal distress due to tracheal irritation plus irritation of other mucous membranes. Respiratory depression will occur, as will hypotension. As the oxygen overload continues, neurological signs will become more evident, and eventually bronchopneumonia and death may occur.

NURSING INTERVENTIONS TO MAINTAIN OXYGEN AND CIRCULATION

The most important measure in treating hypoxia is oxygen administration. However; it is important to monitor the client closely to prevent the administration of too much oxygen. Essential components of oxygen therapy include: careful observation of respiratory status, vital signs, and reaction to therapy; use of aseptic technique[5] to assist in preventing infections; thorough explanation to the client of the procedures being used; and understanding and correct usage of the equipment being utilized.

The fact that the client is receiving oxygen therapy should not cause his other needs to be ignored. Positioning for comfort and correct body alignment is one area of continued importance. In addition, the client with respiratory difficulty will usually assume the position whereby he can get maximum ventilation. This is usually an upright position, sometimes leaning slightly forward. Postural drainage[6] is often of assistance in facilitating drainage of pulmonary secretions and thus improving ventilation.

[5] Aseptic technique, explained in texts on nursing skills, is designed to hinder the transfer of disease-producing microorganisms from one person or place to another.

[6] A complete discussion of postural drainage can be found in Marcia Rie, "Physical Therapy in the Nursing Care of Respiratory Disease Patients," *The Nursing Clinics of North America*, September 1968, pp. 465-69.

The importance of maintaining an open airway cannot be overemphasized. If an open airway is not maintained, then no other therapeutic measures can be effective. Care in giving oral fluids and food, positioning to prevent accumulation of material in the airway, and suctioning of the airway when needed are means of achieving the goal of maintaining an open airway. Figure 7.1 demonstrates how hyperextension of the head facilitates opening of an airway.

The deleterious effects of both physical and emotional stress on clients with cardiovascular and pulmonary dysfunctions have been discussed earlier. Careful explanation by the nurse of any care being given, a calm, confident, and supportive manner on the part of the nurse, and as calm a physical environment as possible go a long way toward alleviating much of the stress encountered by the client.

The nursing process guide is an effective tool for planning optimal care for the client. Table 7.3 is an example related to some expected behaviors of a client with cardiovascular and pulmonary disruption. The example concerns a client

TABLE 7.3
Nursing Process Guide Related to Oxygen Need for Male Client Admitted to Hospital With Myocardial Infarction.

| Behavior | Influencing Factors | | |
	Focal	Contextual	Residual
1. "Anxious" expression on face. 2. Skin pale, cool, and moist. 3. B.P. 90/40 4. P. 130 & thready 5. Respirations 30 6. States pain in left chest area diminished after morphine administration. 7. Insists on being elevated on two pillows "in order to get enough air." States, "I can't get my breath."	Damage to cardiac muscle resulting in decreased circulatory effectiveness.	1. Unfamiliar surroundings and people. 2. Large amount of activity being carried out in immediate environment. 3. Attached to cardiac monitor and I.V.	1. Obese. 2. Smoked two packs of cigarettes a day over a 20-year period. 3. Sedentary—has not regularly participated in physical exercise. 4. No previous history of heart disease or hospitalization.

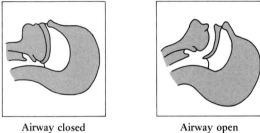

Airway closed   Airway open
                               (head hyperextended)

Figure 7.1   Position to maintain an open airway.

admitted to the hospital following a myocardial infarction, or heart attack. The behaviors exhibited are indicative of early shock. Emphasis is given in this

Problem Identification	Goal	Interventions	Evaluation
Hypoxia due to shock resulting from myocardial damage and decreased circulatory effectiveness.	Having decrease in symptoms of hypoxia. Having a decrease in demands being made on the heart by decreasing anxiety.	1. Provide additional oxygen by mask. 2. Monitor response to oxygen and adjust flow rate accordingly. 3. Observe closely to be sure airway is kept open. 1. Explain to client procedures being performed. 2. Reassure him he will not be left alone. 3. Act calm and confident and move purposefully. 4. Keep room environment cool and prevent buildup of "clutter" as much as possible. 5. Keep client draped both for comfort and modesty as much as possible.	1. Facial expression became less tense. 2. Skin pink and warm. 3. B.P. 130/70. 4. P. 84. 5. R. 20. 6. "Dull ache" over left chest.

nursing process guide to nursing interventions which can be effective in helping to modify the stimuli causing the behaviors. These nursing interventions are in addition to carrying out the medical orders for medication and treatment, which are not listed here.

The behaviors exhibited by this male client reflect his adaptation to the various stimuli affecting him at any given time. To have any effect on the behaviors the nursing interventions must concentrate on the stimuli determined to be causing them. In the example it is possible to initiate nursing interventions focused on the focal stimulus and on the contextual stimuli. Those factors listed as residual may have contributed to the onset of the myocardial infarction and to the anxious response of the client; however, nursing interventions directed at them would not be appropriate at this time in light of the behaviors being exhibited, which demand immediate attention. The nursing diagnosis identifies hypoxia, regardless of the cause, as being the primary problem, and therefore the goals are related to reducing the hypoxia. This is accomplished by interventions aimed at (1) directly reversing the hypoxia, and (2) reducing the oxygen needs of the tissues by reducing stress. Evaluation of the nursing interventions is accomplished by identifying the client's behaviors observed after the interventions have been carried out. If there was no change in behaviors, or if the change was undesirable, the process would have to be repeated and revised as required.

SUMMARY

In this chapter we have seen that man's essential need for oxygen is met by the functioning cardiovascular and pulmonary systems. Behaviors to observe in assessing this need and the factors influencing it have been identified. Some major adaptation problems related to oxygen need, such as hypoxia and shock, have been outlined. Finally, nursing intervention to meet this need has been discussed.

REFERENCES

Beall, Cheryl E. and others, *Physiologic Bases for Respiratory Care.* Missoula, Mont.: Mountain Press Publishing Co., 1974.

Cecil-Loeb, *Textbook of Medicine.* 13th ed., P.B. Beeson and W. McDermott, eds. Philadelphia: W.B. Saunders Company, 1971.

Ganong, William F., *Review of Medical Physiology.* 3rd ed. Los Altos, Calif.: Lange Medical Publications, 1967.

Guyton, Arthur C., *Textbook of Medical Physiology.* 4th ed. Philadelphia: W.B. Saunders Company, 1971.

Helming, Mary G., ed., "Nursing in Respiratory Disease," *The Nursing Clinics of North America,* vol. 3, no. 3. Philadelphia: W.B. Saunders Company, 1968.

Holaday, Duncan A., "Oxygen Therapy," *Anesthesia Rounds,* vol. IV, no. I. Ayerst Laboratories, 1972.

Judge, R.D. and G.D. Zuidema, eds., *Physical Diagnosis: A Physiologic Approach to the Clinical Examination.* 2nd ed. Boston: Little, Brown and Company, 1968.

MacBryde, Cyril and Robert Blacklow, *Signs and Symptoms: Applied Pathologic Physiology and Clinical Interpretation.* 5th ed. Philadelphia: J.B. Lippincott Company, 1970.

Pinneo, Rose, ed., "Concepts in Cardiac Nursing," *The Nursing Clinics of North America,* vol. 7, no. 3. Philadelphia: W.B. Saunders Company, 1972.

Wade, Jacqueline F., *Respiratory Nursing Care: Physiology and Technique.* St. Louis: C.V. Mosby Co., 1973.

8

Regulation of Temperature

Mary Poush

KEY CONCEPTS DEFINED

Homeothermal: Warm-blooded and able to maintain body temperature independent of the environment.

Temperature: Measurement of heat being produced by the chemical reactions occurring in the tissues.

Radiation: Transfer of heat by means of electromagnetic waves.

Conduction: Transfer of heat from one molecule to another by direct contact.

Convection: Carrying away of heat by currents of air or fluid.

Vaporization: The evaporation of water from the body surface and respiratory tract, thus utilizing energy in the form of heat.

Thermostatic Center: Physiological mechanism regulating temperature and located in the hypothalamus.

Fever: An abnormally elevated temperature; also called pyrexia.

After studying this chapter the reader will be able to:

1. Define the key concepts of this chapter.
2. Describe the process of normal temperature regulation.
3. Identify behaviors indicating elevated and subnormal body temperature and list factors influencing these behaviors (see Appendix I).
4. Specify nursing interventions to be used in problems of fever and hypothermia (see Appendix II).

Temperature is one of the vital signs used by the nurse to indicate the state of the human body. It is considered a regulatory physiological need. This chapter will briefly review normal temperature regulation; describe factors for assessment of temperature; explore stimuli that influence normal temperature; and discuss how the nurse may manipulate those identified stimuli.

NORMAL TEMPERATURE REGULATION

Man is a homeothermal animal, that is, he is warm-blooded and maintains body temperature independent of his environment. The body temperature varies (see Figure 8.1) between 97 to 99.5°F (36 to 37.5°C), and is relatively unrelated to the environmental temperature. There is a normal diurnal, or daily, variation in temperature. If one is awake during the day, temperature is at its highest level in the late afternoon or early evening, and at its lowest in the early morning. A woman's temperature usually shows a slight rise from ovulation until menstruation and during pregnancy. The infant's temperature regulation process is immature, so marked fluctuations will be noted.

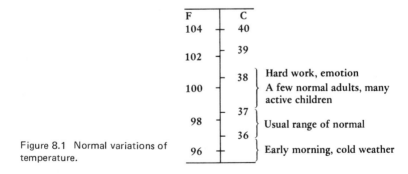

Figure 8.1 Normal variations of temperature.

The heat being measured by temperature is produced by the chemical reactions occurring in the tissues. It reflects a balance between heat being produced and heat lost to the environment. Figure 8.2 illustrates the factors in heat production balanced with the factors in heat loss. Heat production is increased by ingestion of foods containing carbohydrates, fats, and proteins. Heat is produced by the calories in the foods and by their ability to stimulate metabolism. Disease, elevated basal metabolic rate, muscle tension and exercise, including shivering, also increase heat production.

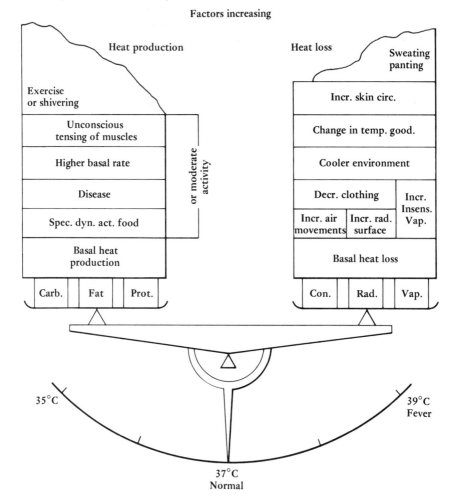

Figure 8.2 The process of normal temperature regulation. (Adapted courtesy of E.F. Dubois, "Heat Loss from the Human Body," Bull. of N.Y. Acad. of Med., xv (March 1939). p. 145.)

Basal heat is lost by radiation, conduction, convection, and vaporization. *Radiation* is the transfer of heat by electromagnetic waves. A medium of transfer is not required since the waves move directly. About 60 percent of body heat is lost by means of radiation. *Conduction* is the transfer of heat from one molecule to another by direct contact. The ordinary object of the greatest amount of transfer of body heat is the air immediately surrounding the person. *Convection* is the carrying away of heat by currents of air or fluid. As air is heated by conduction, it expands, thus becoming less dense. The warm air rises and is replaced by cooler air. In a room of even temperature, without gross currents of air, about 12 percent of body heat is lost by means of conduction with resultant convection. *Vaporization* is the evaporation of water from the body surface and respiratory tract. The conversion of a liquid to a vapor utilized energy in the form of heat to overcome cohesiveness of the molecules. Approximately 20 percent of body heat is lost through the evaporation of sweat.

The processes of heat loss can be increased by such measures as increasing air movements, increasing the surface exposed to the air, increasing insensible vaporization, decreasing clothing, providing cooler environment, or changing the temperature gradient, and increasing skin circulation.

The physiological thermostat for regulating temperature is located in the hypothalamus and is called the *thermostatic center.* The anterior hypothalamus controls heat loss by causing vasodilatation of the skin and sweating when the temperature is rising. The posterior hypothalamus controls heat loss by conserving heat and regulates heat production. Further reading of the physiology of temperature regulation in any noted physiology text is recommended.[1]

ASSESSMENT OF TEMPERATURE

The clinical thermometer is the usual method of determining body temperature. There are two types of thermometers, Fahrenheit and Centigrade. Fahrenheit thermometers have a scale calibrated at $0.2°$ increments extending from $95°$ to $110°$. The average temperature for humans is $98.6°F$. Centigrade thermometers extend from $36°$ to $42°C$, with $0.2°$ increments. The average human temperature on this scale is $37°C$. The thermometer may be placed under the tongue, in the axilla, (under the arm), or in the rectum. The axillary reading is one-half degree lower than the mouth reading, the rectal reading one degree higher. The thermometer should be left in place until a constant temperature reading is obtained. (This varies from seconds to several minutes depending on the thermometer in use.)

A normal (average) temperature will usually correlate with warm, dry skin, regular respirations with an average rate, and an average pulse.

There are several factors to keep in mind to obtain an accurate reading on a thermometer: (1) an oral temperature should not be measured within 30 minutes following the drinking of hot liquids, chewing gum, or smoking; (2) rectal temperature is indicated when an accurate, safe oral temperature is unobtainable

---

[1]Highly recommended is Arthur C. Guyton, *Textbook of Medical Physiology* (Philadelphia: W. B. Saunders Company, 1971), Chapter 71.

(for example, age, mouth breathing due to nasal or oral tubes, nasal or oral surgery, nasal congestion, oxygen administration, poorly fitted dentures); (3) oral temperature is indicated when rectal measurements are inaccurate or unsafe (for example, diarrhea, fecal impaction, rectal or perineal surgery).

Marked deviations below 36°C and above 37.5°C usually require intervention. The nurse should notify the physician, institute nursing measures to regain an adaptive state, and record observations as indicated, every 15 minutes to 2 hours depending on the degree of deviation.

An abnormally elevated temperature—*fever*, 38°C and above—will have several complex related behaviors associated with it. They are: rapid respirations, profuse sweating, hot, dry skin and mucous membranes; hyperemia of the skin, a rapid, full pulse to a weak and rapid pulse; general uncomfortably warm feeling, possibly a hypersensitive skin; chills; headache; general malaise; restlessness; delirium; loss of consciousness; and convulsions (more prevalent in infants and small children). These signs and symptoms are primarily attempts by the body to move back into an adaptive state by getting rid of heat.

A maladaptive subnormal body temperature (below 36°C) will be accompanied by some or all of the following behaviors: pulse either rapid and full or rapid and weak; respirations slower than usual; piloerection (goose bumps) and a pale skin, sometimes cyanotic. The client will have a general uncomfortably cold feeling, numbness in the extremities, and maybe shivering and shaking with teeth chattering. There may be loss of sensation and loss of consciousness. In her first level assessment of temperature, the nurse describes all client behaviors relative to body temperature.

STIMULI THAT INFLUENCE TEMPERATURE REGULATION

Focal stimuli in temperature imbalance are usually disease conditions that affect the production of heat in the body; the loss of heat from the body; and/or the mechanisms that regulate body temperature. Following are examples of each of these categories.

1. Heat production increased:
   a. Increased metabolic rate.
   b. Thyrotoxicosis.
   c. Any tissue injury (trauma) that causes the body to respond with the inflammatory process.
   d. Chills.
2. Heat loss decreased:
   a. Obesity.
   b. Dehydration, causing decreased sweat production.
   c. Skin diseases, preventing sweat production.
   d. Impaired general circulation.

3. Altered regulatory mechanisms:
   a. Head injuries, brain surgery.
   b. Cerebrovascular accidents.
   c. Brain tumors embarrassing the hypothalamus.
   d. Depression of the central nervous system by drugs (general anesthesia, alcohol, sedatives, narcotics).
   e. Emotions.
   f. Heat stroke.
4. Other influencing factors:
   a. Age, both the very young and the aged are more liable.
   b. A high environmental temperature with high humidity prevents cooling by evaporation.
   c. Foreign substances (bacteria, viral, protein) in the bloodstream.
   d. Usual body temperature.
   e. Time of day, as discussed earlier.
   f. Amount of physical exercise (increases metabolic rate and heat production—especially in children).
   g. Phase of the menstrual cycle (and/or pregnancy), higher during latter half of cycle.
   h. Method of measurement—oral, rectal, or axillary.
   i. Amount of clothing worn.
   j. Fatigue

INTERVENING BY MANIPULATING STIMULI

For problems of body temperature, either fever or hypothermia, interventions are based on the mechanisms that decrease body heat (for example, conduction, radiation, convection, and vaporization of sweat) and the mechanisms that produce body heat (for example, metabolism, environment, shivering, and hot food).

Correction or treatment of the disease process (usually focal) is in the physician's domain. The nurse will observe behaviors, report to the physician, and facilitate carrying out his prescribed treatment modalities (for example, giving those drugs that suppress thyroid secretion, thiouracil and related drugs, radioactive iodine, and/or surgical interventions).

Body heat loss may be facilitated (on a short-term basis) by:

1. Lowering the environmental temperature (air conditioning).
2. Decreasing the environmental humidity (dehumidify).
3. Increasing the vaporization of sweat (increased air current, not a draft).
4. Limiting physical activity or any skin friction.
5. Applying liquids that evaporate quickly to the skin (alcohol sponges).

6. Applying cold objects or substances to the skin (ice packs, cool baths, changing clothing or bedding, hypothermia blankets).
7. Administering antipyretic drugs.
8. Administering sedation for restlessness.
9. Administering pain relief measures to decrease physical activity.
10. Removing clothing and linen to a light cotton gown.
11. Exposing a greater amount of skin to the air.
12. Increasing fluid intake to maintain an adaptive fluid balance.
13. Explaining interventions and their results to the patient.

Care must be taken to decrease body temperature gradually or the piloform erection mechanisms come into action, shivering occurs, and metabolism increases with resultant temperature increase.

Body temperature may be increased by the following interventions:

1. Adjusting the environmental temperature (increasing room temperature).
2. Decreasing the vaporization of sweat (eliminating air currents).
3. Increasing physical activity (active or passive) and skin friction.
4. Applying insulating materials around the body (blankets, sweaters).
5. Applying warmed objects to the skin (warmed blankets, thermal pads).
6. Encouraging and providing warm (hot) foods and fluids.

A sample clinical assessment is shown in Table 8.1.

TABLE 8.1
Assessment of Patient With Fever

Regulatory Behaviors	Influencing Factors		
	Focal	Contextual	Residual
T. $102°$ F oral	E. Coli	Room temp. $85°$	4:00 p.m.
P. 110, full	Septicemia	Humidity 70%	52 years
and bounding,		Fluid intake	old
even		previous 8 hrs.	Pathology
R. 26, shallow		100 cc	revealed
Skin: red, dry, hot		Tylenol gr. 10 q 4:	cancer in
to touch, dry,		hr, prn (as circum-	situ cervix
mucous membranes		stances require)	
		40 lbs. overweight	
		Pain from hyster-	
		ectomy 2 days	
		ago	
		Ambulate prn	
		Flannel gown and	
		blanket on	
		Tetracycline	
		500 mg q 6 hr	

The nursing diagnosis would be stated:

Mrs. Baker has a temperature of 102° due to a bacterial septicema. She is in pain, not drinking fluids adequately, the room is warm, and she is dressed warmly. Interventions will be aimed at increasing her heat loss and minimizing heat production.

Goals are stated as:

Mrs. Baker will regain an adaptive temperature range (97° to 99.5°F) by:

1. Having a balanced fluid intake/output.
2. Dressing appropriately to the environment.
3. Decreasing activity caused by pain and movement.
4. Taking antibiotics to reduce infection.

Interventions are:

1. Explain reason for temperature and intervention modalities.
2. Provide Mrs. Baker with cool fluids of choice and praise her for drinking them.
3. Reduce room temperature 72 to 78°F and humidity 30 to 40 percent by air conditioning.
4. Remove flannel gown and blanket and replace with a loose cotton gown and sheet; remove any rubber or plastic sheets from bed, replacing if necessary with soft cotton bath blanket.
5. Administer Tylenol 10 gr. q 4 hr. until temperature is within adaptive range.
6. Administer pain medication as needed to free from pain (see pain assessment).
7. Administer antibiotics on schedule to maintain high blood level concentration.
8. Give tepid sponge bath if desired.
9. Take and record temperature and related observations as indicated every two hours.

Evaluation would be based on whether the primary goal of reaching and maintaining an adaptive temperature range of 97 to 99.5°F was obtained.

SUMMARY

This chapter has reviewed theory related to temperature regulation and illustrated the adaptation nursing process related to temperature control. Readers are encouraged to read pediatric texts, medical-surgical nursing texts, and nursing procedure books for detailed information regarding procedures in the interventions, and the art of taking temperatures.

REFERENCES

Beland, Irene, *Clinical Nursing.* New York: The Macmillan Company, 1967.

Du Gas, Beverly, *Kozier-DuGas Introduction to Patient Care.* 2nd ed. Philadelphia: W. B. Saunders Company, 1972.

Gragg, Shirley Hawke and Olive M. Rees, *Scientific Principles In Nursing.* St. Louis: The C. V. Mosby Co., 1974.

Guyton, Arthur C., *Textbook of Medical Physiology.* Philadelphia: W. B. Saunders Company, 1971, Chapter 71.

Nordmark, Madelyn, and Anne Rohweder, *Scientific Foundations of Nursing.* 2nd ed. Philadelphia: J. B. Lippincott Company, 1967, pp. 130-31.

9

Regulation of the Senses

Jeanine R. Dunn

KEY CONCEPTS DEFINED

Snellen Chart: Chart for measuring acuity of the eye by identification of illuminated letters or objects of varying sizes.

Perimeter: Instrument used to test peripheral vision.

Tonometer: Instrument used to measure intraocular pressure.

Ophtalmoscope: Instrument for visualizing the interior of the eye by directing a small beam of light through the pupil.

Audiometer: Basic instrument for measurement of sensitivity and discrimination of hearing.

Rinne test: Test to compare bone conduction with air conduction.

Weber test: Test to compare hearing of the two ears.

Anesthesia: Loss of feeling or sensation, especially of tactile sensibility.

Hyperesthesia: Excessive sensitivity of the skin.

Paresthesia: Abnormal sensation.

Sensory Input: Stimuli received by the senses.

Sensory Deprivation: Reduction in sensory stimulation.

Sensory Overload: An increase in sensory stimulation to the point of too much.

Distortion: Stimuli without order or predictability.

Monotony: Stimuli that are never changing, being repeated and continuous.

Pain: From a medical viewpoint, a complex physiological response to noxious stimulation mediated through its own neurological equipment. From a nursing viewpoint, the individual's entire response to noxious stimuli including the meaning of the painful stimulation physically, mentally, and emotionally.

Analgesic: Pharmacological agent used to lessen the intensity of pain.

Antispasmodic: Pharmacological agent used to lessen the intensity of painful smooth muscle contractions.

Narcotics: Pharmacological agent whose action inhibits pain perception as well as other cerebral-cortical functions.

Palliation: A means of providing relief until the cause of pain can be determined or when the cause cannot be removed.

After studying this chapter the reader will be able to:

1. Define the key concepts of this chapter.
2. Identify behaviors indicating altered sensation of the eye, ear, and skin, and list factors influencing these behaviors (see Appendix I).
3. Discuss the two goals set up for a client with altered sensation.
4. Describe behavioral responses to sensory deprivation and list factors that influence these responses.
5. Explain the process of assessing the client in pain.
6. Specify nursing interventions to be used in problems of altered sensation, sensory deprivation, and pain (see Appendix II).

The senses provide man with information necessary to interact with his environment as related to himself, as well as, internal information concerning himself in relation to the environment. These sensory stimuli initiate the person's regulatory processes, thereby promoting adaptation.

The nurse must utilize all of her own senses to observe client behaviors, identify influencing stimuli, formulate a nursing diagnosis, and design an individual care plan with appropriate interventions in each of the adaptive modes. Her goal is to promote adaptation in health and illness. This chapter deals with relating this nursing process to man's need for adaptation concerning the regulatory mechanism of the major human senses—sight, hearing, and touch.

THE EYE

Vision enables man to move about freely, safely, and independently in his world and to perform his daily activities. An impairment in the structure and function of the eyes will result in alterations in a client's needs; for example, it can impose limitations on an individual's independence, change his perception of the environment, and have detrimental effects on his ability to communicate emotional feelings. The eye is closely associated with other sensory modalities, especially touch and kinesthesia, that is, the sensation of position and movement of body parts. A detailed analysis of all the objects comprising our environment (size, shape, color, form, texture) is achieved through the visual process.

Behavioral Assessment of the Sense of Sight

The first level assessment involves observing behaviors that can be confirmed by the use of instruments and by questioning the client. Both of these methods should be employed in assessing and validating behaviors in the physiological mode. Quantitative information regarding the status of the sense of sight can be gained by both external and internal tests.

The external, or functional, examination includes the ability of the eye to move in its orbit and the reaction of the pupil to light and accommodation. The function of the eye may be tested by use of the *Snellen Chart,* where the client is asked to identify illuminated letters or objects of varying sizes. Since the acuity of each eye is measured separately, the other is occluded with an opaque card. A *perimeter* is an instrument used to test the client's peripheral vision, which indicates how far to the side he can see without moving the eye. Hence, this test is conducted with the client's vision fixed with test objects moved in from the far periphery. To test *color vision,* the client is asked to identify colored figures or colored light patterns that can be discriminated only if the client can identify colors.

Internal examination of the structural part of the eye is done in several ways. A *tonometer* is used to measure the intraocular pressure, which normally is 11 to 22 mHg. The interior of the eye may be seen with an *ophtalmoscope,* which directs a small beam of light through the pupil. Refraction tests ascertain the ability of the lens and cornea to focus on the retina.

Adaptive and maladaptive behaviors revealed by these tests are summarized in Table 9.1.

Factors Influencing Adaptation of Sight

Many pathological factors, both external and internal, affect the visual process. The most frequent cause of eye trauma is a foreign body, particularly dust or dirt particles, which if in the conjunctiva may be easily removed without danger to sight. (See any basic text on first aid). Contact with toxic chemicals and penetrating wounds or lacerations of the eye may also be factors temporarily or permanently affecting vision. Infections such as conjunctivitis often affect

TABLE 9.1
Measurement of Visual Acuity: Behavioral Data

Test	Behavior	
	Adaptive	Maladaptive
Snellen Chart	One eye correctly identifies letters of size 20 at 20 feet when asked to read the chart.	Not able to identify letters of increasingly smaller size at same distance.
Perimeter	Responds to visual cues in the periphery.	Limited vision at the sides.
Color	Correctly identifies colors of objects presented.	Colors are subjectively translated into another portion of the spectrum, or there is lack of color discrimination.
Refraction	No abnormalities in eye or lens structure or function.	Defective vision, objects are not correctly focused on the retina.
INSTRUMENT		
Tonometer	Tension in 11 to 22 mHg range.	Marked increase in intraocular pressure.
Ophthalmoscope	Interior of eye is clear, blood vessels are of normal size.	Inflamation of blood vessels, tumor, cyst may be present.

vision, as does strabismus, or crossing of the eyes. Glaucoma is a group of diseases characterized by increased pressure within the eye. Its incidence is increasing in proportion to the increase in the older population. However, glaucoma is the most preventible cause of blindness if diagnosed and treated in the early stages. In the case of cataract, there is a loss of transparency of the lens. Retinal detachment is a condition in which the retina falls away from its normal position in the back of the eye. Most detachments are caused by tears or holes in the retina, which may result from trauma or from degeneration.

Some of these pathological conditions—namely, lacerations, strabismus, cataracts, retinal detachment, and occasionally glaucoma—are treated surgically. Postoperatively one or both eyes may be covered. The treatment itself thus becomes a factor influencing vision.

The age and onset at which a person experiences visual impairment, whether partial or total, will affect his adaptation. The person who is born blind is unable to form visual concepts. A person who loses his vision suddenly as the result of an injury or accident has had no time to adjust to the loss or to prepare for it. He may go through a period of grief, as described later.

The type of rehabilitation given to the person suffering impairment of vision becomes an important factor influencing adaptation. A program geared to the total needs of the individual has a greater chance for success than one which uses standardized approaches to limited aspects of the client's problem.

Thus the sense of sight can be assessed by observing given behaviors and factors influencing these behaviors.

THE EAR

Normal hearing, provided by the functioning of an intact auditory system and of the brain, enables man to perceive the multiple sounds of his environment. These sounds may include warnings of environmental hazards, orientation to new aspects of a person's world, as well as continuation of information on routine ones. Hearing facilitates verbal communication and influences interpersonal relationships. It provides a person with pleasurable sounds, such as music or voice. Characteristic changes in the ability to hear may be observed as the person progresses through developmental stages. The degree of impairment may be assessed on the basis of behaviors.

Behavioral Assessment of the Sense of Hearing

Testing to ascertain the degree and type of hearing loss (function) may be carried out by an audiologist, a physician, a nurse, or other appropriately trained personnel.

The selection of a screening test is usually dependent upon the age of the patient. Hearing tests for the infant (1 to 3 months) require the child to respond to some sound; from 3 to 12 months to respond to localized sound; from 18 to 24 months to respond to a voice test; and from 1 to 2 years to respond to specific requests. Audiometric screening tests may be performed for children 3 years of age and older.

The most common hearing test to determine the specific type of hearing defect is the audiogram. The basic instrument for the measurement of hearing is called an *audiometer*. Two types of stimuli (pure tones and actual words) are presented to measure the sensitivity (acuteness of hearing) and discrimination (how clearly the ear distinguishes different sounds) of the person's hearing. The *Rinne test* is used to compare bone conduction with air conduction, and the *Weber test* to compare hearing in the two ears. Behaviors noted with these tests are summarized in Table 9.2.

In addition to the behaviors noted on testing, the nurse should also be alert to the following behaviors which may be indicative of difficult hearing: faulty speech, inattentiveness, unresponsiveness, strained or intense facial expressions, and a tendency toward withdrawal.

TABLE 9.2
Measurement of Hearing Acuity: Behavioral Data

Test	Behavior	
	Adaptive	Maladaptive
Spoken Word	Can hear selected words correctly over 50 percent of the time. Can hear selected list of words at a level optimal for the patient.	"You are speaking too softly; I don't understand you." "The words are loud enough, but they run together and I can't understand them."
Audiometer	Can hear selected tones correctly over 50 percent of the time.	Gives erroneous responses, or no response to the tones presented.
Rinne	Tone produced by tuning fork is heard approximately twice as long by air as by bone conduction.	Tone heard for much shorter time overall; tone heard twice as long by bone conduction indicates conductive loss; tone heard longer by air conduction indicates perceptive loss.
Weber	Tone produced by tuning fork is heard with equal loudness by both ears.	Sound heard in poorer ear indicates conductive loss; sound heard louder in better ear indicates sensorineural loss.

Factors Influencing Adaptation of Hearing

Many factors influence hearing, the most important being the intactness of the structures and functioning of the hearing apparatus. Pathology that interferes with this intactness includes: foreign bodies, otitis media, mastoiditis, ocosclerosis, and neural damages due to toxic drugs, head injury, viral infections, and prolonged noise.

As in the case of sight, the age of onset and the suddenness of hearing impairment greatly affect the person's ability to adapt. Again the type of treatment and rehabilitation used are significant factors affecting adaptation.

THE SKIN

Most of our contacts with the environment are through the skin, which is the largest organ of the body. Among its many functions are the reception of pressure (touch) and temperature. The skin contains end organs of many of the sensory nerve fibers, by which means a person becomes both physiologically and sometimes actually aware of parts of the environment. The surface of the skin contains numerous sensory spots. Each sensory spot serves a specific sense; that is, the sensory nerves of the skin mediate different qualities of sensation—pressure, cold, heat, and pain. Sensitiveness of the varieties of cutaneous sensation differs in different parts of the body.

The temperature receptors consist of two groups: those for cold, which are located superficially in the skin; and heat receptors, located deeper within the skin. Both heat and cold receptors readily adjust to stimuli which are not severe. For example, if the hand is placed in warm water, the sensation of warmth quickly diminishes due to the receptor's adaptive ability. Pain receptors, on the contrary, do not have any adaptive ability. The lack of adaptability to pain is in fact a safeguard, since pain represents a danger signal indicating adverse internal or external conditions. The extremes of heat and cold input are also received as pain. Tolerance of skin temperature varies with individuals. Certain areas of the skin are more tolerant of temperature than are other areas. Parts of the body where the skin is thinner are usually more sensitive to temperature than exposed areas where the skin is thicker. The body is able to tolerate extremes in temperature when the length of exposure is short. The larger the area involved in heat or cold application, the less tolerant the skin is to temperature extremes.

Anesthesia is the loss of feeling or sensation, especially tactile sensibility; the term may also be used for loss of any of the other senses. *Hyperesthesia* is excessive sensitivity of the skin. *Paresthesia* is abnormal sensation. Each of these conditions is assessed by the self-report of the client when various stimuli are applied to the skin.

Cutaneous sensory dysfunctions result primarily from impaired sensory nerve function and/or central nervous system involvement caused by injury or disease. Mechanical injury, such as severing of the nerve, or disease of the peripheral sensory nerves result in total loss of sensation, local anesthesia, within the area of the distribution of that nerve. Restoration of sensation may result as nerve regeneration progresses, although this is a slow process. Injury from compression or penetration, or disease processes affecting the brain or spinal cord, will either greatly curtail or prohibit cutaneous sensation.

MAJOR ADAPTATION PROBLEMS OF THE SENSES

Man uses his senses to perceive his environment, and the stimuli therefrom, to regulate his responses, and promote his adaptation. Various disruptions of the structure and functioning of the senses have been noted as factors influencing sensation. Basically these are medical problems with associated medical interventions. However, these conditions result in major adaptive problems for the client which are within the realm of the nursing process of assessment and intervention. These problems may include: altered sensation, sensory deprivation, and sensory overload, including pain.

TABLE 9.3
Nursing Process Guide for Tommy's Problem of Altered Sensation

Behavior	Influencing Factors		
	Focal	Contextual	Residual
No vision in left eye.	Hit in eye with baseball.	Sudden injury. Good vision in right eye. Generally well coordinated for his age. Supportive family.	Age: 9 years

Altered Sensation

The problem of altered sensation is identified on the basis of the behavioral manifestations concerned with each of the senses outlined in this chapter. The type of altered sensation must be cited, together with the factors influencing it. Specific goals are set for the outcome expected of the client. Then appropriate intervention to reach these goals is carried out. In general, for the client with altered sensation, the nurse includes the following two goals: (1) the client will be safe from injury, and (2) client behaviors will indicate accommodation to altered sensation. These general principles can be illustrated by the following example.

Tommy, a nine-year-old, is being seen in the outpatient clinic of a large city hospital for care following the acute hospital treatment of an eye injury sustained during a softball game. The child has lost his vision permanently in the affected eye. The discharge planning nurse of the hospital has worked with the nurses who cared for Tommy and prepared a summary of the adaptation problems identified during hospitalization, and the progress made in solving these problems. The summary states that Tommy has experienced the grieving process for the loss of his sight in one eye in a very appropriate manner for his age.[1] This problem is considered temporarily resolved, but there is a note to the clinic nurse to re-evaluate it at a later time, since it is too soon after the loss experience to assume that it is permanently resolved. Problems relating to Tommy's roles as schoolchild and peer have been identified and still need nursing intervention.[2] In regard to the senses, the discharge planning nurse provides the clinic nurse with the data summarized in Table 9.3.

Based on this report, the clinic nurse plans that Tommy's visit to her will be spent evaluating the outcome of the short-term goals set by the hospital nurses, modifying approaches as necessary, and breaking down the long-term goals into manageable segments with appropriate interventions. Specifically in regard to

[1]This process is discussed in detail in Chapter 13.
[2]Role problems are reviewed in Chapter 20.

Problem Identified	Goal	Intervention
Altered sensation: loss of sight in left eye due to injury.	Short-term: Tommy will be able to travel to and from school safely.	Provided Tommy and his mother with booklet on safety for the partially sighted, (Carried out in hospital).
	Long-term: Tommy will be able to participate in classroom and school activities safely and effectively.	Spent ten minutes each day with Tommy practicing walking in an area with obstacles. Referred Tommy to Junior Blind Club.

the problem of altered sensation—loss of vision in the left eye—the nurse will evaluate whether or not Tommy has been able to travel to and from school safely. Based on his success with this task, she will plan with Tommy and his mother those goals involving other specific activities, and will carry out specific approaches to meet them.

In this way the nurse uses her nursing process to promote adaptation when there is a problem of altered sensation.

Sensory Deprivation and Overload

In the problem of altered sensation we considered situations in which disruptions in the structure or functioning of one of the senses caused an alteration in the reception of data by the senses. There is also the possibility that the environmental stimuli may be modified in such a way that there is likewise an alteration in the reception of data by the senses. In either case the additional problems of sensory deprivation and overload are possible.

Sensory input, stimuli received by the senses, varies in both amount and predictability. Amount may be described on a continuum from absolute reduction in sensory stimulation, the strict definition of *sensory deprivation,* to an increase in sensory stimulation to the point of too much, or *sensory overload.* Predictability ranges from stimuli that have no order or predictability, called *distortion,* to stimuli that are never changing, being repeated and continuous, termed *monotony.* This relationship is illustrated in Figure 9.1.

Since continuous input of meaningful sense cues is necessary for the organization of human behavior, it is obvious that problems occur whenever a person is receiving cues at either end of the amount or the predictability continuums. We will consider primarily the problems of deprivation and overload, but will recognize the related problems of distortion and monotony.

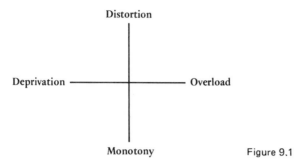

Figure 9.1

Behavioral responses to sensory deprivation extend from mild to extreme. Mild reactions from reduced or increased sensory input include: boredom, restlessness, irritability, fatigue, drowsiness, mental confusion, and occasional anxiety. In more extreme cases—for example, when researchers have placed subjects in a black, soundproof box—drastic cognitive, emotional, and perceptual responses have been reported. Cognitive responses include delusions, primary process thinking, and the inability to think. Emotionally the subjects became labile, or unstable. Perceptual hallucinations were frequent.

The focal stimulus for these problems is, of course, the amount of sensory input as described above and illustrated in Figure 9.1. Specific examples of situations encountered by nurses are: (1) deprivation—blindness, eye patches, deafness, isolation, and traction; (2) distortion—scarred cornea, partial deafness, and strange hospital noises; (3) overload—admission day and special care units; and (4) monotony—same position, one eye patched, and respirator.

One important contextual factor influencing the behavioral response to variations in sensory input is the amount of concurrent social contact. In the black box experiments, the subjects had less drastic effects if they were in contact with the experimenter. If input through one modality is reduced—for example, if the eyes are patched—then input in other modalities are contextual stimuli. One researcher found that eye-patched clients with hearing impairments had greater reactions to the deprivation than eye-patched clients with normal hearing. Others have noted that immobility at the time of deprivation increases its effect. Some studies have shown that certain drugs have been precipitating factors in responses to deprivation. Some investigators have validated the expectation that length of time of deprivation is significant. For clients whose eyes were patched for less than 24 hours, only 35 percent had one or more mental symptoms. However, when the time was increased, as in the case of surgery following a detached retina, 100 percent had one or more symptoms of deprivation. One study found that knowledge of the length of time deprivation will last also lessens the symptoms.

Residual factors which may possibly affect behavioral responses to variations in sensory input are: age—older persons seem more susceptible; sex—women seem to tolerate disturbance longer than men; and premorbid personality factors, as for example, the compulsive person has a greater need to structure the environment.

Identification of a problem of deprivation, overload, distortion, or monotony is made on the basis of the behavioral responses noted, and the known influencing factors. The goal of reducing the effect of the variation in sensory input is then set up. Appropriate interventions are carried out by manipulating the influencing factors that have been noted. This process is illustrated in the following case study.

A 72-year-old female patient, Mrs. Kate Jackson, is admitted to a general surgical unit after surgery for retinal detachment because the eye surgery floor is filled. She is placed in a room alone at the end of the corridor; she is on bed rest; her movements are restricted; and both eyes are patched.

At meal time, a nurse enters the room with a tray. The patient refuses the tray and insists on sitting up. The nurse leaves the room, but checks to make sure that the side rails are up, since the patient seems slightly confused. When the nurse checks back later, the patient is attempting to sit up and wants to get out of bed to go to the bathroom. The nurse applies soft arm restraints, and a sedative medication is given to relax the patient.

By late evening, the patient is struggling to sit up, attempting to remove her eye patches and sees a "big black bug." The nurse clinical specialist from the eye surgery floor is called, and she quickly assesses the patient's problem as being one of sensory deprivation. With the nursing staff she works out the following analysis of the situation and nursing process guide as outlined in Table 9.4.

Thus a problem that could have been avoided by a nurse who was experienced with these situations was resolved, and the clinical specialist was able to teach the staff about an important adaptation problem.

Pain

One form of sensory overload that deserves separate discussion is the problem of pain. It involves excess input to certain sense receptors. The chief problem in formulating a satisfactory definition of pain is that it can be considered from either a physiologic or a psychologic approach. Consideration of pain by one approach without regard to the other is not complete. Pain is a perception, subjective and individual. It varies in different races of people and in the same individual, with changes in physical and emotional equilibrium. Pain can be evaluated only by the individual experiencing it. To each person it conveys a variety of feelings, sensation, and situations unique to him.

From a medical viewpoint, pain can be considered as a complex physiological response to noxious stimulation — a sensory experience separate and distinct from other sensations and mediated through its own neurological equipment. A workable definition of pain for nurses can be simply stated: "Pain is whatever the experiencing person says it is and exists whenever he says it does." It is the individual's entire response to the noxious stimuli, and it is determined by what the painful stimulation means to him, physically, mentally, and emotionally.

Assessment of Behaviors In assessing the pain experience, the nurse should be alert to: (1) picking up overt (open and observable) and convert (concealed or hidden) behavioral cues given by the client; (2) discovering the nature of the pain, as well as its location, type, duration, and intensity; (3) determining the probable meaning of the pain to the patient or her own impression as perceived by the patient's response to her; and (4) obtaining knowledge of the kind of help she is able to give to the patient.

A variety of observable behaviors will help the nurse to validate whether or not pain is being experienced. The "fight or flight reaction," is a pattern of physiological responses often initiated by pain. These responses are due to activation of the sympathetic nervous system and include an increase in pulse and respiratory rates, a rise in blood pressure, pallor, dilated pupils, and cold perspiration. If the duration of the pain is long, the nurse may note that the pulse rate and blood pressure are lower than before the pain occurred. A form of physiologic adaptation occurs if the pain-activating stimulus is repetitive or lasts for a long time, resulting in a decrease in the sympathetic responses.

Other behavioral responses to pain include verbalization, physical activity, reflex responses, and withdrawal. The client may or may not make statements about his pain. He may be very vocal, or the ability to communicate may be altered by a language difference, brain damage, or drug-induced lowering of the level of consciousness. Some patients immobilize a part of their bodies or the total body in a particular position that they feel will minimize their pain. Reflex

TABLE 9.4
Nursing Process Guide for Mrs. Jackson's Problem of Sensory Deprivation

Behavior	Influencing Factors		
	Focal	Contextual	Residual
Refusing meals.	Bilateral eye patches.	In private room at end of corridor.	Age: 72
Struggling to get up.		Bed rest.	Daughter states she is compulsive type.
Attempting to remove eye patches. Seeing "big black bug."		Movements restricted (restrained). Sedative medication.	

responses may be either involuntary movements and/or voluntary flight reactions, such as shielding the endangered part, or actual flight from a threatening situation. These are types of protective responses. Purposeless body motions—kicking, flailing arms, restless moving and turning in bed, beating on something—are all behaviors that may accompany pain. Other persons use a type of rhythmic or rocking motion or a rubbing to alleviate the pain being experienced. For example, a teething baby chews on an object, or a person with abdominal pain rubs his abdomen. The patient's response to environment and his interaction with other persons may decrease as the feelings of pain intensify. The client may focus only on his body and on those measures being done to lessen the pain.

Assessment of Influencing Factors The nurse must first establish the focal cause of the pain. She does this by asking questions and making observations concerning the nature of the pain: its location within the body; its type—dull, burning, sharp, stabbing, cramping, or throbbing; the duration—long or short, its constancy—steady or intermittent; and the intensity—mild or severe, as perceived by the client. This step in the nursing assessment is extremely important. Orlando (1961) gives an example of failure to assess the nature of the client's pain, which resulted in ineffective nursing intervention. A postpartum patient stated that she was in pain. The nurse assumed that the focal cause was uterine cramps and gave the patient the medication ordered for pain. When the pain was unrelieved, the nurse further assessed the situation and found the cause to be the fact that the patient had put on a girdle that was too tight.

Contextual and residual stimuli that may influence pain perception are sociocultural, psycho-emotional, and physiological factors. The presence of pain is a complex problem for an individual. There are multiple influencing factors that the nurse must acknowledge and validate if they are a part of this individual's pain experience. These stimuli are summarized in Table 9.5.

Problem Identified	Goal	Intervention
Sensory deprivation due to bilateral eye patches.	Mrs. Jackson will stop exhibiting behaviors indicative of sensory deprivation and will comply with medical orders.	Move Mrs. Jackson into a double room close to the desk. Spend time twice each shift having Mrs. Jackson carry out movements she is able to do, such as leg motions. At the same time converse with her about her family. In the morning plan with her a structure for her activities for the day.

TABLE 9.5
Stimuli That May Contribute to the Pain Experience

Contextual Stimuli	Residual Stimuli
1. Anxiety	1. Genetic endowment
2. Environment	2. Age
3. Social interaction patterns	3. Cultural orientation
4. Availability of effective drugs	4. Past pain experiences
5. Client's perception of pain	5. Coping mechanisms
6. Client's actual knowledge regarding his or her pain	6. Sex
7. The pain site	7. Religious beliefs
8. General body condition	
9. Presence of trusted person	

Stimuli may be contributory factors in various ways, both contextual and residual:

1. Anxiety. Irving L. Janis (1958) reports that a moderate level of anxiety is helpful for the patient during anticipation of pain. It puts the body in a state of readiness to deal with the pain experience. When anxiety is maintained over a prolonged period of time, or when it is excessive, its protective function is outweighed by the deleterious effect it produces.
2. Environment. Extremes in environmental stimuli, either sensory overload or deprivation, may contribute to the intensity of the experience of pain.
3. Social interaction patterns. A person's skill in interpersonal relationships, his basic trust in other people, and the ability to communicate effectively in the same language may contribute to either the sensation of pain or the ability to cope with the pain.
4. Availability of effective analgesics or narcotics to use in diminishing the pain experience.
5. The client's perception of the pain experience. What is the cause? How long will it last? When will it stop hurting so badly? Can I tolerate this much pain? These are all questions that contribute to the behaviors manifested by painful stimuli.
6. The client's actual knowledge regarding his pain. What is the cause of the pain? What methods are available for controlling it? Will it increase in intensity? Knowledge enhances normal coping mechanisms and adult cognitive functioning.

7. The pain site. Cutaneous pain usually causes the fight or flight response; visceral pain elicits a withdrawal type of behavior that tends to decrease the pain.

8. General bodily condition. Fatigue increases the perception of pain, while at the same time decreasing the ability to employ usual coping patterns effectively.

9. The presence or absence of a supporting, trusted person. The pain threshold is increased when pain is experienced in the presence of a peer group. Young children can more easily tolerate pain if a trusted, caring person is present. A woman in the final stages of labor can more effectively maintain control during contractions with a supportive nurse and/or husband assisting her.

The following stimuli are discussed under "residual," because it may be more difficult for the nurse to validate their actual effect on the pain experience. Once validated, they would be termed contextual stimuli and might be manipulated in intervention. Residual stimuli may have one or more of several origins.

1. Genetic endowment. Pain thresholds are relatively constant cross-culturally. However, some persons are more acutely aware of other environmental stimuli—noise, light, irritating clothing—which may contribute to the perception of pain.

2. Age. Pain tolerance usually increases for many persons with increasing age.

3. Cultural orientation. A number of authors have demonstrated how behaviors reflecting pain may be similar, but the meaning of the pain and the interventions expected and accepted frequently vary between cultures.

4. Past pain experiences and how they were resolved may or may not contribute to this pain experience.

5. Coping mechanisms. People often have learned unique ways of dealing with pain.

6. Sex. Many women and girls in our culture are allowed greater freedom in expressing pain than that expected from men and boys. This factor, however, is in the process of change for many men and women, especially those who identify with the so-called feminist movement of the 1970s.

7. Religious beliefs. The stoic manner of dealing with pain may be associated with devoutness of belief in God. Pain may be viewed as a punishment for some wrong doing, and thus aid in guilt resolution. Or it may be seen as an unjust punishment. Consequently religious beliefs may bring comfort or may inversely contribute to the pain experience.

An example of a nursing diagnosis for pain is illustrated by the following case description. Peter Swartz is verbalizing pain in his incision; is holding his body rigid; his blood pressure has increased to 160/90 and his pulse to 98, due to the pain in the surgical site. He is in his third postoperative day following a cholecystectomy (gall bladder surgery). Mr. Swartz has a friend who had similar surgery, and who needed "pain shots" for six days. Demerol, 75 mg I.M. (intramuscularly) every 3 hours, is ordered for Mr. Swartz. The sun is shining brightly into the window of his room, which is situated across from the elevator.

Client goals appropriate to this pain experience might be stated as:

1. Mr. Swartz will have intermittent periods of rest and feel relatively comfortable.
2. He will ask for help in dealing with his pain when he feels he needs help.
3. He will ask questions and verbalize his feelings about the pain.
4. He will be able to verbalize the meaning and outcome of the pain.

Nursing Intervention in Pain   Pain rarely responds to a single nursing intervention. Selection of a nursing intervention, to prevent, relieve, or remove the cause of pain, is based on an assessment of factors that influence the client's pain sensation and behavioral responses to pain. The suggested nursing interventions for pain are: (1) to establish a relationship of trust with the client; (2) to be with him during the pain experience and offer emotional support, which helps to relieve anxiety and fear; (3) to aid the client in dealing with the nature and meaning of his pain (intensity, duration, location, mode of onset); and (4) to remove the source of the pain and decrease the pain-causing stimuli. This goal of pain relief can be achieved further by nursing interventions that promote the general comfort of the client.

The many specific interventions could include the following: involving the client in the decision-making process regarding which interventions to implement; handling the client gently and carefully; repositioning him to preserve blood circulation and to maintain correct anatomical alignment; insuring general body warmth and relaxation, perhaps by giving a back rub to relieve sore and tense muscles. The nurse might promote bowel or bladder elimination, and maintain a therapeutic environment, which would include optimum temperature, use of color, soft lighting, proper ventilation, diversional activities, and control of visitors. She may need to change soiled linen that is irritating to the skin, loosen a tight binder if permissible, explain all procedures to the patient in order to enlist his cooperation, relieve localized pain perhaps by elevating the affected part, or by applying heat, cold, and counterirritants as prescribed. She should encourage the client to participate in prescribed exercise programs for the maintenance of a normal range of motion, safeguard him from further injury, and provide sensory input. If the client has been experiencing a form of sensory restriction, a normal level and variety of meaningful stimuli may be adequate in producing relief from pain.

Active evaluation of intervention for pain needs to be done in from 15 to 20 minutes after the intervention. Were the client goals reached? Modification and reassessment are indicated if the client remains uncomfortable. An objective description of a nursing intervention (on a Kardex, for example) is important because if effective, it can be repeated and communicated to other health team members, or if ineffective, it can be evaluated and revised.

Medical measures for the relief of pain are *symptomatic treatments* because they are designed for the relief of subjective discomfort, and dictated principally on the basis of the physiological or psychological disturbances responsible for the symptoms of illness. Two types of treatment may be employed, physical measures and pharmacological agents. These two methods may be used simultaneously.

Physical measures include: (1) immobilization of a specific part or the entire body, complete bed rest, for example (the immobilization of areas where there is inflammatory disease avoids the pain-producing stimuli of mechanical friction and local pressure); (2) positioning the client or a specific part of his or her body—for example, in the treatment of joint lesions, local pressure may produce severe pain in the joint, pain is lessened by placing the joint in a position of semiflexion, thereby decreasing the pressure of the synovial fluid in the joint; and (3) application of heat and cold.

Pharmachological agents[3] may include the use of analgesics to reduce the intensity of the pain and discomfort, antispasmotics to lessen the intensity of painful smooth muscle contractions, or narcotics whose action inhibits not only the pain perceptions, but other cerebral-cortical functions as well. Either tranquilizers, antidepressants or sedatives may be given in place of, or in addition to, an analgesic to promote the relief of pain. As a supplement to other measures, *palliation* of pain may be used. It is a means of providing relief until the cause can be determined, or when the cause cannot be removed. The nurse is expected to administer medications, usually written prn, for the relief of pain in an expert manner and to use her professional judgment as to when they are indicated.

SUMMARY

In this chapter we have considered man's regulatory mechanism of his senses. The function of the major senses and the assessment of them were described. The nursing process was specifically applied to the major adaptation problems of altered sensation, sensory deprivation, and overload, including pain. Based on this knowledge the nurse whould be able to plan and carry out care for clients suffering adaptation problems involving the senses.

[3] These medications are discussed further in basic pharmacology texts.

REFERENCES

Janis, Irving L., *Psychological Stress.* New York: John Wiley & Sons, Inc., 1958.

Orlando, Ida Jean, *Dynamic Nurse—Patient Relationship.* New York: G.P. Putnam's Sons, 1961.

ADDITIONAL READINGS

Carini, E. and G. Owens. *Neurological and Neurosurgical Nursing.* St. Louis: C. V. Mosby Co., 1970.

Choldel, J. and B. Williams, "The Concept of Sensory Deprivation," *Nursing Clinics of North America,* vol. 5, no. 3, September 1970, pp. 453-64.

Conover, M. and J. Cober, "Understanding and Caring for the Hearing-Impaired," *Nursing Clinics of North America,* 5/3: 497-506, 1970.

Crawley, Dorothy, *Pain and Its Alleviation.* Copyright 1962, Regents of University of California supported by NLN grant.

Francis, G. M. and B. Munjas, *Promoting Psychological Comfort,* Dubuque: Wm. C. Braun Company, 1971.

Greenberg, B. "Reaction Time in the Elderly," *American Journal of Nursing,* vol. 73, no. 12, December 1973, p. 2056.

Jackson, C. V. Jr. and R. Ellis, "Sensory Deprivation as a Field of Study," *Nursing Research,* vol. 20 January-February 1971, pp. 46-54.

McCaffery, Margo, *Nursing Management of the Patient with Pain.* Philadelphia: J. B. Lippincott Company, 1972.

Myklebust, H. R., The *Psychology of Deafness.* 2nd ed. New York: Greene and Steaton, 1964, pp. 3-11.

Saunders, W. H. and W. Havener, C. Fair, J. Hickey, *Nursing Care in Eye, Ear, Nose and Throat Disorders.* St. Louis: C. V. Mosby Co., 1968.

Schultz, D. P., *Sensory Restriction—Effects on Behavior.* New York: Academic Press, Inc., 1965.

Solomon, Philip, and others, *Sensory Deprivation.* Cambridge: Harvard University Press, 1961.

Veninga, Robert, "Communications: A Patient's Eye View," *American Journal of Nursing,* vol. 73, no. 2, February 1973, pp. 320-22.

Wolff, H. G. and S. Wolf, *Pain.* 2nd ed. Springfield, Ill.: Charles C. Thomas, Publisher, 1958.

Wu, Ruth, *Behavior and Illness.* Prentice-Hall Scientific Foundations of Nursing Series. Englewood Cliffs, N. J.: Prentice-Hall, Inc., 1973.

Zborowski, Mark, *People in Pain.* San Francisco: Jossey—Bass, Inc., 1969.

10

Regulation
of the Endocrine System

Edda Coughran and Sonja Liggett

KEY CONCEPTS DEFINED

Hormone: Chemical substance from a gland carried by the bloodstream, which assists in the control of involuntary and self-regulating processes.

Metabolic Processes: Chemical and physical changes going on in the cells.

Feedback Mechanism: The process by which the hormones act as messengers to regulate their own production.

Master Gland: A term used for the pituitary gland since it directly controls the secretions of all the endocrine glands except the adrenal glands.

Hypersecretion: Increased production of a hormone.

Hyposecretion: Decreased production of a hormone.

Menstrual Cycle: The hormone-controlled cycle from the development of graafian follicle through the discharge of the menstrual phase.

Graafian Follicle: A small, round sac in the ovary that contains the ovum.

Endometrium: Lining of the uterus.

151

Proliferative Phase: Part of the menstrual cycle (5th to 14th day) in which the thickness of the endometrium increases; also called follicular or estrogenic phase.

Secretory Phase: Part of the menstrual cycle (14th to 28th day) in which the uterus is prepared for gestation by swelling of the glands of the endometrium and by an increase in its blood supply; also called progestational, luteal, or premenstrual phase.

Menstrual Phase: Part of the menstrual cycle (1st to 5th day) in which there is a discharge of blood from ruptured small blood vessels, superficial fragments of the endometrium, and the secretion of glycogen and mucin from the glands.

After studying this chapter the reader will be able to:

1. Define the key concepts of this chapter.
2. List behaviors indicating structural or functional maladaptation of the endocrine system.
3. Described Selye's concept of the "general adaptation syndrome" and relate this to stress as a focal stimulus.
4. Delineate contextual and residual factors that may influence endocrine adaptation (see Appendix I).
5. Specify nursing interventions to be used in problems of endocrine imbalance (see Appendix II).

The maintenance of adaptive processes in the endocrine system is like the functioning of an intricate piece of machinery. When all of its interrelated parts are running smoothly, adaptive behaviors can be observed. But let one part become disrupted, and other parts of the endocrine system and the body as a whole may be affected. Adaptive endocrine behaviors involve the blending of many different processes all aimed at one major goal or need—to maintain a life-sustaining environment for the cells.

This chapter reviews briefly the normal structure and function of the endocrine system as a basis for assessing the adaptive regulation controlled by this system. The assessment of significant behaviors and influencing factors is outlined. Nursing interventions are discussed. Finally the adaptation nursing approach to the patient in endocrine imbalance is illustrated in two case studies.

NORMAL STRUCTURE AND FUNCTION

Because of the importance of the structure and function of the endocrine system for the nurse's assessment of client adaptation, this aspect of the regulatory physiological need will be discussed.

The endocrine system is composed of the hypothalamus, pituitary, thyroid, parathyroids, Islets of Langerhans, the adrenals, and the sex glands. These glands perform the intricate functions of coordination and integration of body functions. The endocrine system assists the autonomic nervous system in the control of involuntary and self-regulating processes by secreting chemical substances called *hormones* from the glands directly into the bloodstream on route to specific physiological and anatomical structures.

Maladaptive behaviors may be caused by basic types of pathological conditions and can be observed clinically by behaviors indicating hyperactive or hypoactive hormone secretion. Maladaptive behaviors are seen when the originating hormone site or target tissues are dysfunctional.

The endocrine system is concerned primarily with *metabolic processes,* that is, the chemical and physical changes going on in the cells. The action of each hormone is specific. The entire systemic metabolic process may be affected by one hormone, such as thyrosin, while another hormone, such as parathormone, may have only a regional effect. The endocrine system also has a *feedback mechanism* whereby the hormones act as messengers to regulate their own production. For example, the thyroid gland may secrete an excessive amount of thyroxin if the blood level of this substance is low. When the serum thyroxin level is within normal limits, thyroxin secretion is decreased. This reciprocal feedback mechanism is essential if an adaptive state is to be maintained.

The pituitary gland is commonly referred to as the *master gland,* in that it may, to some extent, directly control the secretions of all the endocrine glands except the adrenal glands. The pituitary gland is composed of two lobes, anterior and posterior, and is located in the cavity of the sphenoid bone just below the brain center.

The anterior pituitary secretes six hormones essential for adaptation. Obviously, maladaptive behaviors can be observed when the rate of secretion is disturbed. These disturbances may be *hypersecretion* (increased production) or *hyposecretion* (decreased production). The six hormones are:

1. *Somatotropic hormone* (STH), also known as growth hormone (GH). This hormone affects nutritive metabolism and growth of the skeletal system. The maladaptive behaviors exhibited by the dysfunctional secretion regulation is dependent upon the age of the client. If hypersecretion occurs before maturity, the client exhibits behaviors of gigantism. However, if hyposecretion occurs before maturity, the client exhibits behaviors of dwarfism. After maturity an increased secretion of the growth hormone results in excessive growth of flat and terminal bones. This disease process is termed acromegaly.

2. *Adrenocorticotropic hormone* (ACTH). Stimulates the adrenal cortex, which in turn secretes the adrenal steroids necessary to maintain life.

3. *Thyrotropic hormone* (TSH). This hormone is often referred to as the

thyroid-stimulating hormone. It is necessary for the thyroid function of maintaining an adequate metabolic rate.

4. *Follicle-Stimulating hormone* (FSH). Stimulates the development of ovarian follicles and in combination with the luteinizing hormone it stimulates the growth and development of male testes and spermatogenises.

5. *Luteinizing hormone* (LH). Primarily functions in conjunction with FSH to stimulate growth and development of male testes and spermatogenises. It also has a role in ovulation and development of the corpus luteum during the menstrual cycle.

6. *Luteotropic hormone* (LTH), also referred to as prolactin. Stimulates the mammary glands for the production of milk. During the menstrual cycle it initiates and maintains the secretion of progesterone from the corpus luteum.

Two hormones are secreted by the posterior lobe of the pituitary—oxytocin and antidiuretic hormone (ADH). Oxytocin primarily is noted for its ability to contract uterine muscles and is thought to enhance milk secretion by the lactating mammary gland. ADH, also referred to as vasopressin, affects the renal reabsorption of water. With hyperactivity of the pituitary, ADH is decreased in blood concentration and clients have been observed to void 20 liters of urine per day. With hypersecretion of ADH, the individual may exhibit water retention.

As one can readily see, the anterior and posterior pituitary hormones are essential for adaptive processes of the body. For example, dysfunctions of ACTH may cause Cushing's disease (marked by rapidly developing obesity), diabetic tendencies, and problems in essential nutrients metabolism.

In some cases an hypophysectomy, the excision or obliteration of the pituitary, may be indicated. Therefore, it is essential for the nurse to know which body functions are affected by each hormone. Also, it is important to know which hormone will be supplemented by medication.

The thyroid gland is composed of a left and right lobe connected by a narrow isthmus located anterior to the trachea and inferior to the larynx. This gland has an abundant supply of arterial flow. Two hormones secreted by the thyroid gland are thyroxine (T_4) and triodothyronine (T_3).

Although triodothyronine is more potent than thyroxin, its action is less sustained in blood concentration. Thyroxin is more important physiologically. It is formed in the thyroid by the synthesis of iodine, which has been absorbed from the bloodstream. The thyroxin in the blood combines with a protein, globulin, and becomes protein binding. Thyroxin is the principal circulating hormone of the thyroid gland.

The thyroid hormones are essential for metabolism in most cells by regulating oxidating processes. As stated the anterior pituitary secretes TSH, which stimulates the release of the thyroid hormones. Therefore, maladaptive behaviors of the thyroid gland can be caused by dysfunctions of the anterior pituitary or the thyroid gland itself. Diseases of hyposecretion are cretinism and myxedema.

Grave's disease, or exophthalmic goiter, are hypersecretion functions.

The parathyroid glands, numbering from four to eight, are located around the thyroid gland. The hormone of the parathyroids, parathormone, controls the blood concentration of calcium and phosphorous. Parathormone also affects calcium metabolism in the body. Hypofunctioning of the parathyroids produces increased neuromuscular irritability due to the decrease of serum calcium and phosphorous. This dysfunction is termed tetany. Hyperfunctioning of the parathyroids increases the serum calcium and decreases the serum phosphorous levels. This deprives the bone of calcium and makes it very susceptible to fractures.

The pancreas is an organ located posterior to the stomach and anterior to the first and second lumbar vertebrae. The pancreas, from its Islets of Langerhans, secretes two endocrine hormones necessary for cell metabolism—insulin and glucagon. Insulin is secreted from the "beta" cells; glucagon from the "alpha" cells.

The primary function of insulin is to assist glucose in its entry into the cell for cell metabolism. Insulin also assists in carbohydrate metabolism. Carbohydrates, fats, and protein are broken down into the end product of glucose, which is the primary form of carbohydrate that can be utilized by the cells for energy. Insulin lowers the blood glucose level and enables the glucose to pass through the cell membrane for metabolism. The primary disease of the beta cells is the hyposecretion of insulin, known as diabetes mellitus.

The primary function of glucagon is to increase the breakdown of glycogen into glucose to be used by the cells for energy. Therefore, its action is the opposite of insulin in that it increases the blood glucose level.

The adrenal glands are located superior to the kidneys, with one on the left kidney and the other on the right. Each gland is divided into the outer tissue, called cortex, and the inner tissue, called medulla. The adrenal glands are the only glands not directly stimulated by the pituitary.

The adrenal cortex secretes chemical substances known as steroids, which affect the synthesis of protein, carbohydrates, and fats. There are three major categories of these essential steroids:

1. Glucocorticoids, which primarily affect carbohydrate metabolism.
2. Mineral corticoids, which affect the metabolism of minerals.
3. Adrenosterones, which stimulate growth of sex-related tissue.

Hyperfunction of the adrenal cortices causes Cushing's disease. Hypofunction results in Addison's disease, marked by a bronzelike skin pigmentation and progressive anemia.

The adrenal medulla secretes the hormones epinephrine and norpinephrine. Not necessary for maintenance of life, they are helpful in enabling man to adapt to stressful situations. Epinephrine is less potent than norpinephrine but has a longer lasting effect. It is the primary circulating hormone of the adrenal medulla. Epinephrine increases blood pressure by increasing myocardial contraction and increasing cardiac output. Norepinephrine constricts the arterioles, resulting in an increased peripheral resistance that increases the systolic and diastolic blood pressure.

Since these two hormones are not essential for life, hypofunctioning of the adrenal medulla is insignificant. However, hyperfunctioning results in the disease called pheochromocytoma, a life-threatening elevation of systolic and diastolic blood pressure.

The last glands of the endocrine system to be discussed are the *sex glands,* referring to all structures that secrete the sex hormones.

In the female the two important sex hormones are estrogen, secreted by the graafian follicle, and progesterone, secreted by the corpus luteum. The function of estrogen is to develop the sex organs at puberty and to establish and maintain the secondary sex characteristics; for example, the growth and distribution of hair, texture of skin, distribution of body fat, growth of the breasts, and character of the voice. During the menstrual cycle, estrogen is responsible for the thickening of the endometrium. Progesterone prepares and maintains the lining of the uterus for the implantation and nourishment of the embryo.

The male sex hormones are called androgens. Androsterone is secreted by the adrenal cortex in both men and women. Testosterone is secreted by the testes in the male. These hormones function in the development and maintenance of normal states of the sex organs and in the appearance of secondary sex characteristics.

The interrelatedness of the endocrine system is illustrated by the hormonal control of the normal *menstrual cycle* (see Figure 10.1). The anterior lobe of the pituitary gland secretes the FSH hormone from the 5th to the 15th day of the cycle, thus stimulating the development of the *graafian follicle,* one of the small, round sacs in the ovary that contains the ovum, or egg. This follicle manufactures increasing amounts of estrogen. Simultaneously the lining of the uterus proliferates markedly. Immediately following menstruation, the *endometrium,* or uterus lining, is very thin. However, as the cells on the surface become taller and the glands become longer and wider, the thickness increases six- or eightfold. This phase of the cycle is variously called the *proliferative phase,* the follicular phase, or the estrogenic phase. The LH hormone, also secreted from the anterior pituitary gland, together with FSH causes maturation of the graafian follicle, and ovulation, which is the discharge of the ovum from the developed graafian follicle. LH then promotes the formation of the corpus luteum. A third pituitary hormone, luteotrophin, initiates and maintains the secretion of progesterone from the corpus luteum. This hormone adds to the action of estrogen and prepares the uterus for gestation by swelling the glands of the endometrium with a secretion containing large amounts of glycogen and mucin. Simultaneously the blood supply of the endometrium is increased. This phase, from the 14th day to the 28th day, is called the *secretory,* progestational, luteal, or premenstrual phase.

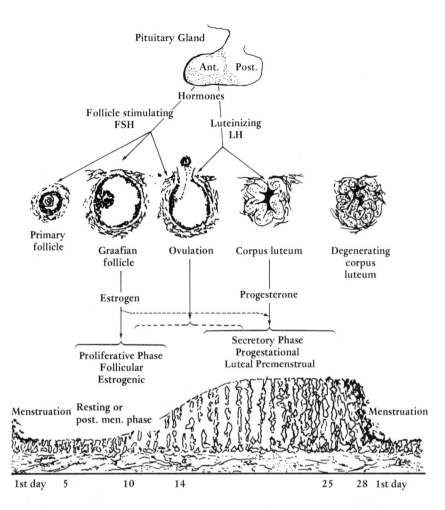

Figure 10.1 The normal menstrual cycle as influenced by hormones. (Reprinted with permission from Fitzpatrick, Elise, Sharon Reed, and Luigi Mastrovanni, *Maternity Nursing*, 12th ed., J.P. Lippincott Co., Philadelphia, 1971, p. 59.)

If the ovum is not fertilized (that is, pregnancy does not occur), the corpus luteum stops secreting progesterone and estrogen about the 25th day of the cycle. Since these hormones have been responsible for the proliferation of the endometrium, their cessation causes a degeneration. The result is a discharge of blood from ruptured small blood vessels, superficial fragments of the endometrium, and the secretion of glycogen and mucin from the glands. This discharge characterizes the menstrual phase of the cycle from the 1st to the 5th days.

ASSESSMENT OF THE ENDOCRINE SYSTEM

Based on her knowledge of the normal structure and function of the endocrine system, the nurse will observe and record adaptive versus maladaptive behaviors. Specific manifestations of dysfunction or maladaptation can be summarized as follows:

1. *Structural Maladaptation*
   a. Observe for dysfunction of soft tissue development, for example, thickening of the facial tissue (acromegaly), changes in skin pigmentation (Addison's disease).
   b. Observe for increase in adipose tissue (hypothyroidism) and enlargement of glandular tissue (hyperthyroidism).
   c. Observe for dysfunctions of skeletal system development, for example, enlargement of flat bones (acromegaly), skeletal decalcification (hypersecretion of parathormone), and hypertrophy, or increased size of the arms and legs (gigantism).
2. *Functional Maladaptation*
   a. Observe for changes of the blood pressure, pulse, respiration, and temperature. Increase in the blood pressure may denote an adrenal medulla tumor; increased heart rate may denote hyperthyroidism. Respiratory changes may signal a decrease in the rate of insulin secretions. Temperature changes may denote dysfunction in the hypothalamus or thyroid gland.
   b. Observe neuromuscular responses. Restlessness and tremors might be indicative of hyperthyroidism or pheochromacytoma. Lassitude and drowsiness may be indicative of diabetic coma or hypothyroidism. Fatigue is a vague complaint that may be observed in many endocrine dysfunctions.
   c. Observe for hyper-or hyporenal responses; they may indicate pituitary, pancreatic, or adrenal dysfunctions.
   d. Observe for lack of control of emotional responses, which may indicate adrenal or pituitary problems.
   e. Observe for changes in the menstrual cycle or in sexual development. Such changes may be indicative of pituitary dysfunction or of hypogonadism (decreased secretion of sex hormones).

The nurse uses her skills of observation, the measurement of internal and external responses, and interviewing to gather data regarding adaptive and maladaptive endocrine behaviors. Often this information is used in referring the client to the appropriate person for a medical diagnostic work-up. Always, the behaviors she notes and the factors influencing them are important in her plan for nursing care of the client with a medically diagnosed or suspected endocrine imbalance. Behaviors in other adaptive modes which are affected by the endocrine imbalance are also assessed.

The structural and functional maladaptive endocrine behaviors noted above are most directly influenced by the focal stimulus of glandular dysfunction, such as hypoplasia (decrease in cell multiplication), hyperplasia (increase in cell multiplication), atrophy, infection, trauma, inflammation, and hypertrophy. Specific pathologies of these glands are discussed in detail in medical science textbooks.

Environmental and emotional stress may also be focal factors affecting endocrine function. The effect of stress upon the endocrine glands has been well documented by Hans Selye (1963). His work began with observations of sick people. Selye noted that certain manifestations, such as watery eyes and flushed or pallid skin, were common to many illnesses. Later he did biological research on rats and found that various physiological and psychological stresses had common effects on the body, notably adrenal enlargement, gastrointestinal ulcers, and thymicolymphatic involution (degenerative changes in certain tissues). When body defenses were activated by stress, Selye called this the "general adaptation syndrome." His use of the term "adaptation" is somewhat different, although not unrelated to the use of the term in this book.

Selye divided the general adaptation syndrome into three stages: alarm reaction, in which the body defenses are mobilized; resistance, which involves adaptations to control the invader; and exhaustion, the result of severe and prolonged stress, ending in death. During the adaptation syndrome the bodily responses are influenced by the secretion of the ACTH hormone by the pituitary gland and the secretion of anti-inflammatory corticoids such as cortisone and of pro-inflammatory corticoids such as aldosterone by the adrenal cortex. A stress situation may thus be the focal cause of endocrine activity, which is eventually maladaptive for the person.

In assessing the factors influencing the endocrine system, the nurse also searches the internal and external environments for factors that are contributing to the behavior caused by the focal stimulus; that is, she also looks for contextual and residual stimuli. Thus the changes in blood pressure caused by an adrenal tumor may be potentiated by the anxiety the client feels upon learning of the diagnosis. The temperature changes noted in dysfunction of the hypothalamus or thyroid gland may be increased by changes in environmental temperature and humidity. Similarly, the lassitude which is evidence of hypothyroidism may be augmented by a socially impoverished milieu.

Based on this type of assessment of behaviors and influencing factors, the nurse will make her plan for care.

NURSING INTERVENTION

In any form of endocrine imbalance, the nurse has two types of intervention: dependent functions, which are carried out under prescribed orders by a physician; and independent functions, which, although accomplished in conjunction with the medical regime, are initiated independently.

Medically dependent interventions include the following:

1. Assistance in medical diagnosis.
   a. Physical preparation for diagnostic tests such as basal metabolic rate (BMR) or thyroid scans.
   b. Physical preparation for laboratory tests such as catecholamine testing of urine or serum tests for thyroxin.
   c. Reporting of signs and symptoms as noted above in assessment of structural and functional maladaptation.
2. Administration of specific therapeutic measures.
   a. Administering prescribed hormones and other indicated drugs to supplement deficiencies and administering antagonists that control excess excretion.
   b. Assisting at surgical procedures as indicated.
   c. Providing prescribed diets such as low carbohydrate, low calorie, or low protein diets for diabetic or hypothyroid clients.
3. Evaluation of physiologic responses to therapy by recording all behaviors and responses to therapeutic measures.

Further discussion of these functions may be found in medical textbooks. What are viewed here as independent nursing interventions in relation to endocrine imbalance can be classified into five basic approaches:

1. To promote normal functioning of the body, especially the skin, renal, and gastrointestinal systems. When any one endocrine gland is affected, physiologic effects can be observed within other body functions. Thus the increased perspiration of the client with hyperthyroidism will necessitate that the nurse plan for frequent cleansing of the client's skin. Likewise, nursing measures to promote bowel elimination (see Chapter 5) will be initiated with the client whose hypothyroidism causes sluggish peristalsis.
2. To teach the client and his family about anatomical and physiological changes that are occurring. Research has shown that most clients will have a less traumatic illness experience if they are aware of the progress of their bodily functions. The information should be on a level which the client is able to understand. Also, time should be allowed for the client to ask questions. Emotional support is essential for the client who witnesses daily changes in body appearance and function. Disruption in body image is a major concern of clients with endocrine imbalance. Obesity, coarse features, hiruitism, and deepened voice are just a few body image disruptions that may occur. (See Chapter 13 for interventions.) The health teaching carried out at the time of menarche and menopause are examples of the type of intervention used frequently by nurses in the problem of disturbed physical self-image).
3. To teach the client and family about the diagnostic tests and procedures, laboratory examinations, and medications. The client must know why

these therapeutic measures are necessary, how they affect body functions, and the procedures necessary for the successful completion of the therapeutic measures. This is especially important for medications, diet, and activity levels. The client will usually be responsible for self-administration of drugs and diet, therefore thorough knowledge and understanding are very important. Also physical limitations should be stressed with emphasis on the positive aspects of activity. The client should be aware of possible behaviors or complications, such as diabetic coma or insulin shock, if medication, diet, or activity levels are neglected. Education of the client to specific therapeutic measures will prevent the possibility of complications and maintain optimum adaptive behaviors.

4. To promote role mastery in the areas frequently disrupted in endocrine imbalance. Problems in completing the client's role as mother, father, wife, husband, or employee often become real threats. Some endocrine problems may cause mood swings that may threaten a wife-husband relationship. Other endocrine problems may induce impotence, which may affect sex relations and prospective mother or father roles. These role problems may be caused by increased dependency needs of the client. For example, if the client is unable to work for a period of time due to fatigue, the spouse or a relative or friend may be required to supply more manual, financial, or emotional support. (See Chapter 20 for intervention in problems of role function.)

5. To evaluate and promote a positive emotional response to therapy and the acceptance of the limitations of the sick role. Effective physiological treatment is dependent to a great extent upon the client's response to therapy. The nurse observes this response and the factors influencing it. She manipulates the factors influencing that response until a positive or adaptive response is made. (Interventions in sick role failure are discussed in Chapter 20.) The nursing process is completed, as always, with an evaluation of whether or not the nursing interventions have been successful in promoting client adaptation. Modification of approaches is planned and carried out as needed. Use of this nursing process with clients having endocrine imbalance is illustrated in the two case studies that follow.

CASE STUDY 1

There are some situations in which a nurse may intervene directly in a state of endocrine imbalance. This is illustrated in the case of 16-year-old Betty White who consulted her doctor because she had not started to menstruate. The doctor examined Betty and found no abnormalities. He also suggested that Betty might like to talk with his office nurse.

The nurse began the talk with the behavior of apparent delayed onset of menses. With her understanding of the factors that influence onset of menses, the nurse interviewed Betty to find the factors that were significant in her situation. She learned that Betty's mother had begun talking about menstruation to Betty when she was twelve years old. In fact, for some time she had instructed Betty always to carry a large purse equipped with sanitary napkins for the "big day." Her mother referred to menses as "female sick days." She herself usually took medication and often claimed that she had to stay in bed at this time. Betty admitted that she did not understand the total process and was very fearful of it. Within the past year Betty and her family had moved from a lake area to a low desert climate. Most of Betty's friends had begun to menstruate. Betty was working at a part-time job in addition to her schoolwork and had a busy extracurricular schedule. The nurse's first and second level assessment is summarized in Table 10.1.

TABLE 10.1
Nursing Assessment of Betty White

| Behavior | Influencing Factors | | |
	Focal	Contextual	Residual
Apparent delayed onset of menses.	Fear of "sick day."	Change in climate. Fatigue. Lack of understanding of physiological process. Expectation of menstruation at younger age. Most peers past menarche.	Mother's behavior and attitude during menses.

The nurse, together with her client, set the goal that Betty would comfortably begin her menses within a year. The nurse began by dealing with the contextual stimuli. She explained that changes in climate and fatigue are known to affect normal menstrual function, and the onset of menarche as late as 17 years old could be within normal limits. Betty showed real interest as the nurse used charts and a pamphlet to explain the anatomy and physiology involved in menstruation. The nurse intended to use the knowledge as a way of reducing fear. Betty asked to have the pamphlet to show to her best friend. The nurse encouraged her to do this and to return again in a week to discuss any additional questions she had.

Betty phoned the nurse three months later to report that she had started menstruating and that she felt fine.

CASE STUDY 2

Very often in dealing with the patient in endocrine imbalance, the nurse's focus is indirect in promoting adaptation; that is, she intervenes in all the other adaptive modes that are affected by the imbalance. This is illustrated in the case of Laura Hart, a 29-year-old married woman with one child. Mrs. Hart is diagnosed as having hyperthyroidism. Looking at all the physiological needs of this client can also serve as a summary of Part II of this book. Behaviors noted by the nurse in the various areas of the physiological mode can be outlined as follows:

1. *Oxygen and circulation* Mrs. Hart has increased blood pressure, increased heart rate, palpitations, increased respirations, dyspnea, and decreased hemoglobin.
2. *Nutrition* The nurse notes increased appetite with a weight loss. Mrs. Hart also has nausea and vomiting occasionally.
3. *Elimination* The client has frequent bowel movements, or diarrhea and polyurea.
4. *Rest and exercise* The client complains of fatigue and insomnia. She has muscle weakness when climbing stairs. She complains of nervousness and feeling irritable. There are tremors of her hands.
5. *Fluid and electrolytes* Mrs. Hart has polydypsea, decreased electrolytes, excessive sweating, dependent edema, and increased calcium.
6. *Skin integrity* The client has mild eyelid retraction, brownish areas on her lower extremities, sweaty and warm palms, flushed, thin, moist skin, and she complains of heat intolerance. She has fine, straight hair and grooving of her nails.
7. *Regulatory and endocrine systems* The client has menstrual irregularities (oligomenorrhea), increased temperature, an enlarged thyroid gland, and inability to focus mentally.

The focal stimulus of all these maladaptive behaviors is the hyperthyroidism, and the client presents the common symptoms of hypersecretion of the thyroid gland. (The client's psychosocial adaptive modes, also disrupted, will not be discussed here.)

Contextual stimuli would include her previous level of activity, knowledge of the disease and its treatment, emotional stability, and environmental stress. Residual stimuli are her previous health state and the attitude of her family support system.

The primary nursing diagnosis of the client is endocrine imbalance. Maladaptive behaviors are illustrated in all the physiological needs due to this hyperthyroidism. Nursing diagnoses can also be made in the relation to these needs: oxygen deficit, increased appetite with occasional nausea and vomiting, diarrhea, fatigue and insomnia, excessive perspiration, and pyrexia and heat intolerance.

The goal of intervention of the health team is to restore the client to her level of wellness by restoring normal function of the thyroid gland. Interventions would be divided into medical and nursing. Medical interventions would include diagnostic tests, surgery, drugs, or irradiation. The nurse would participate directly in meeting this goal of the health team by carrying out the medically dependent interventions listed earlier, namely, assistance in medical diagnosis by preparing the client for diagnostic tests and reporting of signs and symptoms; administration of specific therapeutic measures such as drugs, diet, and surgery; and evaluation of physiologic responses to therapy.

However, in this case study, we are highlighting the nurse's role in promoting client adaptation in relation to the physiological needs during Mrs. Hart's illness. Indirectly this will contribute to the overall goal of restoring the client's level of wellness. These independent nursing interventions are based on manipulating the stimuli influencing each physiological need. Interventions for each diagnosis are summarized in Table 10.2.

TABLE 10.2
Summary of Nursing Interventions for Mrs. Hart

Diagnosis	*Intervention*
1. Oxygen deficit	1. Semi-Fowler's position. Plan activities to decrease expenditure of energy. Encourage foods higher in iron.
2. Increased appetite with occasional nausea and vomiting.	2. Provide high calorie diet in small, frequent feedings of bland foods.
3. Diarrhea	3. Help patient avoid high roughage foods. Cleanse anal orifice after each defecation.
4. Fatigue and insomnia.	4. Provide quiet atmosphere with reduced environmental and emotional stresses.
5. Excessive perspiration.	5. Cleanse skin frequently, and change clothing.
6. Pyrexia and heat intolerance.	6. Provide cool room and light clothing and bed covering.

Thus, both directly and indirectly, the nurse may carry out the adaptation process of nursing for clients having endocrine imbalance. The nurse strives to promote adaptation in relation to all physiological needs when changes in health or illness status bring about adaptation problems.

REFERENCES

Selye, Hans, "Perspectives in Stress Research," from *Life and Disease: New Perspectives in Biology and Medicine,* Dwight J. Ingle, ed., New York: Basic Books, Inc., Publishers, 1963.

ADDITIONAL READINGS

Beeson, P. G. and W. McDermott, eds., *Cecil-Loeb Textbook of Medicine,* 13th ed. Philadelphia: W. B. Saunders, Company, 1971, p. 1718.

Fitzpatrick, Elise, Nicholson J. Eastman and Sharon Reeder, *Maternity Nursing,* Philadelphia: J. B. Lippincott Company, 1966.

Guyton, A. C., *Textbook of Medical Physiology.* 4th ed. Philadelphia: W. B. Saunders Company, 1971, Chapters 75-79.

Moidel, Harriet C., G. E. Sorenson, E. C. Giblin and M. A. Kaufman, *Nursing Care of the Patient with Medical Surgical Disorders.* New York: McGraw-Hill, Inc., 1971, pp. 807-75.

Neher, F. H., *Endocrine System and Selected Metabolic Conditions.* The Ciba Collection of Medical Illustrations, vol. 4. Summit, N. J.: Ciba Pharmaceutical Company, 1965.

Williams, Robert H., ed., *Textbook of Endocrinology.* 4th ed. Philadelphia: W. B. Saunders Company, 1968.

III

Self-Concept

Nancy Zewen Perley, *Coordinator*

In addition to adaptation regarding physiological needs, when a person changes his condition of wellness or illness, he will have to adapt as a total person. When the Roy adaptation model of nursing views the total person, the psychosocial adaptive modes are added. Therefore, in this text introducing the adaptation concept of nursing, it is important to explore each of these modes to the extent that they have been developed to date.

This part deals with the self-concept adaptive mode. Knowledge considered essential for nurses regarding the theory and development of self-concept is discussed in Chapters 11 and 12. The remaining five chapters of this section focus on problems that nurses frequently identify in their clients in this adaptive mode. Each problem is viewed according to the adaptation nursing process; that is, behaviors manifesting the problem and factors that influence it are discussed. Finally, specific interventions to be used by the nurse in helping the client cope with the problem are pointed out.

11

Theory of Self-Concept

Marie J. Driever

KEY CONCEPTS DEFINED

Inner Cell of the Self-Concept: Those perceptions about self which seem most vital; fundamental, important aspects of the individual.

Phenomenal Self: The inner cell of the self-concept and in addition all the perceptions that an individual holds about himself regardless of their importance.

Perceptual Field of the Self-Concept: All the perceptions that one has about oneself, plus those perceptions that are outside the self (the not self).

Looking-glass Self: The person's perception of himself which results from the way he perceives the responses of others toward him.

Significant Others: Those who provide rewards and punishments in a person's life.

Self-Concept: The composite of beliefs and feelings that one holds about oneself at a given time, formed from perceptions particularly of others' reactions, and directing one's behavior.

169

Physical Self: The person's appraisal of his physical self including physical attributes, functioning, sexuality, wellness-illness state, and appearance.

Moral-Ethical Self: That aspect of the personal self which functions as observer, standard setter, dreamer, comparer, and most of all evaluator of who this person says he is.

Self-Consistency: The part of the person which strives to maintain a consistent self-organization, and thus to avoid disequilibrium.

Self-Ideal/Self-Expectancy: That aspect of the personal self component which relates to what the person expects himself to be and do.

Self-Esteem: The individual's perception of his worth.

After studying this chapter the reader will be able to:

1. Define the key concepts of this chapter.
2. Explain the theories of self-concept proposed by Coombs and Snygg and by Cooley, Mead, and Sullivan.
3. Synthesize the views of self-concept presented into a description of the Roy adaptation model view of self-concept.
4. List and explain the components of the self-concept mode.
5. Identify behaviors in ordinary life situations which illustrate the various components of the self-concept mode.
6. Discuss the data gathered in assessing the client's self-concept.

"Who am I? What am I?" Among all of the living things on this earth, man alone has the ability to reflect on who and what he is, and thus abstract an idea as to the nature of himself. This abstraction may be referred to as a person's self, a concept of self, or the self-concept. Although this reflection may appear very real to the individual, in actuality, he can neither see nor touch his own or another's concept of self.

The term "self-concept" is more commonly utilized than the simpler term "self," because man cannot always be aware of his true or actual self. Instead, an individual holds certain beliefs or concepts of himself which may coincide or differ greatly from fact. For example, a young man may view himself as dashing, witty, and clever; whereas the consensus among his peers is that he is actually "pushy" and boring.

Because of the fluid and abstract nature of the self-concept, theorists have had much difficulty in formulating a definition of it. Nonetheless, many social scientists believe that a definition is necessary because it provides a more concrete perspective from which to understand an individual's behavior. This definition is especially important for us in looking at man's response and adaptation to his environment.

This chapter uses various theories of self-concept to develop an eclectic definition that is useful in the Roy adaptation approach to nursing. The components of self-concept will be explored, and the behaviors and stimuli in this adaptive mode will be outlined. In the next chapter the development of self-concept is reviewed with more specific focus on behaviors and influencing factors during the process of maturation.

RELEVANCE OF SELF-CONCEPT TO ADAPTATION NURSING

Just as man adapts physiologically to his environment, he also adapts through self-concept. The nurse is dealing with a whole person. That person has a concept of himself. The concept is affected by and is also used to cope with situations of health and illness. For example, if a man who thinks of himself as physically and morally strong suddenly becomes paralyzed from the waist down, his concept of his physical strength will have to be modified. However, it is his moral self-determination that will allow him to cope with the disability and to develop a satisfying new way of life.

If the nurse has a framework for assessing her client's concept of himself, she may be able to predict some problems the client may have in the temporary or permanent adaptations he will have to make in situations of health and illness. In addition, she may help her client to use the strengths of self-concept to cope with the situation. In this way she promotes his adaptation.

THEORIES OF SELF-CONCEPT

Coombs and Snygg   In the self-concept theory developed by Arthur Coombs and Donald Snygg (1959), what one thinks and how one behaves are largely determined by the concepts one holds about oneself and one's abilities. The pivotal point of this theory is on perception. These authors believe that each person continually attempts to achieve an adequate concept of self in order to preserve psychic integrity. Because of this fundamental need, perceptions of self have a tremendous influence in determining behavior. How a person acts in any given situation depends on how the individual perceives himself.

Coombs and Snygg postulate that the perceptions a person has at a particular time are dependent upon the concepts that this individual holds about himself and his abilities. Thus, for these theorists, the self-concept is a basic variable affecting and controlling perceptions, which eventually affects the behavior of man. In turn, behavior and perceptions affect one's concept of self in an ongoing circle. This process is further illustrated and explained in Figure 11.1.

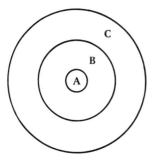

Figure 11.1 Coombs and Snygg
perpetual theory of self-concept.

Circle A   This central portion or *inner cell of the self-concept* includes those perceptions about self which seem the most vital, fundamental, important aspects of the individual. Examples include: "I am a capable mother," "I am fat," or "I am stupid."

Circle B   This encompasses the inner circle and in addition includes all the perceptions that an individual holds about him- or herself regardless of their importance. This particular concept has been termed the *phenomenal self* or the perceived self. Examples of perceptions about self that are not vital include: "I can cook well," "I am always punctual," or "I have a good sense of humor."

Circle C   The final circle illustrates the total *perceptual field of the self-concept* by including all the perceptions that one has about himself (Circles A and B) plus those perceptions that are outside the self (the not self). The not self may be exemplified by the following statements: "The United States is a wonderful place in which to live," "People who are kind to others are usually happier."

In addition to describing their hypothesis of the nature of the self-concept as being derived from the phenomenal self (Circles A and B) and the perceptual field (Circle C), Coombs and Snygg postulate the following characteristics of the phenomenal self:

1. Perceptions of the phenomenal self have the feeling of being very real to to the individual. On the other hand, this individual is probably never able to perceive the total organization of his self-perceptions clearly at any one moment. Instead, he perceives those concepts of self that emerge from time to time as he attempts to satisfy needs.

2. Perceptions of self vary in sharpness for the individual. These perceptions may be cloudy and vague in nature or clear and sharply defined. An example is a woman who identifies herself as "Teddy's mother," as contrasted with one who sees herself as "a good mother." The first example is sharply defined; "a good mother" is unclear and may mean many different things. Another example is an adolescent male who wavers between perceiving himself as a man or boy, thus contributing to a vague concept of self.

This vague concept of self may cause an individual great difficulty. Coombs and Snygg believe that the self-concept continually develops with greater and greater clarity throughout one's life. This clarity assists the person in discovering who and what he is.

3. Some self-perceptions appear to be more basic to a person than others, as illustrated in Circle A. Because the perceptions are central to the person's self-concept, he will most likely resist attempts to change these core perceptions.

4. Another characteristic of the phenomenal self is consistency. Once the phenomenal self is established, it serves as a fundamental frame of reference and has a high degree of stability. Even an unsatisfactory self-organization is likely to prove highly consistent and resistant to change.

In summary, Coombs and Snygg's theory views the self-concept as a map that each individual consults in order to understand himself, especially during moments of crisis and/or decision. It also may be seen as a shorthand approach by which man may symbolize and reduce his own vast complexity to workable, usable terms so that he may be able to perceive and manipulate effectively.

Cooley, Mead, and Sullivan Social interaction theorists provide another focus from which to examine the nature of self-concept. These theoriests, notably Cooley, Mead, and Sullivan, assume that interaction with others, especially significant others, control and alter the individual's appraisal of himself or concept of self.

Cooley (Epstein, 1973) introduced the concept of the *"looking-glass self"*—the person's perception of himself results from the way he perceives the responses of others toward him. Thus if one thinks of oneself as slow-moving, it is because one perceives that others react as if one *were* slow-moving.

Mead (1934) expanded Cooley's concept and saw self-concept as an outgrowth of the individual's concern about how others react to him. He postulated that the way the self achieves an appraisal of itself is to take the role of the "generalized other." Thus a person puts himself in the shoes of those who interact with him and takes on their attitudes toward him. One is motivated to do this because one is concerned about what others think.

In a similar way, Sullivan (1953) sees the self as arising out of social interaction. He emphasizes the interaction with significant others as the key to formulating the self-concept. He identifies *significant others* as those who provide rewards and punishments in a person's life. Based on these rewards and punishments, the person forms a "reflected appraisal" of himself. In other words, Sullivan's premise is that the way in which a person is treated or judged by significant others will determine the way he sees himself. For example, if a mother sees her child as frail and weak and incapable of undertaking tasks that require strength, the child will view himself in that manner.

Whereas Coombs and Snygg focused on the self as a constellation of perceptions, the interactionists emphasize the perceptions of the responses of significant others.

The goal of this brief review of selected theories on the nature of the self-
concept is to provide a basis for an eclectic approach that is appropriate for the
adaptation framework. This was accomplished by utilizing and synthesizing
certain components of the major schools of thought presented.

THE ADAPTATION FRAMEWORK OF SELF-CONCEPT

The Roy adaptation model assumes that man has a need for psychic integrity. This need is met by the person knowing who he is and feeling that this
self is an adequate self. Thus the person must define himself. This self-definition is called one's self-concept. It arises out of perceptions, particularly out of
the perceptions of how he feels others see him. This concept of self then affects
one's behavior. The behavior in turn affects how one sees oneself. For example,
if a person is treated by others as a follower, he is likely to see himself as a follower, and thus assumes the behaviors of a follower. If, however, others place
him in the position of behaving as a leader, he will begin to see himself as a leader. Self-concept is the result of the social experiences the person has over a
lifetime. At any given time, it is the composite of feelings and beliefs the person
holds about himself. It includes the individual's total appraisal of his appearance,
background, abilities, resources, attitudes, and feelings.

For our purposes, then, self-concept is defined as the composite of beliefs and
feelings that one holds about oneself at a given time, formed from perceptions
particularly of others' reactions, and directing the person's behavior.

COMPONENTS OF SELF-CONCEPT

To understand the self-concept adaptive mode more accurately and to provide a framework for the nurse to assess this mode in her clients, we will identify
the components of self-concept. These components are parts of the self which
contribute to the overall concept of self that the person holds. The nurse assesses each component to determine how the client views himself at a given time and
to identify problem areas within the self-concept mode.

The two basic components of self-concept are the physical self and the personal self. The personal self is further divided into the moral-ethical self, self-consistency, and self-ideal/self-expectancy.

Physical Self One of the first perceptions of self is an awareness of one's
body through sensorimotor experiences. In fact, throughout the person's life,
physical perceptions remain a key factor in the sense of self. Physical self is the

person's appraisal of his physical being, his image of himself physically. It includes physical attributes, functioning, sexuality, wellness-illness state, and appearance. Physical self has been referred to in nursing literature as body image. The nurse should recognize that a person's image, or mental picture, of his body may not correspond to actual body structure. For example, someone who has been overweight for any length of time, and then loses weight, will automatically choose clothes and movements used while he was heavy. This person has not yet incorporated a "thin" image into the image of his physical self.

Reva Rubin (1968) identifies two aspects pertinent to the physical self. These are: (1) capacity for functioning—biological structure and functioning determine the individual capacity for functioning, and (2) capacity to control that functioning to appropriate time and place. Timing is crucial in the individual's functioning. As part of the child's socialization, both time and place are conditions of adequate functioning. There is an appropriate time and place for each action, whether evacuating the bowel, running, or shouting. This control of bodily functions according to time and place is a lifelong requirement.

Capacity for function and control thus become important aspects of a person's evaluation of his physical self. Already we can see that there are possible problems for the self-concept of the child, the very ill adult, or the elderly patient who is unable to control bodily functions. Similarly when a given bodily function is lost, there is a need to reorient the physical self and to substitute a different way of carrying out that function. The establishment of the new process physiologically may be easier than the necessary adjustment of the physical self-concept that must accompany the change. For example, the surgical procedure of developing an opening on the abdominal wall for elimination of feces has become relatively simple with a fairly rapid recovery rate. However, accepting a view of oneself as having a bodily function that is carried out differently from most people may take a very long time.

To summarize, physical self is the person's image of self as a physical being and of his capacity to use himself to accomplish what he wishes to do when (timing) and where (place) he wishes to perform that behavior. Problems in physical self are often experienced as loss.

Personal Self As we know, the personal self is divided into the moral-ethical self, self-consistency, and self-ideal/self-expectancy. The *moral-ethical self* is that aspect of the personal self which functions as observer, standard setter, dreamer, comparer, and most of all evaluator of who this person says he is. The moral-ethical self judges the desirability or undesirability of perceptions. It also evaluates the person's behavior in terms of how the person's behavior measures up against the person's consistent image of self. The judgments that the moral-ethical self makes influence the value or esteem the individual feels about himself. For example, it is this aspect of the personal self that judges whether being heavy or thin is desirable for this person. The moral-ethical self includes values held, especially religious values. The value placed on suffering according to one's religious code may be a particularly relevant value in illness. Problems in the moral-ethical self frequently take the form of guilt.

The notion of *self-consistency* is drawn from the theory of personality described by Prescott Lecky (1969). His main premise is that self-consistency means that the person strives to maintain a consistent self-organization, and thus to avoid disequilibrium. Lecky theorizes that the person has a need, and therefore motivation, to maintain a consistent or stable self-image, whatever that self-image may be for the person. This explains why someone who achieves a loss of weight maintains an image of being heavy. It is only after repeated consistent experiences of feeling "thin" that gradually the person changes his concept of self from "heavy" to "thin." According to this aspect of the self, anything that threatens the consistency of the self-image causes the person to experience anxiety. Anxiety, then, is viewed as an adaptation problem of self-consistency.

Self-ideal/self-expectancy is that aspect of the personal self which relates to what the person expects himself to be and do. It is also the person's ideal of what he wants to become. Each person achieves his self-ideal and self-expectancy by incorporating into himself the perceptions of what significant others expect of him. The person takes these images into himself so that the images become what he sees as his self-ideal and self-expectancy. These images of what a person expects of himself, and wishes to become, guide his behavior toward achieving the identified goal.

For a given individual the actual self-image held may differ from his self-ideal/self-expectancy. Also, during their life experiences persons may have difficulties in achieving their ideals and expectancies. To have this difficulty is to feel powerless. Thus, client problems of powerlessness arise out of this aspect of the personal self.

SELF-ESTEEM

Self-esteem is an important concept to consider in examining the self-concept adaptive mode. Generally, *self-esteem* refers to the individual's perception of his worth. It is integral to each component of the self-concept. We have implied that capacity and control of bodily function affect feelings of self-worth. Similarly moral-ethical judgments about the self affect one's esteem. It is only when the person has a consistent concept of self that he is able to place value on that self. Fulfilling self-ideal and expectancies directly influences levels of esteem the individual feels.

Conversely, a given level of self-esteem will change the various aspects of the self-concept. For example, the person with low self-esteem may view himself as ugly and is likely to have a limited view of his self-ideal and minimal expectations. The nurse will have to be aware of problems of self-esteem and their relationship to a client's adaptation in health and illness.

ASSESSMENT OF SELF-CONCEPT

The assessment of self-concept, as in other adaptive modes, involves gathering data about the client's behavior and the factors influencing that behavior. Basically, the nurse determines the client's description of himself in reference to the physical self and personal self.[1] From an internal frame of reference, the person can describe himself in relation to these questions:

1. What am I?
2. How satisfied am I?
3. How do I behave?

Beginning with physical self, to elicit responses to the first question, the nurse may ask the client, "Describe yourself to me physically," or "Give me a word picture of yourself physically." She may assist responses by asking, "Generally, do you consider yourself healthy or sickly; fat or thin; neat or sloppy?" The nurse could ask the following questions for determining the client's satisfaction with self: "Are you happy with your appearance?" "What would you change if you could?" "What would you like to be?" For determining the client's behavior, the nurse might ask for examples of the word description given earlier. An example of responses related to a description of "I am healthy" might be, "I play tennis, golf, and swim a lot."

The nurse follows the same process for the personal self. The descriptive items she is looking for may be expressed by such adjectives as: calm/nervous; nice/hateful; happy/sad; easygoing/anxious; intelligent/dumb; good/bad; honest/dishonest; trustworthy/liar; and consistent/unpredictable. This self-report supplies data for the nurse to identify problems of the self-concept mode in its attempts to adapt to situations of health and illness. For example, the person who sees his moral-ethical self as generally "bad" is likely to suffer feelings of guilt about illness. This simple view of how the client sees himself will also show the self-concept as a factor influencing other adaptive modes. This might be illustrated by a client who sees himself as unpredictable and thus has a difficult time with the consistency required in an intensive rehabilitation program. His self-concept in this case is a residual stimulus for a failure to carry out what is required of his sick role.

To carry out second level assessment, the nurse will look at the focal, contextual, and residual factors influencing self-concept. Focally, she is concerned about factors in the immediate situation which are influencing the client's self-concept. The importance of interaction with significant others has been empha-

[1]This discussion is drawn from work by Katharine Thompson, consultant to the Nursing Department, Mount St. Mary's College, summer 1970.

sized. The nurse may look for the reactions to the client and his situation of health and illness given by family members, the client's physician, and other significant persons. One person's reactions may be focal and the reactions of others may be contextual. Changes in body function may be focal to the physical self-concept. Likewise the situation of illness itself will be a stimulus for changes in the personal self, especially the self-consistency and self-ideal. The client's development of self-concept will be a pervading residual factor in his current view of himself. Self-concept development and the stimuli influencing it are discussed in the next chapter.

SUMMARY

Based on the theoretical background of this chapter, the nurse can identify the client's beliefs about what he is and does. His feelings of satisfaction with these are of concern in promoting the client's adaptation in health and illness. The nurse knows that situations of health and illness will affect the client as a total person and that his physical and personal self are key factors in the adaptations he must make. The nurse is aware of the immediate and past interactions with significant others as shaping the current self-concept of the client. Problems of the self-concept identified by the Roy adaptation approach to nursing have been mentioned and are explored in greater detail in the following chapters.

REFERENCES

Coombs, Arthur and Donald Snygg, *Individual Behavior — A Perceptual Approach to Behavior.* New York: Harper Brothers, 1959.

Epstein, Seymour, "The Self-Concept Revisited or a Theory of a Theory," *American Psychologist,* vol. 28, no. 5, May 1973, pp. 404–16.

Hall, Calvin S. and Gardner Lindzey, *Theories of Personality.* New York: John Wiley and Sons, Inc., 1970.

Lecky, Prescott, *Self-Consistency: A Theory of Personality.* New York: Doubleday and Company, 1969.

Mead, George Herbert, *Mind, Self, and Society.* Chicago, Ill.: The University of Chicago Press, 1934.

Rubin, Reva, "Body Image and Self-Esteem," *Nursing Outlook,* June 1968, pp. 10–23.

Sullivan, Harry Stack, *The Interpersonal Theory of Psychiatry.* New York: W. W. Norton & Company, Inc., 1953.

ADDITIONAL READINGS

Fitts, William H. and others, *The Self-Concept and Self-Actualization.* Nashville, Tenn.: Dede Wallace Center Monograph III, July 1971.

Norris, Catherine M., "The Professional Nurse and Body Image," in *Behavioral Concepts and Nursing Intervention,* Carolyn Carlson, ed. Philadelphia: J. B. Lippincott Company, 1970, pp. 39–66.

Ziller, Robert and others, "Self-Esteem: A Social Construct," *Journal of Consulting and Clinical Psychology,* vol. 33, no. 1, 1969, pp. 84–95.

12

Development of Self-Concept

Marie J. Driever

KEY CONCEPTS DEFINED

Maturation: The process of growth and development.

Growth: An increase in physical size of the whole or any of its parts.

Development: The progressive increase in skill and capacity of function.

Learning: Behavioral change that is dependent upon rewards.

Normal Development: The term used when a person performs behaviors he is expected to be able to do at a certain age.

Cephalocaudal Trend: Control proceeding from the head downward.

Proximal to Distal Trend: Development from the parts closer to the center of the body before peripheral parts.

Generalization: The process that occurs during learning whereby the person responds in a specific way to a nonspecific stimulus.

Discrimination: The process by which the person makes a more specific response.

Task: Some specific work that tests the person's strength or ability.

Crisis: Turning points, points of change that involve the use of judgment.
Trust: A feeling of confidence in the sameness, continuity, and predictability of the environment.
Autonomy: The result of strivings to become a self-governing and an independent person.
Initiative: The quality of undertaking planning, and "attacking" a task for the sake of being active and on the move.
Identification: Incorporating into the concept of self the strengths and weaknesses of the adults on whom the child is dependent.
Industry: Adjustment of oneself to the inorganic laws of the tool world, or learning to win recognition by producing things.
Identity: A new self-definition that allows the adolescent to make adult decisions and to cope with adult life stresses.
Intimacy: Developing an ability to achieve a close relationship with a special person.
Generativity: Concern with establishing and guiding the next generation.
Ego Integrity: Feeling satisfied with one's life and decisions; an acceptance of one's life cycle.

After studying this chapter the reader will be able to:

1. Define the key concepts of this chapter.
2. Discuss the principles of growth and development and of learning.
3. Describe the developmental tasks of selfhood.
4. List and describe the eight stages of crises that Erikson proposes.
5. List factors influencing self concept development.

This chapter focuses on the development of the self-concept adaptive mode. For each of the psychosocial modes we will be looking at how they develop through a combined process of maturation—growth and development—and learning. Maturation and learning together form the process whereby self-concept, role function, and interdependence are developed.

Within the forward movement of maturation and learning, the life cycle is marked by stages. Each of these stages has its transition point or maturational crisis. One view of the stages of psychosocial development is outlined by Erik H. Erikson (1963). His view of these stages with their developmental crises will be used in our discussion. Thus, in this chapter we will be looking at the development of self-concept as a process of maturation and learning within the life cycle. The factors influencing this development, including the maturational crisis, will also be explored.

PRINCIPLES OF GROWTH AND DEVELOPMENT

The principles of growth and development that are basic to the development of all the adaptive modes can be summarized as follows:

1. *Growth* refers to increase in size; *development* implies an improvement in skill and function.
2. *Normal development* is the term used when the person performs behaviors he is expected to be able to do at a certain age.
3. Within each *stage* of development there is a *range of time* for achieving given behaviors. For example, the child may begin to walk anywhere from 9 to 18 months of age and still be considered to be developing normally.
4. The *cephalocaudal trend* marks a person's mastery of body and environment. That is, control proceeds from the head downward; for example, the child lifts his head before sitting up.
5. There is also a *proximal to distal trend* to development. The parts closer to the center of the body develop before peripheral parts. Thus, control of the arms comes before control of the fingers.
6. Behaviors develop in a *sequence,* with one behavior building on the accomplishment of another. For example, development of the pincer grasp (thumb to forefinger) allows for feeding behavior.
7. *Genetic and environmental factors* influence growth and development.
8. The *family* is an important environmental factor influencing growth and development.

PRINCIPLES OF LEARNING

In addition to maturation, learning is an important factor in the development of the adaptive modes. *Learning* is a change of behavior through the process of reinforcement. The following list includes principles that are important in the learning process.

1. *Generalization* is the process that occurs during learning whereby the person responds in a specific way to a nonspecific stimulus. If the mother repeatedly uses the word "bad" with the child, he is likely to feel that the word relates to his total person.
2. *Discrimination* is the process by which the person makes a more specific response. The mother may be able to help the child understand that the word "bad" relates only to the action of hitting his baby sister and not to the child as a person.
3. *Spaced trials* over a period of time are generally more effective than one concentrated session of learning. For example, the mother's consistent

response to her child is more important than one pleasant afternoon spent together.

4. *Active participation* facilitates learning. The child who is able to do something to show competence is more likely to incorporate a competent attitude into his self-concept.

5. *Meaningful material* is learned more quickly than material without meaning. If a person has identified a certain characteristic—for example, dependability—as personally important, he can acquire this trait more readily than a trait personally considered irrelevant, for example, a sense of humor.

DEVELOPMENTAL TASKS OF SELFHOOD

A *task* is some specific work that tests the person's strength or ability. The development of the self-concept involves a specific task for each of its components. Bruce D. Gardner (1964) proposes that in psychosocial development there are three major tasks: physical self-development, which involves the task of learning to live with tools, personal self-development, which implies learning to live with self; and learning to live with others, considered as relevant to the interdependence mode. Each task must be reaccomplished during each stage of development. By the successful or unsuccessful mastery of the two self-concept tasks at each stage, the person gains perceptions of his physical and personal selves. Both of these tasks organize many smaller, more specific developmental tasks. Robert J. Havighurst (1952) postulates a series of concrete demands that the person works on during each stage of development. These general and specific tasks are considered in the following discussion.

The first self-concept task, living with tools, relates to mastering the tools appropriate to each stage of development. Tools come in all shapes, sizes, and varieties. Some tools are tangible and concrete, such as play equipment for the child and technological equipment for the adult. Other tools are less tangible—for example, social customs. Mastery of both tangible and intangible tools involves control of one's body. Thus the infant is controlling his sustenance of life by learning to chew, swallow, and digest solid food.

Living with self is the task that leads to the development of the personal self. This task involves learning to live with the impulses and needs that arise within the self. It includes the person being able to find acceptable ways of dealing with powerful feelings, intense drives, emotional attitudes, conflicts, doubts, and questions that come from within himself.

The person has to learn to live with himself. This means accepting the normality of his feelings and urges. The person must realize that the impulses are there; they are real and valid and will not go away. The person has to "handle" his feelings. This means he must make decisions on what behavior to use to act on or to express his feelings, channel them into other activities, and perhaps find other means of satisfaction. Learning to live with self also includes the developing of awareness of one's resources, strengths, capabilities, and direct feelings.

Thus, at each stage by learning to live with the appropriate tools of the time, and by learning to live with the self, the person will continue to define his physical and personal selves, and thereby his overall concept of self.

DEVELOPMENTAL CRISIS

The word "crisis" is derived from a Greek word which means "to decide." The most characteristic aspect of a crisis is the decision-making experience it provides for, and demands of, the person. *Crises* are turning points, points of change that involve the use of judgment. For the individual a crisis represents a challenge, which demands that the individual recognize how he sees himself in relation to meeting this challenge from his environment.

Erikson (1963) proposes eight universal transition points, or maturational crises, in a person's life cycle. He believes that these crises exist in all cultures and through all times. They are seen as affecting the development of all three psychosocial adaptive modes. They will be discussed in detail here, then referred to later in relation to role function and interdependence.

During the crisis period, the person tries to use previous coping measures and views of himself that were successful in the past but now are unsuccessful. The person then evolves new coping measures and views to reorganize his approach to the environment. If this reorganization is successful, the crisis is met. He now has new ways to cope, see himself, and relate to the environment. The person may use these new ways as tools to keep him healthy and move on to the next crisis. Should the reorganization of the self-concept mode of adaptation be less than successful, the person develops negative behaviors and views of himself, which make him less healthy and less able to adapt successfully to the next maturational crisis or any situational crises that also may be encountered.

The eight stages of crises that Erikson proposes are listed on the following pages.

1. *Trust versus mistrust*   At birth the infant is not capable of conceiving himself as a person in his own right and separate from other persons. He must first develop a close tie with a significant other before he can begin the process of defining for himself who he is.

The infant spends his first year in an almost totally helpless and dependent state. From a consistent and predictable response of a mothering person to his needs, the infant develops a sense of trust. In the routine of daily living, the infant experiences the need for food, warmth, safety, and dryness, and hopefully consistent positive responses to these needs. The long range of this cycle, beyond its immediate implications for survival and well-being, is the general outlook or expectation of life experience that the infant develops. This outlook or expectation should be a sense of trust. A sense of *trust* is a feeling of confidence in the sameness, continuity, and predictability of the environment. The infant trusts that the response of the environment will be, for the most part, positive.

For example, if the infant is fed at regular intervals when he expects to be fed, a sense of trust is encouraged. Should the feelings become sporadic, the infant will become uncertain and anxious about his environment and whether his environment will be positive. This is *mistrust*.

From a sense of trust in his external environment, the infant needs to progress to a sense of trust in himself that his cries will elicit help. The infant needs to feel that he can make something happen, and something that will be personally positive and satisfying. Erikson believes this development of trust is the basic cornerstone of the person's development. It provides the basis for trusting others to trusting self, of being "all right," of being oneself and relying on oneself, and becoming what other people trust one will become. It is the basis of the person learning to use his resources to meet personal needs and depend on others. It involves a balance between trust of self and others.

> 2. *Autonomy versus shame and doubt* Hearing the toddler say "mine" and "no" and seeing him express nonverbally the feeling "I - I - I" is the essence of this stage and indicates what the child is working toward—autonomy.

A sense of trust encourages striving for the sense of autonomy, or the sense of "I." When the infant's motor coordination and mental development become such that he begins active exploration and experimentation, the strivings to become a self-governing and an independent person become the predominant characteristics of his behavior.

The child utilizes a variety of behaviors to fulfill the need to discover how far he can go on his own two feet and still be in control of self and world. Therefore, the nature of this crisis is that the child must have an area in his personal world where he is in charge, where he makes a decision that counts; where when he says "No," the word is respected. The child's "No" that is heard so frequently during this stage is an effort to assist himself, to establish himself as a real person apart from everyone else. The child needs limits in his environment to help maintain trust and confidence in himself and others as he tries out more behaviors and self-control. The danger of this stage is that the child may be "shamed" into "being good" and come to doubt that his impulses are good and can be personally controlled.

> 3. *Initiative versus guilt* Initiative adds to autonomy the facet of undertaking, planning, and "attacking" a task. As the word initiative implies, the crisis of this stage is concerned with developing plans, ideas, and actions.

The child has established himself (if he has a reasonable sense of autonomy) as a real person so he feels good personally to the extent that his ideas and plans count for something.

During the third, fourth, and fifth years, the child is working hard to establish what kind of person that self will be. This is also a time of questioning. "What can I do?" "What can I make of the self which I have discovered and established as a real person?" "What can I be?" "What can I become?" It is a time of imagination and fantasy mixed with the real world of people and things. The four-year-old, for example, has a fluid imagination that he can "be" within a short period of time a tiger or a bunny, or that he can tame a tiger or be the gentle protector of the weak bunny.

During these three years, the process of *identification* develops. It reaches a high point in the child's relationships with the significant adults in his life. The identification process is the way the child strives to experience how adults cope with the complex world. It is an age during which a child incorporates many things into the concept of self that typify the strengths and weaknesses of the adults on whom the child is dependent.

Another key to the child's behavior is his creative activities of all kinds at this time. Through drawing, dancing, and other rhythmic activities, through dressing up and playing parts, through creating roles with other children and living them out in doll play, and through all the building and constructing, the child is exploring the world of possibilities as to what he can do and be.

To fail to achieve some sense of initiative results, in its most gross form, in an overwhelming sense of guilt. The child should develop and manifest some guilt, but there needs to be a balance developed between exploration and the amount of guilt arising from these activities. This is the stage during which the child begins to develop a conscience. Because at this time he is attempting to sort out "good" and "bad" as labels for his actions, the child is vulnerable. The child can be made to feel guilty about too many things. Guidance and discipline relying on shaming the child creates guilt and a decrease in the child's self-esteem.

"I am whatever I can dream about, whatever I can express through fantasy or actions or words, whatever I can imagine myself to be." Those words sum up the sense of initiative the child attempts to master at this stage.

4. *Industry versus inferiority* With a positive answer to "What can I do?" the child has positive feelings and inner strength as "I" is established. He is now ready for the new experiences of school to learn about the routine of the school structure and the skills that go with that experience. For this crisis the focus is on learning to win recognition by producing things. To develop a sense of *industry* is to adjust oneself to the inorganic laws of the tool world. The child can become an eager and absorbed participant of a productive task. Completion of a task is an aim the child develops, which gradually supercedes the whims and wishes of play. He needs to learn steady attention and diligence and how to complete a task. All cultures have or provide some kind of school or educational activity for the child to develop this sense of industry. The

child develops the fundamentals of how to manipulate objects and technology
as he becomes ready to handle the utensils, tools, and weapons used by adults.

The danger at this stage is that the child will develop a sense of inadequacy
and inferiority. The child may despair of how to handle himself and the tools
in his environment. He may come to feel inadequate in being able to control his
body and objects in the environment. This stage of industry is socially a most
decisive one, because industry involves activities with others. It is the stage
where the child needs to learn a sense of how to divide and share.

5. *Identity versus role diffusion*   With the establishment of a good initial relationship to the world of skills and tools and with the coming of puberty, childhood
comes to an end. During puberty and adolescence all sameness and continu-
ities that the person has relied on are more or less questioned due to a rapidly
growing body and genital maturity. The person at adolescence faces most
acutely the question "Who and what am I?" and becomes concerned with what
that identity will be like with the adult tasks ahead. The adolescent seeks to
develop an idea of who he is in light of the feedback received from his peer
group. He is attempting to connect roles and skills learned earlier with new
occupational opportunities of the day.

In searching for a new sense of identity, continuity and sameness, the adolescent has to reword solutions of previous crises. He has to redefine trust, autonomy, initiative, and industry in light of new answers to "Who am I?" This new
definition of self has to incorporate the sexual changes of adolescence as well as
the expectations society has of an adult person. Amidst all this redefinition, the
person has to achieve a new or reorganized concept of self that includes a sense
of confidence. The inner sameness and continuity prepared in the past are
matched by the sameness and continuity of one's self-meaning now.

Adolescence is critical because the individual is reassessing all of his defenses
and adaptive mechanisms. Childhood responses are no longer appropriate; he is
striving for new self-definition. To achieve this he must alter the relationship
with the past, particularly the relationship with parents. This new adult
identity will allow him to make adult decisions and to cope with adult life
stresses.

An inability to develop a new self-definition with which to cope with stress
results in role diffusion. This means the person is unable to consolidate a sense
of self that integrates a variety of expectations and status. He does not have a
solidly formed, but rather a tentative, conclusion of who he is. The individual
feels confusion and anxiety in not having a stable self-definition to use as a basis
for responding to the demands of his environment.

6. *Intimacy versus isolation*   Having achieved a tentatively stable self-definition,
the person is ready to face the crisis of young adulthood — intimacy. To develop a sense of *intimacy* involves developing an ability to achieve a close relationship with a special person. It involves a fusion of one's identity to another

by committing oneself to that person. It also includes developing the strength
to abide by such a commitment even in times of sacrifice and compromise.

Intimacy includes the ability of self-abandonment in close affiliations in sexual union and in close relationships. It involves seeing self-definition enriched by
close relationships with feedback from others.

Avoidance of such experiences of sharing self with another because of the
fear of loss of self may lead to feeling a deep sense of isolation and consequent
self-absorption. This self-absorption blocks the person in being able to continue
to receive feedback and perceptions from significant others to develop more
fully an awareness of who and what one is.

7. *Generativity versus stagnation* Mature adults need to be needed. Thus the
   person must develop the sense of having produced/developed something and
   provided guidance to the achievement of the goal of that production. *Generativity* is the stage where the person concerns himself with establishing and
   guiding the next generation. This focus on producing something to give to
   others need not be solely the having and rearing of children. It can involve
   the generation and nurturing of ideas and objects to pass on to others. Generativity includes, then, productivity and creativity.

Where the person fails in ability to produce something he can give to another
person, in the ability to be needed and supply support, the person regresses to a
point of stagnation and nonproductivity. He becomes more self-absorbed and
concerned with himself, and in a sense becomes his own child that he needs to
guide and support.

8. *Ego integrity versus despair* This last stage of man's development is very much
   dependent on all the previous stages. A person who has mastered some sense
   of trust, autonomy, initiative, industry, identity, intimacy, and generativity is
   ready to meet this crisis of feeling satisfied with one's life and decisions. *Ego
   integrity* involves a person's acceptance of one's life cycle as something that
   had to be. Although the person is aware of other and different life styles that
   give meaning to others, he possesses a feeling of fullness and satisfaction of the
   dignity and completeness of his life. The person is ready to defend his life and
   decisions as the best personal ones.

A person who feels despair suffers a loss of this accrued fullness of self and
fears death. He does not feel that who and what he is, and was, is enough or
right. He has not met self-expectations. The feeling of despair expresses the
feeling that time is now short, too short to attempt to start another life to
achieve alternative ways of developing a sense of integrity, completeness, and
comfort with his definition.

This discussion has implied that each maturational crisis is related to each
other crisis. Each crisis encounter builds on the previous resolution and in turn

contributes to how the person will meet the next crisis. All crises exist from the beginning in some form for the person and each crisis is reworked in succession as the person struggles to master the next one. For example, during the crisis period for the person to master initiative, as the person struggles with this task, he has to redefine how he has learned a sense of trust and autonomy.

FACTORS INFLUENCING SELF-CONCEPT DEVELOPMENT

In the discussion of the theory of self-concept, we have seen that the perceptions of responses by others, particularly significant others, are important in the formation of the self-concept. These perceptions, then, may often be the focal stimuli affecting self-concept development. The developmental tasks and crisis also stimulate the development of self-concept. They may at times be focal stimuli and at other times contextual stimuli depending on the immediacy of their relevance to the developing behaviors. Two other general categories of factors influencing self-concept development are genetic and environmental factors. For example, if it is genetically determined that a person will have short stature, it is unlikely that he will ever include tallness in his concept of physical self. Similarly if one's environment demands robust activity, such as for those living in a mountainous area, strength and prowess may be incorporated in the self-concept.

In summary, contextual influencing stimuli for the development of the self-concept include the following factors:

1. Tools in the environment that the person can learn to manipulate and use appropriate to the person's developmental or situational crises. For example, in learning to feed himself the child needs to have objects and food available that can assist him to develop the muscle control and skill in self-feeding.
2. Self-definers available to the person in the environment. This would include the current feedback from significant others that—hopefully—is positive. It also includes any and all experiences/environmental stimuli that demand and help the person to further experience, become aware of, and define who he is to himself. This might be needed to learn a sport, artistic or craft activity, as well as technical and interpersonal skills that work, family, or social situations might demand of the person.
3. Present self-definition—how positive or negative it is for the person to use as a way of responding to stress.
4. Present coping mechanisms other than self-concept that the person can use, for example, problem-solving ability, ways of handling feelings, and making decisions.
5. The competence of self in situations that the person feels, especially in areas that the person and others value.

Residual influencing factors include:

1. All previous perceptions of feedback about the self from significant others.
2. All previous maturational and situational crises and how the person has reorganized a sense of self-definition in response to these crises.
3. The person's self-expectations and experiences with success and failure.
4. Any experience, especially interpersonal ones, which generate positive feelings and a sense of value and worth, or conversely negative feelings which do not generate a sense of value.

Any of these contextual or residual factors may become focal at some time if they become the factor most immediately affecting the development of self-concept.

SUMMARY

Toffler (1970) postulates that each person will develop "serial selves," that is, a series of different selves developed and discarded in adaptation to a rapidly changing world. From this chapter, we can see that the person develops, changes, and redefines a concept of self in response to developmental crisis. New kinds of behaviors are learned to master the developmental tasks. These behaviors assist the person to resolve the crisis and redefine who he is.

Each crisis provides the person the opportunity to sort out and redefine who he is, and to make decisions of how to act on and present this self to his environment.

REFERENCES

Erikson, Erik H., *Childhood and Society*. 2nd ed. New York: W. W. Norton and Company, Inc., 1963; London: The Hogarth Press Ltd.

Gardner, Bruce D., *Development in Early Childhood*. New York: Harper and Row, Publishers, 1964.

Havighurst, Robert J., *Developmental Tasks and Education*. New York: David McKay Company, 1952.

Toffler, Alvin, *Future Shock*. New York: Bantam Books, Inc., 1970.

ADDITIONAL READINGS

Allerhand, Melvin E. and others, *Adaptation and Adaptability*. New York: Child Welfare League of America, 1961.

Fink, Stephen, "Crisis and Motivation: A Theoretical Model," *Archives of Physical Medicine and Rehabilitation*, November 1967, pp. 592–97.

Fitts, William and others, *The Self Concept and Self Actualization*. Nashville, Tenn.: Dede Wallace Center, Monograph III, July 1971.

Gould, Roger, "The Phases of Adult Life: A Study of Developmental Psychology," *American Journal of Psychiatry,* 129:5, November 1972, pp. 521-31.

Perez, Joseph F. and Alvin I. Cohen, *Mom and Dad Are Me.* Belmont, Calif.: Brooks/Cole Publishing Company, 1969.

Tiedt, Eileen, "The Adolescent in the Hospital: An Identity-Resolution Approach," *Nursing Forum,* vol. XI, no. 2, 1972, pp. 120-40.

Wu, Ruth, "Child Development: A Basis for Nursing Care," in *Current Concepts in Clinical Nursing,* Bergerson and others, eds., vol. I. St. Louis: C. V. Mosby Co., 1967, pp. 269-83.

13

Problems of Physical Self: Loss

Barbara J. Gruendemann

KEY CONCEPTS DEFINED

Loss: Any situation, either actual or potential, in which a valued object is rendered inaccessible to an individual or is altered in such a way that it no longer has qualities that render it valuable.

Object: Includes people, possessions, job, status, home, ideals, parts, or processes of the body.

Significant or Valued Object: Any object that is essential for psychic functioning.

Grief: The series of emotional responses that occur following the perception of or anticipation of a loss of one or more valued objects.

Mourning: The psychological processes that follow the loss of a significant or valued object, or that follow the realization that such a loss may occur.

Stages in Grieving a Loss: Categorizations of behaviors of those experiencing a loss into (1) apprehending the loss, (2) attempting to deal with loss, and (3) final restitution and resolution of the loss.

Shock and Disbelief: An initial stage in grieving a loss in which the reality of the situation cannot be accepted and thus temporary anesthesia serves the useful purpose of not having to face the total grim reality all at once.

Denial: Refusal to accept or comprehend the perceived data.

Unresolved Grief: Behaviors associated with one or more of the stages of grieving are either absent or excessively prolonged.

After studying this chapter the reader will be able to:

1. Define the key concepts of this chapter.
2. Describe the behaviors and influencing factors noted in each stage of grieving a loss.
3. Identify a problem of loss if given a case study illustrating the problem.
4. Specify nursing interventions to be used in the problem of loss (see Appendix II).

Each individual perceives of himself in a different, unique way. These perceptions become a point of reference or a starting point for everything one does. Total appraisal of self ("this is what I am") is self-concept. The feelings and cognitive processes of self-concept involve appearance, background, abilities and resources, attitudes and feelings. These feelings and processes are dynamic forces in directing behavior.

One area of self-concept, separated for study purposes only, is the physical self. The dynamic and penetrating nature of the physical self, portrayed in sensations and body image, is exhibited vividly in a person who has lost some portion of his valued body equipment. Loss of somatic sensations or body image leaves a person exposed and crudely vulnerable. The capacity to use oneself in action for personal accomplishments is disrupted. Expert nursing intervention becomes a must.

It is in this context that the problem of loss is discussed in the first part of this chapter.

LOSS

The nurse frequently encounters clients who experience or perceive some kind of loss. Loss has only recently been recognized as a concept of significant proportions that requires intense study. Loss may occur in varying situations and with differing intensities. At times, it is severe enough to require crisis intervention by the nurse.

Loss is defined as a situation, either actual or potential, in which a valued object is rendered inaccessible to an individual or is altered in such a way that it no longer has qualities that render it valuable. *Object* in its broadest sense includes people, possessions, an individual's job, status, home, ideals, parts and processes of the body. In other words, the loss may be of valued objects, material or psychological, or it may be of abstractions and, most important, of self and the body.

The loss of a significant or valued object is considered to be the event preceding the subjective state of grief and the psychological process of mourning. A *significant or valued object* is any object that is essential for psychic functioning. To lose something of this value may be equated, in the individual, with the loss of self. Loss of self is tantamount to loss of life.

There are many examples of loss. Easily recognized is the loss of a body part or the loss of a spouse, child, or other family member, a close friend, or in the case of a child, loss of a loved object such as a pet. Not so easily recognized are covert losses that may provide just as intense grief responses as overt losses. Sometimes these are not visible by observation alone and are, therefore, incorrectly assessed as unimportant. Examples are loss of body image, function, or control; loss of privacy; birth of a defective child; chronic heart disease, loss of a job, material comforts, or security; uprooting of a family; divorce, retirement; or a terminal illness.

In an infant or child, separation anxiety can be equated to the adult sense of loss. Not to be overlooked are the losses that occur during illness and hospitalization. Not always readily discernible are loss of identity when becoming a client, loss of strength or usual control over the situation, loss of self-confidence and expected outcome. There may also be loss of a care giver, usually the nurse. Termination of a nurse-client relationship may engender grief and mourning in both client and nurse.

The series of emotional responses that occur following the perception of or anticipation of a loss of one or more valued objects is defined as *grief*. Grief encompasses the variety of subjective reactions to significant losses, such as helplessness, loneliness, hopelessness, sadness, guilt, and anger.

Mourning includes the psychological processes that follow the loss of a significant or valued object, or that follow the realization that such a loss may occur. These processes usually lead to the relinquishing of the lost object. Mourning, therefore, includes the processes that are necessary to overcome the subjective states of grief.

Although the general concept of loss could be studied in the context of any one of the four adaptive modes, it is included in the section on physical self. The loss, real or perceived, of part of one's self is so permeating that it is appropriately included here. The experiences of loss touch on and delve into the person's functioning and innermost feelings.

To understand loss, the nurse must realize the stages that a client will experience in the process. She must also assess the progress through the stages and know if the client is exhibiting adaptive or maladaptive behaviors in the work of

dealing with a loss. Although each client will experience loss in a different manner, there are distinguishable patterns that aid the nurse in assessment, diagnosis,
and intervention.

STAGES IN GRIEVING A LOSS
(BEHAVIORS AND INFLUENCING FACTORS)

Behaviors of a client who is experiencing loss can be categorized into
stages: (1) apprehending the loss; (2) attempting to deal with loss; and (3) final
restitution and resolution of the loss (Engel, 1964). Also included in this section
is the topic of unsuccessful or unresolved grief.

Apprehending the Loss

This is the stage of *shock and disbelief;* the reality of the situation cannot
be accepted. It is temporary anesthesia that serves the useful purpose of not having to face the total grim reality all at once (Westberg, 1962, p. 13).

Behaviors usually seen are either those of somatic or psychological distress.
These include transient loss of appetite, inability to sleep, partial disinterest in
one's self and environment, tightness in throat, empty feeling in abdomen, loss
of strength, and inability to concentrate or pursue a task.

Another behavior may be a refusal to accept or comprehend the perceived
data. This is the stage of *denial* and is a normal part of the process. As the client
feels stunned, numbed or shocked (by an unfavorable diagnosis or a perception
of being "different"), he blocks the incoming data from the sense organs and
does not permit any thoughts or feelings that acknowledge the reality of the loss.

One client carries on normal activities in an automatic way as if nothing happened. Another may sit motionless, dazed, and unable to move. The individual
may seem out of contact with reality and it may be difficult to gain his attention. There is a sense of unreality and emotional distance from people.

With the occurrence of flashes of despair and anguish, and with time, the reality of loss penetrates into consciousness (Engel, 1964, p. 95). Sometimes the
initial response is overtly an intellectual acceptance of the reality of the loss.
This may include the making of appropriate arrangements for job changes, alterations in the home situation, or financial plans.

Influencing the shock of loss is the fact that the client will not usually permit
access to consciousness of the full impact of the loss at this time. The anxiety of
this realization is too great. He must at least partially deny in order to cope with
the trauma to himself. The loss is probably recognized but its painful character
is denied or at least muted.

So even though activities that take place at this time may seem inappropriate to the nurse, they serve the client by aiding in this danial of affect. In general, the distinctiveness of this initial phase are the attempts to protect oneself against the effects of the overwhelming stress by raising the threshold against its recognition or against the painful feeling being evoked.

Denial is the most prominent psychological mechanism operating at such times, although such responses are more usual when loss is sudden and unexpected. Denial also occurs when the loss is anticipated although there is more opportunity to work through the initial awareness of the fact of loss, and the shock phase is less prominent or completely absent.

Duration of the first stages varies with each client, but usually lasts a few minutes, hours, or even several days.

Factors influencing grief and mourning include the person's perception of the nature of the threat, its meaning in terms of past experiences, his coping abilities, the responses from significant others, and the help available to him and the family in undergoing the change. Cultural norms are important determinants of behavior. Perceptual capacities affect the experience of loss, as do the losses experienced in the past. Perhaps most important of all is the significance of the valued object to the client — what is its meaning and how intense is this feeling?

Attempting to Deal with Loss

Normally, within a short time, the reality of loss and especially its meaning to the individual begins to penetrate consciousness more and more in the form of acute and increasing awareness of pain and anguish of loss and feelings of something missing or gone.

Many of the behaviors observed in this stage are those of affect and experienced or voiced as acute sadness. Added to these are combinations of feelings of anxiety, helplessness, and hopelessness. The environment seems frustrating and empty. The client is usually unable to relate these to loss of self. Present also is anger particularly toward persons or circumstances held to be responsible for the loss (doctors, nurses, hospital personnel). Anger is also directed toward self; he feels responsible and guilty and that he was the cause of the altered body and image, for example.

Crying is not infrequent, as the client portrays a great deal of anguish and despair. Cultural differences give dictates here: some demand intense show of feelings; others demand no demonstration. In our culture, the wish and need to cry is strong; crying seems to fulfill an important homeostatic function in the work of mourning.

Crying involves both an acknowledgement of loss and a regression to a more helpless and childlike status. Therefore, crying is precise communication, as the client is the recipient of certain kinds of support and still feels self-respect and worthiness. Some clients wish to cry, even feel that they should, yet are unable to cry. This must be distinguished from not crying at all, which may be simply because the loss is not seriously missed. Simply not crying is usually indicative of ambivalence and guilt and shame (Engel, 1964, p. 95).

Other behaviors are feelings and expressions of hopelessness, with accompanying withdrawal and detachment. Some clients are apathetic toward the event related to loss.

Factors influencing this stage may be the same as those of the first stage, especially the time since the loss and the presence of significant others.

Final Restitution and Resolution of the Loss

When loss involves death, the accompanying rites and rituals (for example, the funeral) that initiate the recovery processes demand and give support to the person who is mourning. But even when the loss is other than death, this mutual support is still needed. Many of the behaviors in this stage are associated with rites and rituals that lend this support. Also to be considered is the fact that in our society bereavement is considered "normal" for a period of up to one year. How the client thinks others expect he can and should react will affect his behavior.

With any loss, the client needs to look at reality of the loss to know that it is actual. He may look in the mirror, look at the wound, or see removed parts. Without this, the client is unable to recover. The main work of grief and mourning goes on internally as the reality is acknowledged and accepted. The individual must cope with the painful absence of the lost object, which is felt as a defect in his sense of intactness and wholeness. Resolution involves a number of steps, which proceed haltingly and interruptedly (Engel, p. 95).

First, the client attempts to deal with painful awareness of object loss. This awareness could be a defect of physical self. He may not be fully able to accept a new object, such as a prosthesis or a new opening for elimination, although he may passively and transiently accept treatments and explanations.

The client now indicates more awareness of his own body and experiences various bodily sensations or pains. This is in contrast to the earlier period when he may have been quite numb even to a great physical handicap.

The client's thoughts are exclusively preoccupied with the lost object. The emphasis is on his personal experience with loss and, later, with the object or part lost.

It is necessary for the client repeatedly to bring this up, talk it over, and relate memories of abilities lost. The processes may go on painfully and slowly. Sometimes there is haunting preoccupation with guilty feelings, which led, perhaps, to surgical intervention and the loss.

This preoccupation usually leads to idealization of the lost object, and any negative feelings previously held about it are repressed. Idealization eventually leads to detachment from the lost object because the object slowly becomes an intellectual memory. After many months, the individual becomes increasingly less preoccupied with the lost object and is able to tolerate more ambivalent memories of it. As the dependence and ties to the lost object loosen, there is more and more wish to explore and talk about the "new body" or the new social relationship. Now the client is ready to explore prosthetics, crutches, walkers, new clothing, or different makeup. Interest in a new extension now begins.

Toward the end of this stage, the client can begin to relinquish the pain and the loss. He relaxes and perhaps even jokes about it. The client begins to look outside of himself, to relationships with others and to acceptance of an altered state. The final resolution of loss is signified by the person's ability to again allow himself enjoyment and pleasure. At this point, the individual is able to remember the lost object or relationship realistically and comfortably.

NURSING INTERVENTIONS IN LOSS

When dealing with a client who is experiencing loss, the nurse's prime source of therapeutic usefulness is understanding. She understands that loss brings about certain behaviors and reactions; she understands the varieties of loss and considers the myriad of influencing factors. She sees grief and mourning as healthy, natural responses to loss (grief is a natural part of the human experience, coming almost daily in at least minor situations). She knows that the process is fluid, brings on ambivalent feelings, and that it cannot be rushed or put on a time schedule.

Her explicit role is that of helping the client strengthen his coping mechanisms or providing measures of support until the client is able to use his own resources in the process of adaptation. During the initial stage of shock and disbelief, the nurse may need to make some decisions for the client if she assesses that his coping mechanisms are maladaptive. Her goal, however, is to work toward gradual client responsibility in making realistic decisions.

Of paramount importance is the fact that the nurse must have worked through her own feelings of loss before she can be of any help to another person. Whether or not she herself has experienced loss, she must have thought through her perceptions and her own usual ways of coping with grief and mourning. She will have assessed her behaviors in confronting threats of this kind. To use oneself therapeutically, or helpfully, requires that one's own feelings be worked through before one can give enough of self to be of support to another. Opportunities should be available to both students and staff nurses periodically to discuss these behaviors and reactions with peers and experts. This must be done in an atmosphere of mutual trust and in the absence of any threats to personal responses.

Time is of essence in dealing with loss. The nurse will realize that it takes time for a loss to penetrate, time for full realization to take place. She considers stimuli such as age, significance of the lost object, culture, and severity and duration of the loss. She knows that loss alters reality states to varying degrees and will use this knowledge in planning interventions.

Intervention may consist of mere presence with the client, time when feelings, anger, frustration, and fears are expressed and accepted. The client needs assurance that mourning is a natural, healthy process, and the nurse should never attempt to inhibit or stop stages in the process. For example, the client who cries may express feelings of embarrassment and shame for doing so. Here the nurse makes it clear to the client that this is normal and to be expected, and she will accept him during the crying. Provision of privacy and an atmosphere of nurse availability is crucial. The nurse may ask the client if he wishes others to be called — minister, priest, family member, doctor, or friend. She, however, is the main source of support and should not relinquish this role unless she cannot cope with the situation or finds that she does not know how to handle the information being expressed. Her role in manipulation of the stimuli and creating a nonthreatening environment is foremost.

Intervention may also consist of helping the client to achieve control of a body function that was lost or altered. An example is the client with a new colostomy.[1] As readiness occurs, the nurse assists the client, by small steps, to learn about the new condition, to accept it, and incorporate it into daily activities.

As the client passes through the first stages, the nurse may begin searching for realistic outlooks and alternatives with the patient. Her interviewing techniques include reflection of questions and statements, focusing on strengthening the client's own problem-solving skills. The client makes the decisions; the nurse provides clues and helps in searching out the many possibilities. She relates to the client that the work of mourning a loss is difficult and painful. She may assist in setting realistic goals for the hours and days ahead. All the while she must continually assess and reassess the client's responses for readiness to go on to the next steps.

If nursing care plans are to reflect day-to-day progress, the nurse must revise and note all progress and regression, should it occur. Her charts and reports to other personnel must be up-to-date and pertinent. Continuity of care through thorough communications is vital if the patient is to receive the strong support he or she needs at this time. Family members and significant others are considered and included in the plan of care.

---

[1] See basic text on medical surgical nursing for explanation of this condition.

UNSUCCESSFUL OR UNRESOLVED GRIEF

Unresolved grief may take a number of forms. Usually behaviors associated with one or more of the stages are either absent or excessively prolonged. When the loss is completely denied, there is exaggeration and prolongation of what is normally felt. Refusal to acknowledge constitutes a psychotic response, which largely rejects reality. Some clients completely withdraw or joke and laugh about the situation. Others appear aloof and act as though nothing unusual has happened.

If there is denial of the affect of loss, the loss is acknowledged but the significance is denied, intellectually or effectively. The client may state that the loss doesn't affect him, that it represented no real loss, that he did not (or could not) feel anything. The client may, however, acknowledge that he *should* have felt sad. In this case, the work of mourning cannot take place or it takes place incompletely. A psychotic depression, manic reaction, or other illness may follow months after the loss.

Sometimes clients use vicarious objects to minimize the effect of the loss. The client projects concern on others, especially the family, and relates that a significant other "feels the loss more." When the vicarious object disappoints or leaves the person, depressive responses usually result.

Prolonged unresolved grief can never be completely dissipated by some clients. There is a deep sense of loss and a clinging dependence on the lost object. This person remains in a prolonged, and maybe even a permanent, state of unresolved grief. He continues to miss the lost part, cries at memories of past prowess, and continues to cry when there is any mention of the missing part, even though it has been years since the initial loss. He expresses feelings of sadness, helplessness, and hopelessness, and may even wear attire that was appropriate to the former state but is not appropriate now.

Even though the nurse continues to assess and give support to clients who are exhibiting prolonged grief, this is a complex adaptation problem and she will obtain consultation and assistance from colleagues. Treatment of this client will require intense, sometimes prolonged, therapy.

SUMMARY

In assessing the self-concept of her client, the nurse will consider loss as an important problem of the physical self. She will be alert to recognize the usual behaviors manifested with the problem, and she will use appropriate interventions to assist the patient in resolving the problem of loss. Finally, she will be able to diagnose problems of unresolved grief and to obtain appropriate help for the client.

REFERENCES

Engel, George L., "Grief and Grieving," *American Journal of Nursing*, 64:93-98, September 1964.

Westberg, Granger E., *Good Grief—A Constructive Approach to the Problem of Loss.* Philadelphia: Fortress, 1962, p. 13.

ADDITIONAL READINGS

Corbeil, Madelein, "Nursing Process for a Patient with a Body Image Disturbance," in *Nursing Clinics of North America,* vol. 6, no. 1. Philadelphia: W. B. Saunders Company, 1971, pp. 155-63.

Fisher, Seymour, "Experiencing Your Body: You Are What You Feel," *Saturday Review of Science,* vol. IV, no. 28, July 8, 1972, pp. 27-32.

Gergen, Kenneth J., *The Concept of Self.* New York: Holt, Rinehart and Winston, Inc., 1971.

LaBenne, Wallace D. and Bert I. Greene, *Educational Implications of Self Concept Theory.* Pacific Palisades, Calif.: Goodyear Publishing Co., 1969.

Linn, Louis, "Some Developmental Aspects of the Body Image," *Int. J. Psychoanalysis,* 36:36-42, 1955.

Loxley, Alice Keating, "The Emotional Toll of Crippling Deformity," *American Journal of Nursing,* 72:1839-1840, October 1972.

Murray, Ruth L. E., guest ed., "Symposium on the Concept of Body Image," in the *Nursing Clinics of North America,* vol. 7, no. 4. Philadelphia: W.B. Saunders Company, 1972, pp. 593-707.

Norris, Catherine M., "The Professional Nurse and Body Image," in *Behavioral Concepts and Nursing Intervention,* Carolyn E. Carlson, coordinator. Philadelphia: J. B. Lippincott Company, 1970, pp. 39-65.

Rubin, Reva, "Body Image and Self-Esteem," *Nursing Outlook,* 16:20-23, June 1968.

Spire, Richard H., "Photographic Self-Image Confrontation," *American Journal of Nursing,* 73:1207-1210, July 1973.

Strickler, Martin and Betsy LaSor, "The Concept of Loss in Crisis Intervention," *Mental Hygiene,* 54:301-305, April 1970.

14

Problems of Moral-Ethical Self: Guilt

Nancy Zewen Perley

KEY CONCEPT DEFINED

Guilt: Painful feelings associated with the transgression of an individual's own moral-ethical code.

After studying this chapter the reader will be able to:

1. Define the concept guilt.
2. Discuss the development of the moral-ethical self and its relationship to guilt formation in childhood.
3. List and explain behavioral manifestations of guilt.
4. Identify the various influencing factors associated with guilt.
5. Differentiate between normal and neurotic guilt.
6. Identify a problem of guilt if given a case study illustrating this problem.
7. Discuss the nursing interventions appropriate to guilt (see Appendix II).

The moral-ethical self is a very personal perception of one's own rightness and wrongness, goodness and badness. "I am what I feel I should or must be." When these perceptions are transgressed, guilt feelings will result.

This chapter explores the concept of guilt as it relates to the adaptation nursing process. In addition, specific behaviors, stimuli, and nursing interventions will be discussed.

THE CONCEPT OF GUILT

Guilt may be defined as the painful feelings that result when there is a violation of moral demands against prohibitions that are valid in a given culture. However, one unmarried woman may feel quite guilty about becoming pregnant; whereas another does not, even though the same standard exists for both. Therefore, it must be surmised that in guilt feelings, the painful belief concerns the transgression of a norm which the individual personally recognizes as a norm.

In the very young child (age two to three), there are no internal restrictions against seeking pleasure and acting out impulses. To become a responsible person within society's framework, it is necessary for the child to learn how to control these impulses. The parents or parent substitutes gradually instill in the child such inhibitions, and by doing this assist him in the development of a conscience or superego, as Freud terms it.

Ideally, this superego should serve as a guide and a model as well as a mechanism for adaptive self-criticism. The child learns what he should and should not do in order to remain within society's social and legal codes. Examples of adaptive parental prohibitions include the following: "Don't hit your sister; you are hurting her," or "Don't run across the street; you might be hit by a car." Since the child wishes to receive affection and security from parents and fears punishment, he usually will repress the impulses and conform to their standards. Thus, the parents are endowed with tremendous control over the child during this early period.

Within some families, excessive and/or unreasonable prohibitions are hurled at the child. These prohibitions are almost always accompanied by threats of physical punishment, disgrace and shame, or withdrawal of affection. Examples are: "I'm not going to love you anymore if you continue to walk through the house with your muddy feet!" or "Johnny is a bad, bad boy. He did not eat everything on his plate!" Fearing these threats, the child will attempt to satisfy the excessive unreasonable demands of the parents by eventually conforming to their standards. Due to the nature of these demands, however, the young child will harbor hostility and resentment, which may result in irrational guilt, depression, and even suicide attempts in later life.

In the older child and the adult, the superego resumes the role of the parent and most likely will impose a sense of guilt when a transgression occurs. Although almost everyone will experience some sense of guilt in later life, the degree, frequency, and rationality of it will depend upon how the individual was "programmed" in early childhood.

The nurse has an important role in assisting the client to cope with a disruption of the moral-ethical self. By implementing the steps of the adaptation nursing process, the nurse hopefully can facilitate a realistic alteration of the maladaptive behaviors and a reduction of the internal pain associated with guilt feelings.

BEHAVIORAL MANIFESTATION OF GUILT

As mentioned previously, a feeling of guilt is an expression of the painful belief that a transgression of one's moral-ethical code has been committed. Comparable to anxiety, this expression may occur in a multitude of behavioral manifestations. Since each individual is unique, he has a special way of communicating guilt feelings. These may be overt ("I really feel guilty about putting my father in an old-age home") or covert ("Leave me alone. Why do you always want to bother me?").

In the assessment process, it is necessary for the nurse to be aware of many of the possible responses to guilt in order to assist the client in adaptation. Since many of the responses are covert, careful assessment and validation are essential so that misdiagnoses are avoided. Following is a partial, categorical list of possible behavioral manifestations that have been associated with the diagnosis of guilt.

1. *Physical self*
   a. Less erect carriage and/or less resilient step.
   b. Decreased gastric functioning.
   c. Intestinal sensations possibly resulting in ulcerative colitis.
   d. Bronchial asthma.
   e. Stammering.
   f. Blushing.
   g. Insomnia.
   h. Symptoms associated with anxiety (see Chapter 15).
2. *Personal self*
   a. Expressions of guilt.
   b. Statements of apology and the wish to make amends.
   c. Crying.
   d. Rationalization.
   e. Depression.
   f. Sexual dysfunctions such as impotence, retarded ejaculation, orgastic dysfunction, and denial of sexual pleasure.
   g. Avoidance behaviors—the individual seeks to avoid acknowledging the guilt feelings by physical or mental withdrawal.
   h. Compulsive handwashing—this neurotic behavior is well illustrated in the story of Macbeth, in which Lady Macbeth tries to rid herself of guilt by continuously "washing it away."

i. Masochistic behaviors—the individual may be attempting to "atone" for guilt by inflicting self-punishment. This person seems to invite adverse happenings (mistreatment by peers and family, accidents, illness, loss of money) and may complain that "Everything always happens to me!"

j. Self-recriminating behaviors—there is a tendency for the individual to blame himself for any adverse happenings. The following behaviors result: hurting other people's feelings; being mean, dishonest, and stingy; blaming self for illness ("If only I had gone to the doctor sooner, I wouldn't be so sick now."); pondering endlessly whether or not the "right" thing was said or done in a given situation; being lazy, weak, and unpunctual; degrading oneself ("I am worthless; I just can't do anything right.").

k. Hypersensitivity—if the person feels that his motives are being questioned or criticized or self-recriminating statements are being taken at face value, he will become defensive and extremely angry. In addition, he may throw things, yell, and shout reproaches and accusations to the "attacker."

This list of behaviors shows possible responses that a client who is experiencing guilt may exhibit. Although the list is by no means exhaustive, the nurse should watch for these behaviors when assessing guilt in the client.

FACTORS INFLUENCING GUILT

After gathering data which indicates that the client is experiencing behavioral manifestations of guilt, the nurse needs to assess the stimuli or influencing factors for these behaviors. Then, depending upon the individual situation, the data are classified as focal, contextual, and residual.

As mentioned, almost all individuals, at some time in their lives, experience some type of guilt feelings. In an individual with a generally adaptive self-concept, these transgressions usually occur when some tremendous pressure forces him to violate his prescribed moral-ethical code. This is illustrated in the following examples:

Example #1 A college student was ill two weeks before his final exam and was not able to prepare for it adequately. Because he was afraid that he would fail the exam, he prepared an information sheet to keep underneath his shirt sleeve, even though this was a definite transgression of his moral-ethical code. Although the sheet was not discovered during the exam, the student suffered considerable feelings of guilt for using it.

Example #2 An elderly lady had been generally independent all of her life and was very proud of her independence. Following a stroke, she has hospitalized for an extended period of time and was fed, bathed, and dressed, thus removing most of her independent functions. Because dependence was a transgression for her, guilt feelings ensued.

Example #3 A mother gives birth to an infant with multiple, severe anomalies. Since this child will require almost constant care for the rest of its life, the health team advises the parents to place the infant in an institution. Although the mother realizes that she has other children at home and she cannot possibly care for her infant in the manner necessary, she feels overwhelming guilt in accepting the health team's advice.

Several points need to be considered when assessing the above examples.

Example #1 In this example, a basic ethical code—"Thou shalt not cheat"—is violated. In the individual with a basically adaptive self-concept, there is a serious wish to make amends and refrain from committing the prohibitive behavior in the future. This is contrasted with the disturbed individual who continually commits the transgression in order to obtain some neurotic benefits from the painful guilt feelings.

Example #2 This example illustrates guilt which results from a transgression that is forced upon the individual. This exemplifies the necessity for the nurse to assess carefully the client's moral-ethical self in order to modify, reduce, or eliminate the stimuli associated with forced transgressions.

Example #3 In this case, the transgression that the mother feels she is committing is the abandonment of her child. However, if she does not consent to place the child in an institution, the resulting disruptions may cause an intolerable situation, leading to a breakdown in the family unit. Other examples of this may include the following: an unwed mother decides to place her infant for adoption; a middle-aged couple mutually consent to a divorce; an elderly, disoriented parent is placed in an old-age home rather than living with his children.

In analyzing the stimuli associated with guilt feelings, the topic or neurotic guilt should be reviewed. Although the behavioral manifestations may be suggestive of guilt feelings, the stimuli for such behaviors may not be actual remorse. Due to excessive and unreasonable prohibitions that are inflicted on the young child, he enters adulthood with an extremely hypercritical, possibly hypermoral, appraisal of himself. Since the expectations that the child holds of himself exceed reality, the individual must constantly maintain a facade of perfection, which results in numerous behavioral manifestations. Several of these behaviors, such as masochism, self-recriminations, and hypersensitivity, were discussed in the previous section. A "perfectionist" person is deeply afraid of anyone recognizing his facade. This results in an attempt to anticipate all reproaches and to prevent others from making them.

Another stimulus in neurotic guilt occurs when there is an irrational belief that a transgression has been committed. In many cases, this type of guilt is associated with an unconscious hostile wish that is suddenly but accidentally realized. The following examples illustrate this point:

Example #1   For many years, an adult male harbors resentment against his overprotective father. He continually wishes that his father would leave him alone and "get out of his life." Suddenly, the father dies from a heart attack. As a result, the son suffers considerable guilt, although he does not have conscious knowledge of the source of his painful feelings.

Example #2   An eight-year-old girl deeply resents the attention her infant sister is receiving, and unconsciously wishes that the baby would leave home and never return. When the infant is rushed to the hospital with a severe case of pneumonia, the young girl experiences great pain from guilt feelings.

In both of the above examples, there is no actual transgression of a moral-ethical code. The son did not cause the death of his father; nor did the young girl induce her sister's pneumonia. However, in each case, an unconscious wish was realized and as a result it appears to the individual that a transgression was committed.

In the assessment process, it is important to note that neurotic guilt should be placed on a continuum. At one end, the individual occasionally experiences a minor degree of this type of guilt, which results in some behavioral manifestations with a minimal amount of discomfort. For example, an efficient nurse feels that she just "didn't do enough" in a cardiac arrest case. On the other end of the continuum is the client who is wracked with such self-criticism and irrational guilt that he is almost at the point of being dysfunctional.

Another point to consider in the assessment of the influencing factors of guilt is that the client may be so ashamed that he may be unwilling to discuss the guilt. Since many of the stimuli of the client's guilt feelings are known only to him, it is important for the nurse to establish an environment that is conducive to the discussion of these feelings. This is accomplished by conveying an atmosphere of empathy, trust, and concern. However, a firm refusal to discuss the painful guilt at the present time must be respected by the nurse or it will further increase the client's frustration, depression, and anxiety.

NURSING INTERVENTIONS IN GUILT

Once the assessment data has been collected and the diagnosis of guilt has been established, the nurse is prepared to promote client adaptation by manipulating the influencing factors. Client goals and nursing interventions will be designed to remove or alter the offending stimuli. The establishment of a beneficial nurse-client relationship so that effective nursing intervention can occur has already been discussed in the previous section.

For client adaptation to occur, the client first needs to recognize that the internal discomfort and other behavioral manifestations that he is experiencing are due to feelings of guilt. After the client can freely discuss these feelings, the next step is for him to explore with the nurse the nature of the committed transgression. During this discussion, the client may discover that there are some irrational aspects to the believed transgression and thus gain new insight into his behavior. The client may also express a realistic desire to refrain from committing the prohibitive behavior in the future. If the guilt resulted from a forced choice decision (as in the case of the mother who agrees to institutionalize her child), the client may be able to appraise the situation openly and learn to accept the decision that was made. This discussion of guilt feelings may engender much internal discomfort, thus creating the necessity for the nurse to provide an abundance of support, encouragement, and reassurance.

If the nurse has assessed the client's guilt to be excessive and completely irrational, a psychiatric referral may be considered. One psychiatric approach would be to assist the client in recognizing that he demands the impossible of himself. Over a period of time, the client hopefully will be able to realize that there is a disparity between his facade of perfection and his actual behavior. With this realization, he will be more capable of reversing the maladaptive behavior.

SUMMARY

In this chapter, guilt has been regarded as a transgression of an individual's own moral-ethical code. By applying the adaptation nursing process, the nurse can assess guilt feelings in the client more readily and promote adaptation by the use of effective intervention.

READINGS

Aspects of Anxiety. Philadelphia: J. B. Lippincott Company, 1965, p. 74.

Carlson, Carolyn E., *Behavioral Concepts and Nursing Intervention.* Philadelphia: J. B. Lippincott Company, 1970, p. 71.

Goldman, Douglas and George A. Ulett, *Practical Psychiatry for the Internist.* St. Louis: C. V. Mosby Co., 1968, p. 18.

Horney, Karen, *New Ways in Psychoanalysis.* New York: W. W. Norton and Company, Inc., 1939, pp. 232–45.

Kaplan, Helen Singer, *The New Sex Therapy.* New York: Brunner/Mazel, Publishers, 1974, pp. 140, 260, 327, 384.

Lidz, Theodore, *The Person.* New York: Basic Books, Inc., 1968, p. 160.

Masters, William H. and Virginia E. Johnson, *Human Sexual Inadequacy.* Boston: Little, Brown and Company, 1970, p. 75.

Petrillo, Madeline and Sirgay Sanger. *Emotional Aspects of Hospitalized Children.* Philadelphia: J. B. Lippincott Company, 1972, p. 206.

Schwartz, Lawrence H. and Jane Linker Schwartz, *The Psychodynamics of Patient Care.* Englewood Cliffs, N. J.: Prentice-Hall, Inc., 1972, pp. 51, 74, 141.

Wu, Ruth, *Behavior and Illness.* Englewood Cliffs, N. J.: Prentice-Hall, Inc., 1973, pp. 164–66.

15

Problems in Self-Consistency: Anxiety

Nancy Zewen Perley

KEY CONCEPTS DEFINED

Anxiety: A painful uneasiness of mind due to an impending or anticipated threat.

Real Threat: Present-oriented danger with the threat due to a definite, identifiable object or event.

Imagined Threat: Future-oriented threat not specifically recognized or identified.

Primary Diagnosis: Diagnosis in which behaviors and stimuli are chiefly related to a problem within the given mode, with the overall goal being the reestablishment of the integrity related to the mode.

Secondary Diagnosis: Diagnosis in which presenting behaviors have certain components, but the major disruption lies within one of the other modes.

After studying this chapter the reader will be able to:

1. Define the key concepts of this chapter.
2. List and explain both internal and external behaviors associated with anxiety.
3. Describe the three underlying states of mind associated with an anxious state (isolation, insecurity, helplessness), and give an example of each.
4. Differentiate between real threat and imagined threat.
5. Differentiate between a primary diagnosis of anxiety and a secondary one.
6. Discuss nursing interventions appropriate to anxiety using the three-step approach, and give practical examples (see Appendix II).

Self-consistency is the continuity of self over time. "I am who I am because there is a relationship between the self that is me today and the self that is me tomorrow." Anything that threatens this constancy of self causes anxiety in a person. Thus anxiety is discussed here as the major problem in self-consistency.

Anxiety is a response that involves the total person. In this chapter, then, the assessment of anxiety is related to manifestations in all the adaptive modes. Factors influencing anxiety are reviewed. Anxiety is discussed both as a primary and secondary diagnosis. Finally, nursing goals and interventions for anxiety are pointed out.

THE CONCEPT OF ANXIETY

Anxiety is an emotion that pervades all peoples irrespective of sex, age, or socioeconomic background. Perhaps due to its complexities, this term has many definitions, one of the most comprehensive being found in Webster's dictionary. It states that anxiety is "a painful uneasiness of mind respecting an impending or anticipated ill; concern about some future or uncertain event; a pathological condition occurring in nervous or mental disease . . . synonyms: concern. fear, foreboding, misgiving, worry, solicitude, uneasiness, disquietude . . ." This very powerful emotion is also an extremely personal one because its manifestations are as complex and particular as each individual. For instance, one person may exhibit anxious behaviors by showing signs of restlessness, overeating, and demanding attention; another may laugh and joke whenever discussing his impending operation.

Because anxious behavior is so complex, individualistic, and diverse, it often mimics other diagnoses and may therefore be mistreated. With careful validation, the nurse can implement the steps of the nursing process to facilitate successful adaptation for an anxious client, and thus re-establish his sense of self-consistency. In addition, it is equally important that the nurse be aware of anxiety responses in herself and her colleagues because, for example, an angry, hostile reaction to a complaining, demanding client will almost certainly cloud effective intervention. The nurse must face the anxiety and threat to self-consistency from which her behavior stems.

BEHAVIORAL MANIFESTATIONS OF ANXIETY

Internal Responses   As we know, anxious behavior is a response to a threat to self-consistency. However, before the reaction to the provoking stimulus becomes apparent externally, the autonomic nervous system is activated, resulting in a number of physiological responses. The overall effect of this activation is to prepare the body to respond to the emergency situation by either "fight or flight." The functioning of various bodily systems is altered to allow the individual to react to the perceived threat with greater strength and heightened mental activity. The different events that occur in the body during a "fight or flight" response may be enumerated as follows:

1. The brain perceives the threat and transmits the message down the sympathetic branch of the autonomic nervous system to the adrenal medulla.
2. Increased amounts of epinephrine are released from the adrenal medulla, resulting in deepened respiration, increased heart rate, increased arterial blood pressure, and increased blood glucose levels due to accelerated glycogenolysis and inhibition of insulin release from the pancreas.
3. The hypothalamus exerts its influence by activating the pituitary gland, which results in ACTH secretion, release of growth hormone, and decreased release of gonadotropins.
4. The increased ACTH secretion from the pituitary gland stimulates the adrenal cortices to produce cortisol, which in turn induces production of glucose.
5. Blood is shunted away from the systems of lesser importance (for example, digestive) to the areas of greater importance (brain and skeletal muscles).
6. The spleen contracts, discharging its supply of red blood cells.
7. In addition to the physiological changes previously mentioned, the following occur: the skin blanches and becomes cool to touch, the mouth becomes dry, the hands and skin become clammy due to increased perspiration, there is an increased inclination to eliminate urine and excrete feces, the pupils dilate, the appetite is diminished, and thought processes are enhanced resulting in increased ability to observe, focus attention, and learn.

Two points should be stressed when discussing the physiological changes of a reaction to a threatening situation. The first point is that the brain cannot adequately distinguish between a physical threat or a psychological one. Therefore, whether the individual is faced with an oncoming automobile or with a verbal attack from someone, the bodily responses are the same. Second, it is also important to note that although frequent, inappropriate, and severe anxiety responses serve to hinder the individual from adapting to his environment, all anxiety responses are not detrimental. As long as the person is not impeded from moving ahead to constructive action, the tense, jittery, uneasy feelings that one experiences during an anxiety reaction are actually normal and frequently useful responses of the body. As a result of these responses, the individual is given greater fortitude and alertness, which heighten the ability to react to the threat that he faces, and thus re-establishes the sense of self-consistency.

External Responses   Eventually, the individual exhibits some type of behavior as he attempts to cope with the threat that is faced. Because so many of the bodily systems participate in an anxiety reaction, the nurse should expect in many cases to observe a syndrome of behaviors rather than just one. The behaviors that a client might demonstrate may take one of two courses. First, the client may react to the threat by actually facing up to it either adaptively or maladaptively. On the other hand, he may respond by withdrawing from the disturbing situation, by physically or mentally removing himself.

These two courses represent the "fight or flight" response. In addition, the nurse should consider that this syndrome may include behavior patterns from all four modes, thus making it imperative for her to exercise very careful validation with the client to avoid misdiagnoses. Following is a partial, categorical list of possible behavioral reactions that have been associated with anxiety.

Physiological Mode

1. *Rest and Exercise*
   a. Insomnia. The client may express to the nurse an inability to fall asleep, stay asleep, or have a peaceful, undisturbed night's rest. He may also speak of being plagued by nightmares or a vague sense of uneasiness during the night.
   b. Somnolence. Contrary to the above, the client may sleep or appear to be asleep most of the day and evening as well as during the night. Furthermore, he may refuse care and treatments with statements such as "Please leave me alone and let me sleep" or "I just can't seem to get enough sleep."
   c. Hyperactivity. The client may exhibit signs of extreme restlessness and constant movement. He may continuously fidget, walk around the room furiously, or state an inability to sit still.
   d. Fatigue. The client may constantly complain of extreme fatigue. Whether it be in the hospital, clinic, doctor's office, or the client's home, the nurse may hear the client say "I don't know what the matter is—I'm just tired all of the time" or "I just can't seem to get myself out of bed in the morning."

2. *Elimination*
   a. Polyuria. A frequent desire to urinate may be a behavioral response to an anxiety-producing situation. The client may even state "I get so nervous—it seems that I'm always running to the bathroom even when there's nothing really there!"
   b. Diarrhea. Due to increased peristalsis as a physiological response to a threatening state, the client may be having frequent loose stools. They may be explosive in nature and accompanied by abdominal cramping.
   c. Constipation. The client's anxiety state may precipitate poor bowel habits, which could result in constipation.
   d. Flatus and eructation. Swallowing air in an anxiety reaction often produces gas, which is eliminated by belching and expelling flatus.

3. *Circulation*
   a. Pale appearance. This "white as a sheet" appearance is often associated with anxiety states as the blood is shunted away from the less important superficial arteries.
   b. Tachycardia. Due to the increased amounts of epinephrine being released in threatening situations, the nurse may commonly encounter a pulse rate of 100 or above in anxious individuals.
   c. Palpitations. The nurse may often hear statements from anxious clients or colleagues such as the following: "I get so nervous every time I try to give myself a shot that I can feel my heart pound and pound" or "I get such a funny feeling every time that I have to care for that crotchety old man in 312—it feels that my heart is going to burst out of my chest!"
   d. Heartburn. Excessive acid production in the stomach during a tension state may account for the complaint of heartburn and may even be confused with chest pain.
   e. Premature Ventricular Contractions (P.V.C.s). This cardiac rhythm aberration has often been shown to be associated with anxiety reactions.
   f. Cardiac neurosis. In severe anxiety states, the client may experience intense chest pain, which might lead the practitioner to suspect angina pectoris or a myocardial infarction. However, in these cases, the electrocardiogram would prove to be negative, with the chest pain probably due to muscle spasm.

4. *Oxygen*
   a. Bronchial asthma. There is considerable evidence that tension plays a part in inducing bronchial asthma attacks.
   b. Hyperventilation syndrome and other ventilation difficulties. Anxiety may have its effect on respiration in the following ways: breath holding, dyspnea ("I just can't seem to get enough air in"), deep sighing,

and hyperventilation with a possible consequence of respiratory alkalosis.

5. *Fluid and Electrolytes*

   a. Pseudo-Cushing's disease. As mentioned previously, cortisol is secreted from the adrenal cortices in increased amounts during an anxiety reaction. This phenomena accounts for a pseudo-Cushing's disease, which is accompanied by sodium retention and potassium loss.

   b. Psychogenic polydipsia. Extreme thirst has been noted during anxiety responses.

6. *Nutrition*

   a. Polyphagia (overeating). Many obese or borderline normal weight individuals crave the comfort of food during depressions that accompany tension. The nurse may often encounter a client who has faithfully followed a diet until plagued by emotional or physical trauma or by disgust with his body image. At that time, the client may cast away plans for the diet and plunge into the security that food offers.

   b. Anorexia nervosa. Contrary to the above, some individuals are repelled by the thought of food during anxiety responses and may state to the nurse "Please take this awful food away—I just can't eat a thing."

   c. Cravings. Tension and stress have been known to be contributory factors to the development of excessive cravings, such as for food, alcohol, drugs, and smoking.

   d. Nausea and vomiting. During tension states, many individuals experience varying degrees of nausea even to the point of vomiting. One theorist suggests that this may be due to the body trying to rid itself of a psychologically "poisonous" thought as it would under actual physical conditions. This is consistent with the common statement "I get sick just thinking that horrible thought!"

   e. Gastrointestinal disease conditions. Conditions such as ulcerative colitis and peptic ulcers have been known to have anxiety as a possible precipitating factor.

7. *Regulatory*

   a. *Senses*

      (1) Pain. Whether the pain be a headache, abdominal cramping, or generalized aches and pains, anxiety has been known to initiate, sustain, or increase the intensity of the painful experience.

   b. *Endocrine*

      (2) Amenorrhea. The female individual may experience amenorrhea as a resultant effect of an anxiety reaction. This is probably due to the decreased release of gonadotropins during a stress response.

      (2) Pseudocyesis. This is a phenomenon in which the woman falsely believes and insists that she is pregnant. It has been hypothesized

to be the result of severe anxiety during the oral phase of childhood development.

   c. *Neurological*
     (1) Stuttering, tics, and muscle twitching. These neurological mani-
festations have been noted to be contributory effects of an
anxiety reaction.
     (2) Conversion reactions. Unexplained blindness, paralysis, aphonia,
and others have been associated with severe anxiety responses.

8. *Skin Integrity*
   a. Cold, clammy skin. This stress response has been noted to be due to
blood being shunted away from superficial vessels. An increase in perspiration may be observed on the forehead, periphery, underarms, and
chest.
   b. Rashes and acne. These disruptions in skin integrity have been associated with anxiety. The mechanism involved is not clearly understood.
   c. Alopeccia. This condition—loss of hair on the body—has been known
to occur during situations of great stress.

Self-Concept Mode

1. *Physical Self*
   a. *Body Image*
     (1) Disgust with body. An individual under stress may express dis-
gust with his physical appearance or bodily functions. Statements
of this nature would include "I feel so awful today and what's
worse I can't do a thing with my hair or face!" or "I have enough
trouble and now I have to worry about my bowels functioning
properly!"
     (2) Self-mutilation. An extremely anxious and depressed person may
sometimes angrily try to cope with anxiety by mutilating his
body and may exhibit one or a combination of burns, bruises,
cuts, or stab wounds.
   b. *Senses*
     (1) Sexual difficulties. A lack or lessened ability to perform or
achieve pleasure in the sexual realm is many times related to
anxiety. It has been theorized that these problems may be due
to the past conditioning of the individual in which fear and anxiety constrict him or her from attaining full performance and/or
pleasure. Some of these problems are impotence and premature
ejaculation (male), and frigidity and dysparunia (female).

2. *Personal Self*
   a. Anger. Being a derivative of anxiety, anger serves as a coping mechanism in which the individual tries to "fight" the stress that he faces.
He may do this in a direct manner ("I'm angry with you and I never
want to see you again!") or because of the fear of retaliation, may feel

forced to express anger in a more covert, indirect way ("I'm a little unhappy with what you did today."). Anger is not always maladaptive, for a mild form of it can be just the stimulus that stirs up the individual and initiates him to take constructive action.

b. Denial. In this case, the anxious person copes with the tension-producing stimulus by taking "flight." Until the level of anxiety reduces to the point that he can deal with the reality of the situation, he must physically or mentally withdraw from the trauma and perhaps even deny that it actually exists. Statements that illustrate this may be: "Please leave me alone—I don't want to talk about it" or "Cancer? I don't know what you are talking about."

c. Pseudo-cheerfulness. The individual who laughs and jokes while discussing stressful, tension-producing subjects may also be using a form of denial as a coping mechanism. In this manner, he may be attempting to avert the painful reality of the situation. A typical statement that exemplifies this coping mechanism might be: "Oh, no, I don't mind going to surgery this morning—I get to see some more pretty nurses!"

d. Intellectualism. By intellectualizing, the client tries to cope with the stress by removing the painful emotional tones from the anxiety-producing situation. For example, a client who has diabetes may talk quite knowledgeably about the pathology and clinical nature of the condition. However, when the nurse asks how he *feels* about the condition and what problems it may present for the client and for the family, he may uncomfortably try to change the subject.

e. Crying. This is an emotional response that many times accompanies an anxiety reaction. With the exception of "crying for joy," it usually signifies a state of helplessness on the part of the individual. This response can be either adaptive or maladaptive depending upon what course of action the client takes following the initial weeping. In an adaptive response, the crying behavior helps to dispel some of the frustrations associated with the stressful stimulus, and thus it permits the individual to proceed on to constructive action. In maladaptive crying, the client is "frozen" and cannot progress to solve the stress that confronts him.

f. Guilt. It is not unusual in an anxiety reaction for the client to feel that he may in some way have caused a frustrating, tension-producing situation. For example, a pregnant, unwed, teen-age girl is wringing her hands, pacing the floor, and crying. She states to the nurse, "If I hadn't done *that,* this never would have happened. It's all my fault and I don't know what to do!"

g. Depression. Depression has been defined as a feeling of intense madness, dejection, or melancholy, and is often an accompaniment of anxiety. If the client chooses to express a feeling of sadness to the nurse, a typical statement may be: "I feel so blue today—everything seems so hopeless."

Role Function Mode

1. *Role Failure*. Anxiety may precipitate, contribute to, or be a resultant effect of role failure. Statements that exemplify this are: "I give up! I'm so nervous, I just know that I'll never be a good mother" or "I've failed as a college student — I'll never be able to do anything now!"

Interdependence Mode

1. *Dependent Behaviors*. An anxious client might elicit a syndrome of anxiety-related behaviors that may be classified as dependent behaviors. These behaviors would include complaining, demanding attention, crying, being angry at others, and seeking constant reinforcement.

2. *Independent Behaviors*. Conversely, anxious behaviors in the form of independent behaviors may also be displayed by the client. These might be withdrawal, refusal to accept assistance, sullenness, and anger at oneself.

This list of behaviors shows various ways that the individual tries to cope with a threatening situation. The aim of these behaviors is to avoid, decrease, or relieve anxiety. They may help to lessen the threat temporarily so that the individual can eventually proceed to solving the problem, or they serve to constrict and hinder, thus making a constructive solution much more difficult. In assessing anxiety, then, the nurse watches for these behaviors.

FACTORS INFLUENCING ANXIETY

Behavioral manifestations of individuals experiencing anxiety have been discussed at length. But the stimulus for the behaviors was mentioned simply as a "threat." At this point of the assessment process, the nurse needs to delve more specifically into what is the actual cause of the behaviors.

To assess the influencing factors or stimuli, it is important for the nurse to understand that the threat to the self-consistency is usually associated with three underlying states of mind. These are a sense of helplessness, of isolation, or of insecurity. Many examples would illustrate these three states of mind. A few of them follow.

1. *Sense of Helplessness*
   a. A 68-year-old lady with abdominal pain submits to seemingly endless diagnostic tests which she neither understands nor feels that she personally controls.
   b. A 57-year-old man who experienced a recent stroke is unable to perform previous functions with ease, such as walking, bathing, and feeding himself.

   c. An 18-year-old girl is trying to care for a new baby for the first time with no one to help or give direction.

2. *Sense of Isolation*

   a. A 36-year-old man with a recent heart attack is confined to a coronary care unit with minimal, scheduled visits from family and friends.

   b. A 38-year-old man with diabetes feels that no one really understands what it is like to have a chronic illness.

   c. A 15-year-old girl contracts a venereal disease and feels rejected by her peers and family.

3. *Sense of Insecurity*

   a. A 32-year-old client who has had a breast removed feels that she will no longer be sexually attractive to her husband.

   b. A 28-year-old salesman who recently had surgery for a bowel obstruction is concerned that there will not be enough money to pay the hospital bills and support his wife and three children.

   c. A 42-year-old amputee is worried that he will never be able to earn a living again.

As the nurse gathers the information that is necessary to understand what is causing the anxious behaviors, she needs to classify them as to focal, contextual, or residual. Several points regarding this classification need to be stressed. First, there may be several anxiety-producing stimuli that are provoking the behaviors, not just one. For example:

> Mrs. Alice Forman, a 32-year-old client who had a breast removed, was exhibiting the following behaviors: crying; frequent requests for the bedpan; refusal to have care and treatments; hostile, angry attacks upon the nurses; and unwillingness to see her husband. After observing these behaviors and talking with Mrs. Forman, the nurse assessed these stimuli: focal—fear of loss of attractiveness; contextual—worry over inability to pay hospital bill, dread of recurrence of cancer, and suspicion that the nurses were making fun of her; and residual—expression of anger and hostility is the way she has always dealt with anxiety.

Second, an anxiety-producing stimulus or threat to the self-consistency may be only one of the causes of the behavior, with the other causes being of an entirely different nature. For instance, a client may be having sleepless nights in the hospital because she is afraid that she has an incurable disease, but this also may be due to pain, noise at the nurses' station, and an uncomfortable bed.

The third point to consider is that the nurse may not easily be able to assess the stimuli for the anxious behaviors. Occasionally, the threat is so painful that the client will have difficulty accepting that he is anxious. At this time, the nurse can make only hypotheses of the disturbing stimuli and delay more definite assessment until the client's anxiety level decreases.

OTHER FACTORS TO CONSIDER IN THE ASSESSMENT OF ANXIETY

Before proceeding to diagnosis and intervention, there are several factors that the nurse needs to consider in the assessment process. It may be most helpful for the nurse to ask herself the following questions regarding the data that she has compiled:

1. Is the stress *real* or *imagined?* Although the term "anxiety" is used collectively throughout this section, in the literature a number of differentiations are employed. For simplification, these terms may be divided into categories.
   a. *Real threat* (synonyms: fear, normal anxiety, actual threat). This term connotes a recognized, present-oriented danger with the threat being a definite identifiable object or event. Typical statements that illustrate this include: "The doctor just told me that I have cancer— I don't know what is going to happen to me now!" or "I am overdrawn at the bank and I have no insurance—how am I ever going to pay those hospital bills?"
   b. *Imagined threat* (synonyms: anxiety, neurotic anxiety, perceived threat). This term differs from the above in that the threat is future-oriented and not specifically recognized or identified. Although the individual usually feels in some way that his physiological or psychic integrity is being threatened, he has only a general, vague awareness of what is the offending stimulus. Statements to this nature are: "The doctors try to tell me there is nothing wrong with me, but I just *know* there is!" or "I'm not going to let those doctors operate on me—I'm just sure that they'll make a mistake!"
2. Is the response adaptive or maladaptive? The nurse can assess this by deciding whether or not the behavioral response leads the client to take constructive action to alleviate the threatening situation.
3. Is the response mild, moderate, or severe? The degree of severity of the anxiety does not correlate with whether it is normal or neurotic. It may be distinguished by assessing the client's ability to focus on what is actually happening to him in a given situation. For example:
   a. *Mild anxiety.* In this case, the client is able to focus on most of what is actually happening to him.
   b. *Moderate anxiety.* The client in this situation has limited ability to focus on what is actually happening.
   c. *Severe anxiety.* The degree of anxiety is so great that the client cannot focus on what is actually happening and may be presumed to be in a "panic" state.

NURSING DIAGNOSIS

After gathering and assessing as much of the data as possible, the nurse is ready to establish a diagnosis. Since behavioral manifestations of anxiety occur in all four modes, the practitioner needs to decide which of the modes is the most disrupted in order to determine whether the diagnosis of anxiety is a primary or secondary one. For instance,

1. *Primary diagnosis.* If the behaviors and stimuli are chiefly related to the problem within the self-concept with the overall goal being the re-establishment of the psychic integrity, then the most appropriate diagnosis would be "Anxiety—self-concept mode." An example would be an individual who is so insecure about himself that he feels that he will fail at whatever he attempts. This feeling persists despite encouragement and assistance from family and friends.

2. *Secondary diagnosis.* Although the presenting behaviors have anxiety components, the major distribution may lie within one of the other three modes; namely, physiological, role function, and interdependence. Since these other modes have therapeutic approaches different to that of the self-concept one, anxiety would be considered to be more suitable as a secondary diagnosis. An illustration of this in the role mastery mode would be a student nurse who is shaking considerably and almost on the verge of tears during her first day in the hospital. Her instructor recognizes this and assists in promoting adaptive behaviors by giving role cues. The diagnosis in this instance would be "Role failure with anxiety."

It is also important to consider that due to vague and incomplete data, the nurse may not be able to formulate a definite diagnosis. In this situation, she can establish a tentative diagnosis or hypothesis until new facts are introduced.

GOALS AND INTERVENTIONS

Once the behaviors and stimuli have been assessed and the nursing diagnosis has been established, the nurse is ready to develop goals for her client. These goals will decrease the intensity of the anxious behavior or alleviate it entirely. The interventions will be designed to manipulate or change the anxiety-producing stimuli.

Following is a three-step process of goals and interventions that will facilitate the promotion of adaptive behavior.

1. The client will be able to realize that he is anxious. In order to enact this goal, the nurse needs to establish an environment that is conducive to a beneficial nurse-client relationship. It is important that the client be able to sense an

atmosphere of warmth, trust, concern, and reassurance from the nurse. Of equal importance, the nurse should also examine how she is reacting to her client so that the client's anxiety does not elicit anxious behaviors of her own. It is obvious that the nurse is not exempt from her own feelings of insecurity, isolation, and helplessness. However, if she maintains a conscious awareness that her client's behavior is an expression of personal frustration and is not actually directed at her, she can better keep her own feelings of frustration under control.

The nurse enables the client to realize that he is anxious by first having the client acknowledge that behavior with her. This acknowledgement may need to be initiated by the nurse because the client may feel awkward, hesitant, or embarrassed to do so. In general, the most helpful approach may be one in which the nurse directly confronts the client with his behavior. Opening statements could be: "I've noticed that you've been pacing back and forth in your room today and refusing all meals. Is something bothering you?" or "You seem to be very angry today. Could there be something troubling you?" The level of conversation that ensues as a result of such an introductory statement often depends upon the degree of anxiety that the client is experiencing. Although direct verbalization of the behavior and underlying feelings related to it would be most preferable, the client may not be able to relate on this level at the present time. If the client's response is negative to open verbalization ("No! I'm not angry!" or "Leave me alone—I don't want to talk about it."), the nurse needs to respect this because further inducement to verbalize will only serve to increase the anxiety. However, she should indicate to her client either verbally or nonverbally her willingness to pursue the discussion at such a time that is most comfortable to the client.

2. The client will be able to gain insight into his anxiety. After the client acknowledges that he is anxious and is able to discuss the underlying feelings related to this anxiety, he needs to explore some of the causes (or stimuli) for the behavior. The nurse may be able to assist in this exploration by introducing into the discussion the stimuli she has assessed. These stimuli may be either previously validated or hypothesized. For example: "Mr. Jones, you seemed to be particularly upset when your doctor left the room this morning" or "Do you recall how disappointed you said you were when your brother did not visit you last night?" If the client can identify the source of the anxiety, he will profit through this experience by gaining greater understanding of the limitations of the threat, dispelling some of the energy associated with it, and viewing the threat in a more realistic way. If the client cannot pinpoint the offending stimulus at present, to pursue this line of discussion would only leave him feeling that the situation cannot be resolved, thus resulting in an increase in the anxiety level. However, this individual can still benefit by releasing this anxious energy more adaptively through verbalizations to the nurse.

3. The client will be able to cope with the anxiety in more constructive ways. Once the client has gained greater insight into his anxiety, he will be able to cope

with the threat in more constructive ways, thus promoting adaptive behavior. This may be accomplished by the client exploring with the nurse the following questions: "Have I overestimated this threat—is it really 'that bad'?" or "Can I remove or reduce the source of this threat from my life?" or "Have I considered all possible ways of dealing with this threat?" By carefully deliberating these questions, the client may be able either to eliminate, modify, or reduce the anxiety-provoking stimulus, thus eliciting a change in behavior.

SUMMARY

In this section, anxiety has been viewed as a natural phenomenon that is experienced by all individuals in a multitude of ways. With the application of the adaptation nursing process coupled with the human elements of sincerity, empathy, and concern, the nurse hopefully can assist her client in coping with his anxiety in the most adaptive manner.

READINGS

"Anxiety—Recognition and Intervention," *American Journal of Nursing,* vol. 64, no. 9, September 1965, pp. 135-36.

Aspects of Anxiety. Philadelphia: J. B. Lippincott Company, 1965, pp. 10-11.

Goldman, Douglas, M.D. and George A. Wete, M.D., *Practical Psychiatry for the Internist.* St. Louis: C. V. Mosby Co., 1968, p. 51.

Howells, John G., *Modern Perspectives in Psycho-Obstetrics.* New York: Brunner/Mazel Publishers, 1972, p. 64.

Kaplan, Helen Singer, *The New Sex Therapy.* New York: Brunner/Mazel Publishers, 1974, pp. 126-32.

Kodadek, Shirley, ed., *Continuing Education in Psychiatric Mental Health Nursing for Faculty in Associate Degree Programs.* Boulder: Western Institute for Higher Education, 1973, p. 13.

Leif, Harold, M.D. and Nina R. Leif, M.D., eds., *The Psychological Aspects of Medical Practice.* New York: Harper and Row, Publishers, 1963, p. 284.

McCaffery, Margo, *Nursing Management of the Patient in Pain.* Philadelphia: J. B. Lippincott Company, 1972, p. 223.

Schwartz, Lawrence H. and Jane Linker Schwartz. *The Psychodynamics of Patient Care.* Englewood Cliffs, N. J.: Prentice-Hall, Inc., 1972, p. 405.

Ujhely, Gertrud B., "When Adult Patients Cry," *Nursing Clinics of North America,* vol. 2, no. 4, December 1967, p. 726.

16

Problem in Self-Ideal and Expectancy: Powerlessness

Sister Callista Roy

KEY CONCEPTS DEFINED

Powerlessness: The perception on the part of the individual of a lack of personal or internal control over events within a given situation.

Mass Society: A model of the human community which includes the elements of low control over one's fate, heavy reliance upon specialized experts, bureaucratic authority, and loss of community ties.

Social Displacement: Being outside the social life of which one was formerly a part.

After studying this chapter the reader will be able to:

1. Define the key concepts of this chapter.
2. Differentiate between situational powerlessness and powerlessness as a life philosophy.
3. List and explain behavioral manifestations of powerlessness.

4. Describe the factors influencing powerlessness.
5. Identify a problem of powerlessness if given a case study illustrating this problem.
6. Specify nursing interventions to be used in the problem of powerlessness (see Appendix II).

The final component of the personal self is the self-ideal and expectancy. One is what one would like to be and what one expects oneself to be. To be what one intends means that one has some sense of power or control over one's being. To have a problem of self-ideal and expectancy is to feel powerless. This chapter discusses the problem of powerlessness as assessed and dealt with by adaptation nursing.

THE CONCEPT OF POWERLESSNESS

One important author in the literature on powerlessness, Melvin Seeman, describes it as one of the variants of alienation. He defines powerlessness as "the expectancy or probability held by the individual that his own behavior cannot determine the occurance of the outcomes, or reinforcements, he seeks" (1959). Seeman emphasizes the subjective element of alienation; that is, powerlessness is a perception of the person. Furthermore, there is no implication regarding an objective or subjective value placed upon power. The individual simply does not feel power and may or may not desire power. Seeman intended to limit this meaning of alienation to a statement of man's relation to the larger social order. He seems to see it as a personality trait as indicated by one of the scales he utilized to measure the degree of powerlessness. Seeman and Evans (1962) selected items to represent a general life philosophy of low personal control.

Powerlessness may also represent a situational variable, that is, it may occur only within certain circumstances. Mothers of chronically ill children were studied by means of the Seeman scale of powerlessness and a scale determining feelings of control over health and illness. There was no relationship between the two scales (Grubbs, 1968). Thus mothers of chronically ill children can show a difference between feelings of powerlessness toward life in general and toward the health situation in particular.

The view of *powerlessness* most appropriate to application in nursing practice can be summarized as follows: *the perception on the part of the individual of a lack of personal or internal control over events within a given situation.*

ASSESSMENT OF POWERLESSNESS BEHAVIORS

We begin an assessment of the problem of powerlessness by looking at client behaviors. The behavior produced by various forms of alienation has been a subject of speculation and research. The individual who has a strong belief that he can control his own destiny is likely to: (1) be more alert to those aspects of the environment that provide useful information for future behavior; (2) take steps to improve his environmental condition; (3) place greater value on skill or achievement reinforcements and be generally more concerned with his ability, particularly failures; and (4) be resistive to subtle attempts to influence him (Rotter, 1966). The person who has a low sense of control may then be expected to have opposite behaviors, such as apathy, withdrawal, resignation, fatalism, and malleability.

Seeman pointed out in several studies that powerlessness is related to knowledge. In his study of tuberculosis clients in a hospital (1962) he found that those who were high in powerlessness showed significantly poorer knowledge concerning their health than clients who were low in powerlessness. This lack of knowledge was shown both in a true-false test and in the clients' behavior on the ward, as identified by staff members. Mothers of chronically ill children who scored high in powerlessness had lower scores on knowledge of illness than mothers who scored lower in powerlessness (Grubbs, 1968). Thus another behavior a nurse may note in a situation of high powerlessness is a low knowledge of illness.

A nursing journal describes a nursing assessment of a 65-year-old woman who was hospitalized for removal of a polyp of the colon (Durand and Price, 1966). One nursing diagnosis is "feelings of powerlessness." The authors describe the facts obtained during the nursing investigation as follows: (1) the client talked of coming into the hospital feeling well and now being sick. She said she expected the polyp could be removed by a proctoscope and "now all of this" (the client's expectations regarding hospitalization and treatment have not been met); (2) the client stated, "I'm told it will take time to get well. But I don't know what they mean by time—a day, a week, a month," and "I don't know why I have to have intravenous tubes. The doctor probably knows best" (the client does not feel she can plan what is to come or what she can do), and (3) the client also stated, "All these tubes—I just want to get rid of them so I can be on my own" (the client does not understand or feel in control of her environment). Thus in observing the client's behavior, the nurse may note a pattern of statements reflecting feelings of low control.

Another article describes some observations of client reactions to their provisional existence in a tuberculosis sanitarium (Sorensen and Amis, 1967). Since these clients are to a large extent powerless to control events of their situation and to be what they want to be, their behaviors may be considered indicators of powerlessness.

The typical client feels anxious and uneasy. He is restless and sleepless in bed and wanders around endlessly. He feels frail, victimized, aimless, and powerless to determine his future. He may even feel depressed and that the hospitalization is unnecessary. His feelings of helplessness may lead him to leave the hospital against medical advice. His apathy makes him unable to see choices of existence that are available to him. He is without direction and lacks decision. Thus the following behaviors can be added to the list of behavioral manifestations of powerlessness: anxiety, restlessness, sleeplessness, wandering, aimlessness, and lack of decision-making.

In assessing the clients personal self-concept, and specifically self-ideal and expectancy, the nurse will observe for these specific behaviors related, in practice or theoretically, to powerlessness.

FACTORS INFLUENCING POWERLESSNESS

When the nurse is looking for factors influencing client behavior, she looks for the stimulus most immediately confronting the client (focal stimulus), for all other factors in the environment which also may be affecting the behavior (contextual stimuli), and the values, attitudes, traits, and other past experiences that the client brings to the situation (residual stimuli), which have some undetermined effect.

Although the focal stimulus will change according to the individual client, in general it may be assumed that the very fact of illness has an immediate effect on the development of feelings of powerlessness. Talcott Parsons (1958) has described one aspect of the sick role as: "This incapacity is beyond his powers to overcome by decision-making alone . . . Some kind of therapeutic process, spontaneous or aided, is conceived to be necessary for recovery." In illness the client is not expected to fulfill his normal role responsibilities, which give the individual some control over his life and which help fullfill his self-ideal. The breadwinner of the family may feel he can influence certain family decisions and he may also live up to his ideal of being a good provider by fulfilling his work role. However, when he is ill, he does not work. Thus illness itself may tend to be a focal cause of powerlessness.

Some of the contextual factors leading to powerlessness in the client include: the hospital setting, social displacement, and the gulf between clients and health personnel. Seeman has pointed out the resemblance of the hospital to the mass society discussed by theorists in sociology.

> We took the view that hospitalization for treatment in a tuberculosis hospital, like the medical situation in general, represents a microcosm of the alienative features that are so often discussed in the literature . . . it contains important elements of the model called "mass society"—e.g., low control over one's fate; heavy reliance upon specialized experts; bureaucratic authority; and the loss of community ties (1962).

The client in the hospital has been described as follows: ". . . he becomes subject to rules, regulations, and jurisdictions that are strange to him. He loses perogative and is forced into compliance" (Simmons and Wolff, 1956). Some common expectations of the hospitalized client are dependency and compliance to the hospital rules and regulations, to daily routine and to the decisions that are made for him by the physician and the nurse. The hospital involves a de-emphasis on the external power and prestige that the client had enjoyed outside the hospital.

Social displacement is another experience of the hospitalized client. The client was formerly a part of a certain social life, and is now outside of it. Whether family and friends will visit is controlled by them and by hospital rules. The client has low control over this aspect of his social life. The realization of his self-ideal is built on the reactions of those around the client. His self-concept, then, may depend on the presence of those close to him and the freedom to interact with them. However, this freedom is often denied in the hospital.

Sometimes a gulf exists between the client and the hospital staff. The perspectives of each differ. Illness exaggerates feelings in the client, but his experience is not happening to the others. Staff thinks in terms of the client's future wellness, but the client thinks only of the present. This gulf may be expected to deprive the client of the staff as a means of self-validation and thus increase feelings of self-estrangement. Residual factors influencing powerlessness and alienation include personality variables, age, religion, occupational prestige, education, income, and rural background.

It has been pointed out that Seeman's measure of powerlessness was related to a general life philosophy of low control. Thus powerlessness in the adult may represent a more or less permanent personality trait. A person who had a generalized low expectancy of control in life may be expected to feel even more powerless in illness.

There is a relationship between increasing age and increasing powerlessness. As a person becomes older, there is a gradual giving up of the rights and obligations of relationships. The sphere of influence and control becomes constricted. One author found in his empirical study a small but positive correlation between three components of alienation—powerlessness, normlessness, and social isolation—and advancing age (Dean, 1961). In the same study Dean also found that there was greater alienation among persons who were lower in occupational prestige, education, income, and rural background.

Another study related social and behavioral variables in the alienated Appalachia region (Zwerling, 1968). The author concluded that fatalism is associated with low social status and high religious fundamentalism. Social status and religion may thus influence degrees of alienation in the client.

Thus in assessing the factors influencing powerlessness in the client, the nurse has some guidelines as to focal, contextual, and residual influencing factors. The factors summarized in Table 16.1 can be used in the nursing assessment.

TABLE 16.1
Nursing Assessment Factors in Powerlessness

Behavior	Influencing Factors		
	Focal	Contextual	Residual
Apathy	Illness	Hospital setting	Personality
Withdrawal		Social displacement	Age
Resignation		Gulf between patient and	Religion
Fatalism		staff	Occupation
Malleability			Education
Low knowledge of illness			Income
Statements of low control			Rural
Anxiety			background
Restlessness			
Sleeplessness			
Wandering			
Aimlessness			
Lack of decision-making			

NURSING INTERVENTIONS IN POWERLESSNESS

According to the Roy adaptation concept of nursing, nursing intervention aims at removing the focal stimulus or manipulating the influencing factors to promote client adaptation. It has been stated that the situation of illness is an important focal factor leading to powerlessness. Thus one method for promoting client adaptation is for the nurse to carry out all therapeutic measures which lead toward wellness so that the focal stimuli of illness will be removed from the client as soon as possible.

However, during the time of illness the nurse can aim to remove the specific aspects that lead to powerlessness, namely the low expectancy of control and the constant discrepancy between the client's condition and his ideal self. She can do this by (1) helping the client recognize and learn to use control measures—for example, by letting the client know when he or she may have a say in the scheduling of visitors and/or other activities, and (2) helping the client set realistic goals and expectations for himself—for example, sitting up ten minutes longer each day.

In addition, the nurse may modify the hospital environment, which often contributes to powerlessness. She does this by personalizing nursing care, for example, using the client's name when speaking to or about him, and by consulting the client as much as possible in planning and carrying out nursing care. One example of this is the trend in mental health agencies for the clients to share with the staff the responsibility for the conduct of the ward or hospital. The client should know that he has the right to participate in the decisions that affect his life inside and outside the hospital.

To overcome the effects of the gulf between the client and the staff, the nurse must try to grasp, as fully as an outsider can, the client's individual life experience and try to co-experience the existence of nonbeing and of being-in-the-hospital world. When the client's feelings of helplessness are appreciated, greater efforts will be made to reduce his dependency and the staff will use more carefully their power over clients.

The nurse cannot directly influence the residual factors influencing powerlessness. Personality, age, religion, occupation, education, income, and rural background are all factors that the client brings to the situation. However, the nurse can recognize the clients who are most prone to powerlessness and can plan their care to minimize its occurrence.

SUMMARY

The nurse using the Roy adaptation model of nursing will be alert to assess and intervene to decrease feelings of powerlessness in the client and promote self-concept adaptation. The adaptation problem and nursing process emphasized here are relevant to many situations of illness-induced powerlessness. It should also be recognized that more severe and prolonged forms of powerlessness may occur in client situations. Advanced nursing practitioners and additional nursing literature must be consulted to deal with these situations.

REFERENCES

Dean, Dwight G., "Alienation: Its Meaning and Measurement," *American Sociological Review,* vol. XXIV, October 1961, pp. 753–58.

Durand, Mary and Rosemary Price, "Nursing Diagnosis: Process and Decision," *Nursing Forum,* vol. V, no. 4, 1966, pp. 50–64.

Grubbs, Judy, "Powerlessness Among Mothers of Chronically-Ill Children," unpublished Master's Thesis. Los Angeles: University of California, 1968, p. 31.

Parsons, Talcott, "Definitions of Health and Illness in the Light of American Values and Social Structures," in *Patients, Physicians and Illness,* Gartley Jaco, ed. Glencoe: Ill.: The Free Press of Glencoe, 1958, pp. 165–88.

Rotter, Julian B., "Generalized Expectancies for Internal Versus External Control of Reinforcement," *Psychological Monographs: General and Applied,* vol. 80, no. 1, 1966, pp. 1–28.

Seeman, Melvin, "On the Meaning of Alienation," *American Sociological Review,* vol. 24, no. 6, December 1959, p. 784.

Seeman, Melvin and John Evans, "Alienation and Learning in a Hospital Setting," *American Sociological Review,* vol. XXVII, December 1962, pp. 772–83.

Simmons, Leo W. and Harold G. Wolff, *Social Science in Medicine.* New York: Russell Sage Foundation, 1956.

55 55555555555555555555555555

Sorensen, Karen and Dorothy Bruner Amis, "Understanding the World of the Chronically Ill," *American Journal of Nursing*, vol. 67, no. 4, April 1967, pp. 811–17.

Travelbee, Joyce, *Interpersonal Aspects of Nursing.* Philadelphia: F. A. Davis Company, 1966, pp. 70–72.

Zwerling, Isreal, *Alienation and the Mental Health Professions.* Virginia: Virginia Commonwealth University, 1968, pp. 17–18.

ADDITIONAL READINGS

Johnson, Dorothy E., "Powerlessness: A Significant Determinant in Patient Behavior?" *Journal of Nursing Education*, vol. 6, no. 2, April 1967, pp. 39-44.

17

Problem of Low Self-Esteem

Marie J. Driever

KEY CONCEPTS DEFINED

Self-Esteem: That pervasive aspect of the personal self component which relates to the worth or value the person holds of himself.

Limit Setting: The defining and setting forth by a person the kind of behavior he will allow in himself or others.

Low Self-Esteem: A negative feeling of self-value or worth, which handicaps a person's ability to adapt to his environment.

Self-Definers: The reinforcement or feedback a person receives from others.

After studying this chapter the reader will be able to:

1. Define the key concepts of this chapter.
2. Explain how self-esteem is related to all aspects of the self-concept.
3. Describe two areas of response from significant others that are important in developing self-esteem.

4. Identify the behaviors of and factors influencing low self-esteem.
5. Specify nursing interventions to be used in the problem of low self-esteem (see Appendix II).

At the core of a person's description of who and what he is is the value that the person places on himself. *Self-esteem* is that pervasive aspect of the self concept which relates to the worth or value the person holds of himself. The person experiences self-esteem in the form of a feeling. It is a feeling that can be difficult to isolate and identify because he experiences it constantly. Self-esteem is part of every feeling and emotional response of the person. It is thus a significant concept in the analysis of self-concept adaptation.

THE CONCEPT AND DEVELOPMENT OF SELF-ESTEEM

Abraham H. Maslow (1954) postulates that all people have a need to esteem or value themselves. Whatever view of self a person holds, he seeks to value this concept of who and what he is. People need to be able to place high positive values on the conept of self they hold. This experience helps them to seek and deal with their environmental experiences. If a person has a low value of self, he tends to perceive the environment as negative and threatening. He will perceive stimuli as giving negative feedback and threatening or attacking who and what he is. The person's ability to perceive environmental stimuli and deal with them is disrupted by the attempt to ward off further threat to an already low esteem.

The person will be able to deal more actively with the environment if he values and feels secure with himself. Because he will perceive less stimuli as threatening, and therefore will have less anxiety to deal with, he will find it easier to modify or change aspects of his concept of self. As various maturational and situational crises demand changes, the person will successfully adapt. On the other hand, if a person feels himself to be of little value, he will have an impaired ability to adapt to the changing environment. On a day-to-day level, the person's value of self is challenged by stimuli from maturational and situational crises. The heart of adaptation of self-concept for the person is to achieve and maintain a high positive value of self over time in the midst of ever-changing views or concepts of self. A person with a low self-esteem has, therefore, difficulty or a problem because of impaired ability to adapt.

An examination of what constitures a feeling of value and how the person achieves a level of self-value is necessary to understand the client problem of low self-esteem. Self-esteem is closely related to all aspects of self-concept—the physical self, moral-ethical self, self-consistency, and self-ideal and expectancy. We have already seen the primary influence of perceptions of how others see one in the formation of the self-concept. This influence is particulary significant for development of self-esteem.

An earlier chapter discussed the fact that feelings of loss and consequent depression result from changes in the physical self-concept. When one is depressed about loss of body parts or functions, the person may also question his value. The situation with the moral-ethical self is similar. If one's behavior is consistent with the code of behavior one deems desirable, then the person is able to see himself as a "good" or "desirable" or "valued" individual. If some of his behavior goes against a personal moral code, then he experiences guilt. The experience of guilt causes the person to feel that he or she is "bad" and unlovable, and to have less self-value. The need for maintaining self-esteem within a changing self-concept points to the significance of self-consistency. Prolonged anxiety, which results from threats to self-consistency, can be a cause or effect of insults to self-esteem. In regard to self-ideal and expectancy, if people feel that they have power and control to perform what they expect of themselves, then they feel valuable. This stabilizes or increases their degree of self-esteem. If a person fails, however, to meet personal ideals, then the failure decreases his feeling of worth.

We know that feedback of significant others is incorporated into a person's view of himself. The kind and amount of reinforcement the person receives is particularly crucial in providing a basis for self-valuation. There are two areas of response from significant others that provide ways of communicating worth to the person. In terms of the person valuing himself by the degree of meeting self-expectations and those of others, the first area relates to the kind and ways these expectations are derived from others. One kind of expectation is how one learns to be aware of and handle one's feelings, especially feelings of anger and aggression. Every person learns from others a set of expectations or standards of behavior for handling environment and expressing feelings.

Small children respond to loss of valued objects, usually a significant person such as mother or father, by protesting and acting out angry feelings. Separation or loss, even temporary, threatens the child's feeling of personal and environmental security. The child attempts to deal with this loss/anxiety experience by angry, protesting behavior.

However, persons around the child usually respond to this acting out by trying to control the behavior. They usually tell the child directly or indirectly that he is bad for being angry. Thereafter any time the child feels anger, and acts it out by screaming, yelling, temper tantrums, or other behaviors, significant others reprimand him. Both the unacceptable behaviors and the child's feelings of anger are condemned. Thus, the child learns a pattern of not being able to act out angry feelings, let alone feel them. He can transfer this pattern of awareness and expression to other feelings. Most commonly, the child attributes this pattern to any feelings of asserting or acting out his wishes, goals, ideas, and desires on the environment. So, throughout life when day-to-day situations provoke him to angry feelings, the person feels guilty for having these feelings, and angry and disappointed at himself for not meeting the expectations of others.

When the adult person experiences a loss of a valued object or person, he struggles to deal with the loss of support and feedback. He also has to deal with the response pattern of not showing anger. Such a response pattern makes it difficult to be aware of and deal with the feelings of sadness and anger that the loss provokes. Thus, the person turns the anger and sadness inward and feels less of worth to himself.

The second area of response from significant others from which the child learns some degree of self-value is the limits that the child experiences while growing up. Some generalizations drawn from the research of Stanley Coopersmith (1967, 1968) explain the role that limits have in helping children or persons develop high levels of self-esteem. Limits, or *limit setting,* refer to the defining and setting forth by a person the kind of behavior he will allow in himself or others. A child who grows up with well-defined and enforced limits set on behavior learns many things, such as what reality is by the fact that his behavior results in consequences. He also learns to predict what these consequences will be. The child then can choose what behavior to use based on knowing what consequences can be expected. He not only learns decision-making but also how to get reinforcement. The child learns that positive feedback will be gained if certain behavior is chosen. From this the child learns to trust himself because he can choose behavior that will be successful (get positive reinforcement). The child learns how far he can go and thus learns independence. When problems arise he has these coping behaviors of looking at the consequences of behaviors and decision-making to aid in the self-reliance to solve these problems. Thus, from the experience of having reasonable, strict, defined, and enforced limits set, the child experiences seeing himself as a competent person and one who achieves positive feedback from others. A child who does not have these limits set loses the opportunity to experience competence and positive feedback on which to achieve a high level of self-esteem. As an adult, the person with positive childhood experience with limits is able more easily to set limits for personal behavior and that of others. Such an ability will enable him to have control and direction in interpersonal situations. This will help the person to maintain the high positive self-esteem he has learned to have.

Thus, feedback from significant others in the form of limits and how one should handle feelings, the ability to control bodily functions, the ability to use behavior that brings satisfaction with self-expectancy, self-consistency, and the moral-ethical self all provide the person with data. The data help to achieve a feeling of how competent and secure one is with oneself. Based on the degree of self-competence and security, the person derives a feeling of self-value or worth. How high or positive this feeling is for the person is his feeling of self-esteem. If it is a low or negative feeling, the person has a low self-esteem. A feeling of low self-esteem is a problem because it handicaps one's ability to adapt through the self-concept mode of adaptation.

ASSESSMENT OF LOW SELF-ESTEEM

Table 17.1 identifies the behaviors that a person with low self-esteem would manifest. From these behaviors, one can conclude a picture of someone who perceives himself to be incompetent, unlovable, insecure, and unworthy. There are degrees to the feeling of low self-esteem, determined by the focal, contextual, and residual factors affecting a person's behavior. Depending on the quality, number, and degree of these factors, the person will experience varying degrees of feeling of low self-worth. The degree of feeling will determine the number and degree of behaviors exhibited.

Through observation of behavior and the use of communication techniques, the nurse can assess the degree of self-esteem that the person feels. She completes the assessment by identifying the focal, contextual, and residual stimuli influencing the person. Table 17.1 also lists the focal, contextual, and residual factors influencing low self-esteem behaviors

Generally speaking, these influencing factors can be grouped into three main themes. First, any situation or stimulus causing the person to question self-value is likely to be focal. This is particularly true for any loss the person perceives himself to be experiencing. Second, the kinds of feedback, reinforcement, and the person's awareness of these definers of self and self-value, as well as the pattern of dealing with his feelings, provide the environmental or contextual stimuli. Third, any previous experience with loss, limits, and ability to cope with challenges to how one sees oneself provides the residual stimuli.

A person's own projections of his current level of esteem also becomes a contextual or residual factor in developing new levels of esteem. For example, a person with low self-esteem projects an image of being unlovable and worthless. This often determines the responses of others, which give additional messages of incompetence and worthlessness.

NURSING INTERVENTION IN LOW SELF-ESTEEM

The goal of nursing intervention with the problem of low self-esteem is to help the client to see the focal stimuli as having a positive valuing influence, rather than as being another negative devaluing experience. Nursing interventions can be grouped into actions directed toward manipulating contextual stimuli and those directed toward manipulating residual stimuli.

In working with contextual stimuli the nurse uses communication techniques to help the person to define what kind of reinforcement or feedback is received and from whom. The client needs to identify and answer the question: "What are my self-definers?" He also needs to discover what feelings of sadness, loss, anger, unhappiness, joy, and gladness personally feel like. The client needs to know what they mean personally, and from what situations he derives these

TABLE 17.1
Nursing Assessment of Client Problem of Low Self-Esteem

Behavior of Low Self-Esteem*	Influencing Factors		
	Focal	Contextual	Residual
1. Loss of appetite (often leading to weight loss).	1. Any experience or situation causing the person to question and/or decrease the value of self he feels. Loss experiences are particularly important.	1. Any body changes the person is experiencing—growth or illness.	1. Age and coping mechanisms person has developed.
2. Anorexia or overeating (leading to obesity).		2. The maturational crisis the person is experiencing and how well he is mastering the developmental tasks of maturational crisis.	2. Kinds and degree of threatening situations person has experienced previously.
3. Constipation or diarrhea.			
4. Difficulty in sleeping—difficulty in falling asleep, awakening during night or early morning, inability to return to sleep, no restful feeling after sleeping.			
5. At times withdrawal to bed and/or oversleeping.		3. Any situation that demands the individual to cope and how well he is coping with it as to whether the person will be experiencing a situational crisis.	3. Previous messages of value received from significant others.
6. Complaints of fatigue.			and how well he has coped with them.
7. Poor posture.			4. Previous developmental and situational crises person has experienced and how well he has coped with them.
8. Withdrawal from activities.			
9. Difficulty in initiating new activities.			
10. Decrease in sex drive.			
11. Decrease in spontaneous behavior.		4. Messages, feedback the person receives from significant others as to how worthy, valuable he is.	5. Previous experience with powerlessness and hopelessness and how he has coped with them.
12. Appearance of sadness and/or anxiety, discouragement.			
13. Expression of feeling of isolation, being unlovable, unable to express or defend oneself, and too weak to confront or overcome difficulties.			
14. Fearful of angering others.		5. How well the person meets self-expectancies and those of significant others.	
15. Avoidance of situations of self-disclosure/notice in any way.			
16. Tendency to stay in background, be listener rather than participant.			
17. Sensitivity to criticism, self-conscious, preoccupied with inner problems.			

18. Expression of feelings of helplessness/unable to do what he chose.
19. Expression of being unable to do anything "good" or productive, feeling of badness, worthlessness, inadequacy.
20. Degrading talk, self-depreciating, self-dislike, unhappiness with self.
21. Denial of past successes/accomplishments, present possibility of success of activities.
22. Feeling that anything he does will fail, be meaningless.
23. Rumination about problems.
24. Seeking reinforcement from others, making efforts to gain favors but failing to reciprocate such behavior.
25. Seeing self as a burden to others.
26. Alienation from others by clinging and self-preoccupation.
27. Self-accusating.
28. Demanding reassurance but not accepting it.
29. Hostile behavior.
30. Angry at self and others but unable to express these feelings directly.
31. Decrease in being able to meet responsibilities, do simple tasks.
32. Decrease in interest, motivation, concentration.
33. Complaining of being "boxed in."
34. Taking longer to do tasks.
35. Decrease in self-care, hygiene.
36. Complains of aches, pains of various kinds.

6. Feeling of control the person experiences over reinforcers in environment.
7. The variety and kinds of self-definers the person has, how aware of them the person is, and how he uses them to define self-value to himself. Present limits of self set.
8. Experiences of guilt, shame, powerlessness, and how he copes with these feelings.
9. The kind and number of changes demanded in how he sees himself and how these demanded changes are handled.
10. Awareness of what affects self-concept (e.g., feedback from others) and how he deals with these stimuli.
11. How many failures he allows without judging self to be valueless.
12. How good he feels about himself, how high a self-value, esteem, he holds, how secure with himself.

6. Previous losses and how well he grieves or did or did not resolve the loss.
7. How many and degree of success or failure experienced.
8. Previous experience with meeting self-ideals, expectancies, and standards of behavior set for self.
9. Previous experience of control of self and environment person has had and how he handled it.
10. Previous experience with decision-making and consequences of those decisions.
11. Previous experience with limits person had as a child, whether limits were clear, defined, and enforced.

13. Limits in environment person has, is aware of, and how used.
14. The support from significant others person has and how well he accepts and uses it.
15. How person is aware, expresses, and deals with anger, as well as other feelings.
16. Person's current feeling of hope, comfort with self.
17. Whether person has experiences needed to bring about desirable behavioral changes that will make one useful to self and society.
18. Anything person loses that is considered to be of value to him.

*Indicates that a person with low self-esteem may exhibit any number of these behaviors and to different degrees. The number and degree of behaviors are expressions of the degree of low or decreased value or esteem the person holds of self.

feelings. In addition, he needs to find ways to express these feelings. The nurse helps the client explore this feedback and these feelings and helps him understand in what way this determines how the client feels about himself. Once this is done, the client can separate himself enough to be able to make conscious decisions about what feedback he will allow to affect him and how negative or incongruent feedback from significant others will be handled.

Through the use of communication techniques, the nurse can help the patient to understand what maturational and/or situation crisis he is experiencing, what is expected of him and what the client expects of himself. The nurse can also explore with the client how these expectations can be met and the crisis resolved. The client needs to understand, define, accept, and try out control of the environment that he identifies as comfortable.

The client also needs to develop awareness of what experiences of loss, shame, guilt, powerlessness, and failure feel like, what situations bring these feelings on, and ways that he can cope with them without self-devaluation.

In dealing with the residual stimuli, the nurse uses communication techniques that will help the person to gain a perspective of how the past influences the present. The client needs to see in perspective how in previous experiences when expressing angry feelings, he was made to feel guilty and how that experience has developed into a pattern that he now uses. Feelings, especially anger, are not directly expressed. The nurse helps the person to identify patterns of behavior now used and to resolve the way in which these patterns got started. With the anger example, the person needs to identify how he came to feel bad about expressing those feelings so he can decide if the present patterns of behavior in dealing with angry feelings should be continued.

Through intervention with therapeutic communication techniques, the nurse will help the person to change his view of life. A person with low self-esteem feels that life is just a series of confirming self-degrading experiences. Rather, he needs to see life as unfolding experiences out of which the client can continue to define who and what he is and do so in a meaningful and self-valuing way. The client needs to find ways of finding self-experience (self-perception) as a joyful being.

Helping the person to define these experiences, and how to do so will assist the client to have this perception. Many times the way in which the nurse can do this is by telling the client that experiences of self and environment can be satisfying and that it is all right to have feelings both positive and negative. Above all, through her therapeutic response to the person the nurse needs to help him be aware of what he feels now and help to choose how he wishes to deal with these feelings.

Through therapeutic communication with the patient, the nurse can aid in feeling hope. Sister Madeleine Vaillot (1970) defines hope as the feeling of "to be." To feel hope is to feel a positive level of value or self-esteem, because the person feels he can be and can assert the being to his environment, and that others will respond positively. Thus, the nurse needs to help the person to gain a view of who he is, what he expects of self, and how he can continue this view of self and meet personal expectations by choosing life situations that will allow him to do this. If the choices are limited, the nurse needs to help the client to understand how and why these experiences contribute to valueless feelings. In this way the nurse can assist the client to define himself in a competent, satisfying way and to achieve the feedback to continue that view. With this kind of positive picture of self, the person will be able to change self-views, yet still maintain esteem and thereby adapt through self-concept.

SUMMARY

Self-concept is a core reality experienced by all persons in health and illness. Self-esteem, or value held of self, is significant for adapting self in a satisfying way to the world around us. This chapter has looked at the way that levels of self-esteem are established. Every client will have some level of self-esteem. Low levels often influence rates of recovery, particularly in rehabilitation and psychiatric illnesses. Thus nursing assessment and intervention with the problem of low self-esteem will be an important part of nursing care.

REFERENCES

Coopersmith, Stanley, *The Antecedents of Self-Esteem*. San Francisco: W. H. Freeman, 1967.

————— , "Studies in Self-Esteem," *Scientific American*, vol. 218, no. 2, February 1968, pp. 96–106.

Maslow, Abraham H., *Motivation and Personality*. New York: Harper and Row, Publishers, 1954.

Vaillot, Sister Madeleine Clemence, "Hope: The Restoration of Being," *American Journal of Nursing*, vol. 70, no. 2, February 1970, pp. 268–77.

ADDITIONAL READINGS

Carlson, Carolyn E., "Grief and Mourning," in *Behavioral Concepts and Nursing Intervention*, Carolyn Carlson, ed. Philadelphia: J. B. Lippincott Company, 1972, pp. 95–115.

Crary, William and Gerald Crary, "Depression," *American Journal of Nursing*, vol. 73, no. 3, March 1973, pp. 472–75.

Fraiburg, Selma H., *The Magic Years*. New York: Charles Scribner's Sons, 1959.

Jourard, Sidney, "Suicide, The Invitation to Die," *American Journal of Nursing*, vol. 70, no. 2, February 1970, pp. 269–75.

Lange, Silvia, "Shame," in *Behavioral Concepts and Nursing Intervention*, Carolyn Carlson, ed. Philadelphia: J. B. Lippincott Company, 1972, pp. 67–94.

Lyon, Glee Gamble, "Limit Setting As a Therapeutic Tool," *Journal of Psychiatric and Mental Health Services*, November-December 1970, pp. 17–24.

Mendels, Joseph, *Concepts of Depression*. New York: John Wiley & Sons, Inc., 1970.

Neylan, Margaret P., "The Depressed Patient," *American Journal of Nursing*, vol. 61, no. 7, July 1961, pp. 77–78.

Tiedt, Eileen, "The Adolescent in the Hospital: An Identity-Resolution Approach," *Nursing Forum*, vol. XI, no. 2, 1972, pp. 120–40.

Thaler, Otto, "Grief and Depression," *Nursing Forum*, vol. V, no. 2, 1966, pp. 8–22.

Toffler, Alvin, ed., *Learning for Tomorrow: The Role of the Future in Education*. New York: Vintage Books, 1974.

Travelbee, Joyce, *Interpersonal Aspects of Nursing*. 2nd ed. Philadelphia: F. A. Davis, 1971.

Ujhely, Gertrude, "Grief and Depression: Implications for Preventive and Therapeutic Nursing Care," *Nursing Forum*, vol. V, no. 2, 1966, pp. 23–35.

_____ , "What is Realistic Emotional Support?" *American Journal of Nursing*, vol. 68, no. 4, April 1969, pp. 758–62.

IV

Role Function

Brooke Randell, *Coordinator*

This section deals with the second psychosocial adaptive mode — role function. Theoretical content for the role function mode as presented in Chapter 18 comes from an integration of role aspects described by various role theorists. The purpose of the chapter is to present the selected content of the theorists that forms the basis for the role function mode and describe applications of that content within the framework of the Roy adaptation nursing model. Chapter 19 focuses on the development of roles, both by maturation and role change; Chapter 20 considers the basic role problems.

18

Theory of Role Function

Nancy Malaznik

KEY CONCEPTS DEFINED

Social Integrity: The basic need of the role function mode; it means that one needs to know who one is in relation to others so that one can act.

Role: The functioning unit of our society; it defines the expected behaviors that a person should perform to maintain a title.

Role Performance: Defines the actions taken in relation to expected behaviors of a particular role.

Instrumental Behavior: Goal-oriented and action-oriented behaviors.

Expressive Behavior: Direct, immediate feedback or self-gratifying behavior; behaviors considered to be emotional in nature.

Primary Role: A role that determines the majority of behaviors engaged in by the individual during a particular growth period of life.

Secondary Role: A role that influences behavior in a variety of settings and that is occupied according to the tasks an individual must accomplish to achieve autonomy at a particular time in life.

Tertiary Role: A temporary role of choice that an individual occupies for the purpose of fulfilling some minor task associated with current developmental stage.

Role Problem Identification: A listing of behavior and stimuli made when the entire role performance is not effected.

Role Mastery: Indicates that an individual demonstrates both expressive and instrumental behaviors that meet social expectations associated with the assigned roles.

Role Distance: Implies that an individual demonstrates both instrumental and expressive behavior appropriate to his role, but these behaviors differ significantly from prescribed behaviors for the role.

Interrole Conflict: Occurs when the individual demonstrates instrumental and expressive behaviors incompatible with the expected behaviors for his role as a result of occupancy of one or more roles that require incompatible expected behaviors.

Intrarole Conflict: Occurs when the individual demonstrates instrumental and expressive behaviors incompatible with the expected behaviors for his role as a result of incompatible expectations from one or more persons in the environment concerning his expected behavior.

Role Failure: Occurs when there is an absence of feelings or expressive behavior, and/or a lack of action or instrumental behaviors.

After studying this chapter the reader will be able to:

1. Define the key concepts of this chapter.
2. State the rationale for the assessment of the role function mode.
3. Explain the significance of the partitions in the assessment of the role function mode.
4. Apply Banton's concept of the role tree to the adaptation assessment process.
5. Differentiate between adaptive and maladaptive behaviors in the role function mode.
6. List stimuli other than partitions that influence role performance.
7. Describe the common nursing diagnoses of the role function mode and give examples of each from ordinary life situations.

The Roy adaptation model of nursing has identified role function as the second psychosocial adaptive mode. This chapter explores the theoretical framework of this mode. The work of role theorists is used to outline the process of assessing role behaviors and factors influencing role function. The major problems in the role function mode are defined.

SIGNIFICANCE OF ROLE ASSESSMENT

Before undertaking the presentation of theoretical material, it seems important to identify the reasons why the nurse should assess the role function mode of adaptation. If the role of nursing is to facilitate adaptation along the health-illness continuum, role function is significant in at least three basic ways:

1. Clients frequently are required to take on temporary roles, such as a sick role or a student role.
2. Clients frequently acquire permanent roles, for example, mother or co-lostomy patient.
3. Clients frequently need to alter roles they already occupy either temporarily or permanently —husband/wife or employee role.

It therefore seems obvious that knowledge of role theory and the ability to assess an individual's role performance are essential to the practice of nursing.

DEFINITION OF ROLE

In the assessment of the role function mode the term of major significance is "role." Erving Goffman (1961, p. 85) describes role as consisting of "the activity the encumbent would engage in if he were to act solely in terms of the normative demands upon someone in his position." Position, as described by Parsons, is the smallest element of society organized to reach certain goals—specifically, the individual's title. In the role function mode we have combined the definition of Goffman and Parsons so that the term "role" will be used to mean the title given to the individual—mother, son, student, carpenter—as well as the behaviors that society expects an individual to perform in order to maintain the title.

Role performance, then, is the collection of behaviors observed when an individual with a particular title undertakes those actions which society attributes to that title. Roles are the functional units of society, and by our description the functional unit of the role function mode.

BASIC ASSUMPTIONS

Ralph H. Turner (1966, p. 151) states that "the first essential characteristic of the ideal framework that guides the role-taking process is the view that every role is a way of relating to other roles in a situation." This point of view gives rise to the two basic assumptions on which roles operate. They are:

1. Roles exist only in relationship to each other.
2. Roles are filled by individuals.

Very simply, the first assumption states that to fill a role an individual is dependent on a complementary role (in order to be a student there must be a teacher), and the second says that to occupy a role, an individual must exist (the individual must have a self-perception as an individual so that he may achieve role mastery). For example, if Mary Smith has a perception of herself as a pleasant, bright person, she will be able to choose appropriate role behaviors when confronted with the complementary role of a teacher, and she will achieve role mastery. However, if Mary has an uncertain perception of herself as indicated by behaviors that reflect ambivalence about herself or her intelligence and/or her value to others, she will have difficulty achieving role mastery. In that case, Mary will probably demonstrate a role problem. Quite simply, then, Mary must have a self-concept compatible with the role, and her environment must provide her with a person occupying a complementary role.

These two assumptions provide our formulation of the basic need underlying the role function mode. That need is the need for social integrity; one needs to know who one is in relation to others so that one can act.

ASSESSMENT OF ROLE BEHAVIORS

In describing the process involved in the assessment of the role function mode, we rely on the work of three theorists, Michael Banton (1965) and Talcott Parsons and Edward Shils (1966).

A classification system based on work by Banton divides roles into primary, secondary, and tertiary headings and explains their relation as analogous to a tree with a trunk and branches. Generally, Banton's system appears to be based on developmental theory and therefore allows us to draw relationships between self-concept and role function modes of adaptation.

Banton defines a basic role which we call primary as one that determines most of the way of life assumed by the person. His example of a basic role may be a married woman. The general or secondary role is a branch of the basic and is defined as a role that influences the individual's behavior in a variety of social settings. General roles might include such things as boy's mother and/or minister's wife. Independent roles or tertiary roles are frequently related to general roles. They are defined as roles that are freely chosen and have little or only temporary influence on other roles. These might include such roles as golfer or PTA member.

For the adaptation approach to Banton's role tree, we have made some minor alterations in applied definitions. Using one of our basic premises—an individual must exist in order to occupy a role—we have pulled from the self-concept mode a means of identifying an individual's primary role. As we know from Chapter 11, the self-concept mode gives an indication of the person's perception of himself, and this perception is in part based on the person's success and/or failure in completing the developmental tasks as defined by Erikson. Therefore, we have chosen to equate developmental stages with the concept of primary role. Instead of saying, as Banton might, the primary role equals married woman, our primary roles would include adolescent male, young adult female, generative adult male, and so on. Returning to Banton's definition and our basic premise, *the primary role is one that determines the majority of behaviors engaged in by the individual during a particular growth period in his life.*

Following this same pattern, secondary roles are determined by the tasks associated with each developmental stage. Adolescence, for example, is seen as a time when individuals are striving to achieve their own identities as well as acquire the skills necessary for adult life. The roles associated with these tasks would make up the secondary roles. In the example of an adolescent, secondary roles would include son or daughter, sibling, student, and peer. *Secondary roles influence behavior in a variety of settings and are occupied according to the tasks an individual must accomplish to achieve autonomy at a particular time in life.*

Tertiary roles are temporary roles usually related to a secondary role, but they may be assoicated directly with the primary role. These roles represent the way individuals choose to meet their obligations associated with the two previous role groups. The roles might include hobbies, club or civic activities. An individual occupying a primary role of adolescent male might have the tertiary role of football player assoicated with his secondary role of student. A generative adult female (primary role) might have a tertiary role of PTA member associated with her secondary role of mother, and a tertiary role of woman's libber associated with her primary role. By definition then, *a tertiary role is a temporary role of choice that an individual occupies for the purpose of fulfilling some minor task associated with current developmental stage.*

Tertiary roles of this nature will have varying degrees of importance on nursing care, depending on the setting and the circumstances. However, the sick role, except in the case of chronic illness, fits this category well in that it usually has temporary influence on a secondary role (absence from work, inability to care for household). It is, however, sometimes difficult to say that the sick role is "chosen." Although the individual rarely if ever says, "Today I will have a gall bladder attack," he may be able to choose whether to assume the sick role or to ignore the symptoms.

The first phase of the assessment process, then, is to identify those roles (primary, secondary, and tertiary) occupied by an individual. Once the decision has been made, the nurse can begin to identify those actions in which the individual is engaging to fulfill his needs for social integrity.

The work of Parsons and Shils facilitates the process of behavioral identification. They label roles and role performance as having two major components (1966). These components, the instrumental and the expressive, are not enacted in a mutually exclusive manner, but can be described independently for classification and evaluation. Each of the three roles has both an expressive and an instrumental component.

Instrumental behaviors define behaviors that have a long-term goal orientation. Such behaviors might be comparable to those identified in a job description and are of an action orientation. Instrumental behaviors are further defined by Parsons and Shils as consisting of four partitions. The partitions are:

1. Beneficiary of action—for example, customer;
2. Pay or remuneration;
3. Access to facilities such as raw materials, treatments, place to buy products; and
4. Cooperation or collaboration with others.

The significance of the partitions is that they help to spell out the expected behaviors associated with a particular role.

Using the partitions, let us look at the secondary role of carpenter. A carpenter needs a beneficiary of his actions or trade; in others words, a customer. The expected behavior for his role as carpenter would include advertising, making himself available to potential clients, bidding on jobs, and/or seeking employment with a contractor. Any behavior that helps the carpenter to find or maintain a relationship with a customer would be an instrumental behavior associated with the secondary role of carpenter.

Similarly, behaviors that are goal-directed at receiving payment for his work, such as submitting bills and charging union scale, would be behaviors expected of an individual occupying the secondary role of carpenter. And behaviors demonstrating that the carpenter has access to appropriate resources and the cooperation of others also would be instrumental behaviors associated with the role of carpenter. Examples of these behaviors might include picking up wood at the lumberyard, and calling the architect for blueprints for his project.

The instrumental partitions suggest categories of behavior that should be consider when assessing the goal-directed role performance of an individual who occupies a particular role.

The second behavioral component of role described by Parsons and Shils is the expressive component. The components are similar, but the goal for expressive role performance is for direct and immediate feedback. Expressive role behaviors include those that might be considered of an emotional nature. The partitions, similar to the partitions of the instrumental component, again provide a framework for a description of expected behaviors. The partitions of the expressive behaviors are:

1. An object of affection or consumer (needs to be appropriate and receptive);
2. Response to feedback;
3. Set of circumstances (must be able to accomplish the task); and
4. Diffuse attachment or a cooperative system.

As with the instrumental component, the significance of the expressive partition is that one can more clearly define categories of expected behaviors for the expressive component of a role. Again using the example of the carpenter, he needs an appropriate and receptive person to relate to for immediate feedback. His behavior, designed to achieve or maintain that relationship, then would be appropriate expressive role behavior. These behaviors might include complaining to peers about working conditions or talking to his boss about a promotion.

Similarly, behaviors that are designed to elicit immediate feedback, such as smiling and asking questions, might be considered appropriate expressive role behaviors. The carpenter also needs to engage in expressive behaviors that provide or maintain opportunities for immediate feedback, and that allow him access to other sources of gratification. Therefore, behaviors such as stopping at the local bar on the way home to talk to Joe the bartender or going home to lunch to share experiences with his wife would be appropriate expressive behaviors associated with the role of carpenter.

In summary, the first level assessment of the role function mode involves two operations. The first is to identify the primary, secondary, and tertiary roles occupied by an individual. The second is to identify instrumental and expressive behaviors demonstrated in each role, utilizing the partitions as guides for expected behaviors.

The final step in the first level assessment process is the labeling of behaviors as either adaptive or maladaptive. Whether a behavior is considered maladaptive or adaptive is dependent upon whether the role performance meets the role expectation and allows the individual to achieve or maintain social integrity. Adaptive behaviors are those that meet role expectations, and maladaptive behaviors are those that do not meet role expectations.

ASSESSMENT OF STIMULI FOR ROLE FUNCTION

The partitions as described by Parsons and Shils also provide a structure for the second level of assessment. They tell us what an individual needs within his environment to achieve role mastery. The partitions, therefore define the stimuli for instrumental and expressive behavior.

Again using the carpenter, we know that instrumental behavior is dependent on the presence of a consumer (customer), a reward, (salary of $6.00 per hour), access to facilities (a lumberyard at Second and Main), and cooperation (an architect with blueprints). Similarly, expressive behavior is dependent on a receptive object (an interested boss), the reward (a response from the boss), the appropriate circumstance (the boss has a private office on the building site), and a diffuse attachment (understanding wife at home).

In completing the second level assessment, consideration should be given to the presence or absence in the environment of the partitions for instrumental and expressive behaviors. Having considered these partitions, other stimuli that may influence role performance should be considered.

1. Social norms: the standards or descriptions of behaviors for a position may vary with the society to which one belongs. This takes into consideration different cultural, nationality, economic, religious, or status groups. For example, social norms may dictate differing expected behaviors for the wife role between such groups as black middle-class American and white lower-class Italian.
2. The structure of the individual: things such as age, sex, and developmental stage. For example, a 13-year-old male adolescent will perform the son's role differently than a 40-year-old generative adult male.
3. The individual's self-concept: see Chapter 11 on self-concept.
4. The response and performance of others in respective positions: these stimulate ideals to live up to.
5. The individual's knowledge of what constitutes role expectations.
6. The individual's ability or capacity to fill the role as influenced by physical and/or emotional makeup and well-being.
7. Role performance of expected behaviors of other positions occupied by the individual.

PROBLEM IDENTIFICATION AND NURSING DIAGNOSIS

Identification of role function problems is made, as in previous modes, following the first and second level assessments of the role behavior(s). Role problem identification, a listing of behavior and stimuli, may be made when the entire role performance is not affected. For example, in the example of the carpenter, a simple identification of the problem might be: carpenter unable to complete work assignment because lumberyard was closed and wood was not available. A nursing diagnosis usually indicates either appropriate role function or a major disruption in one or more roles involving many behaviors and stimuli. The nursing diagnoses commonly associated with the role function mode are: role mastery, role distance, role conflict, and role failure.

A diagnosis of role mastery indicates that the individual demonstrates both instrumental and expressive behaviors that meet social expectations associated with the assigned role. The diagnosis of role distance is based on behavior and stimuli very close to role mastery. This diagnosis implies that an individual demonstrates both instrumental and expressive behaviors appropriate to his or her role, but these behaviors differ significantly from prescribed behaviors for the role. The definition and term arise from the work of Goffman (1961), who uses role distance to describe acceptable behavior that deviates considerably from accepted norms. This deviation appears to arise because of the discomfort individuals feel with certain aspects of the roles in which they find themselves. They do not see the behaviors attributed to a role as compatible with their views of themselves.

An example of role distance might be appropriate if the carpenter found it not to be in his "character" to share his frustrations about work with other people, such as boss or wife. Consequently, he might not fulfill a major portion of the expressive component of his role, but shares feelings only with a peer and completes all instrumental behaviors according to expectations.

A diagnosis of role conflict is made under two particular circumstances; consequently we use two definitions for role conflict. The first definition of role conflict is: *Role conflict occurs when a person experiences incompatible expectations from one or more persons in his environment concerning his expected behavior.* Intrarole conflict occurs when a significant other and/or an occupant of the complementary role hold views about prescribed role behavior that are significantly different from those that are held by the role occupant.

The second definition of role conflict is: *Role conflict occurs when an individual occupies one or more roles that require expected behaviors incompatible with another role's expected behavior.* Interrole conflict differs from intrarole conflict in that more than one role is involved.

For the carpenter, intrarole conflict might occur if there is a discrepancy between the boss's and the customer's expectations of his instrumental performance. The boss might expect that the same kind of wood should be used for the cabinets throughout the house, but the customer and the carpenter might favor complementary woods to give a more custom-built appearance. The carpenter experiences conflict because he can't meet the expectations of both the customer, with whose opinion he agrees, and the boss. An example of interrole conflict is commonly seen between a breadwinner role and that of the husband. If the carpenter has a job deadline that he must meet, he may fail to meet his wife's expectations that he get home for dinner on time, or that he attend Little League practice with his son.

The definition of role failure that we shall use is: *Role failure occurs when there is an absence of feelings or expressive behaviors, and/or a lack of action or instrumental behaviors.* Failure may occur if one or both of the above components exist; role failure may be simply expressive or simply instrumental. At this point it also seems important to note that role failure may be the ultimate resolution of role conflict. If that is the case, the diagnosis should remain role conflict, for resolution of the conflict would be necessary to assist a move toward role mastery. Essentially then, the client in role conflict shows an uneven role performance, some adaptive behaviors and some maladaptive behaviors. The client in role failure shows a predominate number of maladaptive behaviors.

Again looking at the example of the carpenter, a diagnosis of role failure would be appropriate if the carpenter arrived at the job an hour late, took an hour and one half lunch instead of the half an hour allotted, and did not complete his work assignment by the end of the day.

SUMMARY

In this chapter, theoretical foundations and definitions of role theorists have been presented for role, role performance, role tree, and components of role as instrumental and expressive. Stimuli affecting role performance have been discussed and methods for evaluation of the behavior as adaptive and maladaptive have been presented. Finally, methods of diagnoses of role mastery, role distance, role failure, and role conflict have been identified. Application of the theory within the framework of the Roy adaptation nursing model through use of examples has been included. When first and second level assessments and diagnosis of role function behaviors have been completed, nursing interventions that manipulate the stimuli causing or contributing to the role behavior can be directed toward the client goal of adaptive role function behaviors or role mastery. Thus the need for social integrity will be met.

REFERENCES

Banton, Michael, *Roles: An Introduction to the Study of Social Relations.* New York: Basic Books, Inc., 1965.

Goffman, Erving, *Encounters.* Indianapolis: The Bobbs-Merrill Company, 1961, p. 85.

Parsons, Talcott and Edward Shils, Editors. *Toward a General Theory of Action.* Cambridge, Mass.: Harvard University Press, 1951.

ADDITIONAL READINGS

Gross, Neal, Alexander McEachern, and Ward Mason, "Role Conflict and Its Resolution," *Role Theory: Concepts and Research,* Bruce Biddle and Edwin Thomas, eds. New York: John Wiley and Sons, Inc., 1966.

Parsons, Talcott, "Role Conflict and the Genesis of Deviance," *Role Theory: Concepts and Research,* Bruce Biddle and Edwin Thomas, eds. New York: John Wiley and Sons, Inc., 1966.

_____,*The Social System.* New York: The Free Press, 1964.

Ruddock, Ralph, *Roles and Relationships.* New York: Humanities Press, 1969.

Turner, Ralph H., "Role-Taking, Role Standpoint and Reference Group Behavior," *Role Theory: Concepts and Research*, Bruce Biddle and Edwin Thomas, eds. New York: John Wiley and Sons, Inc., 1966.

Winton, Rolph, *The Study of Mom.* New York: Appleton-Century-Crofts, 1936.

19

Development of Role Function

Brooke Randell

KEY CONCEPT DEFINED:

Role Change: The experience of undergoing the development of a new role.

After studying this chapter the reader will be able to:

1. Relate the developmental tasks of Erikson to the assumption of roles.
2. Define role change.
3. List behaviors associated with the secondary roles of a young adult woman experiencing a role change to the role of mother.
4. Explain the significance of expressive behaviors in the role change process.
5. List stimuli relevant to the role change to the role of mother and explain the relationship between these stimuli and the partitions of role.
6. Formulate a diagnosis of beginning role mastery if given a case study illustrating this situation.
7. Specify nursing interventions to be used in supporting the adaptation of beginning role mastery (see Appendix II).

Role has been defined as the functional unit of the role function mode. This chapter will take a developmental focus, looking at the roles people occupy at varying stages of their lives and at the process of role change, the normal acquisition of a role previously unoccupied by an individual.

MATURATIONAL APPROACH TO THE DEVELOPMENT OF A ROLE

Using a developmental approach to the assessment of role function allows the nurse to operate on some assumptions when evaluating a client's behavior. Our society is organized in such a manner that there are minimal expectations of the very young and the very old. With increasing age through the middle years an individual has increasing responsibility, and somewhere around the age of 65 or later these responsibilities begin to change and diminish. These divisions may seem arbitrary but they are well-founded in current sociological theory in which the years from 0 to 30 are regarded as preparatory, those from 30 to 65 as contributory, and those from 65 on as supplementary.

Operating from the above premise, plus the concept introduced earlier that roles are the working units of our society, it seems reasonable to measure or evaluate social integrity by ability to acquire and relinquish roles. For the purposes of assessment, every client will occupy a primary role and that role should be more or less compatible with his chronological age. And if the primary role is equivalent to the developmental stage, the individual should occupy secondary and tertiary roles that allow him to complete the tasks society associates with progression from infant, toddler, to preschooler. The tasks of this period generally involve the individual's achievement of a sense of self and autonomy. Given these tasks and the responsibilities allotted the very young, an individual of this age occupies few secondary roles. These would probably include son or daughter, grandchild, sibling, and possibly during the preschool period a beginning peer role. It is unlikely that such a young child would participate in any tertiary relationships.

With increasing social responsibility and interaction comes a dramatic increase in the number of secondary and tertiary roles occupied by an individual. At the age of five or six the youngster assumes the primary role of school-age child. He retains previous roles but adds secondary roles of student and peer and will rapidly add tertiary roles with each additional year in school (club member, music student, athlete, class officer, parents helper). During the school years there is a steady increase in the number and complexity of secondary and tertiary roles. This process continues during the period the individual occupies the primary role of latency-age child culminating in adolescence, where the individual begins to take on secondary roles that will prepare him for adult responsibilities. As he assumes the primary role of adolescent, the individual probably adds secondary roles such as part-time employee and girl or boy friend, with associated tertiary roles.

During the postadolescent years the individual takes on the primary role of young adult. The tasks of this period usually involve preparation for adult roles as well as beginning performances of these roles. It is expected that the young adult will add secondary roles, which may include college student, trainee, apprentice or employee, fiance, spouse, and parent. He will also alter tertiary roles to assume the adult form of club member, community member, team member, apartment dweller, home owner, and the like. This young adult period represents the culmination of the years of rapid growth, which are marked by constantly changing and steadily increasing role responsibilities.

As the individual enters the primary role of generative adult, he is expected to perfect the roles he has been acquiring over the preceding 25 or 30 years. Secondary and tertiary roles associated with this period remain fairly constant and change only with respect to the changing needs of social group and environment.

The final primary role an individual assumes is that of mature adult. Gradually the demands of secondary roles are diminished and the individual must alter performance to meet this change. He is moved from active participant to a position of advisor and consultant, so that as social responsibility and interaction decrease, old roles are lost or altered and a very few new (secondary and tertiary) roles are acquired.

In summary, during the birth to 5-year-old period, the individual occupies several primary roles and a few constant secondary roles. His task is self-oriented and the pressure for social interaction is minimal. Role problems seldom occur here. With increasing demand for social participation, the 5-to-12-year-old assumes the primary roles of school-age and latency-age child, as well as a variety of secondary and tertiary roles which make him a beginning member of society. Student and peer role problems are predominant during this period. The assumption of the primary role of adolescent (13 to 18 years) marks the beginning performance as a contributing society member. A few secondary and tertiary roles are added and the quality of previous role performance is increased. This period may produce multiple role problems, especially in newly acquired secondary roles or the student and son/daughter role. The 20-to-30-year-age group assumes the primary role of young adult and the secondary and tertiary roles essential to becoming a productive member of society. A variety of role problems may occur here, most commonly associated with secondary roles of employee, spouse, and/or parent. From 30 to 65 years, the generative adult maintains a set of rather constant secondary and tertiary roles, which he utilizes to function as a productive member of society. Many role problems can occur during this period, generally related to situational crises and previously unresolved role problems. From about age 65 onward, a steady alteration of roles occurs. Role problems are frequent here and usually associated with the need to give up a major secondary role, such as employee.

Thus an obvious developmental pattern has been identified with the achievement of social integrity. The nurse's familiarity with this pattern and the social structure within which she functions will facilitate her client's adaptation in the role function mode.

ROLE CHANGES

Role change is the experience of undergoing the development of a new role. Nurses frequently assume responsibility for the care of clients acquiring a new role. The remainder of this chapter will deal with the process involved in the assessment, diagnosis, and intervention of a healthy role change. Utilizing the theory from Chapter 18 and the studies of Reva Rubin (1961[2], 1963, 1967, 1970), we will go through the adaptation process with a new mother.

First Level Assessment in Role Change

When assessing a client in the role function mode, we first identify the most appropriate developmental stage. This is most easily accomplished by utilizing an individual's chronological age. In some cases that will give the correct information, but other social data cannot be ignored. For example, if you are assigned a 40-year-old female client, you might assume her primary role to be that of a generative adult female. In reviewing her chart you find she has been married 18 years, has three teen-age children, works part-time for an insurance agent, and makes a place in her home for her aging mother-in-law. All of these facts confirm your selection of generative adult female as her primary role. In another situation you might be caring for a 17-year-old girl. You might assume that her primary role is that of adolescent female. However, you are caring for her on a postpartum unit following the delivery of her infant son. You also learn that she has been married for one year, has worked as a secretary, and will return to part-time work when her baby is six months old. Although this client is chronologically an adolescent, the tasks with which she is dealing are suitable to the young adult. Consequently, this client's primary role would be young adult female. Utilizing this process, we can begin to assess a client taking on the mother role.

Our example will be common and uncomplex—a 25-year-old married primapara (woman with one pregnancy). From initial contact with the client you learn she has been married for four years. Until five months ago she worked full time as a teacher of a fourth grade class. Her husband teaches in a high school, and the couple recently purchased a new home. Based on this data you assign the client the primary role of young adult female. Having identified the primary role you must identify secondary and tertiary roles currently occupied by the client.

The tasks associated with the primary role of young adult, to separate self from family and establish a family of one's own, and to take on adult roles, implies that the client would occupy the following secondary roles: wife, daughter, daughter-in-law, possibly sibling, employee, and mother.

As you identify each of these roles, you begin mentally and on paper to classify client behaviors according to the roles for which they are most representative. In our example you will look for:

1. *Wife role behaviors* indicative of a positive relationship with partner in parenthood (that is, asks if husband may hold baby, verbally shares with husband new facts she has learned about baby).
2. *Daughter and female sibling role behaviors* indicative of a positive relationship with "role models" (asks mother questions about baby, shares her new experiences).
3. *Employee role behaviors* indicative of a positive disengagement from this role (states pleasure at not having to return to work immediately, voices slight regret at loss of work relationships).
4. *Mother role behaviors* indicative of a move from self to other orientation; from passivity to activity, in short, "taking-in" and "taking-hold" (see Rubin, 1963, for theoretical development).

You will notice on the sample in Table 19.1, as in previous sections, that behaviors are labeled adaptive or maladaptive. This will continue to help you identify problem areas and formulate a nursing diagnosis. Role behaviors are also labeled expressive (E) or instrumental (I). As you recall, these labels will be helpful in identifying expected behavior and in the second level of assessment. In our example, with the client taking on the mother role, it seems important to note that the assumption of this new role requires the client to learn a great number of instrumental tasks (for example, infant care) but also involves an intense emotional experience; hence you will see both expressive and instrumental behaviors in the mother role. In the other roles, beginning behaviors will be primarily expressive with instrumental behaviors increasing as the client becomes more confident in the role she is developing. This is a traditional pattern associated with the addition of any new role. The client must first feel the role (expressive) before he can act (instrumental).

As we learned from the preceding chapter, some or all of four ingredients must be present in the environment for role mastery to occur. These environmental components are similar, but vary slightly for instrumental and expressive behaviors. Before beginning the second level of assessment you must identify adaptive and maladaptive behaviors to determine which roles evidence role mastery and which indicate role problems. You should also determine if the role mastery and/or role problems are primarily related to instrumental or expressive factors, or a combination of both. As an adaptation nurse you want to support adaptive behaviors and to assist the client to change maladaptive behaviors. To

TABLE 19.1
Simple Healthy Role Change Assessment

| Client: | Sally Mason | Delivered 8 lb. 6 oz. normal |
| Age: | 25 years | male infant. |

First day postpartum

First Level Role Mastery
   1. Primary role: young adult female.

Secondary Role: Wife
1.	Takes husband to view baby.	(E/A)
2.	Asks nurse if husband may hold baby.	(E/A)
3.	Calls home to tell husband good night at 10 p.m.	(E/A)

Secondary Role: Daughter
1.	Asks mother's advice about position for feeding infant. "Is he okay this way?"	(E/A)
2.	States, "I'm so glad you finally got to be a grandmother."	(E/A)

Secondary Role: Mother
1.	Asks for second sandwich at lunch.	(I/A)
2.	States, "My husband brought a milkshake instead of flowers, isn't that terrific?"	(E/A)
3.	Asks nurse if she did her Lamaze techniques correctly, during labor and delivery.	(E/A)
4.	Discusses labor with roommate: "My pains woke me up about 2:00 a.m. but I didn't come to the hospital until 2:00 p.m."	(E/A)
5.	Holds baby carefully, but slightly away from her body.	(I/A)
6.	Touches baby's feet with her fingertip and states, "You've got your daddy's feet."	(E/A)

---

accomplish this purpose you must search the environment for stimuli, a second
level assessment.

Second Level Assessment in Role Change

When you can answer the questions, "Where are the maladaptive behaviors?" "Where are the adaptive behaviors?" (in one role, evenly distributed in all roles, and so on), "Are these behaviors predominately expressive or instrumental?" (all instrumental, both instrumental and expressive), you are ready to begin searching the environment for the stimuli effecting your behavioral observations. At this time it is important to recall our second theoretical assumption: Roles exist only in relationship to each other. Your search should be designed to discover if the individual has the appropriate environmental setting to achieve role mastery.

For example, if the problem appears to be in one role and is concerned primarily with expressive behavior, you should be sure that your second level assessment includes: 1) an appropriate receptive consumer; 2) the receptiveness of these consumers as well as the receptiveness of doctors, nurses, and visitors; 3) a consideration of the set of circumstances, and 4) identification of diffuse attachment and how their presence or absence is affecting behavior. (For a review of this theoretical material, see Chapter 18.) The process of searching the environment is the same regardless of the number of roles disrupted or whether these disruptions are instrumental or expressive. As the number of disrupted roles increases, however, so does the complexity of environmental stimuli.

Once all these possibilities are considered, let us complete the second level assessment on our 25-year-old primipara.

The literature tells us that certain environmental ingredients are necessary for a woman to assume the mother role successfully. To make an adequate second level assessment, you must identify environmental components essential to instrumental and expressive mother role functions. Instrumental components seem the most obvious. You should include: a responsive baby, a physically well woman, infant care items (diapers, blankets), knowledge concerning infant care, as well as resources to acquire more information as necessary, financial security, previous experience for opportunity to practice, and the presence of a trained staff.

TABLE 19.2
Second Level Assessment for Development of Mother Role. Sally Mason

Focal	Contextual	Residual
1. Delivery of a healthy 8 lb. 6 oz. male infant.	1. Normal pregnancy. 2. Normal vaginal delivery. 3. Voided spontaneously twice. 4. Ambulated in hall. 5. Husband states this is the greatest experience. 6. Mother visits client daily, doesn't give directions, appears supportive, will stay with client one week postdischarge. 7. Client has self-concept of mother (has read lots of books, has all necessary equipment in nursery). 8. Plans to use disposable diapers. 9. Babysat for neighbor during pregnancy. 10. Feels pediatrician is good, visited his office 3 weeks ago. 11. Same nurse and shift giving primary care to mother and baby during entire postpartum.	1. Caucasian. 2. Middle income. 3. Progressive ideas on child rearing. 4. Mormon.

Expressive components seem less obvious but may be considered more significant. If expressive components are absent from the environment, clients usually are unable to fulfill both expressive *and* instrumental behaviors. So, should you have a client with any difficulty assuming the mother role, search the environment carefully for expressive components. Your search should include: a responsive infant, a physically capable woman, an available male with a positive attitude, significant others—especially mothers or mothers-in-law with positive attitudes, access to significant others as desired, a woman with the self-concept of mother (see Rubin, 1967, on pregnancy), confidence or positive feelings toward health care persons, and easy access to health care persons. You will then have identified a consumer of the product, the response or feedback, the set of circumstances, and the diffuse attachment (see Table 19.2).

TABLE 19.3
Nursing Process Guide for Development of Mother Role. Sally Mason

Diagnosis	Goal	Intervention
1. Role mastery behaviors (wife/ daughter) due to adequate environmental components.	1. Client will maintain positive relationship with significant others as evidenced by mastery of mother role and maintenance of I and E wife/daughter role behavior.	1. Nursing staff will allow client time alone with husband and/or mother. 2. Primary care nurse will verbally praise appropriate behaviors (sharing infant with husband; using mother as resource). 3. Primary care nurse will do some teaching and/or demonstration when significant others are present (cord and circumcision care).
1. Beginning mother role mastery behaviors due to adequate environmental components.	1. Client will continue to progress toward mother role mastery as evidenced by daily additions of expressive and instrumental role behaviors.	1. Primary care nurse will give a bath demonstration, allow mother to participate as desired. Praise all attempts at participation. 2. Primary care nurse will be present at beginning of each new experience (holding, feeding, diapering). 3. Primary care nurse will withdraw assistance as soon as mother indicates desire for independence. Allow mother and baby privacy, but be responsive to mother's need for support. All staff will give verbal praise for normalcy of client situation and her increasing skills.

This done, you have completed your second level of assessment and should be ready to formulate a nursing diagnosis.

In the healthy situation initially described, your first and second level assessments would probably be positive, so you would have a diagnosis of role mastery for all roles observed and a diagnosis of beginning role mastery in the mother role. As an adaptation nurse your function would be quite simple, to provide support and teach new skills as the need arises (see Table 19.3).

The diagnosis in Table 19.3 tells the adaptation nurse that her client's role behaviors are appropriate and that the environment is sufficient to facilitate role mastery. The nursing process guide indicates that a diagnosis of role mastery does not relieve the nurse of responsibility, but instead identifies for her which behaviors she should support and which environmental components she must maintain.

SUMMARY

This chapter has shown how the concept of the role tree is used as the basis for identifying client roles in a developmental framework. A specific example of the role change involved in the development of the mothering role was analyzed according to the Roy adaptation nursing model. Thus we see that roles are developed throughout life, often with the possibility of a role problem occurring.

REFERENCES

Rubin, Reva, "Attainment of the Maternal Role," Part I—Process, *Nursing Research*, vol. 16, no. 3, Summer 1967, pp. 237–45.

_____ , "Maternal Behavior," *Nursing Outlook*, 1961, pp. 683–86.

_____ , "Maternal Touch," *Nursing Outlook*, November 1963, pp. 828–31.

_____ , "Puerperal Change," *Nursing Outlook*, December 1961, pp. 753–55.

_____ , "Cognitive Style," *American Journal of Nursing*, vol. 70, no. 3, March 1970, pp. 502–8.

ADDITIONAL READINGS

McFarland, M. and J. B. Reinhart, "The Development of Motherliness," *Children*, March-April 1959, pp. 48–52.

Reeder, Sharon, "Becoming a Mother—Nursing Implications in a Problem of Role Transition," *A.N.A. Regional Clinical Conferences*. New York: Appleton-Century-Crofts, 1967, pp. 204.

Robischan, P. and D. Scott, "Role Theory and Its Application to Family Nursing," *Nursing Outlook*, July 1969, p. 52.

Stone, A., "Cues to Interpersonal Distress Due to Pregnancy," *American Journal of Nursing*, vol. 65, no. 9, 1965, pp. 88–91.

20

Problems of Role Function

Ann Schofield

KEY CONCEPTS DEFINED

Sick Role Mastery: The client demonstrates both instrumental and expressive behaviors appropriate to his stage of illness and position on the health/illness continuum.

Sick Role Distance: The client demonstrates both instrumental and expressive behaviors appropriate to his stage of illness and position on the health/illness continuum, but these behaviors differ significantly from prescribed behaviors for the role.

Sick Intrarole Conflict: The client fails to demonstrate the instrumental and/or expressive behaviors appropriate to his stage of illness on the health/illness continuum as a result of incompatible expectations from one or more persons in the environment concerning client's expected behavior.

Sick Interrole Conflict: The client fails to demonstrate instrumental and/or expressive behaviors appropriate to his stage of illness and position on the health/illness continuum as a result of occupation of one or more roles that require expected behaviors incompatible with sick role behaviors.

265

Sick Role Failure: Occurs when the client demonstrates an absence of feelings
or expressive behaviors and/or actions or instrumental behavior appropriate
to his stage of illness or position on the health/illness continuum.

After studying this chapter the reader will be able to:

1. Define the key concepts of this chapter.
2. Describe the instrumental and expressive patient role behaviors as well as
    the stimuli that would lead to a diagnosis of patient role mastery.
3. List the instrumental and expressive behaviors, as well as the stimuli, that
    lead to a diagnosis of role distance.
4. List the instrumental and expressive behaviors, as well as the stimuli, that
    lead to a diagnosis of patient role conflict.
5. Describe the instrumental and expressive behaviors, as well as the stimuli,
    that lead to a diagnosis of patient role failure.
6. Differentiate between behavior and stimuli when a patient is experiencing
    role conflict as opposed to role failure.
7. Restate the theories of Parsons, Lederer, and Wu, and explain their signi-
    ficance in the assessment of the patient role.
8. Specify nursing interventions to be used in the diagnoses of patient role
    mastery, patient role distance, patient role conflict, and patient role fail-
    ure (see Appendix II).

Practitioners of nursing undertake to evaluate and intervene for a variety of
roles and role problems. This chapter will deal with the aspects of role theory
that provide the nurse with tools for dealing with her clients. The theory to be
discussed is applicable to any role problem that may confont the nurse, whether
it concerns the role of father, adolescent, retiree, or breadwinner. For purposes
of illustration, consideration will be given to what has been called "sick role,"
or patient role.[1] Application of role theory will be made to the patient role.

What constitutes mastery of the patient role?

What are the contributing factors that promote behavior leading to mastery of the patient role?

What is patient role distance? Patient role conflict? Patient role failure?

How does the patient in role failure act that is different from the patient
experiencing role conflict?

This chapter will attempt to answer these questions. Having explored behaviors and causative factors, attention will be directed to posing interventions

[1] Because in this chapter we are dealing with role changes in illness, we refer to the
client as "patient," the term commonly used in literature related to the sick role.

for the various role problems and evaluating the success of such interventions.

Several assumptions are made of which the reader should be aware: one is that role theory as presented in Chapter 18 has been mastered; another is that the development of roles as described in Chapter 19 is understood; and finally that the way the individual achieves role mastery is clear.

As in all roles, the sick or patient role is an interactional position. The role involves a set of complementary expectations concerning the patient's own actions and those with whom he interacts. Our special interest will be the interaction between the role of patient and that of the nurse, doctor, family, friends, and the environmental setting, which must be conducive to being a patient. We must learn how manipulating the environment around the patient contributes to role mastery and how the absence of certain conditions produces role problems.

In attempting to manipulate the environment and assist patients in the achievement of patient role mastery, we have utilized the works of several contemporary theorists, Talcott Parsons (1966), Henry Lederer (1965), and Ruth Wu (1973). These experts help to provide us with the prescribed behaviors for the sick/patient role that will assist the nurse in arriving at a diagnosis of role distance, conflict, failure, or mastery. A brief description of the concepts we employ follows. The reader is referred to the original sources for further clarification.

Parsons describes behavior that should be "taken on" by the sick person. The sick person should: (1) give up a degree of social responsibility (primary and secondary roles); (2) let others take care of him (assume a tertiary role of being sick); (3) want to get well (the sick role is temporary); and (4) seek medical advice (cooperate with the experts).

Lederer describes this process in defining a general pattern of illness in which each individual experiences three fairly well demarcated stages. They are the transition from health to illness, the period of accepted illness, and the period of convalescence.

Wu also alludes to a process that implies certain steps in the movement from wellness to illness and back again. Her description is different in that she ascribes the behaviors of becoming ill to the illness role and the behaviors of illness to the sick role. Illness behavior is seeking help for a problem that the person cannot manage alone. Illness behavior may involve taking action and relieving symptoms, simply doing nothing, considering taking action but doing nothing, or proving that nothing is wrong. When the individual finally sees himself as ill, he begins to act out activities seen as appropriate to the sick patient role.

When acting on the premises stated in these theories, that there are degrees of illness and man must past through certain stages in order to master the sick role and become well, we shall look at some specific behaviors associated with the nursing diagnosis of sick role mastery.

ROLE MASTERY

How does one know what a patient is in role mastery? Our definition of role mastery is *the patient demonstrates both instrumental and expressive behaviors appropriate to his stage of illness and position on the health/illness continuum.*

First Level Assessment of Mastery of the Sick Role

From the adaptation framework, the following assumptions are made. The person just becoming ill must admit to being ill and must learn to enact the behaviors of the patient role. In the stage of transition to illness the following are examples of adaptive behaviors that contribute to role mastery: acknowledging the possibility of illness, talking of symptoms, seeking advice from colleagues, temporarily relinquishing partial responsibilities, and seeking medical advice. These behaviors are instrumental in nature. In addition, expressive behaviors that may be present are: expressing feelings of illness and what it means to the individual, testing significant others about their feelings of his illness, asking that special favors be performed, and seeking sanction of illness from peers, employer, and family.

Having demonstrated the behaviors associated with transition, the individual must then begin to display behaviors indicative of "being sick," the stage of accepted illness. Examples of adaptive instrumental behaviors during this stage are: following a prescribed therapeutic regime, accepting help from nursing staff and others as needed, and asking questions about the illness and the agency to facilitate the ability to follow the prescribed role. In addition, there must also be expressive behaviors such as: continuing to voice fears and concerns of his body and dependent position as a patient, asking for reassurance of loved ones, voicing appreciation of attention given, crying or voicing anger about the situation, and expressing the desire for a speedy recovery.

During convalescence the patient must put sick behaviors behind and relearn old behaviors or modify them as the situation demands. He begins to assume more control of the immediate situation. Instrumental behaviors increase in number. Role mastery is evidenced by daily living, trying out strength (endurance) and abilities, and gradually taking on responsibility for roles previously held and to which he may return. The role of breadwinner is one example; spouse is another. Expressive behaviors center around the pleasure of relief felt as symptoms subside and autonomy is once again experienced; speaking of progress and what it means to him, voicing ambivalence about the strength to regain old roles and responsibilities, and seeking confort and praise from loved ones.

In the case of the person whose life-style must be altered because of illness—such as the diabetic who will need medication and dietary restrictions—the pattern of progression through the stages of illness will remain the same. During the actual stage of illness, there must be an acknowledgement by the patient and an understanding of the changes to be made. The actual stage of illness may be extended, and the stage of convalescence begins as the patient begins to learn new behaviors and to plan to restructure old relationships and initiate new ones.

Second Level Assessment of Mastery of the Sick Role

As we stated in Chapters 18 and 19, a role assessment involves a search of the environment to determine if the necessary components are present to achieve role mastery. We do not yet know all the conditions that must be met to allow role mastery to occur. However, when a number of stimuli are absent or rejected by the person, the chances for role mastery are diminished and the individual may be headed for role problems.

Components associated with patient role performance might include the following: the consumers usually fall into two major groups, members of the helping profession (doctor, nurse) or significant others (parent, sibling, husband, wife, friend); the rewards in these interactions should represent a gain for the patient, a service rendered, relief from symptoms provided by the helping persons or assurances of love; and temporary relief from responsibilities and/or attention from significant others. The set of circumstances should include access to hospital, clinic, medical experts, supplies, medications, and the ability to accept help from experts. Objects of diffuse attachment may include a baby-sitter, mother-in-law, partner, or substitute. This list is certainly not exhaustive and is not meant to include other items necessary for assumption of the sick role. However, it should offer some rather traditional examples of stimuli essential to the achievement of sick role mastery.

To help utilize this information, we have chosen a patient who demonstrates role mastery, and have included in Table 20.1 some actual patient behaviors and contributing environmental circumstances.

Mrs. Nina Gray is an 83-year-old woman admitted to the hospital two weeks ago with a diagnosis of arteriosclerotic heart disease (ASHD). Her adaptive instrumental behaviors include daily trips to physical therapy, ambulation on request, taking medication and diet as ordered, and agreement to insertion of a pacemaker. Expressively she voices appreciation of attention, requests reassurance, and expresses pleasure at her progress. Environmental circumstances include the fact that she has been on bed rest since her admission, and is said to be cooperative and knowledgeable about her illness and treatments. The patient's chart indicates that she is 40 pounds overweight, wears dentures, and dislikes her soft diet. Mrs. Gray lives with a married daughter and is used to the activity of a family. Confinement to bed makes her lonely, and she has a strong desire to return home.

TABLE 20.1
Behaviors and Stimuli Illustrating Role Mastery. Mrs. Gray

Behaviors	Stimuli*	
	Focal	Contextual
Instrumental		
1. Goes to P.T. daily. (A)	1. Wants to get well and lead a "normal" life. (b)	1. Bed rest for two weeks in hospital. (c)
2. Walks as requested. (A)		2. Overweight 40 lb., 5' tall, age 83, ASHD. (c)
3. Takes medicine as prescribed. (A)		3. Understands action of medicine. (c)
4. Tries to eat all of diet. (A)		4a. Mature adult, through aging process lost her teeth. (c)
		4b. Soft diet is not appealing to her. (b)
5. Agreed to insertion of pacemaker. (A)		5a. Heart block from arteriosclerotic heart disease. (c)
		5b. Cooperates with physician whom she considers an expert. (a)
Expressive		
6. Says she enjoys visits from daughter, who comes daily. (A)	6. Family encouraged by staff to return again. (b)	6a. Illness causes restructuring of relations with children. (b)
		6b. Lives with daughter, husband, and 4 grandchildren. (a)
		6c. Lonely in the hospital. (b)
7. Tells staff "good job" when they please her. (A)		7. Immobility − need for dependence on staff. (a)
8. Tells nurse of pleasure her progress gives. (A)		8a. Wants to go home. (b)
		8b. Cooperation and collaboration needed in role relationship. (d)

*Key for stimuli: a) Consumer   c) Set of circumstances
                     b) Reward   d) Cooperation and collaboration

Given these behaviors and circumstances, this patient demonstrates positive instrumental and expressive patient role behaviors. It would appear that her desire to return home is the focal stimuli and that she possesses a variety of adaptive contextual stimuli.

The consumers in this instance are the nurses, the physician, and the patient's family. The obvious reward is a speedy recovery to what the patient calls a "normal" life. Other rewards are physiological benefits from the medicine she is taking, and care and attention from the nursing staff. Lack of rewards include her loneliness in the hospital, her soft diet, the lack of family relationships. Her set of circumstances include her hospitalization, her diagnosis, her age, and her weight. Except for age, these stimuli are being changed by medical and nursing measures. The objects for cooperation and collaboration revolve around her family, who provides her with hospitalization, love, and support. However, her contact with them is limited.

Nursing Intervention in Mastery of the Sick Role

Of necessity, a diagnosis of role mastery is based on adaptive behaviors exhibited by the patient. Nursing intervention must assure that the stimuli causing the adaptive behaviors remain as part of the patient's environment. As the causative stimuli are identified, the nurse must note which need to be supported. As seen in Table 20.1, examples of such factors are the physical care and medications given to the patient and the attentions she receives from her nursing personnel. Some stimuli are supported or provided by other people. In Mrs. Gray's case, her doctor, her physical therapists, and her family play important parts in the performance of her patient role.

In addition to stimuli which need to be supported so that they remain constant, other stimuli may be strengthened or manipulated. Given some attention, a stimulus may give added impetus to the patient and therefore increase adaptive behaviors. For instance, Mrs. Gray's contact with her family is minimal. Perhaps by working with her family, the nurse can encourage them to visit more frequently. They can give more love and attention and encourage the patient to continue participation in her care plan. Dealing with the factors so listed will strengthen those components in the environment, which are necessary to insure adequate role function. Summarily these factors are (1) reward, (2) consumer, (3) set of circumstances, and (4) cooperation and collaboration. See Table 20.2 for an example of a completed care plan for this patient.

ROLE PROBLEMS: ROLE DISTANCE

Role mastery is the appropriate diagnosis when an individual demonstrates adaptive patient role behaviors. When an individual demonstrates maladaptive patient role behavior, the practitioner has three diagnostic choices when defining

TABLE 20.2
Examples of Nursing Process Guide for Diagnosis of Role Mastery — Mrs. Gray

Goal	Intervention	Evaluation	Modification
1. Mrs. Gray will continue to demonstrate instrumental behaviors.	1 a. Bring walker and give aid as needed. b. Encourage ROM Bid. c. Contact dietitian to vary diet as possible and introduce new foods. d. Praise efforts.	1. Interventions are successful, patient continues behaviors desired.	1. None at this time.
2. Will visit with family 3 to 4 hours daily.	2. Talk with family about possibility of staggering visits to increase hours of contact with her.	2. Successful, family will divide day and visit separately instead of all together.	2. None at this time.
3. Mrs. Gray will continue to verbalize satisfaction regarding progress.	3 a. Discuss progress with her. b. Encourage her to express feelings.	3. Successful, verbalizations of satisfaction continue. States she still feels lonely.	3. Increase time of patient contact by assigning various personnel to visit during day.

the role problem: role distance, role conflict, and/or role failure. Role distance will be the first considered because it comes closest to approximating role mastery.

How does one know when a patient is in role distance? Our definition of sick role distance is *the patient demonstrates both instrumental and expressive behaviors appropriate to his stage of illness and position on the health/illness continuum, but these behaviors differ from prescribed behaviors for the role.* The patient in role distance does not see the behaviors of the sick role as fitting or appropriate for himself.

First Level Assessment in Role Distance

By description and definition, expected instrumental behaviors for role distance will be essentially the same in all three stages as those described for role mastery. The essential difference would probably be the degree of response. The person in role distance would wait until the last possible moment to acknowledge the possibility of illness, accept help only when he has no other alternative, and would relinquish the patient role at the earliest possible moment. Essentially the patient in role distance functions just above role failure; he does the minimal number of acceptable behaviors.

Expressively, role distance differs more obviously from role mastery in that the individual sees the patient role as incompatible with self-concept. His expressive behaviors are designed to make him more comfortable with this undesirable role. The patient may choose to belittle the role, make consumers (helpers and significant others) uncomfortable with the complementary roles they occupy, and withdraw and barely acknowledge his feeling in regard to this unacceptable role. Behaviors that might be indicative of role distance are excessive joking, puns, inappropriate comments, flirting, seduction, giggling, and remarks such as, "I've never been sick a day in my life."

Second Level Assessment in Role Distance

As in first level assessment, the second level assessment in role distance and role mastery should be remarkably alike. Usually appropriate consumers include the following: present rewards are obvious and readily available, the set of circumstances is appropriate, and objects of diffuse attachment are available. If patient behaviors are suggestive of role distance, however, the nurse's search of the environment should indicate a lack in the area of diffuse attachment in that assumption of the patient role is seen as a threat to self. This will probably become consistently the focal stimuli in dealing with the complementary role.

In assessing the environment, a male client may be found to have access to consumers, doctors, nurses, and wife, but some disruption in his reward system.

He is showing progress, hence is willing to follow the prescribed medical regimen. However, the usual feminine response he receives from his wife is altered and he perceives himself to be in a nonrewarding situation with regard to other females in the immediate environment. He has an appropriate set of circumstances with access to necessary facilities to perform the client role, but this is his first experience with illness, so he has no previous behavior upon which to rely. Most importantly, in terms of diffuse attachment, he is experiencing a threat to his sense of self as a man.

Nursing Intervention in Role Distance

When the nurse arrives at a diagnosis of role distance, her primary concern is to deal with the uneasiness the person is experiencing in trying to cope with the patient role. During the hospitalization of the above-mentioned patient it is unlikely that his perception of himself will be altered. Therefore, nursing efforts should be aimed at making the patient role more compatible with his perception of himself, and therefore less threatening. At the same time, the nurse wants to continue to support stimuli that are maintaining adaptive behavior. Table 20.3 shows such a typical role distance situation.

In Paul James's case, the nursing approach should be threefold: (1) to continue to support adaptive instrumental behaviors; (2) to encourage client to seek assistance more actively; and (3) to decrease role distance by making the sick role less threatening to his masculinity. See Table 20.4 for a specific nursing process guide. With a diagnosis of role distance, the presence of consumers should be maintained, rewards for patient role behavior increased, circumstances maintained, role cues increased, and the threat to diffuse attachment diminished.

ROLE PROBLEM: ROLE CONFLICT

We have said that a client experiencing role distance has difficulty completing the behaviors prescribed for patient role mastery. A client having a diagnosis of role conflict also fails to perform prescribed patient role behaviors, but the underlying reason is different. In role distance, role performance was a threat to self-esteem; in role conflict the client has received conflicting messages regarding appropriate role performance.

How does one know when a client is in role conflict? In Chapter 18 we saw that the diagnosis of role conflict results under two different circumstances. One definition of sick role conflict is *the patient fails to demonstrate instrumental and/or expressive behaviors appropriate to his stage of illness on the health/illness continuum as a result of incompatible expectations from one or more persons in*

TABLE 20.3
Assessment of Role Distance. Paul James

Behaviors	Stimuli	
	Focal	Contextual
Instrumental		
1. Lifts self in bed using trapeze when requested to do so. (+)		1. Open reduction Fx. femur.
2. Takes medication when administered. (+)	Desire to get out of hospital.	2. Hospitalized one week, never been physically ill before.
3. Requested pain medicine first day postop. (+)		3. Understands treatment and reason for medicines.
4. Never uses call bell but will request help if someone in room. (+)		4. Has been told he may have shot or pain pill every 4 hours.
Expressive		
5. Calls female staff "sweetheart" and frequently uses other terms of endearment.(-)	Patient role is threat to masculinity.	5. Call bell within reach at bedside.
6. Asks personal questions of unmarried nurses about social life. (-)		6. In 2-bed room, roommate 70 years old.
7. Requests nurses to pull curtains around bed so they can talk privately, then tells jokes and re-counts his experiences with women. (-)		7. Staff members enter room approx. once per hour.
		8. 32-year-old male, married, two sons (6 and 2 years), wife visits every day.
		9. Female staff expresses discomfort.

the environment concerning expected behavior. Using the patient role as an example, the following might create patient role conflict: If the individual occupying the patient role believes that a client ought to be as independent as possible
and ask for assistance only when absolutely necessary, he will experience conflict if wife and nurse hold opposing views. For example, if the significant other
and the complementary role occupant (nurse) feel that patients should be pam-
pered and waited upon, confusing messages will result and none of the role occu-
pants will experience role mastery.

TABLE 20.4
Nursing Process Guide for Role Distance. Paul James

Goal	Intervention	Evaluation	Modification
1. Mr. James will continue to demonstrate adaptive instrumental behavior.	1 a. Encourage patient to lift self in bed during linen change and twice during every shift. b. Administer stool softener and muscle relaxants as necessary. c. Offer pain medicine every 4 hrs. requesting he identify type and source of discomfort.	1. Lifts self in bed 3 times each shift.	1. None at this time.
2. Mr. James will be aware that he make requests of staff as needed.	2 a. Explain to patient the purpose of call bell at beginning of each shift. Identify who will answer. b. Always place bell at upper left corner, pinned to pillowcase. c. Assigned nurse will go into patient's room x 1 q shift to talk. Sit down at bedside, initiate social conversation. Patient enjoys skiing and talking about sons. Close curtains only when bathing patient. d. Explain to patient the type of pain medicines ordered, frequency he may receive, type of pain medicine most effective.	2. Stool softener BID, muscle relaxant Tid, pain med. x lq 8 hr. Patient occasionally requests curtains pulled. Does not tell jokes when nurse initiates conversation. Responds to compliments. Mr. James requested pain med. x 1 (date).	2. None at this time. No change. Identify patient progress—that he will return home and to work soon. D.C. explanation by nurse at beginning of each shift—tell patient what is available and how often—encourage to request if necessary.
3. Mr. James will decrease seductive behavior and relate to female staff in appropriate manner.	3 a. When patient calls staff "sweetheart" or any other term of endearment, matter of factly state you prefer to be called Ms. Jones, or Jane if you prefer. b. Staff will answer personal questions with which they feel comfortable—decline to answer others. State you do not care to share that information.	Patient continues to call staff "sweetheart," but is beginning to use first names with some nurses. Behavior continues.	None at this time. No change at present. Be consistent—do not become angry or frustrated.

A second circumstance that would be considered role conflict occurs as follows: *failure to demonstrate instrumental and/or expressive behaviors appropriate to his stage of illness and position on the health/illness continuum, as a result of occupation of one or more roles that require expected behaviors incompatible with patient role behaviors.*

Using the above situation, suppose a man trying to assume the patient role has recently been promoted to a junior executive position, and his presence at work is extremely necessary for future success. However, his condition demands absolute bed rest and limited stimulation. Therefore, patient role mastery almost certainly means temporary breadwinner role failure.

In summary, patient role conflict occurs if a patient role occupant and others hold conflicting perceptions of prescribed behaviors or if the patient's other societal roles prescribe conflicting behaviors.

First Level Assessment in Role Conflict

Utilizing the above descriptions, the instrumental and expressive behaviors demonstrated by a person in role conflict reflect confusion about prescribed behaviors. A patient in intrarole conflict consistently emits instrumental behaviors that reflect his expectations as well as those of the significant other and/or the occupant of the complementary role. Therefore, a client may vascilate from behaving as he wishes to behaving as others wish him to behave. On the other hand, an individual may choose to submit totally to the beliefs of others or to oppose completely the views of others and behave as he wishes.

Whichever instrumental response the patient chooses, the expressive behaviors performed reflect how he feels about the conflict he is experiencing. The patient who is trying to please himself as well as others often responds in a confused manner: "I would like to be up and about sooner, but I guess it's better if I rest," whereas the individual pleasing solely himself or solely the other will often respond with anger and confusion: "Why are there so many visitors?" "Why don't you visit every day?"

Second Level Assessment in Role Conflict

By definition, it seems apparent that second level assessment becomes very important. The environment essentially determines the kind of conflict the individual will experience.

In both intra- and interrole conflict, the consumer is an important stimuli to consider. In interrole conflict the sources of contradictory information are usually consumers and those necessary for cooperation so that a role can be performed. The client may be told one thing by the doctor, who neglects to convey to the nursing staff a desire for a change of orders. The nurse insists on what she knows. A conflict develops. Parents, even though meaning well, may give instructions to children that conflict with the nurse's expectations. Information given by two persons to a third may be the same but may be perceived by the third person as being different. There is in one case a difference of information given, and in the other a perception of conflicting information. The result is the same—confusion and conflict.

In intrarole conflict the patient has different consumers to supply or please, and he must choose or is forced to choose a behavior pattern that causes him to neglect one role in order to preserve the other. Thus the mother of a small child may refuse to take on the sick role and be admitted to a hospital. As she attempts to enact the sick role at home and continues to perform the mother role, conflict may ensue unless she has some aid.

In role conflict we must also consider the set of circumstances in that the patient usually has all the necessities for the patient role, perhaps with the exception of an appropriate consumer as mentioned above. However, he often lacks the circumstances to which he is accustomed in performing other roles. The patient is not at home or at work, and has limited access to the materials he is accustomed to utilizing.

At the same time rewards for role performance are significantly altered. Individuals consistently choose to perform behavior that is most rewarding. A patient who values the rewards of his wife over those of his doctor or nurse will choose to behave in the patient role prescribed by his wife. Likewise the mother who desires the rewards of mothering over those of the sick role continues in the mother role until the symptoms of illness are strong enough to force her to seek medical attention.

To assist the reader in utilizing some of these concepts, see Table 20.5, which offers patient behavior and environmental stimuli that would lead to a diagnosis of intrarole conflict.

Tim is an eleven-year-old boy hospitalized for hepatitis. He demonstrated adaptive instrumental and expressive client behaviors for the accepted phase of illness. He states facts about his illness and treatments, takes medications readily, and accepts bed rest and isolation. He states that he doesn't feel too bad and enjoys the company of personnel. From the second level assessment, the environment supports this role mastery. Tim has a knowledgeable doctor, who explains things to him, a nurse who spends extra time with him, his condition is improving, and he has a history of good health and a strong desire to get well. Despite apparent patient role mastery, there is role conflict between the patient role and his roles as a school-age child and friend.

As a school-age child, Tim is expressing his conflict by not studying his math, despite expressing the wish to do so. He fears that he will fall behind his peers and yet, due to the change in circumstances, he is not completing assignments. Tim has his books and supplies, but is not in the usual classroom setting, lacks his

TABLE 20.5
Assessment of Secondary and Tertiary Roles for Role Conflict

Primary Role: Tim, male, aged 11 years

Assessment for Secondary Role: School-age Student

Behaviors	Stimuli*	
	Focal	Contextual
Expressive		
1. Wants to learn math.	1. To remain on the same level as peers. (b)	1. Enjoys feeling of success. (b)
2. Feels that he is falling behind in math while hospitalized.		2a. Lack of usual energy due to disease progress. (c)
		b. Mother encourages him to "do a little." (d)
		c. Previous motivation of peers, teacher, family lacking. (a)
Instrumental		
1. Has math books with him.	1. Usual schedule missing. (c)	1a. Believes he will study. (a)
		b. Teacher expects him to keep up with class. (a)
		c. Mother brought his books with him. (d)
2. Does not study.		2a. Until yesterday felt "sick." (c)
		b. Usual rewards of school and home missing. (b)
Secondary Role: Friend, as an 11-year-old-boy		
Expressive		
1. Talks of fun he has with friends.	1. Is afraid friends will reject him. (b)	1a. Family encourages friendships. (b)
		b. Is expected behavior for 11-yr.-old-male. (c)
2. Does not tell friends he is hospitalized.		2a. He is jaundiced and has lost weight. (c)
3. Does not express feelings about being apart from friends.		3a. Family visits him 1 hour per day. (d) & (a)
		b. Nurses do not spend time with him. (a)
Instrumental		
1. None observed.	1. No access for friends. (a)	1a. Can't interact with other patients. (a)
		b. No reward. (b)
Tertiary Role: Patient, accepted phase of illness		
Expressive		
1. Says he doesn't feel "too bad."	1. Enjoys company.	1a. Hepatitis is subsiding from lab reports. (d)
		b. Has history of being healthy. (c)

2. Thanks nurse for
   staying with him.

Instrumental

1. Knows facts of illness, how he got sick, and treatment for hepatitis.	1. Previous teaching by his doctor explained his expectations. (c)	1. Nurse taught him, too. (a) and (d)
2. Takes vitamins.		2. Has always taken vitamins. (c)
3. Accepts bed rest and isolation regime.		3a. Feels "tired." (c)
		b. Cooperates to get well and go home. (b)

Key for stimuli: a) Consumer   c) Set of circumstances
              b) Reward   d) Objects of cooperation

---

usual energy, and misses the rewards of peers, teachers, and family. In summary, the circumstances and rewards are right for being a patient and less desirable for being a student.

As a friend Tim has only expressive behaviors—talking about friends and their importance to him. As well as his desire not to have friends know of his illness, Tim has a strong desire for contact with others, but due to changes in reward and circumstances, he is not attempting to meet this need. Tim is in isolation, is jaundiced, and has lost weight. He has the normal desire for socialization; his family visits one hour per day; and other patients cannot interact with him due to isolation. Again, the circumstances and rewards are right for being a patient and less desirable for being a friend.

Nursing Intervention in Role Conflict

In this situation, the overall goal of nursing intervention is to help the patient resolve his role conflict and move into role mastery. By focusing on the maladaptive behavior demonstrated, and dealing with the stimuli producing the behavior, the nurse can facilitate this move. Broad areas of intervention to be considered include helping the patient come to grips with the conflict felt and with its resolution. His expectations and the expectations of others must be evaluated to determine how realistic they are. The adequacy of environmental factors contributing to role behavior must be determined and strengthened when necessary.

The concern for Tim is that he continues to maintain adaptive instrumental and expressive client behaviors. His patient role is a temporary one that he will soon relinquish; therefore we do not wish him to master this role at the expense of his more permanent roles of student and friend.

Nursing intervention, then, is designed to make all roles as compatible as possible, thereby reducing feelings of conflict. Table 20.6 summarizes the process

TABLE 20.6
Nursing Process Guide for Role Conflict. Tim

Goal	Intervention	Evaluation	Modification
Student Role:			
1. Tim will evaluate expectations of his teacher.	1. Talk with him to provide motivation for study. Consider his concern to keep abreast of his peers, and teacher's expectations for his progress.	1. His enthusiasm began to show. He says teacher's expectations are realistic.	1. None needed, continue interventions.
2. Tim will follow a plan for studying.	2. Plan a schedule for him to follow. He says that 10:00-10:30 a.m. is quiet time and he will study math; 2:00-2:30 p.m. also quiet, can read or study math then. Praise accomplishments and plan assignment for next study time.	2. After ½ hr. of study, checked his progress. He asked a few questions. He had completed the math problems we had picked out. He smiled and looked pleased with himself. It worked! He says he will have "no problems."	2. Talk with family. Encourage them to reward his behavior.
3. Tim will have reinforcement from entire nursing staff so he will continue to progress with studies.	3. Record interventions on Tim's care plan and communicate success to team leader.	3. Team leader was receptive.	3. Have a team conference and explain plan to total team.
Friend Role:			
1. Tim will express feelings about being with friends.	1. Stay with him after bath completed and allow time for discussion.	1. Successful, says he misses friends much.	1. Try to provide contact with friends.
2. Tim will discuss possible rejection by his friends.	2. Explore realism of this thought. Point out likelihood is small.	2. Successful, he said he wouldn't reject his friend if situation was reversed.	2. None needed.
3. Tim will call his friend on phone.	3. Be firm and insist.	3. Done! Friend will call back tonight. Consumer and reward established.	3. Enter plan on Kardex.

guide for nursing care of Tim. In a case of role conflict, the excess energy spent in dealing with the conflict drains away the energy needed for getting well. Thus conflicts experienced as a result of health/illness situations, even though not in the patient role, are significant areas for nursing intervention.

ROLE PROBLEM: ROLE FAILURE

We have said that conflicting expectations or multiple role expectations can cause a client to experience role conflict. This results in an uneven or confused pattern of an individual's performance of prescribed behaviors. Role failure is distinguished from role conflict by an absence of adaptive role behaviors and/or an abundance of maladaptive behaviors.

How then does one know when a client is in role failure? Our definition of sick role failure is: *sick role failure occurs when there is an absence of feelings or expressive behaviors and/or a lack of action or instrumental behaviors appropriate to the patient's stage of illness and his position on the health/illness continuum.* Using the sick role as an example, sick role failure might be demonstrated by the patient who cannot verbalize fears about impending surgery, and will not allow himself to be comforted by significant others and/or refuses treatments and medication, and does not follow doctor's orders.

In summary, patient role failure occurs when a patient fails to enact instrumental and expressive behaviors appropriate to his circumstances.

First Level Assessment in Role Failure

Based on the definition of role failure the practitioner would formulate such a diagnosis if the patient is not completing the tasks (instrumental and/or expressive) associated with the assumption of the sick role. The individual would probably deny the presence of illness, fail to follow prescribed regimes, avoid expressing feelings of illness and seek inappropriate means of receiving attention and comfort. Essentially, the person in role failure does not follow the prescribed pattern that theorists have described as the role of patient.

Second Level Assessment in Role Failure

In assessing the environment of the patient experiencing role failure, evaluation of the set of circumstances is essential. One of the most frequent causes of role failure is the patient's lack of knowledge regarding role performance or the patient's lack of skill in performing prescribed behaviors. Simply stated, the patient's circumstances are such that failure is inevitable.

The nurse should also give serious consideration to the patient's reward system. This is especially true during transition and convalescence. In transition an individual frequently sees little reward for beginning assumption of the sick role until his symptoms become so severe that adaptive role performance occurs only to relieve discomfort. On the other hand, patients giving up the sick role and moving into convalescence see no reward for adaptive behavior. The rewards are a return to responsibility, increased activity, and loss of attention. These are not considered as positive by a great number of patients. Therefore role failure frequently occurs because adaptive behaviors are not rewarded by the helping professions or significant others.

Another important circumstance is the individual's perception of the consumer. Patients frequently experience role failure when they perceive the consumer as inappropriate. Instrumental role failure may occur if the patient sees the individual who occupys the complementary role as incompetent or unqualified. Expressive role failure may occur if the client sees the consumer as an inappropriate recipient of an expression of feelings.

In conclusion, diffuse attachment or cooperation and collaboration also influence an individual's role failure. The presence or absence of a support system will frequently determine whether a patient can move from role failure to role mastery.

Again to assist in utilizing these concepts, we have included an example of a patient demonstrating instrumental role failure and have identified pertinent stimuli (see Table 20.7).

Mrs. Weber is a 27-year-old woman ten days postoperative following a cholecystectomy. She is currently being cared for by a student nurse. Mrs. Weber's expressive behaviors were appropriate in that she frequently voiced her fears regarding her recovery, stated her dislike of the sick role, and frequently expressed her love for significant others and her desire to return home. Her instrumental behaviors, however, were consistently maladaptive and included repeated questions about medication, refusal to do activities of daily living, refusal of treatments, and directed staff, especially student nurse, during technical procedures.

In viewing Mrs. Weber's environment, her problems seem to arise in two areas. Her set of circumstances seem to be lacking in that she has little knowledge of the increased independence demanded during convalescence or the nature of the surgical healing process in relation to her condition of being ten days postoperative. At the same time she views her consumer as appropriate for expressive behaviors but not for instrumental behaviors. She feels the student nurse could listen and talk to her, but she doubts her technical competence. In terms of rewards, Mrs. Weber's environment seems adequate in that she is progressing satisfactorily and has a strong desire to return home. However, her fear arising from her set of circumstances and the inappropriate consumer negates some of the reward value. Finally, her attentive family and her apparent attachment to them provide the necessary cooperation and diffuse attachment.

TABLE 20.7
Assessment of Role Failure. Mrs. Grace Weber, in Convalescent Stage of Illness

Behaviors	Stimuli	
	Focal	Contextual
Instrumental		
1. Questioned nurse about 5 medications she was receiving. (A)	1. Fear of a mistake being made. (b)	1a. Considered nurse inexperienced. b. Need to test nurse.
2. Refused to let student nurse remove Foley catheter. (M)		2. Fear of being hurt.
3. Instructed and directed nursing staff in carrying out her activities of daily living. (M)		3a. Fear of disturbing surgery. (b) b. Cholecystectomy 10 days ago.
4. Refuses to do activities of daily living that she can do alone. (M)		4a. Healing process is occurring as expected without complications. (c) b. 27-year-old female with husband and 3 children at home. (d) c. Family revolves around her needs at home; personnel are substitutes for family. (a)
Expressive		
1. Voices fears and other thoughts often. (A)	1. Believes she needs help from nursing staff since she is not yet fully recovered.	1a. Fear of being hurt. b. Student nurse is available to listen and ask questions. (a)
2. States dislike of sick role.		2. Separation from family.
3. Said on phone to husband, "I love you and miss you, too. I want to come home." (A)		3a. Task of nurturing and being nurtured in being wife. b. Separation from family. (d)
4. Thanked nurse for help. (A)		4. Her own capabilities not realized by her at this point. (b)

In summary, role failure seems to have resulted due to the patient's perception of the consumer and a lack in her set of circumstances. Therefore, interventions designed to manipulate these stimuli should result in the patient's movement to convalescent mastery.

TABLE 20.8
Nursing Process Guide for Role Failure — Mrs. Weber

Goal	Intervention	Evaluation	Modification
1. Mrs. Weber will discuss her fear of being hurt by the student nurse, personnel, or any other way she perceives.	1a. Pursue perceptions of fear. b. Ask about her knowledge of student nurse and R.N.s. c. Fill gaps of knowledge about skills she may have.		
2. Mrs. Weber will discuss why she directs nursing staff in carrying out their duties.	2a. Share perceptions of her controlling behavior. b. Ask for her ideas. c. Ask for her reasons. d. Explore establishing schedule for nurses to follow.		
3. Mrs. Weber will bathe herself, feed herself, and give own oral hygiene.	3a. Identify her knowledge of the healing process of her wound. b. Give information she lacks. c. Identify her knowledge of turning, exercising, ambulation, and requirement of food intake. d. Give information she lacks. e. Teach her that staff wants her to assume more and more of her care in activity of daily living as days progress. f. Discuss with her what she can expect of her progress in the next few days, stressing recovery as her reward.		
4. Mrs. Weber will talk about her relationship with her family and the amount of contact she now has with them.	4a. Determine how dependent she is on them. b. Determine if the same dependency is expected of the nursing staff. c. Discuss possibility of increasing her contact with family by extending their visits.		

Nursing Intervention in Role Failure

Nursing intervention for role failure must encourage the appearance of the behaviors necessary for role mastery. By manipulating the stimuli causing the maladaptive behaviors, adaptation is facilitated. In the example of Mrs. Weber, the behaviors that need to be dealt with are: (1) her refusal to let the student nurse remove the Foley catheter, (2) her behaviors that attempt to control the staff as they care for her, and (3) her refusal to perform some of her own physical care. One might question how maladaptive these behaviors are since they do acquire for the patient what she needs—care and attention. However, if her behaviors persist, there is great risk of Mrs. Weber alienating her consumer, in this case, the nursing staff. If alienation occurs, it is doubtful that she will remain in an adaptive state. It seems better to consider the behaviors as maladaptive and to deal with the situation now rather than to allow estrangement to occur. There are various stimuli that can be manipulated in this case. Some include her fear of being hurt and disturbing the surgery, and her view of the student nurse as being inexperienced. Other stimuli are her uncomplicated healing process, her relationship with her family at home, and how that relationship affects her expectations of the nursing staff.

In Table 20.8 we see examples of interventions for Mrs. Weber. The nurse will explore her fear and distrust. She will teach Mrs. Weber what is expected of her, giving her role cues. Also necessary for exploration is the patient's expectation of the nurses—her consumers. To prevent further role failure, expectations of the patient and the nurse must be congruent. Rewards can be strengthened as the patient begins to consider that she is indeed recovering and can rocognize signs of continued progress in the next few days. Her relationship with her family, once explored, should be encouraged within the limits of hospitalization as much as possible. The presence of her family in the hospital will allow her dependence upon them to continue and should decrease her dependence upon the nursing staff.

SUMMARY

The nurse is concerned with problems of role function in her total approach to promoting client adaptation in health and illness. This chapter has outlined the nature of these problems and how the nurse assesses and intervenes in cases of role mastery, role distance, role conflict and role failure. Illustrations of each patient situation have been used to help the nurse in making practical applications of the theoretical material presented throughout Part IV.

REFERENCES

Goffman, Erving, "Role Distance," *Encounters.* Indianapolis: Bobbs-Merrill, 1961, pp. 85–152

Lederer, Henry, "How the Sick View Their World," *Social Interaction and Patient Care,* J. K. Skipper and R. C. Leonard, eds. Philadelphia: J. B. Lippincott Company, 1965, pp. 157–67.

Parsons, Talcott, "On Becoming a Patient," in *A Sociological Framework for Patient Care,* J. F. Folta and E. S. Deck, eds. New York: John Wiley and Sons, Inc., 1966, 246–52.

Wu, Ruth, *Behavior and Illness.* Englewood Cliffs, N. J.: Prentice-Hall, Inc., 1973.

ADDITIONAL READINGS

Bell, Robert, "The Impact of Illness on Family Roles," in *A Sociological Framework for Patient Care,* J. F. Folta and E. S. Deck, eds. New York: John Wiley and Sons, Inc., 1966, pp. 177-89.

Martin, Harry and Arthur Prange, "The Stages of Illness: A Psycho Social Approach," in *Nursing Fundamentals,* Mary Meyer, ed. Dubuque: William C. Brown Co., 1967, pp. 33-44.

Sweetser, Damian, "How Laymen Define Illness," in *A Sociological Framework for Patient Care,* J. R. Folta and E. S. Deck, eds. New York: John Wiley and Sons, Inc., 1966, pp. 220-27.

Tagluicozza, D. L., "The Nurse from the Patient's Point of View," in *Social Interaction and Patient Care,* J. K. Skipper and R. C. Leonard, eds. Philadelphia: J. B. Lippincott Company, 1965, pp. 219-27.

Van Kaam, Adrian, "The Nurse in the Patient's World," in *Nursing Fundamentals,* Mary Meyer, ed. Dubuque: William C. Brown Co., 1967, pp. 51–57.

V

Interdependence

Mary Poush, *Coordinator*

The final adaptive mode to be considered is the mode of interdependence. Observation of human behavior makes it apparent that from infancy to senescence there is a constant struggle between the drive for independence and the desire to remain dependent. Struggles in this area of human behavior are frequent during fluctuations in health and illness. Thus the nurse will view her client in regard to this important dimension in his life. As the basis for her assessment of clients and her planning of intervention in their behalf, the nurse must understand interdependence from a theoretical framework. Chapter 21 focuses on this theoretical framework, and Chapter 22 looks at the development of interdependence. Chapters 23, 24, and 25 examine common problems in interdependence adaptation.

21

Theory of Interdependence

Sister Teresa Marie McIntier

KEY CONCEPTS DEFINED

Interdependence: The comfortable balance between dependence and independence in relationship with others.

Dependence: Enjoying other people as satisfying and rewarding; motivated by the need for affiliation.

Independence: Behavior manifesting self-reliance and self-assertiveness; motivated by the need for achievement.

Need for Affiliation: Need to be associated with others in a dependent way.

Need for Achievement: Need to accomplish tasks on one's own without others.

Coping Style: The development of a pattern of response used to meet a need.

Balanced Coping Style: An admixture of dependent and independent behaviors.

Dependent Coping Style: A predominant use of dependent behaviors.

Independnet Coping Style: A predominant use of independent behaviors.

Regulator Mechanism: A straightforward and almost automatic response that prepares the body for an approach, fight, flight, or avoidance reaction.

291

Cognator Mechanism: Man's problem-solving mechanism.

Cognitive Dissonance: A way of changing perceptions to handle problem stimuli.

Ego Defense Mechanisms: Unconscious adaptive efforts to help cope with the psychological stress that arises from conflict.

Help-Seeking: A dependent behavior whose purpose is to stimulate another to aid or assist the client to reach a goal.

Attention-Seeking: A dependent behavior whose purpose is to be noticed by others.

Affection-Seeking: A dependent behavior whose purpose is to be responded to by another and/or establish an in-depth interaction with another person.

Initiative-Taking: An independent behavior whose purpose is to begin and work on a task by oneself.

Obstacle Mastery: An independent behavior whose purpose is to complete a simple to difficult task by oneself.

After studying this chapter the reader will be able to:

1. Define the key concepts of this chapter.
2. Illustrate dependence and independence with examples from ordinary life situations.
3. State the needs and drives underlying dependence and independence.
4. Describe the three coping styles in the interdependence mode.
5. Discuss the factors influencing interdependent behavior and give an example of each category.

This chapter introduces the interdependence adaptive mode by discussing the theory of interdependence. The needs for affiliation and achievement and the drives related to each are explained. Patterns of coping within this mode are explored along with the mechanisms for handling the changing environment. Finally, categories of dependent and independent behaviors are outlined.

NEEDS AND DRIVES RELATED TO INTERDEPENDENCE

Interdependence by definition is the comfortable balance between dependence and independence in relationships with others. The adult will at times be independent; at other times, dependent.

Dependency comes from the Latin *pendere*—to have weight from something, therefore related to something. Whenever a person gives evidence that people as people are satisfying and rewarding, it may be said that such a person is behaving dependently. Behind this mode of adapting is the social need to be related to other people. This need is called the *need for affiliation.* By it we mean that man needs to be associated with others in a dependent way. The child with a bruised knee will cry for his mother. With her signs of attention and affection, the child will stop crying, in spite of the fact that the condition of his knee remains the same. The need for affiliation at the time of hurt was primary for the child.

Some theoretical authors refer to dependency as a motivational construct. Here, dependency refers to a unitary discriminable drive. The drive is secondary, that is, learned rather than primary or innate. Essentially, it is an acquired drive of dependence that emerges from the interactions of child and caretaker during infancy and early childhood. A second view of dependency may stem from this secondary drive. Behavioral scientists also use dependency to denote a group of response tendencies that are instrumental in obtaining social reinforcement of being nurtured. Used in this way, dependency is a behavioral construct. It is a category or process that may be applied to many different kinds of activities, such as affection-seeking, help-seeking, and attention-getting. Development of this secondary drive and response tendencies is discussed in the next chapter.

In looking at the dependency part of the interdependency adaptive mode, we envision the ring of a target (see Figure 2.1), which has behind it the need for affiliation. The energy for meeting this need originates in the secondary drive of dependency. Stemming from this drive are a group of response tendencies, also identified as dependency.

On the other hand, independency means the absence of weight on the nonhanging free object, and is unrelated to anything. Whenever a person's behavior manifests self-reliance and self-assertiveness (that is, he seeks relatively infrequently to be nurtured by other people and manifests initiative and achievement) that person is said to be *independent*. In recognizing this aspect of interdependence, we are recognizing that in addition to man's need for affiliation, he also has a *need for achievement.* A person must accomplish tasks on his own without others. The child with the bruised knee who cried for mother may have been hurt only because he attempted the task of jumping across a wide ditch. At that point his behavior was unrelated to any other person. A personal need to achieve was primary.

The authors postulate that the drive behind the need to achieve is aggression. *Aggression* is defined as a state of inner tension causing some discomfort to the individual and energizing him to overcome environment, often using gross motor behavior.

The nature of the aggressive drive is such that one must develop patterns of control over it. These patterns are the independent response tendencies. The development of this pattern is discussed in the next chapter, and problems of dyscontrol of aggressive behavior are outlined in Chapter 24.

Thus independence can be looked at as the part of the target ring (refer to Figure 2.1) that has behind it the need for achievement. This need receives energy from the aggressive drive, and the person subsequently develops independent response tendencies.

The meanings behind these definitions of dependency and independency come from rather extensive studies in the behavioral sciences. These studies explore interdependent adaptive balance by looking at the two states of which it is made: dependency and independency.

To achieve a balance, one has to have elements of quite separate entities. To have interdependence, a person must at times be dependent, at other times independent. These two disparate but not mutually exclusive states can be described as response tendencies or behavior patterns.

The theoretical concept of interdependence presented here can be summarized in Figure 21.1.

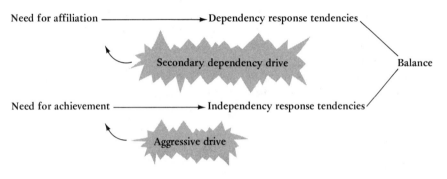

Figure 21.1   Theoretical framework of interdependence mode.

PATTERNS OF INTERDEPENDENT BEHAVIOR

By young adulthood, an individual's predominant coping style to meet affiliative and achievement needs will have emerged. In general, a *coping style* is a pattern of response used to meet a need. This *interdependence pattern* will occur with predictable frequency and consistency. How it develops is the topic of the next chapter. Here we can say that there are three styles of coping: first, the *balanced coping* pattern, which exhibits an admixture of dependent and independent behaviors; second, the *dependent coping* pattern, which manifests a predominant use of dependent behaviors; third, the *independent coping* pattern, demonstrated by the consistent use of independent behaviors. These patterns are the response tendencies developed to handle the secondary dependency drive and the aggressive drive.

American society tends to value independence. Dependent behavior is allowed or sanctioned generally only in the following circumstances: infancy, early childhood, old age, physical or mental disability, and for some, the female sex. (With the advent of the feminist movement of the 1970s, the female sex for many is no longer thought of in terms of dependency.) However, for many persons life situations are such that dependent coping patterns emerge and are highly functional. In comparison with infantile dependency, this mature form is more controlled, less anxiety-driven, and more flexible. It is appropriate to the situation.

Each coping pattern is designed to meet needs, and can be considered adaptive. It is only when changes, such as movement on the health/illness continuum, make the coping style ineffective in meeting needs that the person's coping style may prove nonadaptive.

CAUSES OF INTERDEPENDENT BEHAVIOR

In his interdependent adaptive mode, man responds throughout life in characteristic ways to meet affiliative and achievement needs. The response that will demand the least energy is to use the predominant coping pattern. The focal stimulus for the behavior will be a combination of the environmental change demanding the response and the internal stimulus of his usual coping style. Contextual and residual stimuli will be many, including the factors that lead to the coping style, as described in the chapter on interdependence development.

What happens, however, when behavior resulting from usual coping styles is maladaptive? These problems are discussed in greater detail in later chapters. At this point we can look at the theoretical process that will underlie the subsequent interdependence behavior.

When the environmental demands are such that they are in conflict with the internal coping patterns, the person's major adaptive mechanisms will be activated. For example, when the highly independent business executive is ordered on bed rest, his usual style of coping is inadequate and his adaptive mechanisms must respond to develop new forms of adaptive behavior.

The major adaptive mechanisms of the regulator and cognator were introduced in Chapter 1. The *regulator mechanism* responds in a straightforward and almost automatic manner. The body's sensory apparatus receives a set of stimulus signals and the regulator mechanism prepares the body for an approach, fight, flight, or avoidance response. However, this initial reaction will be inadequate in most circumstances of interdependence problems. The decidedly more complex cognator adaptive mechanism influences and even modifies the regulator response.

The *cognator* has been described as man's problem-solving mechanism. In the total problem-solving process, man uses his perceptions to describe and analyze situations. Leon Festinger (1957) has described the theory of *cognitive dissonance* as one way of changing perceptions to handle problem stimuli. This may be looked at as one operation of the cognator adaptive mechanism. In terms of this theory, when the stimuli confronting the person forms a discrepancy with the person's unique perceptions, values, and/or cognitive organization, the mind acts to reduce the dissonance and to make an adaptive response. Thus the cognator mechanism may be called upon to modify the individual's awareness of the stimulus, or alter the person's unique perception and/or values in such a way that the two stimuli become congruent. If the intellect continues to favor one perception over another, then the will acts to value the one and depreciate the other. By activities of intellect and will, the person may consciously reduce the dissonance experienced in the conflict between environmental stimulus and his own cognitive structure. The use of this type of mechanism will be demonstrated later.

In addition to the coping response on the conscious level, the cognator response in the unconscious domain needs to be considered. Psychological research has designated a series of cognitive mechanisms that unconsciously enable an individual to meet environmental demands. Labeled *ego defense mechanisms,* these unconscious adaptive efforts help to cope with the psychological stress that arises from the conflict between important demands. By resorting to a defense mechanism a person engages in self-deception about the nature of these conflicting demands, and in this way appears to resolve the conflict and reduce the stress it produces. These self-deceptions of defenses enable the individual to deceive himself about actual circumstances or about impulses he cannot personally accept. In this manner, the individual partially solves the conflict dilemma, because he no longer has to acknowledge its existence. Hence, the person gives up, and alters or denies external demands that are at variance with his internal style of coping.[1] These mechanisms will be considered in part of the nursing assessment process of problems of interdependency.

Thus we see that interdependent behavior results from environmental changes demanding response and the internal stimulus of usual coping styles, as these are affected by contextual and residual stimuli. At times when environmental demands and coping styles conflict, the regulator and cognator adaptive mechanisms will be activated to develop new adaptive behaviors.

---

[1] A list of these ego defense mechanisms can be found in any introductory psychology textbook.

CLASSIFICATION OF DEPENDENT-INDEPENDENT BEHAVIORS

There are many ways to meet affiliative and achievement needs. Thus there are many forms of dependent and independent behaviors. Affiliative and achievement needs will be met through the roles a person assumes.

A person may recognize that he prefers to work alone and thus chooses work that allows him to make independent decisions as well as work alone for major periods of time.

One may also express physiological or self-concept behaviors in either a dependent or independent manner. A person with a nutrition behavior of 40 pounds overweight may lose the weight by a self-program or may join a weight-reduction program involving meeting and sharing with other people. This same person might, under body image, frequently ask others, Do you like my dress, my hair? Or the person might manifest independent behaviors of liking what she is wearing, having decided upon the outfit alone and not needing the approval of others.

A behavior therefore may have more than one meaning. It may be manifesting both dependency or independency *and* a role prescription, psychic integrity, or a physiological need. However, it is possible to look at behavior in clients and determine the client's interdependence adaptation. Thus dependent and independent behaviors are described in their own right.

Dependency commonly refers to such behaviors as seeking attention, seeking reassurances, and seeking physical contact. Each of these goals can be achieved in numerous ways. For example, one child may shout to a teacher, "See me!" while another child may silently force his way to the front row to be directly under the eyes of the teacher.

Another example of dependent behavior is the child who is unable to create unusual forms (during a clay modeling class) without copying a formal procedure. Investigative studies indicate that high-dependent children show more imitative behavior than do low-dependent children.

Similarly, independence manifests itself in many different ways. According to the theoretical framework presented, we are talking about response tendencies to overcome the environment on one's own. Thus, the man who designs his own home is acting independently. And so is the child who makes a sand castle.

Using the work of Sears (1957), Heathers (1955), and Clough (1974), the following classification seems appropriate in assessing dependent behaviors of both adults and children.

1. Help-Seeking: The purpose is to stimulate another to aid or assist the client to reach a goal.

a. Physical help. Although help may or may not be required in relation to the client's physical capabilities, the person seeks assistance. Physical help may be obtained by remaining inactive when confronted with the expectation of the nurse to help oneself. This may be expressed by ignoring the nurse, turning away, calling for help, pointing to what the client needs, whining, crying, or excuses such as, "I don't feel up to it." An important consideration is that when help is offered or initiated by the nurse, it is not refused. If help is refused, or if the client states a preference to bathe after breakfast, for example, the behavior would be classified as independent.

b. Psychological help. The person solicits and/or follows advice, suggestions, decisions or reassurances from others. An example is, "How would you do this?"

2. Attention-Seeking: The purpose is to be noticed by others.
The individual may request extra services that are not needed. He may say "Hi" to everyone that passes by, since this usually supplies attention from others. These two examples do not provide prolonged proximity, in that a brief hello or the bringing of an extra tissue does not necessitate someone staying nearby. Nor do these examples provide praise and approval, for the behaviors may be rated as demanding or annoying by the staff. Speaking loudly, wearing "loud" pajamas, talking excessively, giving unasked-for information, complaining, asking irrelevant questions, and displaying immodest behavior also provide attention, but again, not necessarily approval.

3. Affection-Seeking: The purpose is to be responded to by another and/or to establish an in-depth interaction with another person, and has characteristics of protection, caring, proximity, physical contact, recognition, praise, and approval.

a. Seeks physical contact. The person verbalizes the need for physical contact or initiates touching behavior. Touching with the hands is a major element. "Bumping" or "brushing against" another person also fulfills the need, but the problem of intent becomes a handicap in determining whether physical contact is being sought. The person may also accept physical contact initiated by others in that he does not withdraw from contact. We may respond to contact by squeezing the hand offered by another or by reaching for the hand. Touching incurred as a result of physical help, such as a bath, is not included to purify the component. Seeks proximity—the person verbalizes the need for proximity by asking the nurse to draw up a chair, sit close, or be present during painful procedures. He may tell involved stories to the nurse to keep her in the room, even though she states that she must go or is approaching the door. The displaying of get well cards, family pictures, or religious articles may be observed. The client tells the nurse that she is the favorite, which could make the nurse return to the patient to fulfill expectations of a "good nurse." Speaking softly to whispering also helps to meet the need, for another person must remain close in order to hear the client. Approaching other people to listen to conversations is another method of meeting proximity needs.

b. Seeks recognition, praise, and approval. The individual exhibits behaviors that elicit positive attitudes or response on the part of others. It is differentiated from psychological help, attention, and proximity in that the goal is to avoid scorn or disapproval. Behaviors include the soliciting of recognition, praise, and approval for personal appearance, personal status, and accomplishments. By initiating the interaction, it can be separated from independent behavior. If the nurse said, "You're wearing a pretty robe today," she would have initiated the interaction, and the client's need would be met, if it existed. However, if the client initiated the interaction by asking if the nurse liked the new robe, the intent of seeking recognition is clear. Again, if the nurse asked the client if he ate all of his lunch, the reply of "I ate all my lunch" cannot be differentiated from the seeking of praise or the offering of required information. The person may also exhibit behaviors that include seeking recognition through the accomplishments of others, such as "My daughter is a nurse, too"; by conforming to hospital routines, thereby avoiding disapproval; by making indirect comments to elicit recognition such as "I decided to wear my new robe today"; and by offering gifts or offering to help others. Offering gifts is considered here because it can denote a "buying" of approval. Helping others is also considered because praise is not given for self-help or a striving for return of one's own capabilities, but for lightening the nurse's burden.

The classification of independent behaviors follows.

1. Initiative-Taking: The purpose is to begin and work on a task by oneself.

   The person seeks activity when in a state of need and manipulates the environment successfully. Examples include recognition of something needed to be done, decisions to engage in activities, and the initiation of activities on one's own. He rarely discusses actions, therefore does not need to stimulate help from others. Beginning the bath by assem-

bling needed equipment without reminders is a specific example, as
is initiating discussions of health care with a nurse and informing others
of plans made.

2. Obstacle-Mastery: The purpose is to complete a simple to difficult
    task by oneself. Characteristics are persistency, firmness, stubbornness,
    repeated effort, and constant reappraisal to try new methods.

    a. Overcomes obstacles. Exhibits the desire to solve problems. Both
        nonhuman and human obstacles may be overcome. Examples of
        nonhuman obstacles include going to replace defective articles and
        replenish supplies. A burned-out light bulb, since it prevents an
        individual from reading or seeing well, is considered an obstacle.
        Examples of human obstacles include visitors who do not allow the
        client sufficient rest, nurses who do not allow for privacy, and
        nurses who do not allow the client to help himself in accordance
        with physical limitations.

    b. Persistence. The person tries to carry activities to completion that
        are within physical/mental limitations. He will write or talk about
        achievements. Demonstrates perseverance by continuing after the
        ebb or normal energy flow. It is not a prerequisite that an individ-
        ual initiate the activities in which persistence is being observed.
        For instance, the nurse may have set up the bath basin for the cli-
        ent; however, the bath must be completed by the client within phys-
        ical limitation to qualify as persistence. If activity restrictions pre-
        clude bathing oneself completely, as in the case of the cardiac cli-
        ent who is not permitted to bathe his legs for the first two weeks
        after a heart attack, washing the rest of the body with the excep-
        tion of the legs is rated as persistence. When the cardiac client ac-
        cepts help offered to bathe his legs, he is not exhibiting dependence,
        because dependence has been defined as the seeking of help that is
        not required.

All of these behaviors are used by everyone in their attempts to adapt to
changes that affect their mode of interdependence. The nurse must be able to
recognize and assess these behaviors and the problems they manifest. Recall
that one isolated behavior may or may not be significant; a pattern of behaviors
reflects dependency and independency.

SUMMARY

This chapter has focused on the theory of interdependence, which will be
basic to the process of planning care to handle problems of clients who meet con-

flicts in this mode during fluctuations of health and illness. Affiliative and achievement needs, basic to this mode, have been discussed. The secondary drive for dependency and the aggressive drive have been identified as sources of energy in meeting these needs. The resulting patterns of interdependent behavior were pointed out. Finally, categories of dependent and independent behaviors were identified and causes underlying these behaviors were outlined.

REFERENCES

Clough, D., "A Longitudinal Study of Dependence and Independence in Surgical Patients," unpublished Master's Thesis. Los Angeles: University of California, 1974, pp. 27–29, 45–48.

Festinger, Leon, *A Theory of Cognitive Dissonance.* Stanford: Stanford University Press, 1957.

Heathers, Glen, "Acquiring Dependency and Independence: A Theoretical Orientation," *The Journal of Genetic Psychology,* vol. 87, 1955, pp. 277–91.

Sears, Robert R., E. Maccoby, and H. Levine, *Patterns of Child-Rearing.* New York: Harper and Row Publishers, 1957.

ADDITIONAL READINGS

Baldwin, Alfred L., *Theories of Child Development.* New York: John Wiley and Sons, Inc., 1968.

Baller, Warren R. and Don C. Charles, *The Psychology of Human Growth and Development.* New York: Holt, Rinehart and Winston, Inc., 1961.

Cameron, Normal, *Personality Development and Psychopathology: A Dynamic Approach.* Boston: Houghton Mifflin Company, 1963.

Engel, George L., *Psychological Development in Health and Disease.* Philadelphia: W. B. Saunders Company, 1962.

Garrison, Karl C. and others, *The Psychology of Childhood.* New York: Charles Scribner's Sons, 1967.

Hartup, Willard W., "Nurturance and Nurturance Withdrawal in Relation to the Dependency Behavior of Preschool Children," *Child Development,* vol. 29, 1958, pp. 191-201.

Kahn, Jack H., *Human Growth and Personality Development.* 2nd edition. New York: Pergamon Press, Inc., 1971.

Lewis, Donald J., *Learning Approaches to Therapeutic Behavior Change.* Chicago: Aldine Publishing Company, 1970.

McCandless, Boyd R., *Children Behavior and Development.* 2nd edition. New York: Holt, Rinehart and Winston, Inc., 1967, p. 435.

Palermo, David S. and Lewish P. Lipaitt, *Research Readings in Child Psychology.* New York: Holt, Rinehart and Winston, Inc., 1963.

Parke, Ross D., ed. *Readings in Social Development.* New York: Holt, Rinehart and Winston, Inc., 1969.

Singer, Robert D. and Anne Singer, *Psychological Development in Children.* Philadelphia: W. B. Saunders Company, 1969.

22

Development of Interdependence

Janet Dunning

KEY CONCEPTS DEFINED

Operant Responses: Original effective responses that trigger learning.
Primary Reinforcement: Reward that meets a basic need, usually intrinsic.
Secondary Reinforcement: A learned reward, usually extrinsic.
Task of the Interdependence Mode: Task of living successfully in a world of other people.
Interpersonal Self: The self with the task of living with others.

After studying this chapter the reader will be able to:

1. Define the key concepts of this chapter.
2. Contrast the maturational and learning approaches to the development of interdependence.
3. Describe the major task of the interdependence mode.

4. Illustrate the relationship between the developmental crisis and the development of dependent and independent behaviors.
5. List factors influencing interdependence development.

Before birth, the zygote or fertilized ovum is a free-floating organism. As soon as the embryo attaches to the uterus, the independence is lost and the embryo is completely dependent on the mother for maintainance of life. From this point on in development, man alternates between periods of independence and dependence. The development of interdependence, as with the other adaptive modes, is a result of both maturation and learning. It involves fulfillment of the human task of living with others. The developmental crises described by Erikson (1963), which were discussed earlier, are also significant turning points in the development of interdependence. This chapter focuses on the development of interdependence from the framework of maturation and learning within the stages of the life cycle.

MATURATIONAL APPROACH TO DEVELOPMENT OF INTERDEPENDENCE

The maturational factors of growth and development are one approach to discussing the development of interdependence. The dependency of the infant is primarily a function of immature strength and skill for self-care. As the child increases in size, strength, and skill, he has increasingly frequent and wide-ranging opportunities to master the environment, thus allowing more independent and achievement behaviors. As strength and competency decrease with old age, there may be a necessary increase of dependent behaviors. This influence of growth and development is reflected clearly in the discussion included later, which describe dependent and independent behaviors as they develop by ages. Although maturation is not the only factor in the development of interdependency, it must be considered a prerequisite to the learning process that accompanies it. The child cannot learn verbally to demand attention until vocal cords and vocabulary have matured sufficiently to allow the use of this skill.

LEARNING APPROACH TO DEVELOPMENT OF INTERDEPENDENCE

The skills acquired through maturation often become the *operant responses* (original effective responses) that trigger learning of dependent and independent behaviors. The child's behavior is responded to by parents. If this response is rewarding or gratifying, the child will repeat the behavior. We say that learning has taken place.

The first operant responses of the infant are sucking or mouthing movements, clutching and grasping reflexes, seeming random vocalizations, and postural adjustments to being moved and held. Maternal responses to the infant are more complex since they are designed to achieve many caretaking ends—feeding, bathing, cleansing, warming—as well as many mother-gratifying experiences such as cuddling, fondling, and being clutched. Not only does the child get fed, a *primary reinforcement*—a reward that meets a basic need—but he begins to associate the mother's total response to him with feeding. Thus an interpersonal relationship becomes a *secondary reinforcement,* or learned reward. Many authors have emphasized the early feeding experience, in the context of a social relationship, as a most significant factor in learning to relate to others.

This learning process is the rationale behind stating that man has a secondary dependency drive. The process is so deeply engrained that it becomes a strong motivating tendency providing the energy for meeting the affiliative need. The particular set of response tendencies that the person develops to meet this need is contingent upon which behaviors are reinforced in this early stage, and how this pattern is modified by learning in later stages.

We have also stated that man has an aggressive drive that provides the energy behind the need for achievement. This drive also results in operant responses for the child. To relieve an inner state of tension, the child is activated to overcome the environment. Initially, this may be done by kicking feet in the air; later it may mean chewing the rails of the crib. Again, these behaviors elicit parental responses, and patterns of control over this drive are learned. As the child's skill in mastering the environment increases, the parents are likely to transfer their rewards gradually from dependent to independent behavior. When the toddler succeeds in placing one block on top of the other, he experiences the intrinsic reward of achievement, and also may be highly praised by parents.

Throughout life, then, the intrinsic and extrinsic rewards experienced following dependent and independent behaviors are responsible for learning particular patterns of these behaviors. The predominant pattern used has been referred to as the person's coping style. Some specific factors influencing the development of each particular style are discussed later. In general we can say that the development of interdependence is based on both maturation and learning.

The major *task of the interdependence mode* is the task of living successfully in a world of other people, as defined by Gardner (1964). The task encompasses recognizing one's own dependent and independent needs as well as those of other people. Living successfully with others incorporates many components of interaction. These include language skills, nonverbal communication skills, and the ability to recognize the feelings and attitudes of others. The development of sympathy and caring, as well as sharing, are inherent in successful interactions. An individual must also be able to stimulate other people. One thrust of the secondary or social self is the satisfaction that stems from the awareness of group action and cooperative behavior.

Interaction patterns are learned in the family unit. The child then moves to secondary groups with maturity, enhancing and adding to patterns of interaction. The importance of peers, clubs, and social organizations will be explored in relation to each age group during the discussion of developmental tasks as influencing factors.

The mastery of learning to live with others is manifested by feelings of security and adequacy in the individual. Problem areas arising from the nonmastery of the task of living successfully with others are: aggressiveness, rivalry, competitiveness, hostility, loneliness, disengagement, dominance, exhibition, and rejection.

DEVELOPMENTAL CRISIS RELATED TO INTERDEPENDENCE

We have pointed out that the life cycle is marked by stages, each with its transition point or maturational crisis. The eight stages marked by specific psychosocial crises, as described by Erikson (1963), were explored in relation to the developing self-concept. The self that develops is also an *interpersonal self;* that is, it is a self with the task of living with others. Each stage has a significant other person with whom the person deals in an affiliative way; for example, in the stage of identity versus identity-diffusion, the peer group and models of leadership are important. Similarly, each stage has an element of achievement, although some stages are more centrally focused on this need, for example, the sense of initiative versus guilt and the sense of industry versus inferiority.

Thus the discussion that follows relates the development of dependent and independent behaviors to each of these stages.

Interdependence Development: The First Two Years of Life

The behaviors during the first two years of life may be reflex in nature, a physiological response to stimulation, or geared toward eliciting a response from the mother to meet biological needs. However, they may also be a means of obtaining emotional gratification from the mother. By the age of six months, the infant distinguishes mother from other women and from father. Soon he begins to want mother near and cries when she is absent. Although the infant is very dependent at this stage, many developmental milestones, such as sitting and walking, enable him to obtain some independence. Behaviors indicative of dependence and independence during these first two years are many.

Interdependence Development: Two Years to Three Years

Throughout this stage of early childhood, the child has two tasks to accomplish in relation to interdependence. He must become autonomous physically, while remaining strongly dependent emotionally. As the young child is learning to develop better mastery of such skills as walking, talking, and bowel and bladder control, he finds the new environment frightening and must have the support of others. Even though the child needs support, he often must adjust to less attention as a result of the births of siblings.

Interdependence Development: Three Years to Six Years

During the years from three to six, the child learns many affiliative behaviors, such as showing affection and interacting with other age mates. The rapid development of verbal and motor skills makes these behaviors possible. *This developmental stage is in actuality a critical period for developing interdependence.* The conflict is overt and between the affiliative and achievement needs. Gardner (1964) describes this conflict very clearly. The child is ambivalent; he wants to be big, strong, independent, achieving, productive, expansive, and self-actualizing; he seeks responsibility and joyously enters into relationships with the world of people and objects. But at the same time the dependent part of the child desires to be small, protected, dependent, secure, and nurtured by the strength of others. He seeks to avoid responsibility, and protects himself against the intrusion of the world. During these dependent times the child avoids encounters with the strange, the novel, and the threatening.

The developing independent traits enable the child to expand the environment, and as a result he enlarges the circle of relationships, especially with other children. Play groups, nursery school, kindergarten, and the first years of primary school provide a social structure in which the child interacts. The parental role at this point is to assist the child in moving toward independent, achievement behaviors.

Interdependence Development: Six Years to Pubescence

During the time that the child moves from age six to pubescence he takes on the task of freeing himself from primary identification with adults and develops peer relationships. Once a child feels secure by being accepted by others, receiving affection, and having a good feeling about himself he is ready to deal with his peer group in a happy and healthy manner. He is no longer physically dependent, and he is much less emotionally dependent. He now has the initiative to be more self-directed and can free himself from primary identification with his parental figures.

Interdependence Development: Adolescence

Duvall (1965, p. 35) states that "the teen years represent a fundamental dilemma of life — to grow and mature or to stay and be secure . . ." Even though the adolescent is trying to free himself from parental authority, he needs to feel the support of family and that he can return home for love and guidance. The adolescent is trying out new patterns of affiliation with both peers and family. At the same time, he experiences new difficulties in channeling aggressive drives. The adolescent may have violent outbursts in the home, particularly when habitual activities are interrupted or when he fails to accomplish the personal goals set. Sometimes angry displays are attention-seeking devices or reactions to authority. Pacing the floor, going for a walk, and sulkiness are more often utilized with the peer group, since they are more acceptable.

Interdependence Development: Twenty Years to Thirty-five Years

This period actually marks the beginning of a state of interdependency. The adult will at times be independent and at times dependent. No longer building independent or dependent patterns into the total personality, he is working with the patterns that have been established up to this point. One task that the young adult usually tries to accomplish is to build a strong affectional bond with a possible marriage partner. Most often this is done by union through marriage. For some, marriage is not the answer, but affiliation in some type of community life seems better to accomplish this task. For the single person, close affiliations with friends, professional colleagues, and family may best help to meet this need.

Interdependence Development: Thirty-five Years to Sixty-five Years

During this middle period, parents, parental figures, and older friends may be lost through illness or death. In addition, children are growing up, and the mother and father may experience varying degrees of depression due to separation as they go off to college, join the military service, or leave home for work and/or marriage. Affiliative patterns with aging parents and growing children are changing. Along with this change comes the need for marriage partners to rediscover each other.

Interdependence Development: Sixty-five Years and Older

One of the tasks of older age in this mode is to accept the help of others as powers fail. It is desirable at this time to maintain as much independence as possible, as demonstrated by doing as much for oneself as one is capable of. The individual cannot deny the changes of aging, and with this comes the realization that help will have to be acquired from others. Also during this time the person may have to adjust to the death of a spouse and to establish an affiliation with one's own age group.

The preceding section has outlined dependent and independent behaviors as they develop through the life cycle. The influence of maturation and learning is evidenced in the sequence of these behaviors. We may now look at more specific instances of factors influencing interdependence development.

FACTORS INFLUENCING INTERDEPENDENCE DEVELOPMENT

Maturation has been viewed as a necessary prerequisite to the development of interdependence behaviors. Behaviors emerge on the basis of size, strength, and skill of the person. In addition there are numerous other factors influencing interdependence development. Perhaps the most significant are the developing self-concept of the person, and the affection and reinforcements received from others.

We have seen that the infant and young child are very dependent both physically and emotionally. Meeting these dependency needs affects the child's self-concept and interdependence development. Inadequate gratification of dependency needs at this age can make a child feel insecure. Even though the child is becoming more independent, he is dependent on parents to buffer or help in working through the harmful experiences that occur along with this new-found independence. If the infant feels confident that someone will help in these periods, he will develop trust and will feel more comfortable in new explorations. If he feels insecure, the child will respond by becoming nervous, irritable, and given to crying. This in turn precipitates a cycle of events in which the mother sees the baby as difficult and hard to handle. These feelings affect the entire mother-child relationship and the child's concept of self, as well as his ability to relate to others.

By the age of 3 to 6 years the child's concept of self and personal ability to relate to others is dependent upon acceptance by others, receiving of affection, and achievements.

The young child is dependent on himself and the environment to meet affiliative and achievement needs. If he has a physical defect or a deformity, which is a handicap to doing what his age mates do, or a discrepancy between ability and the goals set for himself, there may be problems in meeting both affiliation and achievement needs. If he is taken away from friends who are giving affection, or if there is a breakup in family structure, the significant others on whom he is dependent for receiving a positive self-concept and affection will be missing.

As the child grows older, if he is not pleased with the personal handling of the tools in his environment, and does not perform well in relation to peers, he will be discouraged from identification with them. The child may develop persistent feelings of inferiority and as a result isolate himself. This in turn precipitates a cycle of events in which the child sees himself as less desirable in spite of what he tries to accomplish, and thus becomes less internally motivated.

Any withdrawal of love by significant others tends to make the child feel insecure, and as a result there is a greater inclination toward behavior indicative of attention-seeking and affection-seeking. There are various ways in which the child can be deprived of affection. The more usual expressions of rejection are neglect, unrelenting criticism, overprotection, and overindulgence. Sears (1957) maintains that if children are frustrated in the need to acquire affection, high rates of dependency occur in preschool and school-age youngsters. Levy (1962) states that overprotection yields high rates of dependent behavior, as it prevents the child from exploring his environment.

If the adolescent has established a good self-concept and has satisfactorily completed the tasks of interdependence up to this period, he will probably not have a great deal of difficulty in developing new ways of meeting affiliative and achievement needs. If the adolescent does not feel good about self, overidentification with other personalities is possible to make up for the insecurities that he sees himself as possessing. This may lead to a dependent coping style and less use of independent behaviors.

Several factors can inhibit the young adult from mastering the interdependence tasks. Because of feelings of insecurity about self in relation to other people, he may avoid contacts that permit intimacy and affiliation, or perpetuate excuses that will keep him in social isolation. A disruption in self-concept development in which the individual does not feel worthy of love can prevent him from achieving closeness with any particular person. Intimacy implies loving, nurturing, and taking care of.

When the person moves from early to later adulthood, between the ages of 35 and 65 years, he is likely to rely on whatever coping style was developed earlier. Certain radical changes in life, such as divorce or serious illness, may accentuate the usual style or may precipitate a change in it. The aging process, beyond 65 years, usually emphasizes the person's style for meeting affiliative and achievement needs. One who is accustomed to using initiative-taking and obstacle mastery behaviors predominantly will continue to use them. However, the pace of the activities will be moderated by his diminishing strength. For the person more accustomed to help, attention, and affection-seeking behaviors, failing strength will provide the rationale for intensification of these behaviors. We have pointed out that the death of a loved one is an important stimulus during this time for the development of new ways of meeting affiliative needs.

The principle of learning underlies this development of interdependence. In the beginning, because the child is totally dependent upon parents for gratification of needs, their behavior toward the child is highly valued in his eyes. Their rewards, especially their love, is extremely significant. Later, when the reward value of the parents is reduced, the threat of the loss of their love is also reduced. At the same time, the parents reward his independence, thus contributing to independence development.

Influenced by his self-concept development and the rewards received from others, the person develops a style of coping with affiliative and achievement needs, which is predominantly dependent, independent, or interdependent.

SUMMARY

This chapter has looked at the development of interdependence from both a maturational and learning point of view. The influence of one adaptive mode upon another was seen in the effect that self-concept development has on the resulting style of coping with the tasks of meeting the demands of the successive stages of life. The interdependence mode underlies the development of the other modes. The beginning and ongoing mother-child relationship determines the development of a healthy or unhealthy self-concept. The interaction with other people determines the development of a balanced style of interdependence. The balanced person uses dependent behaviors when appropriate and independent behaviors when those are called for. Understanding this development will assist the nurse in her assessment of clients at all age levels.

REFERENCES

Duvall, E. M., "Family Dilemmas with Teenagers," *Family Life Coordinator*, vol. 14, 1965, pp. 35–38.

Erikson, Erik H., *Childhood and Society.* 2nd ed. New York: W. W. Norton and Company, Inc., 1963; London: The Hogarth Press Ltd.

Gardner, D. Bruce, *Development in Early Childhood: The Pre-School Years.* New York: Harper and Row, Publishers, 1964.

Levy, S. J., "Phases in Changing Interpersonal Relations," *Merrill Palmer Quarterly*, vol. 8, 1962, pp. 121–28.

Sears, Robert R., E. E. Maccoby, and H. Levin, *Patterns of Child Rearing.* New York: Harper and Row, Publishers, 1957, pp. 138–75.

ADDITIONAL READINGS

Aimsworth, M. D., "Patterns of Attachment Behaviors Shown by the Infant with His Mother," *Merrill Palmer Quarterly*, vol. 10, 1964, pp. 57–58.

Breckinridge, M. E. and E. L. Vincent, *Child Development.* 5th ed. Philadelphia: W. B. Saunders Company, 1965.

Combs, A. W., "New Horizons in Field Research: The Self Concept," *Educational Leadership*, vol. 15, 1958, pp. 315–19, 328.

Emmerich, W., "Continuity and Stability in Early Social Development: Teacher Ratings," *Child Development*, vol. 37, 1966, pp. 17–27.

Gessel, Arnold, F. L. Tig and L. B. Ames, *Youth: The Years from Ten to Sixteen.* New York: Harper and Row, Publishers, 1956.

Havinghurst, Robert J., *Developmental Tasks and Education.* London: Longmans, Green and Co., Ltd., 1953.

_____ , *Older People.* London: Longmans, Green and Co., Ltd., 1953.

Horrocks, J. E., *The Psychology of Adolescence.* 2nd ed. Boston: Houghton Mifflin Company, 1962.

Hurlock, E. G., *Developmental Psychology.* New York: McGraw-Hill, Inc. 1968.

Jersild, A. T., *Child Psychology.* 5th ed. Englewood Cliffs, N. J.: Prentice-Hall, Inc., 1960.

_____ , *The Psychology of Adolescence.* 2nd ed. New York: The Macmillan Company, 1963.

MacFarlane, J. L. Allen and M. P. Honzik, *A Developmental Study of the Behavior Problems of Normal Children Between 21 Months and 14 Years.* Berkeley: University of California Press, 1954.

Murray, Edward J., *Motivation and Emotion.* Englewood Cliffs, N. J.: Prentice-Hall, Inc., 1964.

Sears, Robert R., "Dependency Motivation," *Nebraska Symposium on Motivation.* Lincoln: University of Nebraska Press, 1963, pp. 25-64.

Spock, Benjamin, *The Pocket Book of Baby and Child Care.* New York: Pocket Books, 1964.

Tig, F. L. and L. B. Ames, *Child Behavior.* New York: Harper and Row, Publishers, 1956.

23

Problems of Interdependence

Mary Poush and
Sister Joyce Van Landingham

KEY CONCEPTS DEFINED

Internal Stimuli: Internal drives and patterns of control over these drives.

Cognitive Organization: The person's general structures of ideas as they relate to new external demands.

Affective Domain: The person's unique perceptions and values relating to new external stimuli.

Dysfunctional Dependence: The use of dependent behaviors to the detriment of one's well-being.

Dysfunctional Independence: The use of independent behaviors to the detriment of one's well-being.

Insight Therapy: A process by which the client becomes aware of and may resolve conflict.

Interviewing: Purposeful verbal exchange designed to gather data about the client's experience.

Therapeutic Communication: Purposeful verbal exchange designed to facilitate the expression of thoughts, memories, feelings, so that from this expressed complexity the person's behavioral conflict can be defined.

Creative Listening: That technique of therapeutic communication by which the person hears the theme and nuances of meaning that are conveyed indirectly.

Creative Responding: The skill of asking the right questions or reflecting responses to clarify the "music" the nurse has heard; usually uses what, when, where, and who questions.

Behavior Modification: A process of eliciting and rewarding desired behavioral response, and reducing, modifying, or extinguishing ineffective adaptive coping responses.

Social Reinforcement: The use of and manipulation of environmental stimuli to reward desired behaviors in such a way as to increase the probability of their consistent reoccurrence.

Behavioral Control: The active attempt to influence the person directly and explicitly by confronting him or her with environmental conditions designed to produce unlearning of a previous behavioral response and introducing the client to a new and more desirable one.

After studying this chapter the reader will be able to:

1. Define the key concepts of this chapter.
2. Describe the cognitive and affective aspects the nurse assesses in assessing the internal stimuli for interdependence.
3. Identify problems of dysfunctional dependence and of dysfunctional independence if given case studies illustrating these problems.
4. Discuss interventions to be used in the problems of dysfunctional dependence and dysfunctional independence (see Appendix II).

Situations of health and illness frequently demand changes in patterns of interdependence. During illness a person needs to become dependent to conserve energy for healing and moving back to wellness. On the other hand, during convalescence there are new obstacles to overcome, and increased independence is demanded. In Chapter 21 we saw the theoretical basis for interdependence and Chapter 22 illustrated how dependent and independent coping styles are developed. This chapter focuses on the characteristic problems arising when the client's coping patterns result in a conflict with the demands of health and illness. The following two chapters elaborate on examples of specific adaptive problems in interdependence.

The demands of illness can engender maladaption in the interdependence mode even in a person who has developed a balanced interdependence coping style. However, since his response to conflicting and opposing demands for independent or dependent action has been consistently fluid and flexible, this brings about minimal behavioral conflict. That is not true of individuals who have developed one-sided coping patterns, either dependent or independent. Their method of coping with opposing demands has been a rigid use of one-sided behavioral responses, and therefore they face immediate or eventual behavioral conflicts during illness. Behavioral conflict occurs because of the incompatible demands made by the external environment and by their own internal needs. Since such conflict interferes with progress on the health/illness continuum, the nurse uses the process of assessment and intervention to resolve the behavioral conflict and to re-establish interdependence integrity. The commonalities of this process will be discussed. Then these principles will be applied to a situation of dysfunctional independence and to one of dysfunctional dependence.

ASSESSMENT OF INTERDEPENDENCE

The first step in assessment is to observe the client's behavior and determine its frequency and consistency. Which of the behaviors, described in Chapter 21 as dependent and independent, is the client using? That is, are his behaviors help-seeking, attention-seeking, and affection-seeking or are they initiative-taking and obstacle mastery?

Next the nurse looks for stimuli that are influencing behavior. In assessing the stimuli for role function, the nurse looked mainly at the external environment since this is where a person receives cues for role performance. However, in second level assessment of interdependence, the nurse must assess mainly *internal stimuli* since dependency and interdependency behaviors are related mainly to internal drives and patterns of control over these drives. Thus the nurse must get a view of the situation as it is viewed from inside her client.

This view from the inside will have cognitive and affective aspects. Since we cannot view drives and their control directly, we look at the whole picture as the client reconstructs it through the fitter of his drives and patterns. The client's cognitive realm reflects the individual's unique *cognitive organization,* that is, the person's general structure of ideas as they relate to the new external demands. The *affective domain* of the individual expresses the client's unique perceptions and values relating to the new external stimuli.

When addressing herself to cognitive organization, the nurse is dealing with: (1) the client's knowledge of new perceptual data; (2) his comprehension of it, including ability to translate, interpret, and extrapolate the new data; (3) the ability to apply the perceptual data; (4) the ability to analyze the elements, relationships, and organizational principles involved in the new data; (5) the ability to synthesize the new perceptual stimuli; and (6) the client's evaluation or judgment about the value of the parts, as well as the whole, of the new perceptual data.

When the nurse considers the affective sphere, her concerns are multiple. She needs to consider: (1) how the client is actually attending to external stimuli;

how aware he is, how willing he is to receive the data, and, above all, how he usually controls or selectively attends to new environmental stimuli; (2) how the person is responding to new environmental demands, and how he acquiesces, and with what willingness and satisfaction he responds to the new perceptual data; (3) how the client is valuing the perceptual data, how he ascribes value to it and states a preference for a previous value if committed to the new value or only committed to previous values; and (4) how he organizes the perceptual data, conceptualizes the new value, and as a consequence organizes his unique value system.

This assessment of the internal stimuli of the client's cognitive and affective structure of the situation is illustrated in the following example.

Annette Moore is a 14-year-old junior high school student who is on very limited activity due to rheumatic fever with heart involvement. According to the nurses, Annette is continuously going beyond the limits of her restrictions by bathing herself before the nurses come in, by getting out of bed to set her hair, and by writing for several hours a day on an essay for English class. Initially this behavior may look like sick role failure as described in an earlier chapter. However, providing the cues for role performance—that is, supplying the reward, consumer, set of circumstances, cooperation, and collaboration—has not changed Annette's behavior. Thus an alert nurse on the unit suspects that an interdependence conflict may be responsible for the maladaptive behavior.

This nurse spends some time with Annette to reconstruct the situation from her point of view, cognitively and affectively. In regard to the aspects of cognitive organization, the nurse learns the following facts. Annette can recall and repeat information given her on her heart disease, including the effects of activity. She does not see "the little bit I do" as applicable to nonprescribed activity. Because her mother has called her "vain," Annette sees restrictions on the activity of fixing her hair as related to unreasonable parental limitations. She has decided that to continue to take care of herself and achieve in school are valued parts of her life. The fact that she is in the hospital and in bed "most of the time" are seen as being enough to make her well.

Affectively, Annette thinks that what doctors and nurses say should be taken about as seriously as what parents say. That is, they may have a point, but they usually exaggerate. Thus her attention to information from them is limited. She doesn't like to "think about heart damage," but feels it is very important to keep herself looking nice externally. Good health in the future does not have much meaning for her in relation to her strongly expressed feelings of wanting to "be on my own." First and second level assessment of this client's maladaptive behavior is summarized in Table 23.1.

Thus, in assessing interdependence, the nurse uses the same nursing process emphasized throughout this text. However, she focuses her search for relevant influencing factors on the internal stimuli of how the client sees the situation cognitively and affectively in relation to dependency-independency needs.

TABLE 23.1
Assessment of Interdependence — Annette Moore

Behavior	Adaptation Status	Stimuli		
		Focal	Contextual	Residual
Obstacle mastery. Goes beyond activity restrictions — bathing self, setting hair, writing several hours.	M	Conflict of drive for independence with demand for dependency during illness.	Has basic knowledge of illness, but does not see own activity as related to what she knows. Values care of self and achievement in school. Sees hospitalization as supposed to make her well. Feels that doctors and nurses exaggerate like her parents. Avoids thinking about "heart damage" and focuses on looking nice. Feels strongly a desire to be "on her own," but cannot relate effectively to future goal of good health.	Mother calls her vain. Developmental level of early adolescence.

PROBLEM IDENTIFICATION IN INTERDEPENDENCE

After the nurse gathers data on client behavior and influencing factors, she makes a judgment about what the client problem is. At the present stage of knowledge about the interdependence adaptive mode, two types of problems can be identified — dysfunctional dependence and dysfunctional independence.

Dysfunctional dependence is defined as *the use of dependent behaviors to the detriment of one's well-being.* This diagnosis is made tentatively when the nurse observes help-seeking, attention-seeking, and/or affection-seeking behaviors that interfere with movement toward wellness. It can usually be confirmed if data gathered regarding the client's internal structuring of the situation reveal a conflict between the individual's pattern of dependency and the demands of independency made by the health/illness situation. A situation of this type of diagnosis is illustrated later in this chapter, and another form of the problem—loneliness—is the topic of a separate chapter.

Dysfunctional independence is defined as *the use of independent behaviors to the detriment of one's well-being.* Again, the nurse can make this tentative diagnosis when she observes initiative-taking, and/or obstacle-mastery behaviors that interfere with movement toward wellness. Evidence for confirming this diagnosis is obtained from the nurse's efforts to view the client's perception of the situation in relation to his pattern of independence as it conflicts with environmental demands for dependency. This is the diagnosis given for Annette Moore. Dysfunctional independence is further illustrated later in this chapter.

INTERVENTION IN THE INTERDEPENDENCE MODE

From the nature of the assessment and diagnosis described above, it is evident that this adaptive mode requires interventions beyond the manipulation of the environment. That is, modalities must be used that will alter the client's internal stimuli. The behavioral conflict must be resolved to bring about adaptation in the interdependence mode.

Two methods of intervention—*insight therapy* and *behavior modification*—are proposed as ways of achieving this goal. These two modalities are ways of changing behavior. Insight therapy acts directly on the client's cognitive and affective structuring of the situation, while behavior modification works first on outward behavior with consequent internal restructuring.

The goal of insight therapy is to help the client become aware of and in control of his own behavioral conflict and conflict resolution. The process involves three steps. The first step is the facilitation of the person's expression of feelings and perceptions involved in the conflict situation. The second step is the identification and clarification of the perceived and actual conflict involved. The third step is the person's re-education through teaching, translation, interpretation, and extrapolation of perceptual data. The skills needed to carry out insight therapy are interviewing and therapeutic communication. These skills were discussed briefly in Chapter 2 as a means of nursing assessment. Here they are discussed in greater detail as a means of intervention that can be used in the interdependence, as well as other adaptive, modes.

Interviewing separates social chitchat from purposeful verbal exchange. Since the focus of interviewing is on the client's experience, the nurse uses her time and verbal interaction purposefully to gather data about this experience.

An initial purpose of the interview is to establish trust between nurse and client. This is necessary because the two are usually strangers and the nurse cannot expect the client automatically to share his experience. The nurse establishes trust by setting perimeters to the conversation and by providing the client with a measure of predictability. The client needs to know the nurse's name, that she is qualified, what she may be called upon to do or perform, the time limits governing the duration and frequency of nurse/client contacts, and what the nurse plans to do with the information shared (Peplau, 1952).

The skill of *therapeutic communication* continues and enhances the interviewing process. Its purpose is to facilitate the client's expression of complex thoughts, memories, and feelings, so that from this expressed complexity, the nurse can assist in clarifying and defining the person's present behavioral conflict (Lazarus, 1966, 1969). The techniques involved in therapeutic communication are creative listening and responding.

Creative listening is like listening to music. The person hears the theme and nuances of meaning that are conveyed indirectly through sound or hint (Peplau, 1952). *Creative responding,* on the other hand, is the skill of asking the right questions or reflecting client response in order to clarify the "music" the nurse has heard. To respond creatively the nurse needs to facilitate the client's description of what he is actually feeling, thinking, or experiencing. All to often, "how" or "why" questions inhibit or intimidate the person's flow of conversation. Both questions imply a correct or good way of responding; that is, they imply that in order to meet the nurse's "need" the client ought to or must respond in some preconceived or prescribed manner. Hence a feeling of guilt or inadequacy may be engendered. How and why questions also imply that a person should have a correct answer. If the client already knew and understood why or how he came to feel, think, or experience in a certain way, he would undoubtedly be able to identify the conflict and bring about its successful resolution. Creative responding, then, consists of asking questions or reflecting client comments in such a way that they elicit a description of the client's unique perceptions, values, and cognitive organizations.

"What," "when," "where," and "who" questions would aid the nurse in eliciting descriptive verbal expressions. Even stock phrases such as "Tell me about that," "Can you describe it to me?" "What came after that?" "Can you recall?"

or "Go on, please" can help the nurse to become conversant with the person's internal stimuli.

There are some common blocks to creative listening and responding. The troublesome "we," "they," and "us" pronouns form such a block. By their use, the nurse and client identities become merged and confuse the consequent verbal exchange. Another block is the use of automatic knowing clauses such as "I know," "I see," or "I understand" before any client response has been elicited. Such usage terminates the conversation before the client can begin to provide any descriptive data, for these clauses imply that the nurse has preknowledge and does not need the client to describe it further. A third type of communication block is the indiscriminate use of value terms such as "nice," "good," "poor," and "bad." Their use deflects the client's attention from his own value system to that of the nurse. Indeed the nurse will wish to ask the client to describe his own values about the situation or demands, but she will not, in turn, ascribe her own value judgment to the person's descriptive remarks.

Insight therapy, then, should provide a means for helping the client to clarify his own responses to internal and external stimuli to problem solve toward conflict resolution, and to come to his own conclusions about behavioral changes.

The second proposed nursing modality of *behavior modification* also has as its goal to bring about effective behavioral change. It is the process of eliciting and rewarding or gratifying externally desired behavioral responses and to reduce, modify, or extinguish ineffective adaptive coping responses.

The techniques or skills involved in behavior modification are essentially twofold: social reinforcement and behavior control. *Social reinforcement* refers to the use of and manipulation of environmental stimuli to reward desired behaviors in such a way as to increase the probability of their consistent reoccurrence. *Behavioral control* relates to the active attempt to influence the person directly and explicitly. It involves confronting the client with environmental conditions, designed to produce unlearning of a previous behavioral response and introducing the client to a new and more desirable one (Yates, 1970). Behavior control and social reinforcement emphasize re-education and reward, thereby client teaching and conditioning techniques are needed for their implementation.

One conditioning technique is operant conditioning. The following is an example of its use in an independency situation.

The nurse presents a cue or discriminative stimulus to the subject, thereby eliciting the behavior (response) desired. The second step is to reward the behavior (see Figure 23.1).

The positive stimulus response will be more effective in increasing independent behaviors. The nurse is in a prominent position to give cues eliciting either independent or dependent behavior. For example, the client would respond differently if the nurse gave this cue, "You're tired this morning, I'll give you a refreshing bath."

Reinforcers or stimulus responses are an equally important component of the behavior modification process. They must be present for the learning to occur

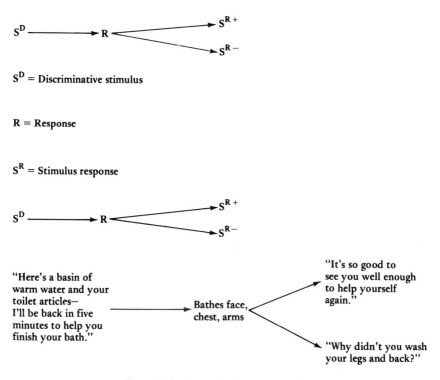

S^D = Discriminative stimulus

R = Response

S^R = Stimulus response

Figure 23.1 Example of operant conditioning in interdependence.

or for behavior to change. The reinforcers must be valued sufficiently to be meaningful to the person who is involved in the behavioral change. (The reader is referred to a psychology text for more detailed information on the techniques of behavior modification.)

The proposed intervention modalities of insight therapy and behavior modification are designed for the purpose of reducing the cognitive and affective blocks to successful conflict resolution and consequent adaptive behavioral change. They address themselves to the direct and indirect manipulation of internal stimuli to assist the client's resolution of conflict and his effective re-establishment of interdependence mode adaptation.

AN EXAMPLE OF DYSFUNCTIONAL INDEPENDENCE

The adult displaying a dysfunctional independence is seen many times a day in a busy medical-surgical unit. The disruptive behaviors manifested due to the stress of the dependent sick role in which he finds himself appear at first deceptively simple to assess and for which to assign appropriate interventions. More is required than assessment of external stimuli if the client's behavior is to be changed significantly. Only limited success will be met unless the internal stimuli motivating the disruptive behavior are also recognized and considered in the total care plan.

Mr. Rodgers typifies the client experiencing dysfunctional independence. He is a 67-year-old self-made businessman, who designed and built his own liquor store. Ostensibly, Mr. Rodgers retired from business two years ago, only to slip back into its strenuous demands because he could not find hired personnel to meet his demands. Mr. Rodgers' usual working day is from 16 to 18 hours. He has few hobbies and rarely relaxes enough to take his wife out for an evening of entertainment.

The demands of a poorly staffed business concern were the reason for Mr. Rodgers' present hospitalization. He injured his back lifting and unloading cases of liquor. Recognizing his need for medical attention after several weeks of painful movement and aching pain in his lower back and right leg, he sought medical advice and was told he had a herniated disc. The doctor explained that the disc, a cartilagineous plate that forms the cushion between the vertebral bodies, may have been injured and/or ruptured, causing its nucleous to push back against the dural sac or against a spinal nerve as it emerges from the spinal column, which in turn causes back and leg pain. Since the pain is due to pressure in the involved nerve area, it is intensified by bending, twisting, and lifting. Continued pressure may produce degenerative changes in the involved nerve. Therefore, the doctor ordered bed rest for both the relief of nerve pressure and relief of pain. He also ordered muscle relaxants and medication to alleviate untoward spasm and increased pressure and pain. Pelvic traction was initiated to relieve nerve pressure and decrease muscle spasms.

Mr. Rodgers' tenth day of hospitalization has shown little improvement. The frequency and severity of muscle spasms are essentially unchanged.

Mr. Rodgers' behavioral pattern during this ten-day period is significant. He consistently gets out of bed for writing material and books. He goes into the bathroom to brush his teeth and shave, and he insists on going to the bathroom for his elimination needs. It depends upon the response to his call light whether Mr. Rodgers waits to be released from traction or whether he releases it himself. Because the nurse's response is rarely quick enough, Mr. Rodgers has contrived an effective means of removing his own traction, and he ambulates where he wishes. The consequences are rather severe, for his combined pain medication and muscle relaxants have contributed to his falling in the bathroom on several occasions.

Despite a repetition of health teaching interventions and re-explanations of the need for bed rest, for rest to the affected part, and for the need of aids or assists to support his muscle and ligaments to reduce pressure and insure healing, Mr. Rodgers continues to exhibit a one-sided independent coping pattern.

Mr. Rodgers' illness dictates a need for him to undergo a dependent phase of activity, to conserve his energy and body movements in order to insure tissue healing. However, Mr. Rodgers' previous coping pattern demands independent meeting of his needs. These conflicting demands result in behavioral conflict and

TABLE 23.2
Assessment of Dysfunctional Independence — Mr. Rodgers

Behavior	Stimuli		
	Focal	Contextual	Residual
Obstacle mastery. Still getting out of bed despite commode and nurse's quicker response to client's call light.	Behavioral conflict due to the demand for a dependent phase of activity with a concommitant demand to be in control by coping in an independent manner (internal vs external stimuli).	Bed rest prescribed for healing and muscle spasm and pain reduction. Patient's need to do everything himself. Patient's knowledge of disease process. His internal value for being independent and in control. Previous attempts by nursing staff to "health teach" about external demands of illness. The nurse (team leader) who was constant. Student nurse (who did an accurate assessment of external stimuli).	Liquor store owner. Retired 2 years ago, came out of retirement 18 months ago. "Can't keep good help at the store." Injured back while operating store and unloading cases of liquor.

militates against an adaptive behavioral response. The behavioral conflict, then, becomes the nurse's primary concern.

After the nurse has spent some time with the client, she makes the assessment outlined in Table 23.2. This assessment reflects Mr. Rodgers' cognitive and affective structuring of the situation.

The diagnosis of dysfunctional independence is made. The nursing goal is to relieve the client's psychic stress, to facilitate his insight into his disruptive behavioral response, to bring about conflict resolution, and to establish interdependence integrity to enable Mr. Rodgers to act dependently until tissue healing is accomplished.

Since the behavioral conflict is the key to the psychic stress and maladaptive behavioral responses, the nursing intervention must be designed for both internal and external stimuli.

First, proposed nursing interventions would manipulate internal and external focal stimuli.

1. *Internal focal stimuli*   Mr. Rodgers need to be in control by using his previous one-sided independent coping style.

The nurse will need to address herself to Mr. Rodgers' cognitive and affective domain. In the cognitive sphere she will use insight therapy to explore his perception of the conflict in his internal and external demands, as well as the anxiety and stress he experiences when he is not in control. Insight therapy in the affective domain will demand that the nurse explore how Mr. Rodgers is actually attending to the external demands due to his illness and, above all, what value he places on these demands and how he conceptualizes them in conjunction with his internal demand to be in control. Then she will look at how he intends to respond to these conflicting demands.

2. *External focal stimuli*   Need to be in a dependent phase due to illness and the doctor's order for complete bed rest.

This demands health teaching and has already been instituted. Clarification in conjunction with insight therapy may be needed here to help clarify Mr. Rodgers perceptual data.

The nurse uses interviewing and therapeutic communication skills to facilitate Mr. Rodgers' insight and help him bring about conflict resolution. To establish interdependence integrity, the nurse will need to employ behavioral modification to help Mr. Rodgers experience a feeling of being in control through dependent activity. Meaningful control through dependent activity will be a new experience for Mr. Rodgers. He will have to see it as valuable and rewarding in order to use it as an effective coping style during his illness phase.

In summary, then, effective nursing occurs only when all the impinging stimuli are manipulated, that is, both the internal and external stimuli confronting the client. Nursing interventions in this mode aim to resolve the conflicting internal and external demands that are made during illness.

AN EXAMPLE OF DYSFUNCTIONAL DEPENDENCE

The person using a dependent coping style is also seen daily in health care situations. He may not be as easily noted because the transitional and accepted stages of the sick role sanction dependent behaviors. The nurse gives care, therefore meeting the dependent needs is not as disruptive to a nursing unit as providing for independent behaviors. The conflict caused by dysfunctional dependence will become overt during the convalescent stage of illness. This occurred with Mrs. Bailey.

Mrs. Bailey was hospitalized for a hysterectomy. The operation was performed successfully, and she was five days postoperative when her dependency became a nursing concern. The nurses on the unit were aware that she was not moving on to the convalescent stage of illness as expected. First level assessment revealed maladaptive behaviors of (1) asking for pain medication every three hours around the clock for incisional pain; (2) putting on her call bell for assistance to the bathroom; (3) refusing to participate in her daily personal care — for example, one daughter arrived at 8:00 a.m. every morning to comb her hair and arrange her flowers, she waited for oral hygiene articles to be brought to her, and she would not help with her bath; (4) holding the nurse's hand and asked many "holding" questions when the nurse was preparing to leave the room; and (5) refusing to carry out the prescribed deep-breathing and coughing regimen.

These behaviors were classified as dependent. Their goal appeared to be attention-seeking, help-seeking, and affection-seeking, rather than sick role failure behaviors. Mrs. Bailey did verbalize a desire to get well and go home, and talked about what she would do at home. She was able to complete her personal care and deep-breathing exercises, but was not doing so.

The nursing process utilizing these behaviors revealed the following: during interview Mrs. Bailey was found to have a dependent coping style: (1) she is used to negating any discomfort quickly, for example, she eats for gratification whether hungry or not; (2) her mother visited and ran the household for three months when Mrs. Bailey gave birth to her daughter; (3) Mrs. Bailey has never been employed; (4) her husband makes the decisions at home, even taking her grocery shopping and making selections. Other stimuli influencing her behavior were (1) the daughter came to visit all day, every day, the husband was taking off work to visit during the day and visiting every evening; (2) husband and daughter frequently ask if she is "in pain," or if they can get anything for her; (3) low self-concept as revealed by self-concept assessment; (4) she has many friends and club members who visit; (5) many cards and flowers in the room; (6) primary nursing practiced on the nursing unit; (7) fifth day postoperative norms are ambulating by self, doing most of self-care; (8) Empirin compound #3 q 3 hours, prn for pain; (9) feels nurse is here to "take care of her," and (10) the nurse is rewarding the lack of cooperation with coughing and deep breathing by coming in and staying with her while she does the exercises. A nursing process record of first and second level assessment is illustrated in Table 23.3.

Mrs. Bailey is manifesting dysfunctional dependency as illustrated by (1) asking for pain medication every three hours; (2) not initiating or participating in activities related to personal care or medical treatments; and (3) using holding questions when staff is in the room. This is due to her usual pattern of dependent coping; the family spending twelve hours a day with her; her feeling uncomfortable when alone; her lack of understanding of her involvement in client role on fifth day postoperative; and her past experience of needing help in stressful situations.

Nursing interventions will be aimed at aiding Mrs. Bailey to resolve her dependency-convalescent sick role conflict and to become aware of her usual coping pattern. The goals are stated in adaptation behavior and are specific and measurable. They reflect the affectional need of the interdependence mode. The proposed goals are:

Short term:
1. Mrs. Bailey will make decisions about, and actively participate in, her personal care.
2. Mrs. Bailey will express feelings and fears about illness to staff.
3. Mrs. Bailey will feel secure and nurtured by calling family when lonely; discussing dependent needs with nurse; appropriate use of pain medications and call light.

Interventions will utilize many of the techniques and skills discussed in preceding chapters. These skills include patient-centered teaching, drug and treatment administration, and communication skills to further explore Mrs. Bailey's feelings. In addition, the two intervention modalities discussed earlier—insight therapy and behavior modification—will be used. The professional nurse (primary) would institute the interventions to reach the goals.

The nurse decided to give Mrs. Bailey her bath and to spend this time for using the insight therapy process outlined earlier. She explored the client's knowledge of new perceptual data, for example, What is a convalescent sick role? How does the client's behavior change during the process of wellness→illness → wellness? How does the nurse fit into the "getting well" process? The nurse talked with Mrs. Bailey specifically about what this meant to Mrs. Bailey—what are her responsibilities regarding her goal of recovery; how can her family help? Therapeutic communication is used throughout the nurse/patient interchange. Cues of unmet dependency needs are observed for both in verbal and nonverbal communication. The intervention interchange alone facilitated the nurse and client deciding

TABLE 23.3
Assessment of Dysfunctional Dependency — Mrs. Bailey

Behavior	Stimuli		
	Focal	Contextual	Residual
Help-seeking:	Conflict of pattern of dependent coping with demands for independence in convalescence.	Daughter/husband in room most of the day and evening.	Mother came in and ran home for daughter and baby for 3 months when child born.
Asks for pain medication every 3-4 hours. (M)		Frequently asked if it hurts. 5th day postop. Empirin #3 q 3 hr prn pain.	
Puts on call bell for assistance to bathroom. (M)		5th day postop hysterectomy.	
Waits for nurse to give bath. (M)		Family in room.	
		Feels nurse is here to "take care of her."	
Does not cough and deep breathe q 2h. (M)		Lung congestion.	
		Nurse comes in every 2 hrs. to check treatment, when not done, stays 5 minutes and verbally encourages client to cough and deep breathe, supports incision with pillow.	
Affection-seeking:		Daughter comes 8 AM to 8 PM. Low self-concept.	Has never worked away from home.
Waits for daughter to come and comb her hair. (M)		Not used to making own decisions.	
Holds nurse's hand when nurse prepares to leave room and asks many questions in order to keep nurse in room. (M)		Husband makes decisions at home—what food will be served, helps her grocery shop.	
		Primary nurse concept on nursing unit.	
		Feels uncomfortable when alone.	

to work primarily with the goal of Mrs. Bailey making decisions and actively participating in her care. Behavior modification in a very simplistic form was utilized by the nurse. Mrs. Bailey put on her call light and asked for assistance to the bathroom. The baseline was known; she always asked for help to the bathroom. The nurse decided to modify the nursing staff interaction with her and interrupt this behavior, establishing a new pattern of going to the bathroom unaided. The procedural plan is outlined.

The nursing staff would answer Mrs. Bailey's request for help going to the bathroom by stating that they would help her with as little help as possible and by verbally praising (valuing) both independent activities (put slippers on by self) and the day in the near future when she could ambulate freely and alone. Any dependent behavior would be assisted, for example, help put gown on, but no verbal interaction would occur regarding the dependent behavior. The plan was implemented first with requests for help to go to the bathroom, then moved into areas of bathing, deep breathing, and personal care.

Evaluation is the collection of current client behaviors related to the goal: Is the client initiating personal care? Is she participating in a cough/deep-breathing program that is effective in decreasing her chest congestion? If behavior has not changed, the nurse must re-examine the stimuli she is manipulating and the manner in which she is manipulating them.

Mrs. Bailey was able, with the help of the nursing staff and her family, to move through the convalescent sick role phase and to assume care for herself. Mr. and Mrs. Bailey were able to recognize the dependent coping style used by Mrs. Bailey and rewarded by her husband. The nurse was able to help them recognize the conflict that this had caused during the stress of illness and the probability of conflict with other stressors.

SUMMARY

This chapter has looked at the major problems in the interdependency mode. The significance of internal drives conflicting with external demands in this mode has been pointed out. Interventions to manipulate internal stimuli have been emphasized and illustrated in the examples of problems of dysfunctional independence and dysfunctional dependence.

REFERENCES

Lazarus, Richard S., *Patterns of Adjustment and Human Effectiveness*. New York: McGraw-Hill, 1969, Chapters 2 and 5.
_____ , *Psychological Stress and the Coping Process*. New York: McGraw-Hill, Inc., 1966, Chapters 3, 4, and 7.
Peplau, Hildegard E., *Interpersonal Relations in Nursing*. New York: G. P. Putnam's Sons, 1952, Chapters 2 and 4.

Yates, Aubrey J., *Behavior Therapy*. New York: John Wiley and Sons, Inc., 1970, Chapters 1, 2, and 7.

ADDITIONAL READINGS

Beller, Emanuel K., "Dependency and Independence in Young Children," *The Journal of Genetic Psychology*, vol. 87, 1955, pp. 23-35.

Cox, F. N., "The Origins of the Dependency Drive," *Australian Journal of Psychology*, vols. 5-6, June 1953, pp. 64-75.

Engel, George L., *Psychological Development in Health and Disease*. Philadelphia: W. B. Saunders Company, 1962, Chapter IV.

Fromm, Erich, *Escape from Freedom*. New York: Holt, Rinehart and Winston, Inc., 1941.

Gewirtz, Jacob L., "A Factor Analysis of Some Attention-Seeking Behaviors of Young Children," *Child Development*, vol. 17 (1), March 1956, pp. 17-36.

_____ , "A Program of Research on the Dimensions and Antecedents of Emotional Dependence," *Child Development*, vol. 27 (2), June 1956, pp. 205-221.

Hartup, Willard W. and E. Duwayne Keller, "Nurturance in Pre-School Children and Its Relation to Dependency," *Child Development*, vol. 31, 1960, pp. 681-89.

Heathers, Glen, "Emotional Dependence and Independence in a Physical Threat Situation," *Child Development*, vol. 24 (3-4), 1953, pp. 169-79.

_____ , "Emotional Dependence and Independence in Nursery School Play," *The Journal of Genetic Psychology*, vol. 87, 1955, pp. 37-57.

_____ , "Acquiring Dependency and Independency: A Theoretical Orientation," *The Journal of Genetic Psychology*, vol. 87, 1955, pp. 277-91.

Jacubczak, Leonard and Richard H. Walters, "Suggestibility as Dependency Behavior," *Journal of Abnormal Social Psychology*, vol. 59, 1959, pp. 102-07.

Josselyn, Irene M., *Psychosocial Development of Children*. New York: Family Service Association of America, 1948, pp. 105-13.

Kagan, Jerome and Howard A. Moss, "The Stability of Passive and Dependent Behavior from Childhood Through Adulthood," *Child Development*, vol. 31, 1960, pp. 577-99.

McCord, William J. McCord and P. Verden, "Familial and Behavioral Correlates of Dependency in Male Children," *Child Development*, vol. 33 (2), 1962, pp. 313-26.

Parsons, Talcott and Robert F. Bales, *Family, Socialization and Interaction Process*. Ill.: The Free Press, 1955, pp. 43-68, 100-101, 215-36.

Redman, Barbara K., *The Process of Patient Teaching in Nursing*. 2nd ed. St. Louis: C. V. Mosby Co., 1972, Chapters 1, 2, and 3.

Sears, R. R., J. W. M. Whiting, V. Nowlis and P. S. Sears, "Some Child-Rearing Antecedents of Aggression and Dependency in Young Children," *Genetic Psychology Monographs*, vol. 47, 1953, pp. 135-234.

Sears, Robert R., Eleanor E. Maccoby, and Harry Levin, *Patterns of Child Rearing*. New York: Harper and Row, Publishers, 1957.

Sears, Robert R., "Dependency Motivation," in *Nebraska Symposium on Motivation*. Lincoln: University of Nebraska Press, 1963, pp. 25-64.

Stitch, Marjorie and Ruth Connor, "Dependency and Helpfulness in Young Children," *Child Development*, vol. 33 (1), 1962, pp. 15-20.

24

Problem of Interdependence: Aggression

Edythe Ellison

KEY CONCEPTS DEFINED

Aggression: The energy or tension behind the need for achievement.

Aggressive Drive: A state of inner tension causing discomfort to the individual and energizing him to take some action vis-à-vis the environment, very often but not necessarily involving gross motor behavior.

Dyscontrol of Aggressive Behavior: Those situations in which there is a marked incongruency between the quantity and/or the quality of the aggressive behavior being manifested and the environmental stimuli surrounding it.

After studying this chapter the reader will be able to:

1. Define the key concepts of this chapter.
2. Explain the basic concept of aggression and illustrate the operation of the drive.

3. Name three reasons for difficulty with the aggressive drive.
4. Describe situations that lead to dyscontrol of aggressive behavior.
5. Discuss assessment of problems of dyscontrol of aggression in relation to the quantity and quality of the behavior.
6. Discuss nursing interventions to be used in dysfunctional interdependence due to the over- or undercontrol of aggression (see Appendix II).

Aggression has been described as the energy or tension behind the need for achievement, one of the basic needs of the interdependency mode. This chapter explores what the author believes to be one of the most important focal stimuli for problems within the interdependency mode — the patterns of control one develops over aggressive drive.

INTRODUCTION

To understand the principles discussed in this chapter one must view aggression in a different light than usual; indeed, in a much broader way. When one hears the word "aggression," one usually thinks first of those situations in which someone shows anger, strikes out or injures another, or uses force to control another person or thing. In contrast, the concept of aggression that will be presented and explored in this chapter includes behaviors that range all the way from passive withdrawal at one end to violent rage at the other and are described in terms of the quantity and quality of control being exerted over one's aggressive impulses. For example, overcontrol of the aggressive drive is equated with inactivity, passivity, and withdrawal; undercontrol, at its extreme, is equated with violent, rageful, destructive behavior. Naturally there is a wide variety of behavior between these two extremes and that is precisely the reason why this broader view enables the nurse to utilize a few basic principles of nursing assessment and intervention in dealing with an extensive variety of human behavior. To do this, however, one must be able to accept the following definition of the *aggressive drive:* a state of inner tension causing some discomfort to the individual and energizing him to take some action vis-à-vis the environment, very often but not necessarily involving gross motor behavior.

During childhood and adolescence the individual develops fairly consistent patterns of behavior that result in the relief of this inner state of tension. When these behavioral patterns are functional the child, adolescent, or adult is able to initiate and maintain interdependency relationships within his milieu which are successful and satisfying. These relationships afford opportunities to affiliate with others and to function as a separate, unique (independent) individual with his own special attributes. Behavioral patterns become dysfunctional when the person finds that due to environmental changes he cannot develop satisfying interdependency relationships within his milieu, and thus meet affiliative and

achievement needs. The development of functional patterns of control are necessary for one to evolve into an independent person from the totally dependent
infancy state that marks the beginning of life for everyone. At this time it
seems important to point out that overcontrol of one's aggressive drive should
not be equated with a high degree of dependency (although they can and often
do occur simultaneously), and undercontrol is not to be equated with high independency. Rather, the terms "overcontrol" and "undercontrol" of the aggressive drive refer to what is presumed to be the cause of dysfunctional
independency or dependency states. For example, the six-month-old infant is
in a very dependent state but does not usually show an overcontrol over aggressive impulses. On the contrary, the child may kick, scream, and fight during
diapering and dressing, and he expends a great deal of energy exploring the environment. By the same token, the adult who has developed little or no control
over aggressive impulses may become entirely dependent upon society either as
a hospitalized psychiatric patient or as an incarcerated criminal.

The terms "overcontrol" and "undercontrol" are also useful in that they
allow the nurse to examine a wide range of behaviors within the same individual
client without resorting to pejorative labels. For example, the "angry" client is
not always angry, and labeling him as such has limited value for the nurse who
finds the client one day to be passive, inarticulate, and withdrawn. And what
about the formerly "good" client who quite suddenly flings the water pitcher
across the room? There are some basic principles that make these seemingly
dissimilar behaviors more understandable for the nurse.

This chapter will (1) demonstrate that it is the aggressive drive that provides
the force or energy behind one's movement on the independency continuum;
(2) identify one main focal stimulus for problems in interdependency as being
maladaptive patterns of control of the aggressive drive (including both under-
and overcontrol); and (3) demonstrate how nursing intervention toward problems of dyscontrol of this drive should have the goal of assisting the patient to
form functional patterns of control over aggressive drive as he moves in either
direction along this continuum. The principles offered are illustrated mainly
within the construct of child development, but are applicable to clients of all
ages and developmental levels.

BASIC CONCEPT OF AGGRESSION

Simply stated, aggression is a drive or force necessary for life. It provides
the energy behind the need for achievement; an individual's striving toward separation and interdependency (Storr, 1968); toward growth and mastery, and
toward assertion of individuality (Thompson, 1964). Aggression that is obviously destructive in nature appears when the goals of obstacle mastery and independence are thwarted; it is then that elements of anger, hate, and rage are seen in

the behavioral manifestations of this drive. Next to sex, aggression is the most controlled of our instinctual behaviors, and it is this learned control, or the quantity and quality of the expression of this drive, with which we are now concerned in the practice of nursing.

Observations of children and their movement from dependency to independency provides an almost pure illustration of how the aggressive drive operates. As an example of this let us look at some incidents which took place during a three-month period with a little girl about 4½ years old, an age when most children are beginning to move out of the narrow confines of the nursery and into the community — the neighborhood, or the school. After observing the child's behavior at this significant time in her development, her mother concluded that it is the aggressive drive which provides the energy and impetus for movement along the independency continuum in the direction of meeting achievement needs.

The girl began the three-month period to which we are referring by listening endlessly to a record of the dramatization of the fairy tale of "Rapunzal," the golden-haired girl who was imprisoned by a witch in a high tower during childhood and adolescence. Also, she began spending more and more time outside of her home, and when she returned she would come through the door with her left arm raised, fist clenched, in a curious way which was labeled the "child power salute." She seemed to be saying, "I'm strong; I'm powerful; and don't you forget it!" Any attempt to control her life was countered with a barrage of statements such as, "You're not my boss; I know what to do myself; quit telling me what to do." These would be accompanied by the bodily stance, facial expression, and tone of voice usually associated with anger. Finally, one day she told her mother in a quiet, kindly way, "You worry about me too much; I can take care of myself."

It was at this point the mother realized her daughter felt at some times that her home must seem like the locked tower of the story of Rapunzal, and with this realization came a deeper appreciation of the amount of aggression her daughter needed to break out of it. Time went by; fewer requests or reminders were made by the family; more responsibility was assumed by the little girl and by the time her fifth birthday rolled around the family found they had quite a different child living with them; one who was very independent, almost totally self-sufficient and was seen to be moving ahead with great strides in many areas both socially and cognitively. She had, in a way, "left home" and she didn't seem angry at all any more.

Some length has been taken to give the reader the flavor of this period of life because the author feels it illustrates so clearly the idea that aggression is a necessary, positive drive that enables us to separate from our parents and become independent individuals (Storr, 1968). In addition, one can see that when the goal of independence is thwarted, the element of anger appears. A spillover of the aggressive drive in the form of anger often causes difficulty within interdependency relationships that are undergoing alterations because of the movement of one individual toward greater independent functioning. This phenomenon is seen not only in the parent-child relationship, but in the adult-adolescent, nurse-patient, teacher-student — in any interdependent relationship between two individuals that is undergoing change.

During these and other critical times in childhood and adolescence the individual develops patterns of behavior in relation to the control of aggressive drive that determine how he will respond as an adult when faced with forced dependency due to illness or hospitalization. These past experiences making up the person's residual stimuli, which are accumulated during childhood, generally fall into two categories: (1) those resulting from how others who are deemed significant are responding to and encouraging this movement from dependency to independency, and (2) those resulting from how these other persons respond to this spillover of aggressive behavior. Is it met with punishment? With stringent controls? With encouragement? With substitute targets? The experiences a child has, plus his own particular temperament, combine to form patterns of control over aggressive impulses that will remain amazingly consistent throughout his lifetime, as has been pointed out in the earlier discussion on coping styles.

DIFFICULTY WITH THE AGGRESSIVE DRIVE

Compared to other species, human beings have an inordinately long period of time in which they are dependent to some degree on others, and there is always a certain amount of resentment accompanying relationships in which one member is notably dependent on the other. The child is dependent on the mother, and to the degree of dependence, she exerts a certain amount of power over the child; hence the development of resentment. Anthony Storr (1968) in *Human Aggression* asserts that our modern civilization (with its highrise buildings, automobiles, and overcrowded, impersonal population centers) forces us to develop patterns of overprotection in caring for our children during this inordinately long period of dependency, resulting in an even more intense situation.

In twentieth-century Western society, we express our aggressive impulses very differently than our ancestors of one hundred years ago. The aggressive drive is what propelled people to hunt, build, explore, and protect a few generations back, but except for those in our modern society who are involved in manual labor, our gross motor and large muscle behaviors are for the most part now sublimated into sports activities.

There are others, of course, but these three factors — the number of years children are forced to remain dependent, the degree to which their natural and exploratory behaviors need to be curtailed because of the inherent dangers of our highly mechanized society, and the ever-lessening need for large muscle activity in day-to-day living — seem to account for a significant amount of the difficulty humans presently have in controlling their aggressive drives, both in childhood and as adults.

SOURCES OF PROBLEMS IN AGGRESSION

Students have found it useful to conceptualize the growth curve toward independence as occurring optimally when the developmental level of the child ("where he is at" physically, psychologically, and socially) is consistently congruent with the opportunities afforded by the environment to achieve and assert independence and individuality. When these two parts are kept in tune, are congruent, are without disparity and held steady, a child will move toward separation and independent functioning without too much trouble. On the other hand, there are many situations that make the growth toward independence difficult and uneven. If one accepts the hypothesis that it is the aggressive drive that provides the energy for this growth, it follows that these situations would be accompanied by some degree of *dyscontrol*[1] *of the aggressive behavior.* A summary of these situations follows:

1. *Lack of successful dependency relationships.*

First among the experiences that seem to be present in the early history of children, adolescents, and adults manifesting chronic problems in the control of the aggressive drive is deprivation and/or abandonment in infancy (Bender, 1953). To move toward independence one must first experience a successful dependency; that is, one must first have had the experience of knowing that one is worthy of being cared for and loved and nourished. Complete abandonment and severe deprivation are not usually encountered in middle-class urban and suburban communities, but another kind of situation does exist there that makes it just as difficult for many children to experience a successful dependency relationship in early childhood. The rearing practices in middle-class American homes seem heavily concerned with how quickly the infant becomes independent — how soon the child walks, how young when weaned, and how early when toilet-trained, for examples. Storr offers the suggestion that "the frequency of depression amongst us may be related in part to our failure to meet our children's dependent needs, and to our puritanical insistence that they shall be independent before they are ready for it" (Storr, 1968). This

---

[1]The term "dyscontrol" is used to describe those situations in which there is a marked incongruency between the quantity and/or the quality of the aggressive behavior being manifested and the environmental stimuli surrounding it.

ambivalency toward providing successful dependency relationships is often observed in nursing practice, especially in the psychiatric setting. For example,
not long ago a heated discussion was overheard taking place in a nursing team
conference concerning Cathy's self-mutilating behavior, which most nurses felt
was designed to get the attention and physical care she so desperately desired.
Only one nurse felt that she would be able to provide the "mothering" behaviors needed by Cathy. The others stated that they were too uncomfortable to
relate to a 15-year-old in that way, and were afraid of fostering too much
dependency in Cathy.

2. *Chronic inequality between one's developmental level and the
opportunities in the environment.*

As an example of this type of situation, consider the child growing up in
extreme poverty, without the materials or playthings necessary to meet his
need for achievement. The environment may have a great deal of sensory
stimuli (such as noise and people), but it is impoverished in the sense that
there are inadequate opportunities for the child to master it according to
childlike abilities. Another example is the hospitalized client. All clients who
are sick and in the hospital experience this type of incongruency to some degree and as the length of hospitalization increases, so does the likelihood that
the client will develop patterns of dyscontrol (either in one direction or
another or both simultaneously) of aggressive drive. One of the worst effects
of long-term hospitalization in psychiatric facilities is the gradual and inevitable pattern of overcontrol that the client develops over his aggressive drive,
resulting in the very low incidence of initiative-taking and obstacle mastery
behavior. The realization of this type of incongruency may have started the
trend toward returning many of these patients to the community setting.
Clients in all settings who chronically experience vast gaps between what they
are capable of doing and what they are allowed to do or expected to do will
have a great deal of trouble fully utilizing the energy provided by their aggressive drives.
Another type of chronic incongruency comes about when one is constantly
pushed to act at levels beyond which one is capable. Arbitrarily held expectations of children because of their chronological age and expectations of client
behavior developed without regard to individual differences are the two most
common causes of chronic incongruencies between client's developmental levels
and what is demanded of them by their environment.

3. *Alterations in the client's abilities.*

Problems in dyscontrol of aggression also occur when there is a sudden alteration of the person's developmental level and no adjustments are made in

terms of what is expected of him by the environment. These alterations can come about because of physical illness, or an accident (especially one resulting in immobilization of a body part), or a surgical procedure. Regression is the term used most frequently to describe the effects of these problems on the personality, and the two most common symptoms seen are withdrawal (overcontrol of the aggressive drive) and/or temper tantrums (undercontrol of the aggressive drive).

When working with adults it is often the client who causes the incongruency by not accepting, even temporarily, his lessened abilities and by not being able to "take in" the environmental stimuli indicating the need for greater dependency. For many clients, the thought of any loss of independency is very threatening, and any or all attempts to force him to be more dependent are met with angry resistance, resulting in a critical situation in some cases. An example may be the client who has suffered a heart attack.

4. *Alterations in the environment.*

If the child's environment is constantly changing because of, for instance, frequent moves with resulting changes in schools and friends; or if the significant others in the child's life are unstable and constantly changing the rules, schedules, and directives under which the child must operate; or if the child loses a parent through death or divorce, then incongruencies will result, at least temporarily, in what the child is capable of doing and what is expected of him. This is because adapting to change takes energy (for the child *or* the adult) and may deprive the child of the necessary amount of energy needed to exert control and direct aggressive impulses appropriately. Clients who have developed patterns tending toward overcontrol of their aggressive drives will most likely respond to excessive amounts of change in their environments by withdrawal and inactivity.

5. *Uneven developmental growth.*

The child who experiences a great deal of unevenness or disparity between physical, emotional, and cognitive growth curves may become an accidental victim of the incongruity between his developmental level and the demands of his environment. Children and people of all ages do not always progress at the same rate on all fronts; hence the need for an accurate assessment of a child's abilities on many levels.

Projecting expected performance levels in many areas on the basis of the patient's performance in one area can result in incongruencies for him which will be manifested by some dyscontrol of aggression. For example, dyslexic children (those with perceptual motor learning difficulties) often go unnoticed until their aggressive behaviors, disruptive in the classroom, single them out from other children.

ASSESSMENT OF PROBLEMS OF DYSCONTROL OF AGGRESSION

Basically there are two steps in the assessment of the behavior of problems of dyscontrol of aggression: (1) examine the *quantity* of the aggressive behavior, and (2) examine the *quality*.

In assessing the quality of aggressive behavior being manifested, one should ask, "Is the aggressive behavior congruent with the incoming stimuli? Is the form of the aggressive behavior appropriate to the situation? Is the target of the aggressive behavior appropriate? Is there congruency between the verbal and nonverbal behavior being exhibited?"

Asking these questions enables the nurse immediately to identify the withdrawn client in the corner of the busy dayroom; the client who delivers an angry barrage at the first "good morning"; the client who insists through tightly clenched teeth that "nothing is wrong," as all exhibiting some dyscontrol in either the quality or quantity of aggressive behavior. The one exception to this method of identifying problems in dyscontrol has to do with the sharp increase in the amount of aggressive behavior exhibited by children or clients during periods of rapid growth or transition from one developmental level to another. The behavior of the little girl described at the beginning of the chapter is called "temporary spillover" and the hypothesis is that this behavior is *inevitable* during periods of rapid growth in children, adolescents, or adults.

After the nurse identifies the client aggressive behavior, she makes a hypothesis about the focal stimulus of under- or overcontrol of aggression. Clients who have developed too little control over their aggressive drives may be somewhat hyperactive and easily frustrated; have very low impulse control, and/or have trouble attending or focusing. Chronic angry, hostile, destructive behavior marks the child, adolescent, or adult with a more severe problem in undercontrol. If the client has developed too much control over aggressive drive, he will very likely be passive, inactive, and reluctant to begin new tasks, will give up easily, and in more severe cases will be withdrawn and regressed.

In general, teachers, nurses, and parents are much more sophisticated in discovering and dealing with problems of undercontrol of the aggressive drive than overcontrol. This is somewhat understandable considering the volumes that have been written about how to discipline children and "manage" hyperactive clients. However, if one can see the relationship between what we have just put forth as evidence of overcontrol of the aggressive drive and childhood and adult depressive states, then the importance of attending to clients who have developed patterns of overcontrol of their aggressive drives is obvious.

The environment and client's background will then be assessed for factors further influencing the behavior. The situations that make growth toward independence difficult or uneven, as discussed in the earlier pages, are important possibilities for consideration. After the behavior and influencing factors have been assessed, the nurse makes the appropriate nursing diagnosis of dysfunctional dependency or dysfunctional independency due to over- or undercontrol of aggression.

INTERVENTION IN DYSFUNCTIONAL INTERDEPENDENCE DUE TO DYSCONTROL OF AGGRESSION

Following are principles of nursing intervention for relief of problems of dyscontrol of aggression.

Principle 1   Manipulate the environment to keep the opportunities for expression of independence and individuality as congruent as possible to the developmental level of the client. An assessment of the environment needs to be approached from the client's point of view, as nurses sometimes become immune to all the little ways clients are guided into greater dependency than is warranted by their physical conditions.

The assessment of the client's developmental level, whether child, adolescent, or adult, should begin with an accounting of *successes* within the area in question; this will become the basis for increased independent functioning.

Principle 2   Provide outlets to siphon off some of the "temporary spillover" of aggressive behavior that accompanies movement on the independency continuum. If the client can find appropriate methods of draining off some of this excess aggressive behavior, then his interpersonal relationships with the significant others in his life (parents, teachers, caretakers) may not be so strained. Any large muscle activity that does not have to be closely controlled lessens the degree of aggressive tension experienced by the young child. Noise (yelling, screaming) and water are two more classical methods of relieving this tension. Adult clients should be encouraged to develop patterns of recognizing and relieving high states of aggressive tensions through physical exercise.

Principle 3   Encourage the development of the client's own personal control system over aggressive impulses, and become a partner in this endeavor rather than simply another provider of outside control. This principle can be expanded to the parent-child and teacher-child dyad. Some examples of fairly successful verbal communication geared toward this goal are: "That behavior cannot be allowed because it is dangerous (or harmful or infringes on the right of others, or whatever). Can you stop yourself? Can you continue here without doing that? If not, I can help you to stop, and someday you will be able to stop by yourself." Or, "I'm going to take that away from you because I see you cannot control yourself with it. When you feel you can, ask me for it."

As the age of the client increases, the communication should change so as to apprise the client of the effect his behavior is having on others ("When you do that, such and such happens") and provide him with alternatives and choices ("Is that what you want?"). An adult client can be brought up to the point of predicting the effects ("What do you think will happen if you do such and such?"), formulating alternatives, and of making his own choices. The nurse provides another view of the reality of the situation, and should encourage the client to express feelings verbally, of anger and/or frustration, as much as possible, and in this way the need to act out these feelings in potentially destructive ways can be lessened.

A number of physiological components of the state of being angry (increased blood pressure and heart rate, greater flow of gastric secretions) will, over time, take their toll from the client who has not developed functional behavior patterns concerning the expression of anger. A five-year-old once remarked, after witnessing an intense temper tantrum by her two-year-old brother, "In our family Joshie gets angry the *goodest!*" Notwithstanding the poor syntax, we are struck by her use of the word "good," because expressing one's angry feelings is indeed good for you, given an appropriately supportive environment.

However, a nurse should never encourage a client to express anger unless she is certain she can supply the needed support of that expression. The client who has developed strong patterns of overcontrol of aggressive behavior and who is depressed and withdrawn often begins to "come alive" after having been encouraged to express that anger. It is as if this begins the mobilization of the aggressive drive once more.

Principle 4   When confronted by behavior in a client indicating that too much control over aggressive drive has been developed, the nurse should encourage the formation of new behavior patterns that will capitalize more on the energy provided by this drive and allow the client to achieve more power. Try to focus on the client's perceptions of his position of weakness and powerlessness, and encourage him to take a position of strength as much as possible. This can be done in a number of ways: by pointing out the temporariness of his present position, by demonstrating that the client is indeed powerful in some aspects of his life, and by together exploring new areas in which he may achieve greater power. Whenever possible, manipulate the environment so that the *patient's actions do make a difference.* Power struggles are antithetical to this principle and should be avoided whenever possible. Most people respond quite negatively when they are deprived of making decisions regarding their basic needs for food, rest, dress, or privacy, so this is always a good place to begin. The child or adult who maintains a position of abject weakness vis-à-vis another's behavior needs to be encouraged to demonstrate his strength against that person and to express feelings and desires in the situation.

"How do you feel when Joey hits you?" "How do you feel when your wife says that to you?" "Can you tell him how you feel?" Encouraging the client to say, "Stop that! I don't like that!" is often the first step in helping him begin to get out of the position as victim for another's aggressive behavior.

Working with children, clients, and students will point out the infinite variety of methods humans utilize in dealing with feelings of weakness and lack of ability to meet achievement needs. The small child uses fantasy and play to help him to cope with the world that is largely dominated and controlled by adults. Adults seem to rely more on their identification with strong, powerful figures in real life and in the worlds of sport, literature, and drama. Religion provides another way, and more and more people are banding together in groups to share these feelings and lend support to each other. The insightful nurse will become aware of her client's methods, support them whenever possible, and provide opportunities for the client to expand his repertoire of these functional achievement behaviors.

SUMMARY

This chapter presents the idea that it is the aggressive drive that propels the child, adolescent, or sick, hospitalized client toward greater independent functioning. Problems in either over- or undercontrol of this drive result, for the most part, when there are basic incongruencies between what an individual is capable or desirous of doing and what the environment expects or allows him to do. When an individual chronically finds himself in such a situation, he develops dysfunctional patterns of either over- or undercontrol of the aggressive drive. In a given situation he may be diagnosed as dysfunctionally independent or dependent. Principles of nursing intervention have been presented, which have as their purpose the assistance of the patient in the development of more functional patterns of control over his aggressive drive and in the meeting of his achievement needs.

REFERENCES

Bender, Lauretta, *Aggression, Hostility and Anxiety in Children*. Springfield, Ill.: Charles C. Thomas, Publisher, 1953.

Jackson, Lydia, *Aggression and Its Interpretation*. Methuen and Company, Ltd., 1954, p. 13.

Storr, Anthony, *Human Aggression*. New York: Atheneum Publishers, 1968.

Thompson, Clara M., *Interpersonal Psycho-Analysis*. New York: Basic Books, 1964, p. 179.

25

Problem of Interdependence: Loneliness

Sue Ann Brown

KEY CONCEPTS DEFINED

Alienation: A condition or feeling of being estranged or separated from self or others.

Lonely: Missing the contact of another who is far from one either by death or other physical separation or emotional separateness.

Lonesome: An adjective used to describe a lonely person.

Loneliness: The exceedingly unpleasant and driving experience connected with an inadequate discharge of the need for human intimacy, for interpersonal intimacy.

Aloneness: A chosen state of being by oneself.

After studying this chapter the reader will be able to:

1. Define the key concepts of this chapter.
2. Explain the relationship between alienation and loneliness.

3. Compare and contrast aloneness and loneliness.
4. Describe the development of loneliness.
5. List factors influencing loneliness.
6. Discuss behaviors manifesting loneliness.
7. Specify nursing interventions to be used in the problem of loneliness (see Appendix II).

There is a saying, "If you can't make it with people you can't make it." Clark E. Moustakas points out its corollary, "If you can only make it with people, and not alone, you can't make it" (1972, p. 48).

This precept indicates some of the problems that exist in the interdependency mode of functioning. This chapter will concern itself with one problem in the area of dysfunctional dependency, loneliness.

From the aged client to the infant, from the wealthiest to the most poverty-stricken, we see the commonality of this adaptation problem. No one is immunized against loneliness; it is a lifelong struggle for everyone to maintain an adaptive level of interdependency. "No man is an island"—we need each other. We need to be affiliated with others. We have seen that this need for affiliation is basic to the interdependence adaptive mode.

To be engaged or to be in contact (we shall use these two terms interchangeably) is a feeling of togetherness or union with self and others. Where engagement exists, the individual is working to maintain his relationships by utilizing functional dependency and functional independency where each is appropriate. Significant others are able to act as affection suppliers. Consequently, the engaged person feels loved and worthwhile and meets his affection and affiliation needs. He has learned how to seek attention, affection, and help in a positive way to fulfill those needs.

Alienation is a condition or feeling of being estranged or separated from self or others. One develops alienated feelings when significant others are not meeting expectations of affection suppliers. This deprivation of contact leads to a feeling of being not wanted, not needed, not appreciated by others, and herein lies the routes of loneliness. The affection supplier may or may not be aware of this lack. Likewise, the alienated one may be asking too much or too little of his suppliers.

Alienation is a serious problem in contemporary society. Many social theorists have written on its extensiveness in American life and on the stimuli that affect this pattern. Among these stimuli are computerization, diminishing of the family as the basic unit of society, mobility, and urbanization. Modern man feels manipulated by others. Every aspect of life enhances this feeling. For example, politically one might say, "Who can I trust? Being a politician means deceiving others for self-gain." Economically, wages, price controls, strikes, cutbacks, paybacks, all seem to be out of one's control. Socially, friends seem to be transient, families physically separated, and, after all, "Who does care what happens to me?" That alienation exists is undeniable. Because of contemporary stimuli (focal, contextual, and residual), the human being has a good to excellent chance of developing one of the variants of alienation—powerlessness, meaninglessness, normlessness, isolation, or self-estrangement, as described earlier in the discussion of problems of self-concept. Any one of these variants can also cause the individual to feel separated from others.

Some individuals can handle these alienated feelings by innovative independency. An example is the young adult who appraises the situation and says things aren't good, aren't the way he would like to have them, but they do not have to remain such and proceeds to become involved in the change process. He might join a political campaign where he has a voice in the platform of the candidate. Or he might pursue an interest in being his own boss and have as a business objective that he will treat each customer and employee as an individual.

Others will use less positive means to deal with alienated feelings. These avenues involve a dependency on things or others to ward off alienated feelings. They include: (1) dependency on life-style that emphasizes withdrawal and retreatism to feel secure; (2) dependency on performing ritualistic behaviors to deal with anxieties of alienation (chain-smoking, overeating, psychosomatic illness, or any activity that is done in excess to stay busy); (3) rebelling against society by joining an altraculture group with subsequent dysfunctional dependency on it (drug culture, alcoholic state, sexual variancy groups); (4) dependency on situations retaining the status quo. This last method involves an individual who sees no possibility for changes and looks at the world through pessimistic glasses.

Some of these alternatives can be so maladaptive as to stimulate self-concept disruption. An example would be the individual who chooses to withdraw from the real world and stay in his own fantasy existence. This condition is referred to as self-alienation and can involve a total collapse of one's self-concept.

Alienated feelings lead to ideas of not being accepted or liked or wanted by others. To develop lonely feelings is the logical next step for the alienated one. For again, to be engaged or to be in contact is the interrelatedness of the person with the society of which he is a member. It is possible to be lonely in many different ways. Thus we will review the terminology relating to loneliness.

TERMINOLOGY ON LONELINESS

Being lonely is missing the contact of another who is apart from one either by death or other physical separation or emotional separateness. Everyone seems to have occasions of being lonely. *Lonesome* is an adjective used to describe a lonely person. Sullivan has defined *loneliness* as "the exceedingly unpleasant and driving experience connected with an inadequate discharge of the need for human intimacy, for interperson intimacy" (in Fromm-Reichmann, 1959, p. 3). This is a severe state unacceptable to most people. It would seem to last longer and be more profound than the state of being lonely. By contrast, *aloneness* is a chosen state, to be by oneself for personal growth, meditation, or for an inspired artistic performance. Aloneness is healthy and should be pursued.

From these definitions, one can visualize a continuum, as in Figure 25.1, where aloneness is the most healthy behavior and psychotic loneliness (also termed self-alienation) is at the far illness end. Midway between these two one finds *lonely*. Contact with others to the left of lonely is definitely healthier. To the right of lonely one finds loneliness, and the defenses we have said are used by some alienated people, and psychotic loneliness.

Aloneness ———— Contact ———— Lonely —— Loneliness —— (Use of distractive responses to loneliness: rebellion, withdrawal, ritualistic activity, etc.) —— Psychotic loneliness

HEALTH ═══ ILLNESS

Figure 25.1

To be in a state of loneliness is an uncomfortable and unpleasant experience. It hurts—it hurts so badly that one tries distractive measures with an ardent fervor if one is not able to use innovative independency. Moustakas (1972) quotes a tenth-grade boy who wrote the following:

> "Loneliness is a depressing state of mind that none desires but we all endure. When I'm lonely it's not because of being shut away from human beings physically but when I'm rejected by those I respect and love. If a close friend turns against me I feel hurt and lonely. When I feel like a square block in a round hole, it brings on a form of loneliness. Sometimes my parents seem unfair; there is no one to turn to and I feel desolate, lost. Loneliness comes every day. When someone makes a thoughtless criticism that attacks one of my weaknesses, it takes the wind out of my sails. I wonder if what they say is really true. I get a small feeling and that's a kind of loneliness."

His usage of terms is different than ours, but he is saying a lot in these few sentences. Reread his words and see if you can define lonely, loneliness, and aloneness for yourself.

POSITIVE ASPECTS OF THE CONTINUUM

It may seem strange to encourage aloneness and define it at the far healthy end of our continuum. If so, reflect on the precept that begins this chapter. If one *always* needs others, one is dysfunctionally dependent. One needs to stand alone at times to be his own person. If one is only able to define oneself as others see one, that person is not in contact with the true self. Moustakas (1972) advocates the kind of self-encounter and solitude one experiences when alone. Many individuals today talk of encounters and groups where one learns to know oneself better. In these groups, however, learning is sometimes restricted to knowing how others see us, not how we see ourselves and how we want to be or to develop. One needs to search one's own mind for direction.

The importance of this state of aloneness may be easier to see if one considers the artist. If he paints only in the physical or emotional presences of others with their advice, comments, or directions, we are robbed of knowing this artist—of seeing his ideas in any kind of pure form—of seeing how one person views a subject. In this case, we see that achievement, another need in the interdependence adaptive mode, depends on aloneness.

The authentic person is the one who *knows* and *is* his true self. He is like a magnet in attracting those who come into contact with him. Such a person's behaviors are genuine; such a person is his own boss in directing his life. Because the person is genuine, he possesses no phoniness and thereby attracts others, and is far less likely to develop alienated feelings or loneliness. However, he may be lonely at times.

DEVELOPMENT OF LONELINESS

The process involved in the development of loneliness can be summarized as outlined in Figure 25.1. The model depicts the process as often a circular one. Alienation leads either to innovative independency or to feelings of loneliness. The results of each response are very different. Innovative independency produces positive contact with others. On the other hand, the feelings of loneliness bring about an interdependency crisis with a variety of possible behaviors to cope with it. Four of these behaviors—rebellion, acceptance, withdrawal, and ritualism—have the possible effect of further alienation from others. If help is sought instead of these behaviors, or if it follows after them, the final outcome may be positive contact with others leading to ability to function independently.

The period of adolescence is used to illustrate the development of loneliness since it has inherent hazards in this direction. Adolescence commences the overt search for identity and independency. Our society emphasizes youth, beauty, and good life, and encourages one to "be happy"—not necessarily "to be." When significant others allow the adolescent freedom to explore himself, his goals, and to develop his own route to accomplish these goals, then he has a start at becoming a genuine person. An adolescent armed with an instinctual urge to find himself may meet role models who foster feelings of rejection and ask that the individual be as they want him to be. He learns that to be accepted is to be as others want him to be and not as he would like to be. Since exploration of oneself has resulted in rejection, the adolescent decides to not take further chances but to "buckle under." Consequently the nurse assessing such an individual can find behaviors denoting dysfunctional dependency; a dependency on others or things that allow him to remain lonely and "safe" from rebuff. The individual learns that the presence of others and the use of others (negative uses of attention-seeking, affection, and help-seeking behaviors) help decrease feelings of loneliness. All of us learn to use others whether we like to admit it or not. However, there is a difference between using a boyfriend to help complete chemistry problems and using a boyfriend to make parents angry and to obtain some attention.

Take the case of Marcia, who uses spectacular attention-seeking behavior to overcome her loneliness and get her father's attention. Marcia lived with her twice-divorced father and one stepbrother. There were other siblings in other households. Her father was on the verge of his third marriage, to an old family friend. Marcia had acted during the past year as homemaker and began to feel her territory was being invaded. She saw not only role loss as an outcome of the pending marriage, but also the loss of a significant other. To call attention to her emerging loneliness caused by role losses, she did the following:

1. Stripped in front of a busy campus center building.
2. Wore black clothing and poured water over herself to "conserve salt."
3. Tried to spread the word among her family that she was having an immaculate conception.

These behaviors succeeded in getting her admitted to a psychiatric unit and thereby getting her father's attention. They forced a delay in his plans, and re-established her dependency on him and his relationship. Marcia used dysfunctional attention-seeking behaviors to point out her dependency. She was not mature (physically or emotionally) and did need to be dependent upon him in some regard; however, it became dysfunctional dependency when she chose "crazy behaviors" to get and maintain his attention.

STIMULI AFFECTING LONELINESS

The next task is to cite specific stimuli responsible for the development of behaviors denoting loneliness. In exploring focal stimuli start by asking these questions: Why is this person lonely at this particular time (why *now*)? What is the reason given by the client for his present behaviors (what *for*)?

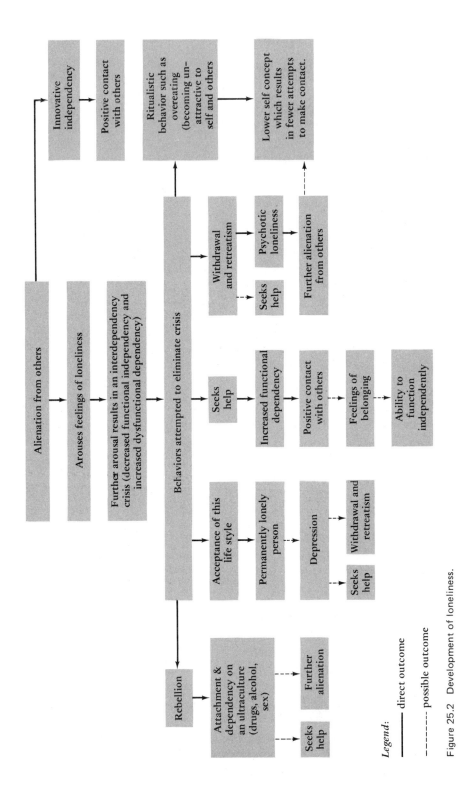

Figure 25.2 Development of loneliness.

Legend:

——— direct outcome

-------- possible outcome

How would the individual rescue himself (what does *he see* as *cause*)? What would you eliminate or add to his life to help the client to adapt (what do *you see* as *cause*)?

The major focal stimulus that has been noted in the development of loneliness is one of the variants of alienation. Although a loss, real or imagined, may seem to be the cause of the alienation, the behaviors of loneliness can be more directly connected with the *way* the loss made the individual feel. In other words, if you identify as focal feelings of despondency about justice or God or life in general following the death of a loved one, it is wiser to view your focal as "feels a great deal of meaninglessness in present life situation due to concurrent loss" instead of "loss of loved one" as focal. One can manipulate and work with the focal stimuli of the feeling of alienation to change assessed loneliness behaviors directly rather than manipulating an event—loss of a loved one. The focal stimuli can be a behavior of another problem area; this commonly happens—stimuli for some adaptation problems are behaviors or labels for another adaptation problem.

Contextually, the stimuli would also vary widely with the individual. Some areas to explore for possible stimuli are:

1. Family communication—is the individual hearing them and/or are they truly hearing him?
2. Physical living condition—does he live alone? How far from significant other? Does he have, or can afford, a means of transportation and communication (car, phone, bus, railway, plane)?
3. Family interdependency—how does the family relate to one another? If unhealthily, is there a family scapegoat? Is there family cohesiveness? In what role does the individual see himself? In what role does the family see him?
4. Does cultural age separation exist? Today an adolescent spending a day with a grandmother probably would be frowned upon by peers. Peer pressure to stay within certain limits of activity is strong, and consequently one is usually surrounded by individuals of the same age.
5. How are the person's lonely behaviors met? (Loneliness and anxiety are unattractive and contagious, and one tends to avoid them.)
6. "Future shock" faces all of us; that is, Toffler's (1970) idea that things are changing so quickly today that the individual cannot adapt to them. How does the individual meet and accept change? Does he try new things, accept new ideas or views?
7. What thing(s) or what person(s) does the individual need? What game(s) is the individual playing to maintain his loneliness?

In considering contextual stimuli it is often the case that although one is not physically removed from others, one may feel lonely in a crowd—may not be able to make contact with anyone. If an individual has many different groups of which he is a member, the chances of finding someone with whom to establish true contact *may* be increased. Both adolescents and adults seem to get into ruts of doing everything with the same people. These contexts tend toward loneliness.

Residual stimuli one may see in the lonely person are usually related to the inadequate parenting that results in poor interdependency development, as described in an earlier chapter. One important stimulus of which to be aware is interactions tending toward withdrawal from others. Recall that roles exist only when they are identifiable by other's presence; for example, a mother can't be a mother without a child. Consequently, if another withdraws or society at large withdraws from someone, he cannot exist in relationship with them. One has difficulty being in contact with a removed person or thing. Lack of contacts could be an aspect in developing loneliness.

An example of such a withdrawal by society would be a man imprisoned. He loses contact with the majority of the population and things that establish feelings of belonging (freedom to be himself, stimulating atmosphere). This type of withdrawal is overt. But society can unconsciously and covertly also withdraw. Examples of this are seen in reactions of some families to terminal illnesses, disfigurement, the physically or mentally disabled. In this regard consider Julie. Julie is a young adult who has a cleft lip and palate. Many surgeries have been performed to aid her physical attractiveness—they have been unsuccessful. Her speech is slurred and one must listen very closely to understand her. No one knowingly gives her clues of being unwanted, but because of the demands of her position (she is a clerk) she meets many individuals who unintentionally (or unthinkingly) give facial and bodily clues that they are repulsed by her. Because they reject her, she in turn rejects them— for example, she might remove herself physically each time they approach her, or pretend that she doesn't hear their requests. It might rightly be concluded that Julie has many problems with her own self-concept, and one may ask what gains, primary and secondary, she receives from working in such a situation. However, this example illustrates how interaction affects our engagement (contact) or discontact from others.

Related to interaction causing withdrawal is the concept of social disengagement. Social disengagement is thought to be a process that has been identified in the aged to understand both their and society's reaction to becoming older. In this theory the individual is accepting society's withdrawal and may even prepare for it by developmental and psychological mechanisms (increased preoccupation with self, physical loss of acute awareness—hearing, vision, cohesive speech, and a decreased interest, even in significant others). Those opposed to this theory are advocates of the activity theory. This theory proposes that older people have the same needs as middle-aged individuals, and the only reason they experience decreased social interaction is because society withdraws. If you accept the disengagement theory, you will let older people withdraw and take on more aloneness and think it is natural and right. If you accept the activity theory you will not allow withdrawal and will formulate nursing diagnoses that entail loneliness, and will instead encourage substitute activities, roles, and loved ones, when established ones are lost.

BEHAVIORS OF LONELINESS

What then can we look for in terms of behaviors in assessing loneliness? The predominant theme that seems to prevail is one of not being able to extend oneself to another for contact. Since one sees one's actions as ineffective, the motivation to do anything decreases. Nothing matters that much to require one's attention. One begins to identify behaviors from other modes— self-esteem diminishes, role failures begin to develop, and physical appearance may become retarded. Symptoms of anxiety—the emotional pain one suffers from viewing one's own dilemma with tunnel vision—will be manifested in different ways by individuals. Another group of symptoms that one could assess revolves around depressive behaviors described in the chapter on loss. How then can you distinguish loneliness as an interdependency problem? Once you have made your first and second level assessment, it should start to become clear what is the *problem* and what is the *symptom*. Anxiety and depressive behaviors may not be our chief concern when we see in black and white that dysfunctional dependency or independency is occurring and is the cause of the anxiety or depression.

Behaviors of loneliness denoting dysfunctional dependency might be: a contentment to let others care for the person, abuse of another's attempt to help (example, monopolizing a staff person's time), a clinging love relationship, a lack of broad interests and only a tacit acceptance of those that could be satisfying.

Dysfunctional independency goes hand in hand with dysfunctional dependency. Very often both can be assessed in the alienated person experiencing loneliness. Dysfunctional independency could be shown in a tendency to manipulate others (the client experiencing loneliness isn't aware, however, of any power over others), and efforts to succeed on one's own without asking for help even though one is incapable of doing something or experiencing something. It is possible to be *too* independent. Lack of contacts via superindependence can also breed loneliness.

Jerry A. Greenwald (1972) has identified several games the lonely person plays to maintain dependency on others and on his loneliness. Among them are:

1. "Someone fill me up" game—feels an emptiness in himself and looks to others to remedy the situation (a negative help-seeking behavior).

2. "Holier than thou" game—refuses contact with others since he perceives own hang-ups as less than those of others (a negative initiative-taking behavior).

3. "Loser-oriented" game—choosing people for contact who are not what the individual really wants in an engagement (a negative attention-seeking behavior).

4. "Being hurt" game—has more than the average fear of rejection; develops a fantasy of what could happen that is overwhelming and unbearable (a negative affection-seeking behavior).

5. "Psycho-anesthesia" game—use of alcohol and drugs to withdraw (a negative help-seeking behavior).

6. "The joker" game—uses humor to keep situation from hitting relevant issues (a negative attention-seeking behavior).

7. "Being present in body only" game—gives only off-and-on attention to an interaction—daydreams the contact away (a negative initiative-taking behavior).

8. "Busy work" game—activities prevent him from experiencing loneliness and working with it (a negative initiative-taking behavior).

9. "Why not ask" game—learns to ask for everything he wants, is insensitive to others, and exceeds the other person's desire to give (a negative initiative-taking behavior).

These games and the behaviors they seem to represent are good criteria to use in assessing a client's communication pattern and interdependency behaviors.

Note behaviors that show loneliness in the following situations:

Case 1 Mrs. Sarah Ames is 63 years old and has been a widow for three years. She has no children. Until she retired last year, she worked part-time in the cafeteria of the local grade school. Thirty years ago she and her husband built the tiny two-bedroom bungalow she still maintains. When Al was alive, he kept the yard up well, they had three dogs and two cats, and were well liked by the neighbors. Two years ago new huge apartment complexes were built on either side of the house. A brick wall, put up by the developers, completely surrounds the yard. Last year the apartment dwellers complained to the city about the five animals. The city filed a nuisance law regulation against Mrs. Ames. She did not get a lawyer and argued the case herself. She lost and was told to get rid of three of the animals, which she did. Mrs. Ames doesn't drive and either walks or takes the bus to get around. Her doctor, an old friend, says she needs cataract surgery. She rejected his advice and told an optometrist to make bifocals for her. In an interview with a public health nurse following a referral from the doctor, Sarah Ames said, "It's all so useless; they patch up one thing and then another goes." "Those people [apartment dwellers] don't want an old lady around, messing up their block."

"Oscar and Shadow [the two dogs she got rid of] were really a big part of my life since Al passed on—I needed them." "You know, Al made all the decisions, now I can't decide what to do with the house, or who to call or visit—I just left that up to him." After two hours, the nurse tried to close the interview several times, and finally got up saying she had to leave. Mrs. Ames said, "You must come again and spend the day, I'll fix a nice lunch for you."

Case 2   Jim is 15 years old and is in isolation on a medical floor for an infection from a wound in his arm. He is not handsome, and is one hundred pounds overweight. His wound was sustained when his ten-speed bicycle fell apart as he rode home from school. Someone had taken a vital nut off the bike, and Jim, not realizing that anything was wrong, was going fast when the bike fell apart and he went over the handlebars onto the pavement. His jaw is wired and he has many contusions. This infection developed two days ago in a large gash in his arm, and at this time he was transferred into isolation. He is a junior in high school, is making poor grades, and has no apparent friends. Nobody can remember ever seeing him with another teen-ager.

Jim is an only child of a father who is an artist and a mother who is a Ph.D. chemist. The parents are middle-class individuals who are social climbers (throw frequent parties, concerned with having everything the Joneses have). Both parents say they are close to Jim. Each has visited once since his admission four days ago and each has phoned once. He spends most of his waking hours watching television. The staff thinks Jim is a "spoiled child" since he sulks and makes only minimal responses when they are in the room. They feel he should be doing more of his own care, and do admit to finding him repulsive.

When a student nurse began a relationship with him, he said: "Why do you want me as a patient?" As the relationship progressed, he made these comments: "I need Mother, at least I'm supposed to." "Well, yes, I do, too, have a friend, it's my television set, without it I'd lose my mind." "Who needs friends, anyhow—money can get you what you want."

Case 3   Ray is a 43-year-old rehabilitation patient with a medical diagnosis of cardiovascular accident, or stroke. He is slowly regaining his speech and the use of his left side. His family lives 100 miles from the hospital, and usually comes to visit weekly. It has been six weeks since his stroke and his progress has been so positive that the doctor anticipates a complete recovery.

Ray has his light on constantly, flirts with all the staff members as best he can, and has developed a meticulous need for his care to be done in a certain way.

Case 4   Linda is a nurse's aide on the surgical floor. She has recently received her final divorce papers. Her marriage was a stormy one that lasted four years. She has two children from this marriage.

A new student nurse finds Linda crying in the utility room. Although the student was quite unsure of herself as a practitioner, she felt the need to ask Linda what was wrong, and if she could do anything to help. Linda's comments during the ensuing conversation included, "I just feel so let down—I didn't think I'd feel any loss, but I do." "There are a lot of men around who will love me and treat me well—I don't know why I put up with it for even four years." "It's awful at night—when the kids are in bed, it's so quiet it frightens me."

In each of these cases we see an individual who wants contact (engagement with others) but who cannot reach out to the people he finds in his sphere. Sarah Ames and Jim seem in some degree not to be in functional dependency. Mrs. Ames is trying to make it all alone. She is at a maturation age when her task is to increase her dependency and decrease her independency, and yet we find her going the opposite. Jim may feel that he has been rejected so much that why should he try; only more pain and loneliness might result. He, too, needs to reach out to engage another (contact). Ray and Linda seem similarly involved in an interdependency conflict—Ray being dependent on the staff to meet his affectional needs and Linda struggling with a need-don't-need situation. The nursing diagnosis, based on the sparse information, would stem from behaviors of loneliness in the first two cases, and from being lonely in the last two cases. Consider each case—what behaviors do you note in the interdependency mode; what stimuli are validated as cause; and what stimuli need to be validated?

INTERVENTIONS FOR LONELINESS

The main aim of interventions dealing with loneliness should revolve around the person, decreasing dysfunctional behaviors, and developing instead functional dependency and independency. One needs to develop contact with others on an adaptive basis to remove feelings of estrangement.

Active friendliness to initiate contact with a lonely person is frequently used as a nursing intervention. In using this method the nurse seeks out the patient to spend time with him although the verbal interaction may be minimal. She does so to increase his social confidence and trust in another. Once trust is established by the nurse's *genuine* concern for the individual, he may feel free to communicate to what degree he is lonely and how helpless he feels. Using this approach the nurse is fostering functional dependence. It is not of a clinging or permanent nature. If the nurse would view herself in the role of an adult and this client in the role of a child, and consequently begin to set goals *for* the patient instead of *with* the patient on an adult-to-adult basis, she is sure to fail. A nurse can be too mothering, too able to foster a clinging dependence. The nurse needs to learn to assess her own effect on the client.

As one is fostering functional dependency, one is also fostering independency. At the same time one is allowing dependency in certain areas, one is pushing independency in others. For example, although the one-to-one relationship is her basic tool, the nurse is also encouraging rapport with families, neighbors, other patients, or significant persons. Part of her one-to-one may be exploring ways to increase contact in the person's present situation - what happens to make a contact rewarding or a happy one, what makes it a failure, what does the individual have to offer others, what or for whom is he lonely, and why.

If an individual is using one of the distractions (keeping too busy, joking off interactions, or using any dependent crutches) to ward off loneliness, this can be worked with by the nurse and the whole health team. The client most likely is not consciously aware of using these mechanisms. However, when you take something away from a client you *must* help him replace it, and he *must* be ready to let it go and replace it.

Much of the appropriate interventions involve getting the person to see himself as he is and wants to be, and helping him problem-solve to get there. Think of Sarah Ames, Jim, Ray, and Linda. Do they need nursing intervention? If so, what interventions would you supply.

SUMMARY

Loneliness is a miserable state. To be in the state of loneliness is to see oneself as unpopular, and to be unpopular relates directly to one's self-esteem. Clients often suffer from this state. If nurses care about the people they meet and care for, they must consider loneliness a high priority problem to be analyzed with the nursing process.

As many have said, the antidote for loneliness is not having an answer, but being open, flexible, and finding a way. The same would seem to hold true for the approaches of the caretaker. The nurse can meet the affiliative needs at the root of loneliness, and thus help the client adapt his interdependency mode.

REFERENCES

Fromm-Reichmann, Frieda, "Loneliness" *Psychiatry*, vol. 22, 1959.

Greenwald, Jerry A., "Self-Induced Loneliness" Voices: *The Art and Science of Psychotherapy*, vol. 8, 1972, pp. 17–21.

Moustakas, Clark E., *Loneliness and Love.* Englewood Cliffs, N. J.: Prentice-Hall, Inc., 1972.

Toffler, Alvin, *Future Shock.* New York: Random House, Inc., 1970.

ADDITIONAL READINGS

Burnside, Irene.M., "Loneliness in Old Age," *Mental Hygiene*, vol. 55, no. 3, July 1971, pp. 391–97.

Cumming, M. Elaine, "New Thoughts on the Theory of Disengagement," *New Thoughts on Old Age*, Robert Kastenbaum, ed. New York: Springer, 1964.

Eisner, Victor, "Alienation of Youth." *The Journal of School Health*, vol. 39, no. 2, February 1969, pp. 81–90.

Francel, Claire G., Loneliness," *Some Clinical Approaches to Psychiatric Nursing*, Shirley F. Burd and Margaret A. Marshall, eds. New York: The Macmillan Company, 1963, pp. 178–83.

Havighurst, Robert J., Bernice T. Newgarten and Sheldon D. Tobin, "Disengagement and Patterns of Aging," in *Middle Age and Aging*, B. Newgarten, ed. Chicago: University of Chicago Press, 1968, pp. 161–72.

Moustakas, Clark E., *Loneliness*. Englewood Cliffs, N. J.: Prentice-Hall, Inc., 1961.

Peplau, Hildegard E., "Loneliness," *American Journal of Nursing* vol. 55, no. 12, December 1955, pp. 1476–81.

Slater, Philip, *The Pursuit of Loneliness: American Culture at the Breaking Point.* Boston: Beacon Press, 1970.

VI

Minority Cultures

In introducing the student and practicing nurse to the Roy adaptation concept of nursing, we have focused on man adapting in relation to his four modes of adaptation: physiological needs, self-concept, role function, and interdependence. The reader has been guided in learning to assess and intervene to promote client adaptation in each of these modes. Of necessity discussion has focused on the usual behavioral responses of the majority of clients encountered in health care settings. However, in the United States many minority groups also enter the health care scene, and the nurse must be aware of any variations in adaptation nursing that exist for them. Such variations may stem from a client's different manifestations of adaptive responses, but may be also due to the role of a nurse from a majority culture caring for clients of a minority group. Minority culture clients, as well as any other patients, have the right to receive care from nurses who are knowledgeable in the application of the nursing process to their needs. Therefore it is essential to include in this text a section on applying the adaptation nursing process to clients from minority cultures.

26

Adaptation Problems in Minority Cultures

C. Margaret Henderson

KEY CONCEPTS DEFINED

Culture: The sum total of shared beliefs, values, symbols, knowledge, attitudes, and habitual behavior patterns transmitted by the members of a particular group.

Minority: Those individuals who belong to a group that differs in one or more characteristics from the dominant culture.

Prejudice: A rigid attitude or emotional response, usually unfavorable but not necessarily so, toward a certain group of people.

Accommodation: A mechanism for coping with prejudice in which the minority person outwardly reconciles himself to majority demands.

Avoidance: A mechanism for coping with prejudice in which the minority person purposely or unconsciously keeps away from unpleasant situations and encounters.

Aggression: A mechanism for coping with prejudice in which the minority person's behavior has the goal of destruction, injury, frustration, embarrassment, discomfort, or annoyance of another person or group.

Obsessive Sensitivity: Viewing the dominant culture with deep suspicion due to repeated experience with prejudice in some form.

Ego Enhancement: A reaction to prejudice in which the minority person goes to the extreme to impress the dominant culture person that he understands the situation.

Self Hatred: A response to prejudice in which the minority person deems it necessary to make negative remarks about someone from his own ethnic group to a person from the dominant culture.

Powerlessness: The result of prejudice in which the minority person feels that he has no control over the dominant culture.

Anger: A feeling of injury or mistreatment; usually the first reaction to prejudice and often accompanied by other coping mechanisms.

Anxiety: A feeling of painful uneasiness experienced by many minority persons when they encounter prejudice.

Culture of Poverty: An adaptation and a reaction of the poor to their marginal position in a class-stratified, highly individuated, capitalistic society; involves behavior patterns and feelings.

Poverty: A state of economic deprivation with a structure, a rationale, and defense mechanisms.

Helplessness: The feeling that there is little one can do to change the situation.

Matriarchy: Dominance by the mother in the household.

Patriarchy: Dominance by the father in the household.

After studying this chapter the reader will be able to:

1. Define the key concepts of this chapter.
2. Describe and illustrate the concept of prejudice and the behavioral reactions of minority persons in coping with prejudice.
3. Relate the concepts of poverty and language to client adaptation.
4. Compare and contrast the Black, Mexican American, and American Indian cultures with the dominant culture in the United States.
5. Illustrate the occurrence of the adaptation problem of powerlessness in minority clients.
6. Give examples of variations in adaptation problems in the Black, Mexican American, and American Indian cultures.
7. Assess the nurse's own stance in relation to care of minority clients.

This text has dealt with the adaptation problems that all clients face in situations of health and illness. We have seen that many factors influence these problems, one significant factor being the client's culture. Madeleine Leineger (1970), a nurse and anthropoligist, advocates that clients have the right to have their cultural backgrounds understood in the same way that they expect their physiological and psychosocial needs to be recognized and understood. The nursing literature of the past thirty years reveals an emphasis on the physiological, sociological, and psychological well-being of the client. More recently there has been increased interest in cultural differences as influencing the meeting of the needs of all clients. In the United States a number of minority groups have cultural backgrounds that differ from the majority of the population. Sometimes the nurse has had limited exposure to these groups. The importance of understanding cultural differences is emphasized by studies such as the one by Gracia S. McCabe (1960), which found that the lack of knowledge about Black clients' perception of illness and hospitalization markedly interferred with the ability of the White nurse to provide adequate nursing care.

For the nurse from the majority culture with limited knowledge and experience of minority groups, questions may arise such as: How do I assess the skin color of my Black client? How do I care for his coarse and naturally styled hair? How am I to understand the behavior of the minority client which may at times be apathetic or resistive? This nurse may ask an even more basic question: How does my being from a different culture affect the client's attitude toward me or the kind of care he is receiving from me? The nurse with these unanswered questions can herself become a focal stimulus for the adaptation problem of a minority client.

The purpose of this chapter, then, is twofold. First, it should assist and give insight to those nurses from the dominant culture so that they do not themselves act as focal stimuli for further adaptation problems of minority clients. Second, the content is organized to help all nurses assess and intervene in selected adaptation problems specifically influenced by the client's minority culture.

MINORITY CULTURE

A client's minority culture will influence the particular form his adaptation problems take. To understand this influence we must define what we mean by culture and by minority. Then concepts related to minority culture—prejudice, poverty, language differences—will be explored. Finally, the Black, Mexican American, and American Indian cultures will be briefly discussed.

Culture

The term "culture" is used by anthropologists and behavioral scientists to specify the complexity of learned behavior patterns that are characteristic of the member of a group. *Culture* can be defined as the sum total of shared beliefs, values, symbols, knowledge, attitudes, and habitual behavior patterns transmitted by the members of a particular group.

The components of culture serve as an adaptive mechanism to meet the needs of individuals in a culture. For example, the wearing of parkas is part of the culture of the Eskimoes that helps them to adapt to the cold climate. Culture is learned and passed from one generation to another. At the same time new situations arise that require adaptation, and thus new habitual behaviors are developed. This is the process of cultural change. For example, with the movement in the 1970s toward a new Black identity, many Black Americans began wearing so-called Afro hairstyles. Thus culture contains the elements of both constancy and change.

MINORITY

Those individuals who belong to a group that differs in one or more characteristics from the dominant culture are referred to as being part of a *minority*. They are singled out from the dominant culture in the society because of their physical and/or cultural characteristics. They may receive differential and often unequal, unfavorable treatment. As a result, they often regard themselves as objects of collective discrimination. The Black, Mexican American, and American Indian comprise the largest ethnic minority groups in the United States. Each ethnic group has developed a culture of its own with its own unique characteristics. However, the groups will have some characteristics in common. When minority groups are oppressed, there is a limit to possible ways of reacting. Since each of these groups is subordinate, they will respond to dominance in somewhat the same manner.

PREJUDICE

The minority group may not, and usually does not, enjoy full participation in the dominant culture. This singling out is generally the result of prejudice. Prejudice leads to unequal treatment in all areas of life, including health care.

Prejudice can be defined as a rigid attitude, an emotional response toward a certain group of people. Hortense Powdermaker (1941) says prejudice means jumping to a conclusion before considering the facts. It is also called an "enemy of society" or an "insidious disease."

One of the widest forms of prejudice that exists in American society is the color caste system. The darker the skin of an individual, the more he is apt to be discriminated against. It has long been a common occurrence that if a Black and a White person with equal qualifications enter an office for a job interview, the person conducting the interview will make a prejudgment that the Black is inferior and less capable. This kind of prejudice is a form of racism. It is difficult to deal with because it is hard to identify and to validate specifically.

Prejudice has a distinct effect on the self-concept development of minority clients. We have seen that perceptions of reactions of others are significant in the development of self-concept. We can apply Cooley's looking-glass theory (Epstein, 1973) to the self-concept development of the minority child. The minority child has two "looking glasses." He may receive a favorable appraisal of himself from family and friends. These impressions predominate up to about three or four years of age. After that, the child, becomes aware of racial differences. The "looking glass" of the majority culture may show him to be an inferior human being. Prejudicial behavior on the part of others transmits this message. The child finds it difficult to make distinctions between these two appraisals. The result may be a questioning of self-worth with resulting low self-esteem. This concept of self may be reinforced by the racism the minority child continues to experience in the supermarket, department store, restaurant, and school.

Members of minority cultures develop ways of coping with the reality of prejudice. Behaviors they may use as coping mechanisms and other reactions are:

Accommodation
Avoidance
Aggression
Obsessive Sensitivity
Ego Enhancement
Self-Hatred
Powerlessness
Anger
Anxiety

Individual minority persons will have their own reactions and responses to the consequences of prejudice. However, the nurse, whether a member of the majority or minority, should understand the possible reactions and how these may affect the client's behavior.

Accommodation Many minority clients come to accept their disprivileged position by not being very aggressive, that is, by outwardly reconciling themselves to majority demands. The behavior that the client displays would be agreeable, yielding, and good-natured. Many clients find it easiest to cope with the dominant society by utilizing this coping mechanism. A situation illustrating the use of accommodation could be as follows. A nurse (from the majority group) may say to a client with intravenous fluids running, "Call me before it runs out completely." The client may appear very agreeable about notifying the nurse. The truth is, the minority client resents having a nurse from the dominant society putting that responsibility on him. However, his accommodation mechanism does not allow the client to say to the nurse that he wants to take a nap rather than watch the intravenous.

Avoidance Many times minority clients will purposely avoid or keep away from unpleasant situations and encounters. They want to avoid the necessity of having to conform to the patterns of behavior prescribed by the caste system. Perhaps avoidance is used by more minority clients than any other coping mechanism. It is sometimes done unconsciously to adapt to everyday living conditions. An example of this mechanism may be the minority client who fails to seek prenatal care from a majority-dominated health care system.

Aggression In this context, the term "aggression" means any behavior whose goal is destruction, injury, frustration, embarrassment, discomfort, or annoyance of another person or group. Individuals no longer accept a subordinate role. Aggression is a form of striking back. It is very unlikely that minority clients could experience prejudice and discrimination without feeling hostility. This hostility may be unconscious, but it may take the form of outward aggression. For example, after waiting three hours in a clinic, a minority client may be verbally abusive to the staff.

Obsessive Sensitivity Often the minority client views the dominant culture with deep suspicion due to repeated experience with prejudice in some form. The minority client then may react with hypersensitivity when coming in contact with the dominant culture. A minority client might not trust a nurse from the dominant culture when she is caring for the client. An example of such behavior might be watching the nurse's every move and not wanting to have his back turned toward the nurse, as would be necessary in having some injections or an enema.

Ego Enhancement The minority client goes to the extreme to impress the dominant culture person that he understands the situation, for example, his medical problem. In reality the client may have many unanswered questions.

Self-Hatred Many times minority culture clients deem it necessary to make negative remarks about someone from their own ethnic group to a person from the dominant culture. An example of this occurs when a Black client says to a White nurse, "I don't want that Black nurse caring for me; you can take better care of me."

Powerlessness Minority clients often feel powerless as a result of having experienced prejudice from the dominant society. The minority client feels that he has no control over the dominant culture, who is prejudiced toward him. The more the minority client experiences prejudice, the more the feelings of powerlessness increase. An example of this response is likely to have occurred in the client whose nurse asked him to watch the intravenous and whose behavior was accommodating.

Anger Anger is usually the first reaction when a minority client experiences prejudice. It is basically a feeling of injury or mistreatment and is often accompanied by other coping mechanisms. The amount of the anger is influenced by the severity of the prejudice. It may be expressed in aggression as described earlier.

Anxiety   Anxiety is not a coping mechanism, but a reaction of painful uneasiness experienced by many majority clients when they encounter prejudice. This behavior can be assessed as described earlier in this text. In addition, when the anxiety level is high the minority client may be unable to utilize the normal coping mechanisms to combat prejudice.

Poverty

The minority person often finds that because of the majority's low estimation of the minority group, he is placed on the lower end of the economic scale. According to Lewis (1969), in addition to the economic consequences of low socioeconomic status, there are cultural outcomes. These outcomes are referred to as the *culture of poverty*. It is defined as an adaptation and a reaction of the poor to their marginal position in a class-stratified, highly individuated, capitalistic society. Lewis's concept puts emphasis on the development of behavior patterns and feelings. This concept can be summarized by the following:

> In anthropological usage the term culture implies, essentially, a design for living which is passed down from generation to generation. In applying this concept of culture to the understanding of poverty, I want to draw attention to the fact that poverty is not a modern concept. Poverty is a state of economic deprivation. It is also something positive in the sense it has a structure, a rationale, and defense mechanisms without which the poor could hardly carry on. In short, it is a way of life, remarkably stable and persistent, passed down from generation to generation along family lines. The culture of poverty has its own modalities and distinctive social and psychological consequences for its members.

The behavior patterns developed in the culture of poverty are likely to be similar to the behaviors used to cope with prejudice. For example, the poor person may avoid contact with the more advantaged person. He may be angry about hiring practices that keep him in a low-paying occupation. In addition, within the culture of poverty, there may be certain behaviors that are specifically adaptive to the economic status but which perpetuate it. For example, a young mother living on Aid to Dependent Children may not have enough cash at times to buy food. However, she can get credit from the local grocery store, who charges higher prices and has less variety than the discount supermarket. When her monthly check arrives, she pays the grocery bill, and then again does not have cash to shop at the supermarket, where she could use her money more economically. So again, she buys the expensive food on credit.

The feelings that accompany this cycle of poverty are often those of *helplessness*. As the poverty and adaptive behavior patterns are passed from generation to generation, so is the feeling that there is little one can do to change the situation. The inability to achieve any concrete aspirations reinforces the helpless feeling.

The culture of poverty has an affect on the client receiving health care, as well as on the care he receives. Studies have shown that minority patients in the low socioeconomic group seek care only when it is vitally necessary. These clients rarely participate in preventive health care services as compared with those of the dominant culture. The health care system, managed by the dominant culture, furthermore has put priority on more drastic types of health services (for example, heart transplants) rather than on expanded services for the poor and minorities. The results of this priority is dramatized by recent mortality rates for nonwhite infants, for example, 31.4 per 1,000 live births—as compared with 17.4 for white infants. Poverty in the minority culture thus has economic, cultural, and health status effects.

Language

It is important that any nurse be able to communicate with her clients. Language is a primary tool of communication. When the client and the nurse do not speak the same language, their communication meets with difficulties.

When a White nurse is giving care to a Black client, she may have to be able to understand Black English. Black English is referred to as a form of non-standard English. For example, an older aged Black client might refer to pain as "miserie." This example can be very important in the assessment of pain.

For the nurse who is not Mexican American or Indian, the communication problem with these two groups, whose first language may not be English, may be even more difficult. The Mexican American or Indian client especially may not be able to speak English at all, or may be able to speak only a limited amount. Many times when the minority client can speak only a limited amount of English, he may be reluctant to use what English is known. The nurse in that case must encourage the client to use what English he does know. The nurse always should be aware of the effect of minority languages on her communication with her clients.

As we have discussed, when we speak of minority cultures we are speaking of peoples who share ways that are different from the dominant society and who often suffer the effects of prejudice, poverty, and language differences. The minority culture will influence the client's adaptation problems. Before discussing such problems, we will look briefly at some specific minority cultures. In looking at the cultures of the minority groups we will be discussing the major cultural components, including such areas as family, education, time orientation and competition.

BLACK CULTURE

Family patterns   The effects of African culture on Black family patterns is no longer apparent. Slavery broke up the basic composition of the Black family.

During this period the Black family was forced to adjust itself to many forms of social organization, such as being bought and sold as individuals or as family groups. Supports for family life varied greatly with the slave owners. Even following the period of slavery, the Black family faced two major factors contributing to its disorganization—poverty and the related social conditions. A disproportionately high percentage of Black families are at the lower end of the socioeconomic scales. On the average, Black American families earn less than most White families. The Black male has the highest percentage of enemployment, partially influenced by the geographical area and availability of jobs.

Unemployment among Black males is related to what has been called the Black *matriarchy*. There is a common assumption that Black families are dominated by the mother in the household. The facts are that the Black female in most cases can find a job faster than can her Black male counterpart. In many Black families the female is either the only breadwinner and/or she is earning a higher income than her husband. Furthermore, there are many more Black families headed by females than there are in the dominant culture. However, in the 1960s and 1970s this concept of Black matriarchy proved to be more of a myth than a reality when it is taken as a whole. When the Black family consists of both father and mother, the family actually tends to be a *patriarchy*, that is, dominated by the father.

The family is an important structure in the Black culture. Its members depend on the family unit for their main nurturing and for positive reinforcement. Black families tend to be larger than in the dominant culture and the extended family concept is important. That is, grandparents and uncles and aunts are often included in the family group.

There has been much written about the fact that Black families are deteriorating. However, studies are few and outdated. It is more accurate at this time to say that the Black family has not been studied adequately and sufficiently.

Education   In the Black culture, education is often stressed as being the hope for surviving and moving ahead. Many young Blacks have found that concept to be invalid. They have stayed in school, have received college educations—and still cannot find jobs. Many times college-graduated Blacks have to take "noncollege" jobs. An example is the fact that many Black postmen have college educations.

Orientation to time   Time is not equated with success in the Black culture as much as it is in the dominant culture. The majority of the Black culture is probably more present-oriented than future-oriented. Socioeconomic class standing influences how future-oriented the Black family might be. Based on this lack of future-orientation, it is not uncommon for clients of low economic status (Black or others) to arrive late for appointments.

Competition   Competition was not as important to the Black culture until Blacks began to move into areas of competition with the dominant culture. Since the 1950s, emphasis has been placed on the need to compete to achieve. However, many older Black Americans who enter competitive situations are not yet as skillful at "playing the games" necessary to survive in the dominant society. Although the value and emphasis placed on competition has changed, this value is not yet totally integrated in the Black culture.

Modesty   Privacy when dressing and undressing is still generally more important in the Black culture than in the dominant group. Similarly, the concept of modesty is important in any physical examination, particularly if the genitals are involved.

MEXICAN AMERICAN CULTURE

The Mexican American, or Chicano, culture is undergoing even more rapid change than is the Black minority. It is a product of both the Spanish and Pueblo Indian cultures, both of which historically functioned in a rural setting. As such, primary, or direct, relationships with people were basic. Stemming from life in rural settings, the following main components of the Mexican American culture have developed: (1) orientation toward people rather than toward abstraction or ideas; (2) individual autonomy within the boundaries created by the culture; (3) the separation of sexes with different roles within the social structure of the family. The male is dominant, and the female's role centers around the home. The man's machismo, or maleness, comes first. Then, he is a husband, father, and breadwinner. He is the one who generally decides how many tertiary roles the wife will take on, such as being a den mother for the community scout troup; (4) present-time orientation. Because of present-time orientation and because human and personal relationships are very important to the Mexican American culture, the individual is flexible and might forgo previous plans if something more interesting comes along, and (5) an emphasis on religion and the Catholic Church with its focus on another world.

A summarization of the differences between the Mexican American and dominant culture has been explained by Bernard Valdez (Valdez, 1973). This is shown in Table 26.1.

TABLE 26.1

Anglo-Urban (Dominant Culture)	*Spanish-Folk* (Mexican American Culture)
The Family	
Marriage Marriage gradually drifting into a partnership relationship with strong considerations of mutual and common interests of concern only to parties involved. Family approval not necessary.	Marriage assumed as an institution with romanticism attendent to folk societies. Consideration of mutual interests secondary. Family approval of great consideration.

Family Roles

Confused family roles resulting from partnership status. Much independence between husband and wife. Dual employment common.

Distinct family roles. Husband is head and provider of family. Wife exclusively concerned with household duties.

Children

Strong tendency toward small families. Children encouraged to become independent at early age. Institutions outside home exercising increasing influence.

Large families considered an asset. Children subordinate to parents, extending into maturity. No external influence.

Extended Family

Extended family relationships increasingly severed upon marriage. Grandparents, uncles, aunts, and cousins not considered part of immediate family.

Very close family ties maintained and extended into several generations. Blood relationships considered part of immediate family.

Education

Tradition

Universal secular education was part and parcel of English tradition at the time of settlement in America. These traditions became an important part of American heritage and moved westward with the covered wagon.

Universal education was not a part of Spanish tradition during the colonization period. Public education did not come to the southwest until after 1880 and to the more remote villages until after 1912.

Emphasis

American education is compulsory, highly competitive, with clearly defined goals to prepare students for continued competition throughout life.

Education in the southwest limited to select few. Oriented to philosophy, literature, and religion. Not competitive or pursued with aggression.

Time Orientation

Personal Goals

In the most industrialized society in the history of man, machines regulate daily routines and time schedules; careful planning and hopes for the future make up the concept of the purpose of life. This purpose is summed up in the word "success."

Personal planning or goals in an agrarian society are limited to daily routine and the rhythms of the seasons. The concept of "success" is part of the personal interrelationships between family or immediate community and does not involve material translations.

Time

The proper use of time is of consuming concern in industrialized society. Time is valuable – time is money. Wasting time is like wasting money. Time should be spent profitably, even when it is leisure time.

Time is a gift of life to be enjoyed to the fullest, and to be enjoyed it must not be postponed. The concept of wasting time is not understood. There is no guilt complex to mar the enjoyment of the present.

The Future

Since the dominant goal in life is success, to achieve this goal we must make elaborate plans for the future. Therefore, the culmination of life is always in the future.

Success, being a part of personal daily interrelationships without material translations, has no significance for the future, The future is entirely in the hands of God. The language is replete with proverbs to fortify this concept.

Competition

Competition is an integral part of achieve-ment concepts. Competition is encouraged beginning within the family and continuing in scholastic endeavor, sports, business life, social life, and even permeating denominational religious organizations.

Competition in agrarian folk societies discouraged. Competition not compatible with family life, or interpersonal relations prevalent in folk cultures. Achievement concepts between individuals in competition not understood.

Leadership and Organizations

Organizations

American life revolves around a complex system of organization. The very foundation of democratic government has a basis of political organizations. Business, commerce, civic endeavors, social life, education, and even churches are founded on this basic principle.

In a patriarchal society, there is no need for organization. In the simplicity of agrarian society, family groups are able to meet their needs without the complexities of organized effort. Also, since organizational goals involve the future, time-orientation limits their use.

Leadership

Organizational experience conditions the individual to function in organized situations. Organizational goals give substance to individual goals, thereby promoting the concept of community achievement and a desire for change and progress.

Lack of organizational experience promotes individualism and thereby reduces the individual's ability to function in organized situations. This has a tendency to limit horizons and stimulation for progress.

Symptoms of Cultural Disintegration

American society is moving and changing very rapidly. Cultural value concepts are modified almost daily. Mobility, mass media of communication, and intensive industrialization are but a few of the factors responsible for these rapid changes. Although these changes are responsible for much of our progress in improved standards of living, they also account for many of the social problems we face today.

The Spanish folk culture values moving from small villages or rural areas to urban centers are immediately challenged at every point. The villager's value concepts about life, family, and personal role within the family are assailed daily. Because of economic conditions, initial contacts with people already in conflict with urban life. Therefore, first view of urban life is generally a distorted picture. Efforts to assimilate distorted value concepts often result in serious consequences.

Family Life

American family life shows symptoms of serious disintegration. Divorce rate is the highest in the world. One out of three marriages ends in divorce. The rate of desertions is estimated to exceed the rate of divorce. Marital insecurity is believed to account for many other social ills.

The ability of the husband to maintain status as head and chief provider of his family is the foundation for the preservation of the paternalistic family. The new arrival from a rural setting is ill-equipped to maintain this role in our industrialized economy. Lack of skills and inability to compete result in low wages, sporadic employment, and inadequate income. Financial pressures soon force the wife into the labor market. This results in the loss of face and self-respect for the husband. The wife begins the inevitable process of emancipation from paternalistic traditions. These conflicts often result in

Emotional Problems

Mental illness is now considered the number one problem in the United States. Much progress has been made in the cure and treatment of mental illness, but we are still unwilling to look at some of the causes of emotional strain. Alcoholism is climbing at an alarming rate.

marital discord. Desertions, separations, and divorce are apt to follow.

The removal of the protective shield of security provided by the family in the folk culture leaves the individual naked and insecure during periods of crisis or emotional stress. Unfamiliarity with institutions and red tape involved in securing assistance add to the frustrations. Mental illness and emotional problems crop up. Alcoholism, as an escape, becomes common.

All of these differences between the two cultures can cause problems in the adaptation of the minority to the dominant culture. More particularly, they can cause adaptive problems in situations of health and illness.

AMERICAN INDIAN CULTURE

There is no one American Indian culture in the United States. The diversity among Indians is more widespread in the North American continent than in any other geographical area.

The average White or minority American knows very little about the real culture of the American Indian. When the majority of Americans think of Indians, they think about cowboy and Indian movies. Anthropologists and sociologists have been puzzled over the reluctance of the majority of American Indians to abandon their own cultural mores and move into the mainstream of the dominant culture. American Indians do have highly developed cultures of their own that do not fit the movie stereotype.

The Indian is a mixture of many peoples — from Southeast Asia, China, Siberia, and many points west. It is not known what really stimulated them to leave their homelands, but they came to the Western Hemisphere in small clans and family groups, beginning some ten to forty thousand years ago (Fellows, 1972).

There are approximately 17 Indian cultures in the North America continent from Panama to the Artic. The following information regarding the components of Indian culture are generalizations referring to the Indians of North America.

The Family The average family, of mother, father, and children, is a social unit characterized by sharing a common residence, economic cooperation, and responsibility for the children's education. The families are classified into three major types: the nuclear family, consisting of parents and children; the polygamous family, which is an aggregate of two or more nuclear families because of plural marriages; and the extended family, which is also an aggregate of two or more nuclear families, but is produced by joining three or more generations of relations. In some cultures, if no children are born after several years, this is often grounds for divorce.

Education   Education in the North American Indian culture has a very different meaning than in most other North American cultures. Education in the North American Indian culture refers to the entire process by which individuals learn the way of life of the society into which he or she is born and reared. This process involves many activities and is not limited to formal school settings.

Discipline   North American Indians are generally very permissive with their children. Corporal punishment is seldom used.

Religion   The Indian cultures are very religious. This may range all the way from an amorphous feeling of reverence to the performance of elaborate rituals where every word and gesture is prescribed in advance. The term "supernatural" is important to the Indian religious culture. Magic is also an important aspect.

Medical Care   Plants, herbs, and witchcraft are still used widely. The medicine man may serve as the doctor. He is an important person in the Indian culture. Most of the people are treated by the medicine man on the reservation. An Indian, however, will take a child to a medical doctor when he or she has an elevated temperature that does not respond to treatment by the medicine man.

As noted, these statements about Indian culture refer in general to the North American Indians. However, each culture within this generalized group is rich in its own traditions and practices. Any nurse working with a particular Indian group would have to study the specific culture involved.

ADAPTATION PROBLEMS IN MINORITY CULTURES

Based on our understanding of minority cultures discussed earlier, we can look at adaptation problems of clients from minority cultures. These problems may be any of the adaptation problems already discussed in this text. However, the influence of the client's culture will be a primary factor in determining which problems are primary and also the particular form the problem may take.

One adaptation problem that occurs frequently among clients of minority status is powerlessness. This problem is related to the frequent experience of prejudice both inside and outside the health care system. This adaptation problem has already been discussed. Behavioral responses of apathy, withdrawal, and resignation may be common manifestations of powerlessness among Blacks, Mexican Americans, and American Indians. However, anger and aggression may also be a way of expressing feelings of powerlessness. In preventing and in intervening in the minority person's powerlessness, the nurse will focus on removing what is often the focal cause—that is, prejudice. Prejudice may be manifested in clinical settings openly, for example, in derogatory remarks; or more subtly,

for example, in delay in answering a call bell. As noted earlier, previous experience with prejudice may also lead the person to interpret ordinary behavior as
prejudicial. The nurse's efforts will focus on giving the minority client some
control over his situation.

To demonstrate further minority culture influence on adaptation problems,
some specific problems with particular relevance for different ethnic groups will
be discussed.

Variations in Adaptation — Black Culture

One variation in adaptation among Black clients is the manifestations of
shock, which differ because of pigmentation. In assessing Black clients' oxygen
and circulatory needs, the nurse will note that shock will be manifested by grayish, ashen skin color, dry, crusty, and whitish-colored lips, purplish-colored nail
beds, and purplish-colored gums, as well as the common changes of pulse, respiration, and blood pressure noted in all clients.

The adaptation nurse will be alert to support the physical self-concept of any
client. Maintaining the client's positive body image includes care of the client's
hair. For the Black client, the variation in this care is in the intervention. The
nurse will be responsible for the care of the hair of children, some geriatric
clients, unconscious clients, and all those who are unable to do this for themselves. The suggested procedure for caring for the Black client's hair is as follows:

1. Take small portions of the hair and brush out all the tangles.
2. Comb the hair in small portions with a large tooth comb.
3. Assess the scalp for dryness and apply oil or petroleum jelly to the scalp
   as needed. This is done by parting the hair in small portions and applying
   the oil with the fingertips.
4. Braid long hair.

It should be noted that oily, shiny hair in the Black client who has coarse hair
is a normal condition. The oil makes the hair easier to comb and it also prevents
the tendency for the hair to split.

In regard to the interdependence of the Black client with the nursing staff, the
nurse's approach should be warm and friendly. However, a too friendly approach
by a White nurse may make the client suspicious. In this case, as in dealing with
any client, the nurse will focus on an honest respect for the individual person
with whom she is dealing.

One point related to problems of self-esteem is the importance of the nurse
asking the Black client for permission to call him by his first name. This is especially important to the older Black client. As for any client, the nurse will not
presume to use the client's first name in most situations, but will be especially
sensitive to this when dealing with Black clients.

One last comment in promoting adaptation in Black clients is that the nurse will be aware that most individuals from the Black culture would like to be with their family members when they die. This stems from the particular meaning of death in the Black culture. The nurse will be alert to notify the family when the client's condition changes so that death is imminent.

Variations in Adaptation — Mexican American Culture

In regard to the help-seeking behavior of many Mexican American clients, the nurse should be especially aware of the effect of language differences on the process of being able to get the help one needs. The nurse must be willing to meet the client where he is in the area of communication. She must provide methods of communication for those who have difficulty with the English language. In some cases this may mean getting an interpreter. In other instances, the nurse can use language that is clear, concise, and uncomplicated. She will be alert for indications that either she or the client is not getting the message across.

Also related to problems of interdependence, the nurse will recognize that the Mexican American culture is generally tolerant of dependency, and, therefore, will place less emphasis on initiative taking and self-determination. When the nurse encourages the Mexican American client toward more self-care, this may be perceived as rejection. The nurse will work with the client to help him to see this process as movement toward getting well rather than as rejection by the nurse.

When we consider the behavior of carrying out the sick role, the nurse will recognize that the lack of time consciousness in the Mexican American culture may lead to problems. Thus she will not give appointments too far in advance of the time they are to be kept. Telephone call reminders may be helpful.

Although modesty is a common cultural value, it is particularly significant for the Mexican American client. The nurse will be mindful that the physical self-concept of the Mexican American includes the value of modesty regarding body functions. She will approach physical examinations and discussions of sexual matters with regard for the client's reserve and modesty. The Mexican American client should be afforded as much privacy as possible in hospitals and out-patient clinics when he is dressing and undressing.

Variations in Adaptation — Indian Culture

One adaptation problem that the nurse will be particularly alert for in the Indian culture is low self-esteem. This problem has been discussed extensively earlier. However, the particular variation that the nurse will find in the Indian culture is caused by the individual and collective lack of positive reinforcement from the dominant culture. Because of the nature of this problem, nurses working with groups of Indians will focus on the building of self-esteem in the Indian child.

Another particular adaptation problem is sick role failure due to a lack of information about illness. The Indian folk culture regarding medical care often leaves the individual without knowledge of how to deal with illness. Health teaching by the nurse is indicated.

SUMMARY

This chapter has focused on minority cultures and on how the nurse can assess and intervene in their adaptation problems. By recognizing the differences in minority cultures, hopefully the nurse will alleviate rather than contribute to a minority client's problems of adapting in situations of health and illness. The nurse may find it helpful to indicate to the client that she is aware of the cultural differences between them—if such differences exist. Beyond this recognition, the nurse will identify her own stance in relation to cultural differences. Her aim in this self-examination will be to come to an appreciation and respect for all individuals. In this way the nurse, whether a member of the dominant or a minority culture, can hope to be a person who will promote adaptation in each client for whom she cares.

REFERENCES

Epstein, Seymour, "The Self Concept Revisited or a Theory of a Theory," *American Psychologist,* vol. 28, no. 5, May 1973, pp. 404–16.

Fellows, Donald, *Mosaic of America's Ethnic Minorities.* New York: John Wiley & Sons, Inc., 1972.

Leininger, Madeleine, *Nursing and Anthropology: Two Worlds to Blend.* New York: John Wiley & Sons, Inc., 1970.

Lewis, Oscar, "The Culture of Poverty," *On Understanding Poverty.* David Monyneham, ed. New York: Basic Books, 1969.

McCabe, Gracia S., "Cultural Influences on Patient Behaviors," *American Journal of Nursing,* vol. 60, no. 8, August 1960, pp. 1101–4.

Powdermaker, Hortense, *Probing Our Prejudice.* New York: Harper and Row, Publishers, 1941.

Valdez, Bernard, *Spanish Americans in Correctional Institutions and on Parole,* Report to the Colorado Department of Institutions, June 30, 1973.

ADDITIONAL READINGS

Allpart, G. W., *The Nature of Prejudice.* Boston: Beacon Press, 1954.

Banks, James and Jean Grambs, *Black Self-Concept.* New York: McGraw-Hill, Inc., 1972.

Bullough, Bonnie and Vern, *Poverty Ethnic Identity and Health Care.* New York: Appleton-Century-Crofts, 1972.

Clark, Margaret, *Health for the Mexican-American Culture.* Berkeley and Los Angeles: University of California Press, 1970.

Driver, Harold, *Indians of North America.* Chicago: The University of Chicago Press, 1969.

Henderson, C. Margaret, "A Study of the Relationship Between Self-Esteem and the Month Prenatal Care was Initiated in a Group of Low Socio-economic Pregnant Mothers," Unpublished Master's Thesis. Los Angeles: California State University, 1972.

Honigmann, John, *Understanding Culture.* New York: Harper and Row, Publishers, 1963.

Johnson, Kenneth, *Teaching the Culturally Disadvantaged.* Palo Alto, Calif.: Science Research Associates, Inc., 1970.

Jones, Reginald, ed., *Black Psychology.* New York: Harper and Row, Publishers, 1972.

Kardiner, Abram and Lionel Oulsey, *The Mark of Oppression.* Cleveland: The World Publishing Company, 1962.

Levine, Stuart and Nancy Lurie, *The American Indian Today.* Deland, Fla.: Everett Edwards, Inc., 1968.

Meier, Matt and Feliciano Rivera, *The Chicanos.* New York: Hill and Wang, 1972.

Moore, Joan, *Mexican-American.* Englewood Cliffs, N. J.: Prentice-Hall, Inc., 1970.

Staples, Robert, *The Black Family.* Belmont, Calif.: Wadsworth Publishing Company, Inc., 1971.

Starlie, Frances, *Nursing and the Social Conscience.* New York: Appleton-Century-Crofts, 1970.

Appendixes

377

I.   NURSING ASSESSMENT BASED ON ROY ADAPTATION MODEL
Cecilia Martinez

Adaptive Modes	Assessment Factors	
	First Level	Second Level

I. *Basic Physiological Needs*

Adaptive Modes	First Level	Second Level

A. Exercise and Rest	Posture.
	Mobility.
	Muscle tone
	Body alignment.
	Equilibrium status.
	Activity level.
	Frustration tolerance.
	Level of concentration.
	Sleep pattern.
	Appearance of eyes.
	Mannerisms, e.g., yawning.
	Complaints of weakness,
	    fatigue, unsteadiness,
	    and dizziness.
		Genetic makeup.
		Developmental stage.
		Role functions.
		Emotional status.
		Stress: physical, emotional.
		Drugs, alcohol, tobacco.
		Cultural orientation.
		Social interaction pattern.
		Coping mechanisms.
		Environment.
		Religion.
		Metabolic rate.*
		Skeleto-muscular status.
		Acute physical illness
		    requiring bed rest.
		Pain.
		Setting: familiarity,
		    lighting, noise.

B. Nutrition	Intake: amount and kinds
	    of four basic foods.
	Body structure (contour).
	Frustration tolerance.
	Skin turgor.
	Muscle tone.
	Weight constancy.
	Elimination pattern.
	Distended abdomen.
	Complaints of nausea,
	    vomiting, anorexia,
	    belching.
	Fatigue, weakness.
		Common assessment factors.
		Eating pattern, habits, and
		    cultural influences.
		Attitude toward weight and
		    body image.
		Peer group influences.
		Moral values associated with
		    food.
		Diet restrictions, allergies.
		Illness or disease process.
		Level of activity.
		Palatibility of food.
		Social setting.
		Food fads.
		Vitamin, mineral deficiency.
		Knowledge about nutrition.
		Pregnancy, lactation.
		Appetite pattern.
		Body structure.

C. Elimination	Stool: frequency and
	    character, quantity.
	Urine: frequency and
	    character, quantity.
	Perspiration: quantity,
	    odor, location.
		Common assessment factors.
		Usual elimination pattern.
		Diet pattern.

*These first 12 factors are common influencing factors in all modes.

Distension.
Bowel sounds.
Complaints of: flatus, pain,
feeling of fullness,
stress, incontinence.

D. Fluids and
   Electrolytes

Intake: amount and
frequency.
Urination: amount and
appearance.
Diarrhea: character,
amount, frequency.
Vomitus: amount and
appearance.
Drainage: source and
amount.
Urine: specific gravity.
Serum electrolyte values.
ECG.
Mucous membrane and
tongue condition.
Muscle tone.
Skin turgor.
Weight change.
Appearance of eyes
(puffy, sunken).
Frustration level.
Orientation status.
Thought processes.
Pulsation rate, intensity.
Energy level.
Temperature.
Appetite.
Respiration rate, type.
Voice changes.
Body fluid distribution.
Complaints of tinnitus,
pain or cramping, thirst,
carpopedal spasm,
paralysis, tetany,
numbness, and tingling
in extremities.
Edema.

Common assessment factors.
Acute illnesses, especially
adrenal problems.
Chronic illnesses, e.g., renal,
congestive heart failure.
Injuries that are massive
and crushing.
Loss of body fluids: gastric
and intestinal juices,
sensible and insensible
fluid, bile, exudates,
pancreatic juice.
Availability of fluids.
Proportion of rest to
exercise.
Nutritional status.
Climate and temperature.
CNS disturbance of
respiratory center.

E. Oxygen and
   Circulation

Respiration: rate and
depth, quality,
secretions, sound.
Chest: shape, equality of
bilateral movement.
Pulse: rate, regularity,
quality, proximal,
peripheral, apical.
Blood pressure.
Skin: temperature, color,
moisture.
Vein integrity.
Level of consciousness.
Sensorium status.
Mood.

Common assessment factors.
Diseases of blood, cardiovascu-
lar and pulmonary systems.
Blood volume loss.
Temperature, climate, and
altitude.
Obstruction of airway.
Muscle tone.
Energy level.
pCO_2 pO_2, pH.

Frustration level.
Thought processes.
Blood loss.
Lab studies: enzyme,
  L.D.H., S.G.O.T.,
  S.G.P.T., C.P.K.,
  H.B.D., hemoglobin,
  hemalocrit, ECG, and
  chest x-ray.

F. Regulation:
   Temperature

Body temperature.
Skin: temperature, color,
  moisture, piloerection,
  hypersensitive skin.
Respiration rate.
Pulse rate.
Perspiration.
Sensorium.
Level of consciousness.
Convulsions.
Frustration level.
Complaints of general
  uncomfortable warm or
  cold feeling, chills,
  shivering, malaise, rest-
  lessness, numbness in the
  extremities, teeth
  chattering.

Common assessment factors.
Head injuries, brain surgery.
Brain tumors.
Diseases: hypothalamus,
  circulatory, vascular,
  glandular (thyrotoxicosis),
  skin diseases.
Climate, temperature.
Clothing.
Body rhythm in relation to
  time of day.
Activity.
Amount and temperature of
  food/fluid intake.
Surgery.
Body trauma.
Obesity.
Dehydration.
Heat stroke.
Foreign bodies, e.g., virus,
  bacteria.
Usual body temperature.
Phase of menstrual cycle,
  pregnancy.
Fatigue.
Mode of temperature
  measurement.

G. Regulation: The
   Senses

Sensorium.
Orientation.
Perceptual abilities of
  sight, hearing, touch,
  temperature, taste,
  smell.
Levels of sensory input.
Level of frustration.
Thought processes.
Pain: location,
  quality, duration.
Blood pressure.
Pulse rate.
Skin.
Pupils/activity level.
Complaints of changes in
  sight, hearing, taste,
  smell, touch, temperature;
  of boredom, irritability,
  fatigue, drowsiness,
  anxiety, pain.

Common assessment factors.
Diseases: impairment, and
  trauma of the sensory organs.
Systemic diseases.
Etiology and age of onset of
  sensory dysfunction.
Pain stimuli.
Past pain experience.
Pain site.
Pain threshold.
Interpersonal response.

| H. Regulation:
Endocrine System | Urine test.
Lab values.
Menstrual cycle regularity.
Basal metabolism rate.
Eye appearance.
Physical and physiological
sexual developmental
level.
Activity level: mental,
physical/emotional.
Pregnancy.
Lactation.
Body fluid distribution.
Aging process.
Skin condition.
Condition of skeletal
system.
Stress tolerance level.
Body tissue distribution.
Blood pressure.
Pulse: rate and quality.
Respiration: rate and
quality.
Body temperature.
Neuromuscular response.
Nutritional status.
Elimination condition.
Rest/exercise pattern. | Common assessment factors.
Diseases: organic and
functional.
Weight/height relationship.
Diet and attitude toward
prescribed diet. |

II. *Self Concept*

| A. Physical Self | Grieving/loss stage.
Weight/height proportions.
General physical
appearance.
Body posture.
Eye contact.
Breathing.
Activity level.
Attitude toward activities.
Mannerisms related to
body part.
Emotional status.
Appetite level.
Sleep pattern.
Reality pattern.
Mood.
References made to body
image, approval or
satisfaction of how client
feels in regard to loss of
body part or function,
helplessness, hopelessness,
guilt, anger, not caring. | Common assessment factors.
Sex.
Residual loss experiences.
Perception of loss.
Degree and extent of loss.
Concept of illness. |
| B. Moral-Ethical Self | Emotional level.
Reality level.
Consistency between
verbal and nonverbal
behavior. | Common assessment factors.
Superego development.
Moral-ethical code. |

	Perceptual level of rightness, wrongness, goodness, badness. Physiological behaviors. Gait and body posture. Sleep pattern. Utilization of defense mechanisms. Mood. Sexual libido and performance. Attitude toward self. Interpersonal patterns. Statements about dissatisfaction with how "ought" or "should" be, feelings of guilt, displeasure with behavior of self, goodness, badness, rightness, wrongness.	
C. Self-Consistency	Activity level. Emotional level. Level of attention and comprehension. Sleep pattern. Interpersonal pattern. Perspiration. Bladder and bowel pattern. Neuromuscular mannerisms. Pulse: rate and quality. Respirations: rate and quality. Blood pressure. Reality testing. Pupils. Skin and mucous membranes. Decision-making. Completion of tasks. Eating patterns. Utilization of defense mechanisms. Sexual libido and performance. Statements about change in performance levels, inability to cope with change or to concentrate, nausea, tremors, headache, heartburn, palpitations, cramps, generalized aches, amenorrhea, chest pain.	Common assessment factors. Unresolved conflicts. Level of constancy of self-concept. Perceived real or imagined threat to one's self-consistency. Future uncertainty. Sense of helplessness. Sense of isolation. Sense of insecurity.
D. Self-Ideal and Expectancy	Utilization of defense mechanisms. Problem-solving. Role adaptation level.	Common assessment factors. Occupational prestige. Education. Income.

Mood.
Activity level.
Sleep pattern.
Eating pattern.
Sexual libido and function.
Elimination pattern.
Statements about percep-
  tion and conflict, how
  one would like to be (in
  any situation), inability
  to cope with life situa-
  tion(s), loss of interest,
  hopelessness, being
  "overcompliant," in-
  ability to control events,
  anxiety, dissatisfaction
  with others and objects.

Disparity between the
  perceived ideal and the real.

E. Self-Esteem

Emotional level.
Interpersonal pattern.
Eating pattern.
Weight constancy.
Elimination pattern.
Sleep pattern.
Social integration.
Body posture.
Activity level.
Sexual libido and
  performance.
Mood.
Feeling level of control
  in one's environment.
Expression of anger.
Utilization of defense
  mechanisms.
Statements about self (and/
  or projected into
  significant others) that
  refer to being incompe-
  tent, unlovable, insecure,
  worthless, fatigue. Feel-
  ings of isolation, inability
  to express or defend self,
  too weak to confront or
  overcome difficulties.

Common assessment factors.
Sense of self-value.
Sense of self-acceptance.
Sense of self-confidence.
Sense of inner security.
Situations leading to
  questions of self-value.
Perceived reinforcement
  from others.
Residual feelings from
  experiences with loss,
  and limits.
Residual experiences to
  his or her expressions of
  anger.

III. *Role Function*

Perception of self in
  relation to expected
  role behaviors.
Perception of role
  expectations imposed
  by others.
Perceived role performance.
Performance and response
  of others in respective
  positions.
Consistency of role
  performance with role
  expectations.

Common assessment factors.
Residual experiences with
  role change.
Social integrity.
Self-concept.
Degree of attachment to a
  primary or secondary role.
Knowledge of role expectations.
Ability or capacity to fill a role.
Primary, secondary, and
  tertiary roles.

Interrole equilibrium.
Role change level.
Role function in relation
to developmental stage.
Disparity in one's expectations and those of others
in the environment.
Congruency of self-concept
and role(s).
Mood.
Emotional response.
Effective utilization of
defense mechanisms/
problem-solving.
Statements relating to
current and former roles.
References or lack of
acknowledgement to a
role, joking, belittling
references.

IV. *Interdependence*

Defense mechanisms.
Mood.
Problem-solving level.
Affection-seeking.
Help-seeking.
Attention-getting.
Emotional responses.
Initiative-taking behavior.
Obstacle-mastery
behavior.
Satisfaction from work.
Autonomous behaviors.
Loneliness behaviors, e.g.,
chain-smoking, overeating,
psychosomatic illness,
ritualistic activity, avoidance of contact with
others.
References made to having
needs met by self or
others, dissatisfied with
achievement, minimizes
help from others, refuses
help, rebellion, of self-
esteem, passivity, apathy,
whining.

Common assessment factors.
Coping styles.
Personality structure:
dependent/independent,
equilibrium, aggressive
pattern.
Autonomy level.
Achievement drive level.
Affiliative need status.
Self-concept.
Perception.
Cognitive organization.
Demands for dependent/
independent action.
Conflict between environ-
mental demands and one's
coping style.
Support by significant others.

II. NURSING INTERVENTIONS BASED ON ROY ADAPTATION MODEL
Sister Callista Roy

I. *Basic Physiological Needs*
  A. Exercise and Rest
    1. Immobility

Position properly.
Provide exercise.
Prepare physically and psychologically for ambulation.

    2. Fatigue

Provide exercise.

    3. Insomnia

Limit fatigue situations.
Provide conditions consistent with habit patterns.
Use comfort measures.
Decrease environmental stimulation.
Relieve anxiety.

  B. Nutrition
    1. Malnutrition
    2. Nutrient deficiency
    3. Overweight
    4. Underweight

Teach nutritional requirements and how to analyze foods client is eating in relation to need and resources.
Explore possibility of dietary supplements as needed.
Let client choose own foods, serve food at correct temperature, on time, attractively, and in pleasant surroundings.
Explore feelings regarding food and dietary restrictions.

    5. Nausea and vomiting

Decrease intake.
Record intake and output.
Offer 7-Up, ginger ale, tea, dry toast, soda crackers as allowed and tolerated.
Keep food or anything producing nausea out of client's sight and smell.
Following emesis, clean client and environment immediately.
Decrease activity.

  C. Elimination
    1. Constipation

Teach to alter life style to accommodate elimination needs.
Encourage diet high in fiber and residue.
Refer for thorough physical and psychological assessment.
Provide enema, suppository, or cathartic.

    2. Diarrhea

Decrease oral intake initially.
Administer parenteral therapy.
Provide bland diet, low in sugar and warm in temperature.
Cleanse anal orifice after each defecation.
Participate in drug therapy.

    3. Anal incontinence

Initiate and enlist client's cooperation in bowel training program.

4. Urinary retention	Provide for relaxed environment privacy and normal position.
	Run water in audible distance, dangle fingers in water, pour water over perineum.
	Relieve anxiety or pain.
	Encourage intake of a minimum of 1,000 to 1,500 cc daily.
	Rub ice cube over the lower abdomen at 2 to 3 second intervals for 30 seconds and brush with soft brush in a rapid manner for 2 to 3 seconds for 30 seconds.
	Catheterize client as necessary.
5. Urinary incontinence	Cleanse perineal area frequently, apply ointment.
	Encourage active and passive abdominal, perineal, and gluteal exercises.
	Initiate bladder training program.
D. Fluids and Electrolytes	
1. Dehydration	Treat underlying cause (manipulate stimuli, for example, control fever).
2. Edema	
	Keep continuous intake and output record.
	Weigh daily.
	Replace lost fluid orally or intravenously or restrict fluids.
3. Electrolyte imbalance	Treat underlying cause.
	Devise goals and implement plan based on total assessment according to adaptation framework, reassess and modify plan as necessary.
	Establish environment conducive to adaptation.
	Institute educational program for the client (e.g., diet counseling).
E. Oxygen and Circulation	
1. Hypoxia	Maintain an open airway.
2. Shock	Administer oxygen (observe respiratory status, vital signs, and reaction to therapy; use aseptic technique; explain procedure to client; understand and use correctly the needed equipment).
	Position for comfort and maintain correct body alignment.
	Initiate postural drainage.
	Explain care and act in calm, confident, and supportive manner.
	Provide calm physical environment.
F. Regulation	
1. Temperature	
a. Fever	Lower environmental temperature, decrease humidity, and increase currents.
	Limit physical activity.

Apply liquids that evaporate quickly (e.g., alcohol sponges) or cold objects to the skin (ice packs, cool baths, fresh clothing or bedding, hypothermia blankets).

Administer antipyretic drugs.

Decrease clothing.

Expose skin to air.

Increase fluid intake.

b. Hypothermia

Increase environmental temperature, eliminate air currents.

Increase physical activity and skin friction.

Apply insulating materials around the body.

Apply warmed objects to the skin (warmed blankets, thermal pads).

Encourage warm foods and fluids.

2. Senses
   a. Altered sensation

Educate to maintain safety from injury.

Educate to promote accommodation to the altered sensation.

   b. Sensory deprivation

Regulate type and amount of sensory input through all sense modalities.

Explain reason for and length of deprivation.

   c. Pain

Establish relationship of trust with client.

Be with client and offer emotional support.

Aid client in dealing with the nature and meaning of the pain.

Remove source of pain and decrease pain-causing stimuli.

Involve client in decisions regarding interventions.

Handle client gently and carefully.

Re-position, give back rub.

Insure general body warmth and relaxation.

Maintain therapeutic environment (optimum temperature, use of color, soft lighting, proper ventilation, diversional activities, and control of visitors).

Apply heat, cold, and counterirritants.

Use analgesics, antispasmatics, or narcotics.

3. Endocrine System
   a. Endocrine imbalance

Prepare client for laboratory and other diagnostic tests.

Report signs and symptoms of dysfunction, and all responses to therapeutic measures.

Administer prescribed hormones and other drugs.

Assist at surgical procedures.

Promote normal functioning of the body, e.g., skin, renal, and gastrointestinal systems.

Teach the client and family about anatomical and physiological changes that are occurring.

Teach the client and family about diagnostic tests and procedures, laboratory examinations, and medications.

Promote role mastery in areas frequently disrupted in endocrine imbalance.

Evaluate and promote positive emotional response to therapy and acceptance of limitations of the sick role.

II. *Self-Concept Mode*

   A. Physical Self-Loss

Understand loss, grief, and mourning.

Strengthen coping mechanism and provide measures of support.

Use self therapeutically.

Work through nurse's own feelings of loss.

Be present while feelings are expressed and accepted.

Provide nonthreatening environment.

Strengthen problem-solving skills.

Communicate for continuity of care.

   B. Moral-Ethical Self-Guilt

Maintain beneficial nurse-client relationship.

Identify feelings of guilt.

Explore nature of committed transgression and help client accept decision.

Provide support, encouragement, and reassurance.

Make psychiatric referral.

   C. Self-Consistency
      Anxiety

Provide atmosphere of warmth, trust, concern, and reassurance.

Keep nurse's own feelings of frustration under control.

Help client acknowledge anxious behavior.

Help client explore causes for behavior so that he will gain greater understanding of the limitations of the threat, dispel some of the energy associated with it, and view the threat in a more realistic way.

Help client to cope with anxiety in more constructive ways by asking clarifying questions.

   D. Self-Ideal and Expectancy
      Powerlessness

Use therapeutic measures to remove focal stimulus of illness.

Help client recognize and learn to use control measures.

Help client set realistic goals and expectations for himself.

Personalize nursing care.

Try to co-experience client's nonbeing and being-in-the-hospital world.

E. Self-Esteem
   Low Self-Esteem

Use communication techniques to identify self-definers.

Help client discover feelings—what they mean, where derived, find ways to express feelings, and cope with evolving self by asking questions.

Help with decision about what feedback client will allow to affect him and how he will handle negative or incongruent feedback by leading client through decision-making process.

Help understand crisis, what is expected, and how client wants to meet expectations by exploring situation with him.

Help to understand, define, accept, and try out control of the environment.

Help gain perspective of how past influences present.

Communicate to his experience of self and environment and that it is alright to have feelings both positive and negative.

III. *Role Function*
   A. Role Mastery

Reinforce and support positive behaviors by verbal praise.

Teach new skills as need arises and provide time and equipment needed to practice skill.

Maintain environmental components that are contributing to role mastery.

   B. Role Distance

Help client deal with uneasiness he is experiencing in the patient role by making clear the expectations.

Support stimuli that are maintaining adaptive behavior.

Explore client's role changes with him so that they will be less threatening.

Increase rewards for patient role behaviors.

Handle behaviors nonappropriate to the client role in a matter of fact or nonreinforcing manner.

   C. Role Conflict

Help client face the conflict felt by asking questions.

Help client determine how realistic are his expectations and the expectations of others.

Evaluate and strengthen environmental factors contributing to role behavior.

   D. Role Failure

Explore with client feelings that block adequate role performance.

Provide role cues.

Explore expectations by client of the nurse and try to bring expectations into congruence.

Strengthen rewards for role mastery behavior.

IV. *Interdependence*
    A. Dysfunctional Dependence
    B. Dysfunctional Independence

Change client's cognitive and affective structuring of the situation through insight therapy.

Change outward behavior by behavior modification techniques.

    C. Dysfunctional Interdependence Due to Over or Under Control of Aggression.

Manipulate the environment so as to keep opportunities for expression of independence as congruent as possible to the developmental level of the client.

Provide outlets to siphon off some of the "temporary spillover" of aggressive behavior.

Encourage the development of client's own personal control system (see examples in Chapter 24).

Focus on client's perceptions of his position of weakness and power-lessness and encourage him to take a position of strength.

Avoid power struggles.

    D. Loneliness

Use active friendliness to initiate contact.

Establish trust through genuine concern.

Do *not* foster clinging dependence.

Encourage rapport with others.

Help client replace distractions with relationships.

Help person to see himself as he is and wants to be, and to problem solve to get there.

Index